CW01367783

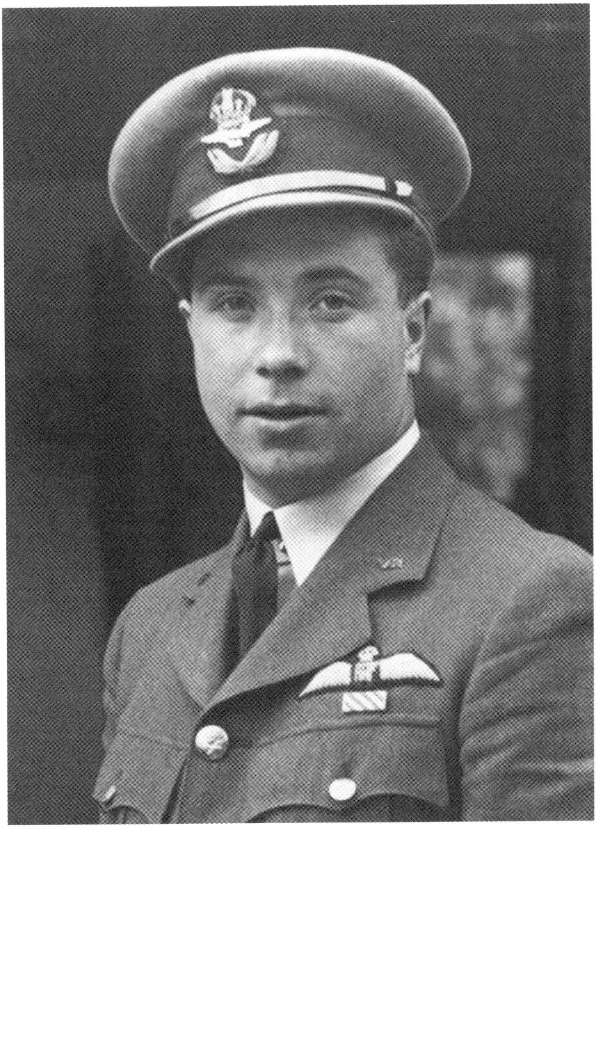

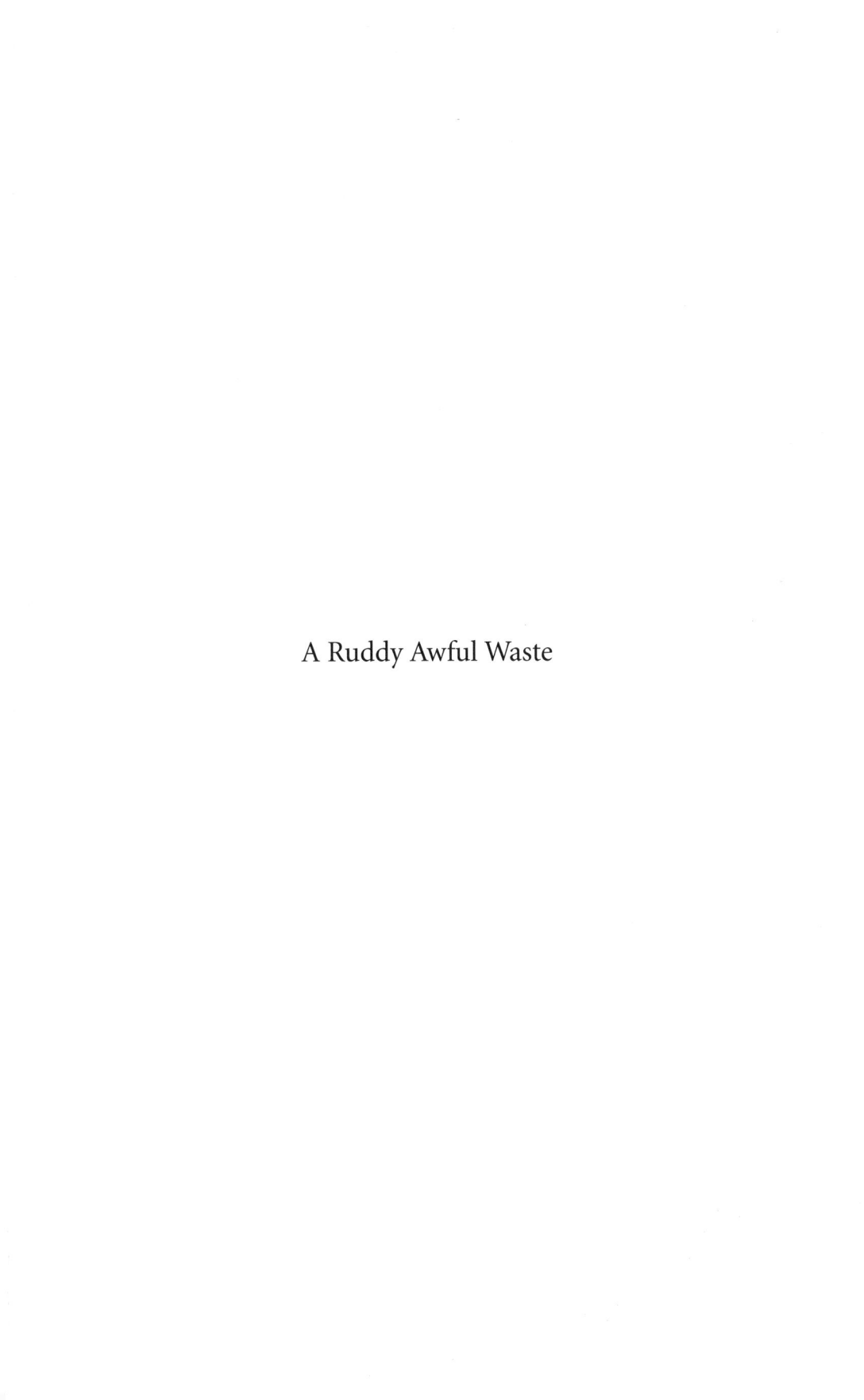

A Ruddy Awful Waste

A RUDDY AWFUL WASTE
ERIC LOCK DSO, DFC & BAR
THE BRIEF LIFE OF A BATTLE OF BRITAIN FIGHTER ACE

BY STEVE BREW WITH MIKE BRADBURY
FOREWORD BY AIR VICE-MARSHAL GARY WATERFALL CBE

Published in 2016 by Fighting High Ltd,
www.fightinghigh.com

Copyright © Fighting High Ltd, 2016
Copyright text © Steve Brew, 2016
Copyright text © Mike Bradbury, 2016

The rights of Steve Brew and Mike Bradbury to be identified as the authors of this book are asserted in accordance with the Copyright, Patents and Designs Act 1988.

The print publication is protected by copyright. Prior to any prohibited reproduction, storage in a retrieval system, distribution or transmission in any form or by any means, electronic, mechanical, recording or otherwise, permission should be obtained from the publisher.

The ePublication is protected by copyright and must not be copied, reproduced, transferred, distributed, leased, licensed or publicly performed or used in any way except as specifically permitted in writing by the publisher, as allowed under the terms and conditions under which it was purchased, or as strictly permitted by applicable copyright law. Any unauthorised distribution or use of this text may be a direct infringement of the author's and the publisher's rights and those responsible may be liable in law accordingly.

British Library Cataloguing-in-Publication data.
A CIP record for this title is available from the
British Library.

ISBN – 13: 978-09934152-3-4

Designed and typeset in Adobe Minion 11/15pt
by Michael Lindley. www.truthstudio.co.uk.

Printed and bound in the UK by Gomer Press.
Front cover design by www.truthstudio.co.uk.

Contents

Acknowledgements VII
Preface XI
Foreword XIII
Introduction XVI

1 Growing Up in Shrewsbury: April 1919 – February 1939   1
2 Flying Training: February 1939 – June 1940   9
3 Posted to Operations: June – August 1940   29
4 Battle of Britain Ace: August – September 1940   43
5 Great Courage: October 1940   93
6 Shot Down and Wounded: November 1940 – June 1941   122
7 Back to Work: June – July 1941   149
8 A Ruddy Awful Waste: August 1941   190
9 Eric's Legacy: The Years Since   197

Appendices:
I A Concise Biography   204
II Victory Claims   206
III The Lock Family: A Brief History   215
IV The Meyers Family: A Brief History   223

Notes to Text   229
Index   238

Acknowledgements

It is likely that this work would not have come about if it were not for Mike Bradbury, who is related to Eric Lock – the subject of this book – through Eric's mother's family, the Cornes. Mike was eager that a formal biography was published about Eric, which corrected a number of errors and encouraged me to put pen to paper, or finger to keyboard as it were. He was instrumental in gaining family support and input, and gathering a significant amount of information, which has been used throughout this work.

Mike also accommodated and was host to me during a week-long research trip to Shrewsbury, took me to a number of locations relevant to Eric's life, and introduced me to members of the extended Lock family. Subsequent to that invaluable trip, he continued to chase up loose ends, undertake further research, contact organisations and authorities, answer my additional questions, and arrange photographs and permissions. He provided a significant amount of assistance and put in many hours of work, including help with proofreading. This biography would likely not have been realised if it were not for Mike's passion and perseverance, and it is not without reason that he is acknowledged on the cover of this book.

I would also like to express my thanks to the following people (in alphabetical order) for their generous assistance with their material, images, time and permissions: Paul Abbot, Tim and Sarah Adkins, Steve Brooking, Emma Cleugh of Knight Frank LLP, Gerald Cock, Jacinta Cole, Clive Crocker of the Midland Gliding Club, Frank Crowe, Simon Davies, Bruce Dennis, Hamish Evans, Nick Fenton, Jessica Hadfield of the East Grinstead Museum, Henry Hand, Bill and Claire Hatfield, David Hatherell of the Bexhill Museum, R. Vince Hogg, Melissa John, Gary Sluffs Johnson, Caroline Lawson, Andy Long, Bob Marchant of the Guinea Pig Club, Philip and Richard Meyers, John and Jennifer Milner, Greg Muddell, Janette Murray of the Church Stretton and Area Local History Group, Bill Norman, Andrew Perkins, Gill and Alan Reynolds, Rosanna Sewell of Knight Frank LLP, Ady Shaw, John Shipman, Nigel Shuttleworth, Jayne Simmons of

Prestfelde School, Andrew Stevens, Peter Toghill, Pete Tresadern, Johnny Wheeler, Caroline Williams of Prestfelde School, and Andy Wright.

Johnny Wheeler also deserves a particular mention as he had done a significant amount of work with the intention of publishing his own biography of Eric, but instead kindly provided his material to assist me with this work instead. His generosity and support are most appreciated.

A sincere thanks also goes to Ray Brown, Mike Bradbury and Allan Hillman for proofreading the entire manuscript, to Bob Marchant for specifically proofreading material relating to Queen Victoria Hospital, skin grafting and the Guinea Pig Club, and to Dr Kate Berry, BM, MRCP, MRCGP, DFFP, for reviewing and advising on material relating to trauma medicine. Their input and feedback have been invaluable.

In particular I would also like to thank 41(R) TES, which has supported and encouraged this work and other publications on its history, and opened their archives to me. Thank you particularly to the officers commanding 41 Squadron while I was researching and writing: Wing Commander (Ret.) Dick MacCormac, MA, MRAeS (2004–2006), Air Vice-Marshal Gary Waterfall, CBE (2006–2007), Group Captain (Ret.) Andy Myers, MBE, MA (2007–2009), Group Captain Rich Davies, MA (2009–2012), Group Captain Mark Rodden (2012–2014), and Wing Commander Steve Berry, MBE (2014 to present), as well as Squadron Leader Jim Harkin, Flight Lieutenants Scott Cotton and Jim Stokes, and Warrant Officer Chris Walster, who arranged permissions, access and transport, for their escorts on station at RAF Coningsby, and for their kind hospitality and generous help. Their support and encouragement throughout has been most appreciated.

I also acknowledge the kind assistance provided by the former officer commanding the Battle of Britain Memorial Flight, Squadron Leader Duncan Mason, Warrant Officer Kev Ball, their photographer Stephen Elsworth and other members of staff at RAF Coningsby, during my visit to the BBMF in June 2015.

I would also like to express a sincere thank you to Air Vice-Marshal Gary Waterfall, CBE, who was Chief of Staff (Operations), Permanent Joint Headquarters, RAF, at the time of writing, for making time in his busy schedule to kindly write the Foreword and lend his formal support to this work.

Thank you especially to Jacqui for her love and encouragement, for her support of this project, for becoming involved, for understanding my passion for 41 Squadron's history and the men who made it, and for helping make this work a reality.

Quotes from documents of 41 Squadron's archives, The National Archives (TNA), and the *London Gazette* that have been reproduced in this work have been licensed under the terms of the Open Government Licence. See http://www.nationalarchives.gov.uk/doc/open-government-licence for further details. The author has sought to establish and acknowledge the copyright holders of all photographs and material used in this work. Should you become aware of any material that you believe has not been correctly acknowledged, the author welcomes contact via the publisher, and all reasonable endeavours will be made to correct the error.

Preface

Flight Lieutenant Eric Lock, DSO, DFC and Bar, was just twenty-two years old when he failed to return from operations over France in August 1941. From anonymity, he rose to become a household name in a matter of months, and readers hungrily followed his climbing tally of victories and stories of his daring combats that were reported in the newspapers.

Very much a celebrity of his time, he was different to those we call 'celebrities' today. Rather than being lauded for some form of physical, oral, or oratorical talent, safely performed under lights within the confines of an auditorium, studio, or concert hall, with an audience and judges, his skills were of a rarer variety. He competed with man pitted against man, and against the elements, with his very life in danger. He used his wits and developed strategies in the air, with no one to rely on, and nothing to save him but his own prowess.

He applied himself both physically and mentally at great altitudes over England, the Channel and France, and there were few if any witnesses to any of his aerial jousting. Indeed, his own reports of his actions give little away about the thinking and planning behind his attacks, about the freezing temperatures and yet the sweat caused by nerves, about the fear and excitement, the exhalation and relief, and the afterthought and realisations following a battle.

In the solitude of the cockpit of a Spitfire, these thoughts were his alone. There was no one to share them with; there was no one to advise him, console him, encourage him or praise him; there was no audience, no judge and no applause. Like the basic human emotions of love and grief, it was personal. Only he could deal with his thoughts and his actions, in his own way. There was no right or wrong way; they were his alone to process and deal with.

Time and time again, throughout the Battle of Britain and beyond, Eric ventured into the sky to engage his opponents, and returned to report yet another successful combat. However, they did not always go his way and he was seriously wounded in action in November 1940. And yet, upon recuperation, he returned to the skies, despite it all, knowing that there was a job to be done and he had a duty to fulfil. Ultimately, he paid the greatest price, but in his short life he displayed the greatest traits that man is measured by. He gave it all for little in return; no one could have asked him for more.

Eric's skill in the cockpit saw him rise from one of thousands of young pilots to become the highest-scoring pilot of the Battle of Britain. In fact, two-and-a-half years after his death, the RAF still considered him the fifth-highest-scoring pilot in the RAF, surpassed only by such greats as Group Captain 'Sailor' Malan, Wing Commander 'Paddy' Finucane (by then missing, presumed killed), Wing Commander 'Bob' Stanford Tuck (by then a prisoner of war), and Squadron Leader 'Ginger' Lacey.

This earned him a number of accolades: a Distinguished Service Order and two Distinguished Flying Crosses, a Mention in Dispatches, and the type of heroic celebrity that the Air Ministry's propaganda machine eagerly fed the British public when it was most needed. However, what were their value against this young life, lost in its prime?

Although married, the war intervened in any effort at family planning, and when Eric was posted missing fourteen months after his marriage, he had no offspring. In time, his distraught widow remarried and his family line was ultimately lost to history. Perhaps this is why the selfless acts of this courageous young man have never been compiled and told in a work solely devoted to him.

Eric is by no means forgotten, though. A street in Shrewsbury is named after him, and he is mentioned in several books, including 41 Squadron's published history of World War II. Most poignantly, perhaps, his name appears on a number of war memorials, alongside too many other young airmen who also paid the ultimate price.

This work now draws everything together in one complete record and tells the full story of Eric's life for the first time, revealing the man behind the legend, dispelling myths and clarifying open questions. We witness his highs and his lows, we feel his joy and his pain, and we grieve with his family as they struggle to come to terms with his loss. It is a comprehensive tribute to a brave young Shropshire airman who died far too young, whose celebrity has perhaps passed, but who deserves an enduring memorial, as he has no known grave where we may otherwise pay our respects.

Foreword by

Air Vice-Marshal Gary Waterfall CBE, RAF

It is a real privilege to write the foreword for Steve Brew's latest book, showcasing once more the mastery, bravery and human spirit of life in Fighter Command during the Second World War. I first had the honour to meet Steve when I took command of 41 Squadron in 2006, while he was researching and writing aspects of 41 Squadron's history. Having already published two large volumes on the 41 Squadron's colourful past from 1939 to 1945, he is now moving into new territory with this biography, by allowing himself the liberty of delving deeper into a specific 41 Squadron pilot's life than his previous works allowed.

His chosen subject is one of the United Kingdom's greatest fighter pilots, Flight Lieutenant Eric Lock, DSO, DFC and Bar, best known perhaps for the significant role he played in the Battle of Britain. Lock's life and career are a worthy focus, particularly when one considers all he achieved in his brief life, and it comes as a surprise to learn that there is no previous detailed biography devoted to this highly decorated pilot. It is a particularly poignant tale for me, as Lock's final squadron, 611 (West Lancashire), previously sat under my command as Air Officer Commanding No. 1 Group. Today, as then, the Royal Air Force Reserve Squadron plays a pivotal part both in peace and in conflict.

Steve provides a detailed account of how an unassuming Shropshire farmer joined the RAF Volunteer Reserve in early 1939 and within eighteen months found himself pitted against the largest air force in the world, fighting for the survival of his homeland in a pivotal battle that, if lost, had the potential to change the course of world history.

It is a portrait of the life of a young pilot, who in spirit, gusto, drive and humour, was not dissimilar to the brave and fearless men and women of today's Royal Air Force: when faced with seemingly insurmountable odds, he rose to the challenge despite his fears, grasped the urgency of the task at hand, drew strength and encouragement from his squadron and his family, and found within himself skills and courage that perhaps even he had not imagined he possessed.

The sixteen-week-long 'Battle of Britain' was perhaps one campaign within a larger war, but it was without a doubt one of Britain's greatest military actions. The first major campaign to be fought entirely in the air, it has become a legend in British history, standing proudly alongside other pivotal actions such as Trafalgar, Waterloo, and Rorke's Drift. These famous campaigns maintain a proud place in the British psyche because of the victories that were seized in the face of determined enemies and overwhelming odds.

However, the Battle of Britain stands apart from other battles as it was not fought on foreign soil, but waged at home, against a foreign tyrant, defending the very existence of the United Kingdom. The surreal aerial ballet fought in the skies over Britain was played out in full view of an admiring and grateful public in the summer and autumn of 1940, who witnessed the coming of age of airpower in the hands of the junior service, and galvanised a nation of 'The Many' who saw directly the strategic effect 'The Few' would have on the outcome of the Second World War.

Struggling against extreme odds, in the face of sheer exhaustion, we might say the men and women of the RAF in 1940 embodied the highest traditions of the service, but as the RAF was only a little over twenty years old at the time, they were in fact writing the legend of the fighter pilot. Their spirit lives on today in their modern descendants; despite significant technological advances, air combat remains a personal and gladiatorial experience among the few who have had the experience in the jet age.

In mere weeks, Eric Lock rose from anonymity to become a household name and hero of the nation. Having flown his first operational sortie in early August 1940, he became an ace within a month. He was awarded a Distinguished Flying Cross in September 1940, a Bar in October, and a Distinguished Service Order in November, by which time he had claimed an astounding twenty-two confirmed victories.

Sadly, however, he failed to return from a routine patrol to France in August 1941 and has no known grave. Steve's choice of title is drawn from 611 Squadron's records and reflects the unit's despair, mixed with the inevitable dark humour of the fighter pilot, that a pilot as experienced and capable as Lock could be lost on such a trivial operation. His untimely death was indeed 'a ruddy awful waste'.

With the support of Lock's extended family across the globe, Steve reveals to us the man behind the bravado of the wartime headlines. He does not pull any punches; he does not spare any detail. Emotions are laid bare and tough questions are posed.

As a serving senior officer and fighter pilot in the Royal Air Force, and as a former officer commanding 41 Squadron, I feel a certain affinity with Eric Lock

FOREWORD

and a sense of awe of all he achieved in his tragically short life. Steve brings him back to life, and on reading I can easily find myself in the pilot seat with him, in the adrenalin-fuelled tension of close-quarters combat in the confines of his cordite-filled cockpit, thousands of feet above sea level.

I also recognise the humanity of the aircrew behind their flying helmets and oxygen masks, their commitment, their exertion, their limits and their emotions. Today's fighter pilots the world over always work and play hard; Eric Lock and his band of brothers are their inspirational forebears as they sought to rationalise the constant danger of mortal combat, retiring each evening for a pint or two of real ale in the local public house. No more so is this epitomised today, perhaps, than by Royal Air Force Reaper (Remotely Piloted Armed Air Vehicle) crews who fly vital missions over Iraq and Syria, taking life when needed to protect others, before returning home for their children's bath time or retiring to their 'local' to discuss the day's events quietly over an ale.

This well-rounded and comprehensive biographical study is a fitting tribute to one of the Royal Air Force's finest fighter pilots. I trust you find *A Ruddy Awful Waste* as enjoyable and fascinating a read as I have.

Air Vice-Marshal Gary M. Waterfall, CBE, RAF
Chief of Staff (Operations), Permanent Joint Headquarters, RAF
(Officer Commanding No. 41 (R) Squadron, April 2006 – June 2007)

Introduction

A detailed biography of Flight Lieutenant Eric Lock, DSO, DFC and Bar, is long overdue. However, this work may not necessarily take the form that some people may expect in a biography. As the author of two volumes of 41 (F) Squadron's Second World War history, in which I studied the lives of all 325 of the unit's wartime pilots, I am a firm believer that understanding a serviceman's life is not just a matter of recording a list of his postings, promotions, incidents and victories in isolation. It is also not a question of placing genealogical data in chronological sequence, but rather an issue of adding order and context to raw facts.

Moreover, it is a study of the people around him and the people he shared his day with. It is also a survey of the events going on around him or in the news that dominated the discussions he had with his contemporaries, and it is a review of the operations and combats he was involved in, which affected his life, thinking and being, and determined both his and his family's future existence. It is a matter of placing his life, career and actions into context, painting them in the larger picture, and showing how he affected others' lives and they affected his.

Eric Lock was a man who made an impact and left a legacy. Since his death in August 1941, his family have dealt with the fallout of that event and witnessed the emergence of a form of legendary status. They have now come together, seventy-five years later, to share facets of his story that only they know, and to provide an insight into Eric – the man behind the legend – as never before. This has been made possible by drawing together memories, stories, letters, newspaper reports and photographs from his extended family. Many have remained hidden from public view as a result of not bearing the Lock surname, but this lack of visibility should not be misconstrued: they are fiercely proud of their legacy, and it is their support and encouragement that has made this work possible.

The extended family wanted his story to be told fully and truthfully, without bravado, but with the respect due to an airman of the Royal Air Force who was not only a fighter ace and a national hero, but also someone who paid the ultimate price in performing his duty. This has also been my aim, and it is therefore hoped that this work will provide a definitive record of the short life of this brave young man, and cement his place as one of Britain's true national heroes.

> With proud thanksgiving, a mother for her children,
> England mourns for her dead across the sea.
> Flesh of her flesh they were, spirit of her spirit,
> Fallen in the cause of the free.
>
> Solemn the drums thrill: Death august and royal
> Sings sorrow up into immortal spheres.
> There is music in the midst of desolation
> And a glory that shines upon our tears.
>
> They went with songs to the battle, they were young,
> Straight of limb, true of eye, steady and aglow.
> They were staunch to the end against odds uncounted,
> They fell with their faces to the foe.
>
> They mingle not with their laughing comrades again;
> They sit no more at familiar tables of home;
> They have no lot in our labour of the day-time;
> They sleep beyond England's foam.
>
> They shall grow not old, as we that are left grow old:
> Age shall not weary them, nor the years condemn.
> At the going down of the sun and in the morning
> We will remember them.
>
> *'For the Fallen'* by Robert Binyon, 1914

Chapter One

Growing Up in Shrewsbury

April 1919 – February 1939

Easter was always a special occasion in the Lock family, but it was particularly so in 1919. On Easter Saturday, 19 April, second son Eric Stanley was born to 40-year-old Dora and 39-year-old Charles Lock in their stone homestead on Bomere Farm, Bayston Hill. He was their first child in twelve years.

When he came into the world, he had three much older siblings: Evelyn, who was fifteen, Herbert, who was thirteen, and Sarah, eleven. It was a large gap between Sarah's arrival and Eric's that day, but birth and death records suggest there were no other children in the intervening years. Sadly, it is most likely that Dora had had some miscarriages.

Life was historically hard on the land and Eric's parents had descended from several generations of farmers. His paternal grandfather had moved from Worcestershire, where the family had lived for several generations, approximately sixty years before Eric was born. His mother's family had its roots in Cheshire and his maternal grandfather had moved south to the Shrewsbury area around the same time. As such, both of Eric's parents were first-generation Salopians.

Charles Edward Lock was born to Anglican parents in Condover in 1880, while Dora Evelyn Lock, née Cornes, had been born to Methodist parents in Shrewsbury the year before. They likely met as a result of the fact that Charles's elder sister and Dora's elder brother were married in 1897, but when their romance started is unknown. The registrar's records reveal they were married in Fylde, Lancashire, four years after their older siblings, in spring 1901.[1]

The newlyweds settled in Bayston Hill, in the parish of Condover, approximately two-and-a-half miles south of the town of Shrewsbury. The ecclesiastical district had a population of 534 at the time, and had existed as a separate settlement to its larger neighbour, Shrewsbury, since Roman times. Archaeological evidence has been unearthed in the Bayston Hill area that suggests the existence of both an ancient Iron Age fort and a Roman settlement on the high ground in the village area. A heavily forested area covering Bayston Hill and nearby Condover district, named the Long Forest, became a royal hunting ground for King Edward the Confessor (c. 1004–66) and Bayston Hill itself was recorded in the Domesday Book in 1086. However, large swathes of land and estates were sold or gifted to various noblemen over the ensuing centuries, and all royal title in the vicinity was ultimately relinquished.

As the village of Bayston Hill grew, amenities were established to cater to its residents' needs. A rope walk and windmill were built in 1835 and, eight years later, Christ Church was erected, built of stone in early English style, with a chancel, nave and a western tower, which contained a clock and a bell. In 1844, Bayston Hill was established as a new ecclesiastical parish of its own, which amalgamated sections from the parishes of St Julian, Shrewsbury and Condover.

However, the locality's greatest assets lay below its inhabitants' feet. Ancient sediments from the floor of a great ocean, which had been fed by ash from numerous volcanoes, were subsequently eroded and broken down by Ice Age glaciers. This produced a fertile soil that made Bayston Hill a successful farming region even in medieval times. The topsoil varied but was generally considered light, while the subsoil contained clay and significant amounts of gravel. By the time of the Locks' settlement in the area, the principal crops farmed in the parish were wheat, barley, turnips, beets and clover, but large areas were also maintained for grazing cattle. All of these elements played a vital role in the Lock family's lives.

Less than three years after their marriage, in January 1904, Dora Lock gave birth to a daughter. They named her Evelyn Dora, but she would become known simply as 'Evie'. By this time, the family was living in a house named 'Tankerville Villa' on Lyth Hill Road in Bayston Hill. Charles Lock ran a general store from the building and is listed in various documents as 'Manager' and 'Provision Merchant'.

In early 1906, Dora brought a boy into the world, who they named Herbert Samuel Charles. For reasons now lost to history, he would become known as 'Jimmy', bearing no identifiable relation to his actual names. A second daughter, Sarah Florence, was also born in June 1907, and in time she would be known in the family as 'Cissy'.

Bayston Hill now had its own sub-post office that received postal deliveries from Shrewsbury at 04:45 each morning, and sent new post into Shrewsbury at 20:45 each evening. However, the nearest telegraph office was still a mile away in Meole Brace. The local coeducational public elementary school had been open for over fifty years already and accommodated over 100 children of the local farming and mining communities. It was here that the Lock children would spend their first school years.

During this period, Charles Lock continued to run his general store from 'Tankerville Villa'. However, around 1909, he also took over the ownership or management of Bayston Quarries, and documents refer to him as the 'Proprietor'. The quarry is located on a shallow spur of limestone and sandstone sedimentary rock, up to approximately 120 feet below the surface, which forms a part of the Longmyndian range. Charles Lock mined pre-Cambrian gravel, which was used for ballast for the railways. The quarry is still operating today and produces high-quality, durable asphalt and tarmac.

It is apparent that Charles Lock's businesses were doing well as, around 1909, he began a long lease on Bomere Farm, which was immediately adjacent to the quarry. At this time, the family was residing in 'Tankerville Villa', and he was working both the quarry and the farm, presumably with a number of employees. During the ensuing years, Charles and Dora continued to work hard on the family businesses, but it was a period of some turmoil for them. While no children were born, possibly suggesting that Dora suffered the horror of a few miscarriages, Charles lost his father in 1913 and Dora lost her mother in 1917.

Great Britain was also drawn into the war just across the Channel, and was soon deadlocked along extensive systems of trenches that stretched from Switzerland to the North Sea, and cut a deadly path across France and Belgium. Owing to their ages, however, the Lock family did not see any service. Their son Jimmy was too young to serve, and Charles, his brothers and brother-in-law were too old. However, their livelihoods on the land were in any case reserved occupations, and they would have likely not been called upon even if they were of age.

It is said that an army marches on its stomach, and significant resources were required to keep the soldiers in the trenches fed. Perhaps it was partially for this reason that Charles Lock relinquished ownership of 'Tankerville Villa' around 1916, and moved his family into the farmstead on Bomere Farm. Sharing the land with a gamekeeper by the name of Alfred Mitchell, its boundaries stretched almost 150 acres, and included very fertile land watered by springs and pools. Its arable land was reputed to have produced an excellent quality of grain and root crops, although Bomere is believed to have been primarily a dairy farm, with cheese production and butter-making. The farmhouse itself was a south- and west-facing, solid brick building with a tiled roof, an entrance hall, dining room, sitting room and large kitchen, the latter with a brick floor. The house also included a cellar, four bedrooms and a bathroom, while the grounds contained an array of separate sheds, barns, stores and stockyards. It was a sizeable holding.

It was here, therefore, on 19 April 1919 – the first Easter that Britain had enjoyed in peace in five years – that Eric Stanley Lock was born. While his older siblings had all been given forenames related to family members, it appears that Eric's bore no relation to anyone in the family, contemporaneously or historically, and they were purely of his parents' own liking. The irony, perhaps, is that none of the Lock children, with the exception of Eric, were ever known by their actual forename.

With his big sisters and brother eleven to fifteen years older than him, young Eric was no doubt spoilt by them, and photos show a happy boy who had a natural affinity with the farm's animals. His father had small crops, horses, cows, chickens and dogs, and no doubt also a few goats, too, and Eric quickly became familiar with them all.

In summer 1922, when Dora Lock was forty-three, she brought another daughter into the world, Ethel Mary Joan, who would become known as 'Joan', although Eric nicknamed her 'Tinky'. He now had a little sister, and owing to the closeness of their ages, and the large gap between them and their older siblings, they would play together as children, and became very close as they grew up. They would often ride horses, play cricket, and make kites together, and in the wintertime they would delight in tobogganing on the hills around the farm. Their childhoods were happy ones on Bomere Farm, and as Charles and Dora were financially comfortable, the family was also able to enjoy a number of trips to the seaside in the family Buick.

The children would also amuse themselves in the woods around neighbouring Bomere Pool, a large kettle-hole mere with a one-mile perimeter, and an almost twenty-five-acre surface area. Adjacent to the lake was Bomere Wood, which itself contained another, though significantly smaller, pool, named Shomere. The shores of Bomere Pool were once home to a Roman army camp, which to this day are reputed to be haunted by a dead Roman soldier. He is considered Shropshire's oldest known ghost. Such stories must have created both fun and horror for the young playmates.

Eric and Joan would often climb trees in the wood to have a look at bird nests, and Eric once made a treehouse. He and Joan would sit in it and eat home-grown apples and nuts. They sometimes fished and made balsa-wood boats to sail on Bomere Pool; in summer they would swim, and in the winter Eric would ice skate as well if the lake was frozen. They would also venture into Shrewsbury at times to visit the public baths.

It was during Eric and Joan's early childhood that romantic novelist Mary Webb (1881–1927) lived in a cottage on Lyth Hill, where she wrote her novels *House in Dormer Forest*, *Seven for a Secret* and *Precious Bane*. Her stories were generally set in the Shropshire countryside, while her characters were broadly based on Shropshire folk and people she knew. The main action in *Precious Bane* took place around Bomere Pool, which Webb referred to in her novel as Sarn Mere. Bomere Farm itself is also mentioned, but named Sarn. Completed in July 1924, when Eric Lock was five, it is not beyond the realms of possibility that she may well have seen Eric and his family on her walks around the pool and woods, gathering inspiration and material for her writing.

In 1926, at the age of seven, Eric was sent to a boarding school named 'Clivedon', in Clive Avenue, Church Stretton, approximately eleven miles south of Bomere Farm. Built on the high ground to the east of the town in 1902, the three-storey building is a typical example of early 20th-century architecture. Its hanging tiles on the first floor external walls, half-timbered external walls on the second floor facing the road, high gables, large windows and three chimneys must have presented an imposing sight to the young Eric as he arrived for the first time, walking up the driveway through its brick garden wall.

The school accommodated approximately thirty-six students, two-thirds of whom were day students, while a dozen boarded. These latter students included Eric, as it was too far for him to travel home every day. Opened around 1905, the school was run by the Pearson sisters – 55-year-old Edith and 53-year-old Evelyn – both spinsters, who were purported to be generous with discipline. There was no running water or heating in the dormitories upstairs, and one can imagine life would have been difficult for young Eric as he struggled with being away from home, and finding himself in a challenging environment.

Nonetheless, he excelled in these surroundings, and it was during his time here that one of the county newspapers ran a painting competition in their children's section, The Playmates' Club, which Eric won with a painting of wild flowers done from memory. His prize was a book, which was awarded to him in April 1927, and inscribed by a lady reporter: 'The men that move the world are those who do not let the world move them'. It proved to be a prophetic statement. A few surviving photos of Eric from Church Stretton show an outwardly happy boy, enjoying the outdoors, including climbs up the Burway to the Long Mynd.[2]

A few months after Eric turned nine, he commenced the new school year much closer to home, at the Shrewsbury High School for Boys. It was housed in the Old Porch House on Swan Hill, close to the Shrewsbury town centre. Dating from at least 1628, the black and white two-storey timber-framed building was originally erected as a townhouse, with an elaborate porch that extended onto the street, from which it had acquired its name. As Eric arrived there in 1928, the 4,000-square-foot house had been a school for at least thirty years, but still included Jacobean wall panelling that was typical of the Charles I period, some of the original doors, latticed windows facing the street, twelve-pane sash windows to the sides, inglenook fireplaces on both floors, an oak staircase and exposed timbers throughout.

Eric's stay at the school was relatively brief, however, as the headmaster's death resulted in the school's complete closure in 1929. On the move again, Eric soon found a place in St Alban's Preparatory School (now Prestfelde School) in Prestfelde House on London Road, Shrewsbury, around 200 yards south-east of the 133-foot-high column built to honour Lord Hill. An independent Anglican day and boarding preparatory school for boys aged between three and fourteen, it had just opened with ten pupils. The headmaster was the Reverend Kendal Dovey, and his sister Edith was both matron and secretary.

It proved a good choice for Eric. It was close to home and he was able to settle and excel academically and physically. He was good at sport, he was popular with both teachers and pupils, and he remained at the school until he completed his education at the end of the 1933 school year.

In October 1929, Eric's father passed Bomere Farm to his eldest son, Jimmy, and moved the family into a house named 'Eastington' on Lyth Hill Road, Bayston Hill, which he purchased for £1,233. It was not far from their previous house, 'Tankerville Villa'. Having married in 1927, Jimmy now had a son of his own, while a daughter was presently on the way. Eric's two elder sisters were also soon married, Evie in 1931 and Cissy in 1932. Perhaps considering it a natural progression with the older children out of the house, Charles Lock moved off the farm and took Dora, Eric, Joan, and briefly Cissy, to live in the village again.

Eric began to do well in sport at school, and at Prestfelde's first annual sports carnival in July 1931 he came second in the seniors' throwing of the cricket ball, beaten only by Price-Owen, who dominated most of the senior sports that day. However, Eric continued to develop his skills and, by the 1933 sports carnival, had improved his results significantly. Despite heavy rain on the day, his accolades included five first placings and one second:

- Swimming Trophy, Junior, 1st place
- 100 Yards, Senior, 1st place
- Long Jump, Senior, 1st place
- Throwing a cricket ball, Senior, 1st place (60 yds 2 ft 10 in)
- Relay Race, 1st place (Wells, Lock, Smith, Woodhouse, Steward, Preece, Millen)
- Hurdles, Senior, 2nd place.

Eric was also a member of the school's football eleven, in which he received his colours, played in the school's cricket team, and was a keen boxer. He was good at woodwork, and purportedly a talented singer, too. He once sang in Latin at the school's Christmas performance. All reports seem to indicate that this was an enjoyable period of his life.

On his fourteenth birthday in April 1933, during his final year at Prestfelde, Eric's father treated him to a 5s, fifteen-minute flight with Sir Alan Cobham's Flying Circus. The aviation pioneer and former RFC pilot ran a series of 'National Aviation Day' displays – a combination of barnstorming, wing-walking, and joyriding – between 1932 and 1935, which were very popular with the public. The 'circus' consisted of a team of up to fourteen aircraft, ranging from single-seaters to airliners, which toured the country and used airfields and, at times, cleared farm fields as a base for their displays. Cobham's shows gave thousands of people their first opportunity to see the world from above, and promoted flying as 'the future of transportation'. His vision was, of course, quite prophetic.

Like many others before him, the brief 'flip' provided young Eric with his first experience of flying, and cemented an interest in becoming a pilot.[3] School friends remembered him building aeroplanes with Meccano and sketching imaginary aircraft in the margins of his school books.

However, his carefree days at Prestfelde came to an end in 1933, and he left school at the age of fourteen for employment in his father's quarry. It is said that Eric enjoyed working in the quarry more than on the farm on account of the opportunities it offered him to drive lorries around the district. The following year, his father was able to take over the lease of Allfield Farm from Thomas Davies. Adjacent to Bomere Farm and the quarry, it was of a similar size, terrain and soil, and allowed Charles Lock to continue doing what he did best, while retaining a close proximity to the quarry and 'Eastington' in Lyth Hill Road.

Eric now helped with the farm, too, and he is believed to have spent most of the ensuing five years working in the fields and with the animals. He was a keen horse rider and was a member of the South Shropshire branch of the Pony Club, which was established in 1929. He also is reported to have ridden his horse to meets of the South Shropshire Hounds, and although hunting was not a passion, he was a very good shot. At one of these meets, he fell off his horse and broke his left arm. Although it was set correctly at the time, he never regained full strength in that limb.

As a teenager, he had learned to drive lorries in his father's quarry, and soon developed an interest in sports cars and motorcycles. Having earned some money of his own, he purchased a Norton motorcycle that had purportedly been ridden in the TT Races on the Isle of Man. The rider had been killed in an accident and Eric bought it cheaply from the man's widow. In time, Eric became such a proficient rider that he would gain sufficient speed on a straight stretch of road, then stand up on the seat and spread his arms out for balance.

Sometime around his eighteenth birthday, Eric afforded himself a motor car, a Singer Nine Le Mans 'Special Speed' model, which carried the number plate CLG 907. A flashy little sports car of 972cc, with a single overhead camshaft that produced 38bhp at 5,000rpm, it had originally been registered in Cheshire in May or June 1935. The vehicle had a light blue body and wheels, ivory wings and blue upholstery, and two spare wheels mounted on its rear. The frame dropped behind the front wheels and was underslung at the rear, and carried a twelve-gallon external petrol tank. Its original purchase price in 1935 would have been £225, plus an additional 15s for a bonnet strap, but it is presumed that Eric purchased it second- or third-hand around 1937. A similar light blue and ivory Singer Le Mans featured in the 1965 film, *What's New Pussycat?*, in which it can be seen being driven through Paris a number of times by actor Peter O'Toole. However, it is reassuring to know that Eric's own Singer, CLG 907, has survived to this day and is owned by a collector in Cheshire, where it was first registered over eighty years ago.

Around this time, Eric began courting a striking eighteen-year-old British-Canadian girl by the name of Margaret Meyers, who was known as Peggy. The daughter of a Canadian First World War soldier and his British war bride, both her parents has passed away by the time Eric met her, and she was now living in Shrewsbury with an aunt and uncle. She was a pretty girl who had entered and won the Miss Shrewsbury competition in 1937. It is believed they met at a dance at the music hall in the centre of Shrewsbury. There were a few other locals that Eric frequented – the George, the Mytton and Mermaid, and the Corbett Arms – so he may also have met her at one of these pubs, although this is perhaps less likely for a single eighteen-year-old female in the 1930s.

Eric's keen interest in flying continued to dominate his thoughts throughout this time, but his parents were less than enthusiastic about the idea. Aside from the safety aspect, and perhaps a perceived lack of career prospects, it was no doubt expected that Eric would continue in the family business. Although Charles Lock could not stop him from having aviation aspirations, it seems he managed to keep Eric from following his ambition almost another two years. Maybe Charles hoped it was a fad he was going through, like horses, hounds, sports cars and motorcycles, but in time realised it was not, and from that point forward there was nothing more he could do. In February 1939, just two months before Eric's twentieth birthday, he joined the Royal Air Force Volunteer Reserve (RAFVR) as an 'Airman under Training Pilot'.

Although the exact date he applied to join the RAFVR is unknown, it is assumed to have been sometime in late 1938. His service record lists a man of 5 feet 6 inches, with a 35-inch chest, dark brown hair, brown eyes and a fresh complexion, whose religion was Church of England and occupation was 'Farmer'. He signed up for an initial five years' service, which would, under normal circumstances, have expired on 16 February 1944. Commencing his service on 17 February 1939 as an aircraftman 2nd Class (AC2), he was promoted to sergeant the following day.

Although Eric initially only served part time, which meant he was otherwise committed to his father's farm and quarry, from this point forward it would be His Majesty, rather than his father, calling the shots.

Chapter Two

Flying Training

February 1939 – June 1940

The Air Ministry launched a major development in its expansion programme in July 1936 when it founded the Royal Air Force Volunteer Reserve (RAFVR). All the major powers were building their air forces, but Hitler's growing strength and menace had re-energised growth, and the threat of another possible war with Germany, less than twenty years after the last, lent an urgency to its efforts.

The history of the RAF's reduction and re-expansion between when Eric was born a few months after the Armistice in 1918, and the outbreak of war in 1939, is a complex one. By 1920, the RAF had reduced its strength from approximately 300,000 men in November 1918 to just over 3,300 officers and 25,000 other ranks. Surplus airfields, aircraft and equipment had also been scrapped, returned to their former owners, or sold off at a fraction of their value, to meet prime minister Lloyd George's War Cabinet's 'Ten Year Rule' that Great Britain would not be engaged in any significant war in the ten years from August 1919.

Based on this policy, the Chief of the Air Staff, Air Chief Marshal Sir Hugh Trenchard, tabled a White Paper in late 1920 in which he laid out his vision for the RAF under this policy: only around twenty-five squadrons would be retained, of which approximately eighteen – about two-thirds – would be kept overseas. Seven squadrons would be based in Egypt, eight in India and three in Mesopotamia. The latter area encompassed modern-day Iraq, Kuwait, north-east Syria, and parts of south-east Turkey and south-west Iran.

In the light of the Treaty of Versailles, which saw Germany surrender the majority of its serviceable fighters and bombers, while Britain and its Allies occupied the Rhineland, it was considered that home defence was, in the immediate term at least, of lesser importance. The RAF combined its Northern and Southern Area Commands to form an 'Inland Area' in April 1920, and a new headquarters was established at Uxbridge.

With much of Europe licking its wounds from the First World War, rebuilding and domestic issues dominated politics during the first years following the conflict. Even though many countries around the world were just forming their air forces, both governments and their constituents had no appetite for war planning or significant military spending, and many an air force was therefore founded with war-surplus aircraft bought in fire sales. Ultimately, however, France's Armée de l'Air became the largest air force in Europe, and therefore formed the benchmark against which the RAF measured itself.

A report in *The Times* in February 1922 indicated that the Armée de l'Air had 300 bombers and a similar number of fighters, whereas at the time the RAF had only around 40 aircraft in Britain. Relations with France were presently somewhat awkward, owing in part to Britain's protectionist policies and proposed free trade regulations, which would have imposed significant tariffs on French goods. The general atmosphere resulted in a resurrection of old concerns about the possibility of aggression between the two nations, and it was argued that the RAF should be expanded to counter a potential flexing of French muscles.

An inquiry was subsequently undertaken by the Committee of Imperial Defence, and Lloyd George announced in August 1922 that the government had accepted a scheme proposed by the Air Ministry to form fifteen new squadrons, nine of which were for home defence, to expand the size of the Reserve, and to equip the RAF with 500 aircraft at an additional cost of £2,000,000 per annum. This would have the net result of fourteen squadrons of bombers and nine of fighters for home defence, and an increase in pilots and groundcrew numbers of around 700 officers and 12,000 men. However, the size of the undertaking, the time to recruit and train men, and develop and build new aircraft, meant a phase-in period of four years was necessary to achieve the plan's ultimate goals.

However, soon after the expansion was announced, a joint subcommittee was set up to study home air defence, based on a proposed force of nine fighter squadrons. When their report was tabled in April 1923, the committee declared in no uncertain terms that its air power would be woefully inadequate to perform the duty it was required to do. The committee therefore proposed a new multi-faceted home defence plan, which included a fifteen-mile-deep defence ring around London that they called the 'Air Fighting Zone'. The city was to be additionally protected by inner and outer artillery zones, which would be defended by large anti-aircraft guns. The cornerstone of the defences was an early warning system provided by observation and listening posts along the eastern and south-eastern coasts.

The plan was accepted by the Committee of Imperial Defence, and the Cabinet transferred the responsibility of the country's anti-aircraft defences to the RAF. Nonetheless, there was still significant argument about the future of the RAF, and indeed about its very existence, but events on the Continent soon began to take priority and ultimately quashed all such discussion.

In January 1923, Germany defaulted on its coal deliveries and France sent troops across the Rhine to occupy the Ruhr Basin and attempt to force Germany to deliver. French troops were supported by a Belgian army division, French colonial Moroccan troops and twenty squadrons of aircraft. While the British government did not intervene, they watched events unfold with awakening alarm. It was necessary for the French to cross the British occupation zone to occupy the Ruhr Basin, which they were permitted to do, but the government feared that if they were drawn into a conflict with France over the Ruhr, it would not have an air force for home defence of sufficient size and strength to repel the Armée de l'Air: it was now the strongest foreign air force within striking range of London.

As a result of these concerns, the Cabinet approved an altogether new scheme to increase the RAF to the equivalent strength of France's air force, and the original fifteen-squadron scheme was superseded by a plan to enlarge the RAF to fifty-two fighter and bomber squadrons. This remained the policy for the ensuing decade, and it was not until 1934 that further expansion was undertaken.

When the 1935 Air Ministry budget was revealed, it had increased by over eighteen per cent, to £23,851,100, in preparation for a new expansion scheme that foresaw the creation of ten new RAF stations, the enlargement or adaptation of twelve existing stations, and the purchase of twice as many aircraft and engines in 1936 than in 1935. The largest part of the increase was allocated to works, buildings and land.

Front-line strength in March 1935 stood at approximately 890 aircraft, with a further 130 in so-called 'non-regular' squadrons. It was planned to add 150 aircraft to the front-line strength in 1935 alone, but the scheme also anticipated the creation or re-formation of forty-one squadrons by the end of the 1938–39 financial year. Before the plan could be actioned, however, an acceleration of the plan was announced in November 1934, which would see twenty-five of the squadrons already formed and operational between 1935 and 1936. By the time the remaining sixteen squadrons were ready, by the end of June 1939, the strength of the RAF's front-line equipment would stand at 1,330 aircraft, plus another 130 in non-regular squadrons.

The expansion plans proved to be a prudent move, and its authors displayed significant foresight. A number of events were occurring, or were about to occur, in and around Europe that were cause for growing concern. These included Hitler coming to power in Germany in January 1933 with his brutal internal policies; Stalin's purge of 1,100,000 Communist Party members in 1933–34, many of whom were tried for treason; Italy's expansionist policies, which saw it invade Abyssinia (Ethiopia) in October 1935; the Spanish Civil War, which broke out in July 1936 and for which both Germany and Italy provided equipment and manpower; and the remilitarisation of the Rhineland in 1936.

In the light of events abroad, and under the wider umbrella of the expansion programme, Air Defence Great Britain (ADGB), which had managed home defence since 1925, was disbanded in 1936 and three new major commands were formed in its place from its domestically based squadrons: Fighter Command, Bomber Command and Coastal Command. The distribution of responsibility was logical enough: Fighter Command controlled the country's fighter force, Bomber Command controlled the RAF's bomber fleet, and Coastal Command protected the country from naval threats, specifically those posed by submarine warfare.

Training Command was also formed to take over a significant amount of the flying training then undertaken by operational squadrons and to take charge of elementary flying training provided by civil schools. All the new Commands were to work cooperatively with one another under the over-arching RAF banner, but this concept of clearly defined responsibilities between four branches of the same service was unique among the world's air forces at the time.

There was another major development within the scope of expansion plans, and that was the formation of the Royal Air Force Volunteer Reserve in July 1936. Created on the basis of a 'citizens' air force', entry was open to middle-class, public and secondary school-educated civilians aged between eighteen and twenty-five. Recruits were often drawn from the areas around newly established Elementary and Reserve Flying Training Schools, and all of them commenced their service as airmen. They would only be commissioned based on merit – ability and leadership qualities – rather than social class, and then only on or after their twenty-first birthdays. This set them distinctly apart from the Auxiliary squadrons, which consisted of officers only – no NCO pilots at all – who were generally of some wealth, and included aristocrats, bankers, landowners, lawyers, and in any case young men of only public school education. It is not without reason that one of the Auxiliary units was nicknamed 'The Millionaires' Squadron'!

The Elementary and Reserve Flying Training Schools were run by civilian contractors, whose instructors were often retired members of the RAF or Auxiliary Air Force. Their task was to provide ab initio training for civilian entrants and feed successful candidates into the RAF's established flying training schools. This would streamline the ultimate objective of providing a rapidly deployable reserve of aircrew in the event of war. On being accepted for training, civilian volunteers took an oath of allegiance and were then inducted into the RAFVR. Once they had attested, they would return to their normal daytime jobs until called up to commence part-time training. Following attestation, recruits were permitted to wear a silver RAFVR lapel badge to demonstrate their affiliation.

By September 1936, the RAF had formed, or re-formed, twenty-six squadrons since the announcement of the expansion programme, which encompassed fifteen bomber squadrons, five fighter squadrons, three general reconnaissance squadrons and three Auxiliary Air Force squadrons. However, Europe continued to heat up and Germany began to emerge not only as the dominant power on the Continent, but also the greatest threat to its tenuous stability. This deemed threat drove further growth in the RAF, RAFVR and Auxiliary Air Force, with an urgency that was not unfounded.

Hitler began to flex his muscles in February 1938 when he threatened to invade Austria if the Austrian chancellor refused to include a prominent Nazi sympathiser in his government. Although the chancellor ultimately complied with the demand, German troops marched into Austria within the month under the guise of re-establishing order, and formally annexed the country on 13 March.

Later that month, Hitler demanded autonomy for the Sudetenland, an area of northern Czechoslovakia containing over 3,000,000 ethnic Germans, who had become a part of the newly created state of Czechoslovakia following the break-up of the Austro-Hungarian Empire in 1918. Germany ramped up pressure on Czechoslovakia throughout 1938, and when British efforts at mediation failed, Hitler demanded that the Sudetenland be annexed to the Third Reich. Czechoslovakia mobilised its troops, but in an effort to avoid war, prime minister Neville Chamberlain and his French counterpart, Édouard Daladier, suggested Czechoslovakia should concede to Hitler's demands. Both France and the Soviet Union had alliances with Czechoslovakia, but neither was prepared to go to war with Germany over the Sudetenland. Britain had similar feelings. Contemporary studies suggest that the government overestimated Germany's military strength at the time, but this was a falsehood that Hitler willingly propagated.

In fact, both Britain and France were stronger militarily, but neither believed they had sufficient manpower and resources at the time to go to war with a reasonable chance of victory. With both in the midst of significant expansion programmes, they felt they needed to buy time to build up military strength to successfully counter the threat that Hitler now posed. In September 1938, therefore, Chamberlain and Daladier travelled to Munich and met with Hitler, where they acquiesced to his demands; Czechoslovakia was not even invited. Believing they had appeased Hitler and avoided a war, the pair returned to their respective countries proclaiming that 'the Munich Agreement' represented the achievement of 'peace with honour [and] peace for our time'.[1] Given the green light, German troops entered and occupied the Sudetenland on 1 October.

However, Hitler was not appeased at all; his success only emboldened him and encouraged him to keep up the pressure and demands. Recognising a swirling vortex of escalating events drawing Britain into a new war with Germany to rid the world of Hitler and his regime, the Air Ministry beefed up its expansion programme with renewed gusto, and ramped up its recruitment of pilots and airmen. This meant the creation of several new training facilities and, in July 1938, *Flight* magazine reported:

New V.R. Centres

The Air Ministry announces the opening of two further R.A.F. Volunteer Reserves training centres. The total of such centres is now 27. The new centres are at Luton and at Meir (Stoke-on-Trent). Applications for training as pilots are invited immediately from candidates resident in those districts. They should be addressed to the Air Officer Commanding No. 26 (Training) Group, The Hyde, Hendon, London, N.W.9.

Candidates must be between their 18th and 25th birthdays, be physically fit and have had an education approximately up to the standard of the School Certificate. Previous flying experience is not required. The initial period of service will be five years, with opportunity of extension. Selected candidates will be entered as airman pilots with the rank of sergeant. Later they will have opportunities of promotion to commissioned rank on merit. Training will be at week-ends and in the evenings with a continuous period of 15 days annually at, so far as possible, the convenience of individual pilots.

Pilots who carry out the required training and reach the required standard of proficiency will receive a retaining fee of £25 a year. Pay and allowances will be given during continuous training and an allowance for expenses at other training times.[2]

Perhaps it was this very article that Eric Lock read, or maybe a different version of the same announcement in his local newspaper, but it was certainly under this programme that he enlisted in the RAFVR and commenced training in February 1939. And it was under brewing storm clouds on the Continent that he took his oath to serve his 'King and Country'.

From a personal perspective, the RAFVR offered Eric an opportunity to learn to fly without the cost associated with such a venture on a private basis; on the contrary, he would be paid to do so. Trainee pilots received 1s per hour for attending evening classes and weekend flying training, but during the two-week annual camp they were paid between 8s and 10s 6d per day, dependent upon rank. Compensation was also provided to cover travelling expenses.

At that time, a man's average annual income was approximately £182, whereas unskilled workers might receive about £100 per annum. Weekday newspapers cost 1d, a men's haircut cost 6d, ten Woodbine cigarettes were priced at 5d, and ten Players cigarettes 7d; a Baby Austin motorcar would set you back £122, a Morris Minor £175, and a Wolseley £215; a furnished bungalow could be rented for 2 to 3 guineas per week, while the average three-bedroomed home could be purchased for between £400 and £500. On a pound-for-pound basis, accounting for indexation alone, the average annual income of £182 in 1939 equated to approximately £10,930 in 2015. However, comparing 1939 prices with those of today suggests the pound had significantly more buying power then than it does now.

Income aside, although it was no doubt an added bonus, it was perhaps the most recent series of events on the Continent that convinced Eric that, should war in fact eventuate, he would want to serve as a fighter pilot. He applied for entry into the RAFVR, was accepted as an 'Airman under Training Pilot', and issued the number 745501. He commenced instruction in February 1939, which was a daunting time to be joining any branch of the British armed forces, indeed any in Europe at the time; war was looking more inevitable as each month of 1939 passed.

Eric was sent to No. 28 Elementary and Reserve Flying Training School (28 E&RFTS), based at Meir Aerodrome[3] in Staffordshire, to begin his flying training. Located approximately forty-four miles from Eric's home in Bayston Hill, and around five miles south-east of Stoke-on-Trent, Meir had initially been established as a civil aerodrome in 1930, but had only recently begun to be utilised by the Air Ministry.

Given the popularity of aerobatic displays throughout the country, a growing interest in the future of flying was encouraged by the *Staffordshire Sentinel* and, in May 1928, it began to promote the idea of an aerodrome for the city of Stoke-on-Trent. Other cities were in the process of doing the same thing, and the newspaper felt it was crucial for the area's future success and prosperity. Only two months later, Stoke Council raised the idea formally at one of their meetings, and agreement was reached to seek an appropriate site for development. Suitable sites were subsequently identified in Meir, Trentham, Weston Coyney, and Wetley Common. Following consultation with the Air Ministry, Meir was chosen in February 1929, and the council purchased an area of land measuring 154 acres, three miles south-east of Stoke, on the southern side of the Stoke–Uttoxeter Road. The ground sloped gradually toward its centre, where run-off collected and it would tend to become boggy, but it was felt this could be overcome. It was considered that the area chosen was large enough for all types of aircraft existing at the time, and that no serious obstructions bordered the proposed landing ground. Preparation of the surface and erection of fencing were expected to cost around £6,250.

Work did not start until January the following year but progress was then swift and the airport was declared open for business on 15 June 1930. National Flying Services offered commercial flights, but continued to provide joyrides all summer. Throughout this period building continued, which included a 70-foot × 90-foot hangar, a number of offices, and petrol pumps in the aerodrome's north-eastern corner, near the main entrance on the Stoke–Uttoxeter Road.

By October, an air taxi service had been inaugurated, an aero club formed, and a telephone installed. Meir was now well and truly established, and Sir Alan Cobham included the aerodrome on his list of destinations for his 'Flying Circus' during his National Aviation Days. On 12 August 1935, the first airline added Meir to its schedule and commenced regular air services to Stoke, when Railway Air Services added the stop on their London (Croydon)–Belfast–Glasgow route, making a stop in each direction. The following year, Midland Aircraft Repairs set up its headquarters at the airfield, and in May 1936 the RAF made its first appearance at Meir as a part of that year's Empire Day celebrations. On that occasion, Gloster Gauntlets of Ternhill-based No. 10 FTS spent the afternoon at the airfield performing aerobatics and demonstrating formation flying.

Around the end of 1937, the Air Ministry began to show an interest in Meir in the scope of its expansion plans. After inspecting the airfield and its facilities, the Ministry informed the council that it wished to establish a flying training school at Meir for its Volunteer Reserve programme and offered a payment of £850 per annum rent for a twelve-year lease. The council unanimously and eagerly accepted the proposal and, in January 1938, purchased another ninety-three acres adjacent to the airfield for £11,000 to prepare for its necessary expansion. To accommodate the flying school the Air Ministry planned to build two hangars of 180 feet × 90 feet – each over twice as large as the existing hangar – as well as a mess and accommodation for personnel.

Preparation moved ahead at a great pace and the school, designated 28 E&RFTS, opened at the beginning of August 1938 with an initial intake of thirty-six trainee pilots. It was one of four such schools that commenced in summer 1938, the others being No. 25 E&RFTS at Grimsby, No. 26 E&RFTS at Oxford and No. 27 E&RFTS at Tollerton (Nottingham). All four units came under the umbrella of Training Command's No. 26 (Training) Group, but in February 1939 the group was renamed No. 50 (Training) Group and transferred to Reserve Command.

Approximately six months after 28 E&RFTS started, nineteen-year-old recruit Eric Lock arrived at Meir for his six-month ab initio training course, eager to learn to fly. By that time, the airfield's facilities had grown to encompass an oil, dope, fuel and gas respirator store, a workshop and ground staff hut, a chief instructor's hut, a fire tender and ambulance garage, a 5,000-gallon petrol store, two Bellman hangars, a Link Trainer, an instructors' and pupils' canteen, locker room and parachute store, a compass platform, a gas chamber and a machine-gun range.

Flying training comprised evening classes and weekend flying instruction provided by the civilian company Reid & Sigrist Ltd, which had at their disposal Hawker Harts and Hinds, Miles Magisters and Tiger Moths. Formed in 1927, Reid & Sigrist had significant credentials. One of the company's managing directors was aviation pioneer Frederick Sigrist, MBE, a founder of the Sopwith and Hawker Aircraft Companies. By his death in 1956, he had also held directorships with the Gloster Aircraft Company, A.V. Roe, Air Service Training and Armstrong Whitworth Aviation.

The other director was Squadron Leader (Ret.) George H. Reid, DFC, who had served with the RNAS and RAF during the First World War. Having led an abortive raid on the Zeppelin sheds at Tondern in Schleswig-Holstein in late March 1916, he was captured on his return flight after he alighted on the sea in his floatplane to pick up a stranded fellow pilot. Developing engine trouble after saving his colleague, he landed on the sea again and drifted for three hours until the German military arrived on the scene. The two men were captured and spent over two-and-a-half years in captivity.

Reid and Sigrist's staff at 28 E&RFTS included the following men:

- Commandant: Hon. Wing Commander Percy Y. Birch, DSO (lieutenant colonel, RARO)
- Assistant commandant: Hon. Flight Lieutenant William D. Hall, MC (colonel, Indian Army, Ret.)
- Chief flying instructor: Flying Officer Lewis S. Tindall, RAFO
- Flying instructors: Flying Officer Alfred C. Richardson and Sergeant Pilot Eric T. Heelas
- RAF examining officer: Flight Lieutenant John E.C.G.F. Gyll-Murray
- Chief ground engineer: James R. Brittan.

By the time Eric joined the school, there were over 100 pilots and around 110 observers and wireless operators undergoing training. Trainee pilots attended lectures two nights a week in the Trentham Institute, a large black and white timber building on Stone Road in Stoke. Subjects included administration, airmanship, armament, bombing, communication, discipline, drill, engines, gunnery (Vickers and Browning machine guns and the service revolver), navigation, parachutes, photography, reconnaissance, rigging, signals and the theory of flight. Several training aids were employed by the instructors, such as diagrams, charts, models and films. Students were also expected to spend at least five hours in a Link Trainer.

Flying on the weekends was understandably the highlight of the training programme, and trainee pilots generally spent about thirty minutes in the air on each occasion. The flying syllabus included taxiing, taking off into the wind, climbing, gliding, formation flying, turns, climbing turns, steep turns, aerobatics (loops, half rolls, slow rolls), side-slipping, night flying, power approaches, gliding approaches and landing. Precautionary measures were also taught, such as stalling the aircraft, restarting a stopped engine in flight without the aid of an electric starter, spinning and recovery from a spin, fire during flight, abandoning an aircraft and forced-landings.

Trainees were expected to fly solo after twenty half-hour flights, or around ten hours, and Eric appears to have met this milestone in his instruction programme fairly rapidly. He took his first solo flight on 3 March 1939, and was presented with an engraved pewter cup marking the occasion, which is still in the family's possession. His skills would have been honed further during a two-week annual training camp at Meir, which was held between 5 and 19 March 1939.

While on camp, however, the clouds darkened further over Europe when German troops entered Prague unopposed on 14 March. Hitler then occupied the rest of Czechoslovakia, and the 'Munich Agreement' became as worthless as the piece of paper it was written on. Prime minister Chamberlain felt betrayed by Hitler and immediately began to mobilise the country's armed forces; France quickly followed suit. Later that month, Hitler demanded that Poland relinquish Danzig to Germany. A part of Prussia since 1793, the city had a large German population, but had been under Polish control since the 1919 Treaty of Versailles. Now fed up with Hitler's demands and broken promises, the British and French governments guaranteed Poland support in case it was attacked by Germany and pledged to protect the country's independence. The alliance emboldened the Polish and ended their willingness to negotiate with Germany, resulting in a rapid deterioration of relations between the two countries, which included threats and border skirmishes.

Realising that war was now inevitable, Britain introduced conscription in May 1939, and training proceeded at Meir with heightened momentum. However, it did not come without its dangers. The students received a stark reminder of the hazardous nature of flying late that same month when the school's 21-year-old Sergeant Pilot Clare Parish was killed in a flying accident. Undergoing further training to become an instructor, he took off from Meir for an air navigation training flight in a Hart, but struck a tree approximately fifteen miles north of Meir while performing aerobatics at low altitude. He lost control of the aircraft and hit the ground on a hillside at Rushton Spencer and, although removed from the aircraft alive, died a short time later. It must have come as a shock to Eric and his fellow students.

On 1 July, the Secretary of State for Air, Sir Kingsley Wood, visited Meir to inspect facilities. As it was a Saturday, Eric was most likely present at the airfield for the occasion. Overseeing a period of significant expansion in manpower, infrastructure and aircraft manufacturing, Wood was pleased with what he saw. He returned to London to announce further development of the airfield with the establishment of a repair depot. Another outcome of the visit was that Stoke Council was asked to camouflage the airfield.

Less than two months after his visit, a rapid sequence of events heralded the pending arrival of the war that many had long expected. Military personnel of the rank of major/squadron leader/lieutenant commander and above were recalled from leave on 22 August, while Reserves and other key personnel were ordered to report a day later. On 24 August, all remaining military personnel were summoned back and issued with gas masks and, the following day, Britain and Poland signed the Polish-British Common Defence Pact. The French government started evacuating children from Paris on 30 August and on the next day the British government did the same in London. In the meantime, Germany had signed a ten-year alliance with Italy and a mutual non-aggression pact with Russia. Thus encouraged, Hitler was undaunted by Britain and France's warnings and fifty-eight Wehrmacht divisions invaded Poland along its entire border before sunrise on 1 September, supported by the Luftwaffe. Europe now stood on the brink of war once again, only twenty-one years after the 'war to end all wars'.

Following the German invasion of Poland, the British government was initially hesitant to make a formal 'Declaration of War' on Germany without the express support of France, despite their guarantees to Poland. As France's intentions were not immediately clear, the British government therefore felt it could only issue Hitler a new ultimatum: if German troops withdrew within two days, Britain would help to open talks between Germany and Poland. However, when Chamberlain announced this to the House of Commons on 2 September, there was great outcry and disapproval. The chief whip told Chamberlain that he believed his government would fall if war was not declared. After bringing further pressure on the French, who finally agreed to emulate any British action, the British government changed its ultimatum to a Declaration of War if German troops were not immediately withdrawn from Poland. When Chamberlain was snubbed by Hitler, who ignored his demand, he was compelled to act. In a brief radio broadcast to the nation over BBC radio from Downing Street at 11.15 a.m. on 3 September 1939, Chamberlain announced to the country:

> This morning the British Ambassador in Berlin handed the German Government a final note stating that, unless we heard from them by 11 o'clock that they were prepared at once to withdraw their troops from Poland, a state of war would exist between us. I have to tell you now that no such undertaking has been received, and that consequently this country is at war with Germany.[4]

The country was going to war once again, and Eric Lock was going to be a fighter pilot.

By this time, the RAFVR comprised 6,646 pilots, 1,625 observers and 1,946 wireless operators. Every man was mobilised and the Air Ministry used the RAFVR as the principal means for aircrew entry from this point forward. Meir Aerodrome was requisitioned and renamed RAF Meir, all civil flying was prohibited, and 28 E&RFTS was disbanded and many of its aircraft placed in temporary storage.

Eric was sent on leave with full pay until further notice to await orders. Noting this was the case with large numbers of Reserve and Auxiliary service personnel, some sections of the British media criticised the move, asking how the country could be at war and yet members of the air force were on open-ended leave on full pay. It was decried as a waste of public funds. The Air Ministry was forced to defend its actions, and went to pains to explain that those sufficiently trained had been posted to active units, but that the remainder would be sent to Initial Training Wings (ITWs) that were in the process of being established. Although a greater number of ITWs could have been set up, the Ministry had to contend with the costs associated with commandeering buildings, assembling instructors, arranging for catering, and similar logistical issues. The Air Ministry further contended that, even if these were not issues and all reservists had commenced training immediately,

> a delay would still have been inevitable, though it would have occurred at a later stage of their training. The governing factor was the capacity of the regular Flying Training Schools to accept pupils for intermediate and advanced instruction. They immediately started working to capacity on a war basis, and it was thought better to give leave on full pay to the remaining V.R. men until they could be sent straight through the course of I.T.W., Elementary F.T.S., and regular F.T.S.[5]

The problem was further exacerbated at the outbreak of war with large numbers of new volunteers joining up and also requiring training. They, in turn, were compelled to wait until pre-war Reservists, such as Eric, moved through the available schools before they could do so themselves.

Eric therefore now returned to Bayston Hill to await his call-up papers. Although no doubt a welcome help to his father on Allfield Farm and in the quarry during this period, his relationship with Peggy Meyers was also beginning to become serious, and he is likely to have spent as much time with her as he could.

Life was rapidly changing as the country moved on to a war footing, something Charles and Dora Lock had seen once before in their adult lives. While their families had remained relatively unscathed in the last war, Eric was now fully committed and Joan had joined the WAAF. This war would have a lasting effect on the family.

Britain imported around twenty million tons of food per year, which equated to about seventy per cent of its annual requirements for its population of approximately forty-seven million people. This included more than half its meat, around seventy per cent of its cheese, fats, sugar and cereals, and eighty per cent of its fruit. Rationing was introduced from early January 1940, and the 'Dig for Victory' campaign was launched to encourage Britain to supplement their food with their own vegetable gardens.

Agriculture and its produce were in demand, farming itself was declared a reserved occupation, and Eric's father would be as busy as ever on Allfield Farm. Although Eric could probably have applied to be excused from wartime service on that basis, he did not even entertain the thought. He had wanted to fly for years and had long ago decided that if there was to be a war, he would want to be a fighter pilot. That dream had now almost been fulfilled and there was no turning back. He was headstrong and determined – traits prominent in the Lock DNA – and there was no way his father would change Eric's mind, even if he tried. And his father knew it.

Ultimately, Eric's leave lasted less than two months, and he received orders to travel to Sussex to join No. 4 Initial Training Wing (No. 4 ITW) on the Channel coast at Bexhill-on-Sea by 30 October 1939. Although he would travel back to Bayston Hill for short periods of leave, this would be the last time he would live at home. This was the end of innocence and the quiet before the storm. A series of events had now been set in place from which there would be no return and no happy ending.

No. 4 ITW had only been established a little over a month when Eric arrived, and it is believed his course was the unit's first. No. 1 Squadron, 4 ITW, was formed on 30 October with a large intake of 246 sergeant-under-training pilots, of which Eric was one. The school's commandant was 47-year-old First World War pilot Wing Commander John S.F. Morrison, who had initially joined the Royal Naval Air Service, but transferred to the RAF upon its formation in April 1918. He had been awarded the DFC in 1918 and the Italian 'Bronze Medal for Military Valour' in 1919 for his service in Italy. He was also Mentioned in Dispatches in 1917, but was retired to the unemployed list in April 1919.

Morrison was a talented sportsman, lauded as an all-rounder, who had subsequently played amateur football for England, first-class cricket for Cambridge University and Somerset, and won the 1929 Belgian Amateur Golf Championship. He was granted re-entry into the RAF for the duration of hostilities with a commission as a wing commander in the Administration and Special Duties Branch only a day after the declaration of war. Just weeks later, he was tasked with establishing a new Initial Training Wing in requisitioned public infrastructure.

Morrison was joined at Bexhill by over 100 permanent staff, which included at least ten education officers, two equipment officers, a sports officer and the following key support staff:

- Administration officer: Squadron Leader Joshua J. Westmoreland (captain, Indian Army, Ret.)
- Squadron leader flying: Flight Lieutenant Patrick J. Bett (lieutenant, Gordon Highlanders, RARO)
- Medical officer: Flying Officer J. Aidan MacCarthy, MB, BCh
- Adjutant: Flying Officer Francis H.L. Searl, RAFO.

The unit was housed primarily in the 1897-built Metropole Hotel on the seafront, but the 1890 Sackville Hotel, the holiday home Roberts' Marine Mansions, the eastern half of the modernist De La Warr Pavilion, the Egerton Park Pavilion, and a part of the Sackville Garage, were also requisitioned for the school.

The De La Warr Pavilion's car park was cordoned off for drill, while its first floor, part of which had been allocated to the Ministry of Defence's Southern Command, was reserved for classroom instruction. Its flat roof was also utilised, while Egerton Park and its pavilion were used for physical training. The whole area and the seafront were defended by a number of anti-aircraft guns located strategically around the town.

The main intention of the school was to introduce Reservists, and subsequently recruits, to full-time service, by instilling discipline, developing esprit de corps and building physical fitness. At this stage of the war, the course only lasted five weeks as the students already had some pre-war training under their belts and displayed a measure of these characteristics. In time, as raw recruits joined up, the course programme was extended to eight weeks.

Life on No. 4 ITW for Eric and his fellow students followed a strict routine, starting with reveille at 06:30 hours Monday to Saturday and ending with lights out at 22:30. Breakfast was at 07:00 and the morning's first parade at 07:55 hours.

The day's training started at 08:00 and continued though to 12:30, with a thirty-minute break at 10:15. The men were then given fifteen minutes to change and prepare for lunch, which was held between 12:45 and 13:30 hours. Training then recommenced and continued through to 18:00, with dinner at 18:15. The men had their evenings free, with the exception of a roll call at 22:00.

Instruction included a regimen of both classroom lessons and physical activity, which encompassed lectures on the principles of flight, engines, navigation, meteorology, aircraft recognition, signals, gas, law, discipline, maths, administration, organisation, hygiene and sanitation. Outside the classroom, the curriculum included physical training, drill, swimming, arms and ammunition, clay pigeon shooting, dinghy drill and inspections. All of these disciplines were subject to a final assessment, which would decide whether a man was suitable to continue his training and advance to Service Flying Training School (SFTS).

Sundays were generally kept as a day of rest. Reveille was held at 07:00 hours, breakfast at 07:45, lunch at 12:45, tea at 16:00 and supper at 18:30, followed by the usual roll call at 22:00 and lights out half an hour later. There was an ecumenical church parade, but there were no lessons. The men were left to pursue their own pastimes and entertainment throughout the day, although some time would no doubt have been spent on study and revision. However, most evenings and Sundays left them ample time to explore the town and enjoy some social activities.

Bexhill had seen significant growth during the 1920s and 1930s, not only as a peaceful location to retire to, or to bring up a family, but also as a holiday resort, and facilities were built to accommodate and entertain residents and visitors. The population stood at approximately 20,000 in 1939, but was now swollen by the staff and students of No. 4 ITW and approximately 700 children. The children arrived soon after the outbreak of war as the town was declared an evacuation zone and several schools were relocated there.[6]

The De La Warr Pavilion, named after one of the town's former mayors, was constructed to provide cultural and musical productions, as well as offering a dance hall. Although briefly closed at the outbreak of war, the pavilion was reopened once black-out conditions had been met and dances were held once again. Similarly, after a brief closure, the cinemas were also allowed to reopen and there were four in the town, all within close walking distance of each other: the Gaiety, the Playhouse, the Ritz and St George's. The town's golf course was mined, as was the beach, which was in any case inaccessible on account of barbed-wire obstructions intended to impede a possible German invasion. However, between the De La Warr Pavilion, the cinemas and a host of pubs, the young men of No. 4 ITW had ample choice for entertainment during their time off.

Having already covered much of the instruction material in his six months at

Meir, Eric passed the five-week course without a problem and was posted to No. 6 Service Flying Training School (6 SFTS) at RAF Little Rissington in Gloucestershire to undertake the next stage of his flying training. He was one of thirty-nine RAFVR sergeants and one officer who arrived to commence Course No. 17 on 9 December. Little Rissington was a relatively new airfield that had been purpose built the previous year in the scope of the Air Ministry's expansion programme. Located approximately nineteen miles east of Cheltenham, the airfield was a good 100 miles south- east of Eric's family home in Bayston Hill. It was established in undeveloped agricultural land on the Cotswold plateau, approximately 750 feet above sea level and, in terms of altitude, was considered one of the highest RAF stations in England. The location was chosen for its commanding views of the Cotswold landscape.

The runway was initially just a grass strip, and as many existing trees were retained within the airfield's boundaries as practicable, or new trees planted to replace those lost in clearing the land. In liaison with the Council for the Protection of Rural England, wherever possible the airfield buildings had been constructed from Cotswold stone, and boundaries marked with drystone walls, rather than standard military fencing, to maintain the style of the local area and its villages.

A guard house stood at the entrance to the airfield, through which all personnel had to pass to gain entry. A sergeants' mess of approximately 8,000 square feet stood opposite the guard house, close to the entrance gates, which was designed to accommodate sixty-five senior NCOs. This is where Eric would spend his nights for the next six-and-a-half months.

In August 1938, No. 6 Flying Training School (6 FTS) had arrived at RAF Little Rissington from RAF Netheravon as a part of the Air Ministry's broader re-organisation and expansion programme. It was the first flying unit to be based at the airfield, bringing with it Hawker Audaxes, Furies and Harts, and Avro Ansons. Approximately three months later, a second unit took up residence when No. 8 Aircraft Storage Unit (8 ASU) was formed there with Airspeed Oxfords. They remained the only units at the airfield until the outbreak of war in September 1939. At that time, 6 FTS changed its name to No. 6 Service Flying Training School (6 SFTS), and 215 (Training) Squadron arrived for a brief stay with its Handley Page Harrows and Vickers Wellingtons. In the meantime, 8 ASU had also changed its name to No. 8 Maintenance Unit (8 MU). The station commander and commandant of 6 SFTS was 53-year-old First World War veteran Group Captain Augustine ap Ellis, CBE. He took up his post from the airfield's opening in August 1938 and remained in command until December 1940.

Now additionally equipped with Harvard trainers, 6 SFTS's Course No. 17 commenced on schedule on 9 December 1939. However, two days after Christmas it was announced that Courses 13, 15, 16 and 17 would be extended by five weeks, and on 5 February 1940 it was made known that Course No. 17 would be extended by yet another two-and-a-half weeks. This was presumably to take advantage of the relatively quiet conditions of the 'Phoney War' then under way, although was possibly also a result of the wintery conditions, which had brought a significant amount of snow.

The syllabus at SFTS included an initial term of intermediate flying training, upon the conclusion of which the successful trainees were awarded their much coveted Pilot Badge, or 'Wings' as they are more commonly known. Following a two-week break, the pilots then returned for another term of similar length for their advanced flying course. The full SFTS course for pre-war RAFVR pilots was originally planned to be nine months long to cover the full curriculum. This was intended to bring graduating pilots up to a standard where they could hit the ground running when posted to a squadron, and become fully operational as quickly as possible. However, operational requirements led to the course being shortened to approximately six months.

This intermediate term included advanced instruction on many of the subjects previously covered in elementary training, thereunder administration, armament, airmanship, photography and signals. In addition, gunnery from a rocking nacelle to simulate air firing, law, maps and charts, meteorology, and simulated bombing, were also added to the syllabus. Armament included Browning, Lewis and Vickers guns, rifles and revolvers, stoppages and dismantling weapons to clear them.

Airborne lessons were also given in solo, dual, formation, instrument and night flying, and navigation. However, one of the problems encountered in executing the training regimen was the fact that most schools were equipped with biplanes with fixed undercarriages, such as Audaxes, Furies, Harts and Hinds, whereas the RAF was in the process of equipping its fighter squadrons with monoplanes fitted with retractable undercarriage, such as the Supermarine Spitfire and Hawker Hurricane. As such, training aircraft often had features or operating procedures that were archaic or were, at the very least, on their way out and steadily losing relevance.

The introduction of twin-engined Avro Ansons, and subsequently Airspeed Oxfords, alleviated the issue to some extent as they were monoplanes with retractable undercarriages, and were better training aids for those pilots selected for Bomber Command and other branches utilising aircraft with more than one engine. For those destined for fighter squadrons, the introduction of two-seater, single-engined Miles Masters and North American Aviation Harvards with controllable-pitch propellers and retractable undercarriages made fighter training more practical.

Many of these issues were being overcome as Eric undertook his own intermediate course, and one surviving photograph captures him with a Harvard in the background. The presence of this aircraft may suggest that he was not required to fly fixed-wheel biplanes during his SFTS course. Regardless of this issue, however, King's Regulations stated that, in order for Eric to gain his Wings by the end of the intermediate course, he had to:

- have logged a minimum of eighty flying hours, of which twenty were to have been on a service-type aircraft;
- be able to fly a service type reliably by day in clear and instrument-only conditions;
- be able to consistently land well;
- be able to execute normal and aerobatic manoeuvres appropriate to the service type;
- be able to recover an aircraft from abnormal positions by the use of instruments;
- have climbed to and maintained an altitude of 15,000 feet in a service type for at least thirty minutes; and
- have flown a service type on two triangular cross-country flights of at least 200 miles.

With little change, these basic criteria were almost identical to those applied to pilots trained in 1916 for the last war. In practice, however, although Wings could be awarded after eighty hours of solo and dual flying, the minimum number of hours had been gradually increased in practice to 120 hours by summer 1940, which may account for some of the extension to Eric's course. As such, by this time Wings were generally only granted at the culmination of the intermediate term at SFTS, not after reaching the required number of hours.[7]

There is no note in Eric's service record of the exact date he was awarded his Wings. However, it is assumed to have probably been sometime in March 1940, and they were most likely presented by Group Captain ap Ellis during a special parade to mark the event. The newly breveted pilots were then sent on two weeks' leave and returned home to celebrate their new status.

Following their break, Course No. 17's pilots returned to 6 SFTS to complete a term of advanced training, on the conclusion of which they would be posted to an operational squadron. During this term, they flew advanced trainer aircraft fitted with machine guns and bomb racks for armament training, and cine cameras for diagnosing faults in air-to-air shooting, rather than the basic and intermediate trainers. They were also required to undertake formation flying and night flying, to fly at a constant altitude and speed for a period of time, fly on a steady course maintaining a compass bearing, operate their aircraft at full weight, and make a bombing run. However, according to the urgency of turning pilots out to operational squadrons to replace losses – perhaps most noticeably following Dunkirk in May/June 1940 and until after the Battle of Britain – the second term was shortened or lengthened as necessary.

Perhaps attesting to the aptitude of the pilots in Eric's class, Course No. 17 was well into its advanced term before it suffered a fatality. On 18 May 1940, twenty-year-old Sergeant Pilot Herbert Megarry of Bangor spun into the ground at Islip, Oxfordshire, in Harvard P5842 and was killed. Tragically, only three weeks later, on 8 June, there was a second death when 26-year-old Sergeant Pilot Joseph Morehen of Tingewick, was killed in Harvard P5841, during a dive-bombing exercise. The latter fatality occurred just twenty-one days prior to the official end of the course.

However, records show that, although the course formally ended on 29 June 1940, all the graduates were posted to various operational units during that month. Ultimately, two officers and thirty-two airmen graduated, suggesting that one officer joined the course after its commencement or was commissioned before its completion. Considering that two NCOs were killed in flying accidents, it is apparent that the remaining airmen failed the course or were discharged at an earlier stage. For his part, Eric achieved 'Pass' with a combined score of 76.29 per cent for both ITW and SFTS.

Twelve of the thirty-two NCO pilots did so well on the course that, upon graduating, they were granted commissions as pilot officers on probation for the duration of hostilities. These dozen young men included 21-year-old Eric, who was issued the commissioned number 81642, and 23-year-old Gerald Langley of Stony Stratford, who was given the preceding number, 81641. The pair was posted together to No. 41 Squadron at RAF Catterick in Yorkshire on 18 June 1940, along with two graduating sergeant pilots, 21-year-old John McAdam of Gillingham, and 24-year-old Frank Usmar of West Malling.

Despite some almost certain excitement on their postings and the chance to see 'some real action', the realisation that the war was no longer flying practice in friendly skies, out of harm's way, was no doubt sobering for all four men and their families. And not without reason: the Dunkirk evacuation had recently ended, and Hitler now controlled western Europe to the Channel coast. He was about to turn his full attention to conquering Britain, and had already made his intentions quite clear in a series of ever increasing attacks on both the RAF and on ground targets in England.

In one of his most famous speeches before the House of Commons, prime minister Winston Churchill forewarned the country of what was coming, and emphasised the gravity of the situation in which Britain now found herself. On the very day that pilots Lock, Langley, McAdam and Usmar were posted to No. 41 Squadron, Churchill announced:

> What General Weygand called the Battle of France is over. I expect that the Battle of Britain is about to begin. Upon this battle depends the survival of Christian civilisation. Upon it depends our own British life and the long continuity of our institutions and our Empire. The whole fury and might of the enemy must very soon be turned on us. Hitler knows that he will have to break us in this Island or lose the war. If we can stand up to him all Europe may be free and the life of the world may move forward into broad, sunlit uplands; but if we fail then the whole world, including the United States, and all that we have known and cared for, will sink into the abyss of a new Dark Age made more sinister, and perhaps more prolonged, by the lights of perverted science. Let us therefore brace ourselves to our duty and so bear ourselves that if the British Commonwealth and Empire lasts for a thousand years men will still say, 'This was their finest hour.'[8]

It was a daunting responsibility being taken on by Eric and his fellow pilots, considering they had not yet flown an hour on operations, let alone seen the Luftwaffe. The victory over Germany would ultimately be realised, of course, but it came at a significant cost. Of the four young graduates of 6 SFTS who were posted to No. 41 Squadron that day, only one would live to see VE Day.

Chapter Three

Posted to Operations
June – August 1940

Eric's first of ultimately two operational postings was to No. 41 (Fighter) Squadron, a unit with an excellent reputation, which had already drawn its first blood of this war and had mourned its first losses. Its history spanned almost a quarter of a century, two wars, and an overseas deployment on policing duties since its formation at Gosport in July 1916.

The squadron's participation in the First World War commenced when it was sent to France in October 1916, equipped with the Royal Aircraft Factory FE8 pusher. It arrived in the dying days of the first Battle of the Somme, and over the remaining twenty-five months of the war participated in the Battles of Arras, Messines, and Cambrai, the German 1918 spring offensive, and the Battle of Amiens. By the time of its return to the United Kingdom in early 1919, the squadron boasted a hard-earned reputation with a respectable record of victories and accolades. The pilots were credited with destroying 111 aircraft and 14 balloons, sending down 112 aircraft out of control, and driving down a further 25 aircraft and 5 balloons. They were awarded four DSOs, six MCs, nine DFCs, four Mentions in Dispatches, and two French and two Belgian Croix de Guerres, while two of the groundcrew also received Military Medals.

Of the 185 pilots of Great Britain, the Empire and the United States who served with the squadron during the First World War, 39 were killed in action or died on active service, 48 were wounded or injured, and 20 became prisoners of war. Their battle honours were 'Western Front 1916–1918', 'Somme 1916', 'Arras and Cambrai 1917' and 'Somme 1918'.

Formally disbanded at the end of 1919, the unit was re-formed at RAF Northolt in April 1923 under the auspices of an Air Ministry scheme to expand the RAF by fifteen squadrons for home defence, increase the size of the Reserve and purchase 500 aircraft. Upon its rebirth, the squadron consisted of one flight of six First World War vintage aircraft, but grew significantly in size and flew seven different service types before the outbreak of the Second World War: the Sopwith Snipe, the Armstrong Whitworth Siskin III and IIIa, the Bristol Bulldog IIa, the two-seat Hawker Demon I, the Hawker Fury II, and its first monoplane, the famed Supermarine Spitfire.

The inter-war years were an exciting and busy time for No. 41 Squadron, during which time approximately 200 pilots served with the unit. This new generation of men experienced all manner of activity in addition to their training, such as inter-squadron competitions, air displays and aerobatics, and were closely involved in the development, growth and maturity of the Royal Air Force. During 1935 and 1936, the unit was also deployed to the Aden Protectorate on air policing duties, and made its first attacks in anger since the Armistice in November 1918.

In late December 1938, now based at RAF Catterick, the squadron was issued with its first Spitfires, becoming the third RAF squadron in history to take delivery of these soon-to-be iconic planes. By early February 1939, the unit had received a full complement of twenty Mark I Spitfires, and the pilots and crews then spent much of 1939 familiarising themselves with the aircraft and their new technology, handling and procedures.

However, following the official Declaration of War in September 1939, the squadron did not play any significant role in the fighting until the evacuation of Dunkirk took place in May/June 1940. Although the pilots were involved in minor skirmishes with the Luftwaffe over northern England and the North Sea prior to this, it was the Dunkirk campaign that constituted the squadron's real baptism of fire in this war.

Stationed at Hornchurch during this period, No. 41 Squadron spent twelve days operating over the evacuation beaches and acquitted themselves well, claiming six enemy aircraft destroyed and one probably destroyed. However, the unit also recorded the loss of its first pilot killed in action, and its first pilot to become a prisoner of war. On its return to Catterick on 8 June 1940, new pilots were needed to replace them. They arrived on 18 June in the form of, not two, but four new pilots, fresh from flying training. Newly commissioned Pilot Officers Eric Lock and Gerald Langley, and Sergeant Pilots John McAdam and Frank Usmar reported to the unit as ordered, but indicative of the state of emergency, had not yet flown a single hour in a Spitfire. Their flying experience had hitherto been limited to inter-war-era biplanes and Harvard trainers.

The four young men arrived on No. 41 Squadron to find a close-knit unit of several 'old hands', who had trained together for some time – in some cases for over three-and-a-half years – and knew each other well. Having flown Spitfires for eighteen months by this time, they were well versed in flying and dogfighting in the aircraft, in the routine of scrambles and pumping up retractable under-carriages, and in handling, tactics and aerobatics. They had lived together, played together and fought together. And they had lost friends. It cannot have been easy for the four young 'greenhorn' VR pilots to have joined the unit at this time, or penetrate the thick skin of experience to be accepted as an equal.

At the time, No. 41 Squadron was commanded by 31-year-old Squadron Leader Hilary R.L. 'Robin' Hood, a Cranwell graduate who had been in the RAF since late 1927. The unit's second wartime officer commanding, he had taken command in late April 1940, having spent several of the previous years as a flying instructor. He had arrived in time to take the squadron to Dunkirk and, 'although rusty in tactics, had the heart of a lion'.[1]

The flight commanders were 25-year-old Flight Lieutenant Norman Ryder, DFC (A Flight) and 24-year-old Flight Lieutenant Terry Webster (B Flight). They were experienced and well-respected pilots. Ryder had claimed his first victory in early April 1940 when he shot down a Heinkel He111 bomber off Whitby, was hit by return fire and compelled to ditch. He was rescued from the sea by a trawler and subsequently awarded the Distinguished Flying Cross for the action. It was the squadron's first decoration of the war. Webster had claimed his first victory, a probably destroyed German seaplane in December 1939, but had seen significant action during the recent Dunkirk evacuation. In the space of two days in skies over the French and Belgian coasts, he had claimed two and one shared destroyed, and one probably destroyed enemy aircraft, and was well on his way to becoming the squadron's first ace.

Upon their arrival, Eric and John McAdam were posted to A Flight, under Ryder, while Langley and Usmar were posted to B Flight, under Webster. Ryder was very particular about his training of new pilots, and was eager for them to learn fast and keep up. He made it a rule that the newest or weakest pilot on an operation must fly as his wingman, so he could take care of him and guide him. He was quite clear in his strategy, later explaining:

> My rule was that he stayed with me to the point of attack, tried to sort out the scene and then broke off, to return to base – this to be done three times. After three returns I asked the young fellow how he got on, 'Fine,' he said, 'I had a 109 filling my screen, then I remembered your orders and returned to base.' I was delighted and certain he would do well. ...
>
> One's eyes became skinned in time, and then you could see things you had no hope of doing so in the early stages. Some would return with bullet holes in their Spits and professed to having seen or felt nothing; those who didn't return – the same explanation possibly.[2]

Eric and John McAdam were now his newest apprentices. Fortunately for them, however, No. 41 Squadron was based at RAF Catterick, in a currently quieter sector of operations, enabling them time to find their feet without being thrown into the proverbial deep end. The airfield was located in 'O' Sector of No. 13 (Fighter) Group, approximately forty-two miles south of Newcastle and forty-seven miles due west of the Yorkshire coast. Also resident at the airfield at the time was No. 219 Squadron, equipped with Bristol Blenheim I (F) heavy fighters. The station commander was Wing Commander Guy Carter, AFC, who had a special affection for No. 41 Squadron as he had served with the unit on the Western Front during the First World War.

RAF Catterick was one of several airfields in the sector, which covered the area north of the Humber and all of Scotland. Its main airfields were Acklington, Catterick, Church Fenton, Grangemouth, Turnhouse, Usworth and Wick, but a number of smaller aerodromes and satellite airfields also fell within its boundaries, such as Abbotsinch, Dyce, Evanton, Hartlepool (Greatham), Leconfield, Leuchars, Scorton, Sumburgh and Thornaby. They all came under the umbrella of No. 13 Group, which was commanded by Air Vice-Marshal Richard Saul, DFC. The group's headquarters and control room were located at RAF Kenton Bar, just north-west of Newcastle.

As Eric, Gerald Langley, John McAdam and Frank Usmar entered RAF Catterick through the Guard Room, they would have passed two hangars on their right, the larger of which was home to No. 219 Squadron and the smaller to No. 41 Squadron. Around the airfield were several bell tents for accommodation, and small marquees that housed the flight offices, the flight commanders and chief engineer. The flight offices were decorated with caricatures of many of the pilots on the squadron, which had been drawn by one of the men employed in the station's officers' mess who had been a commercial artist prior to the war. The squadron's Spitfires were parked nearby on hard standings.

No. 41 Squadron had been based at RAF Catterick since returning from its deployment to the Aden Protectorate during the Abyssinian Crisis, in September 1936, less than two months after Station Headquarters Catterick was first established. On coming back from overseas, several pilots were posted away and replaced with new men; many had come and gone since, and now just one man was still on the squadron from the time of the unit's arrival at Catterick.

The single-seater fighters, to which the four young men were about to be introduced for the first time, had an overall length of 29 feet 11 inches, a wingspan of 36 feet 10 inches, a height of 11 feet 5 inches, and were armed with eight .303 Browning machine guns. They were fitted with Merlin III engines and three-bladed, two-position variable-pitch de Havilland propellers. Speed was dependent upon altitude, and the maximum of 363 mph could be attained at 18,500 feet. The service ceiling was 31,900 feet and the maximum range some 575 miles. By comparison, while the Harvards they had trained on had a similar length and height, and in fact a greater wingspan than the Spitfire, its maximum speed was just 208 mph and its service ceiling 24,200 feet.

By the time of Eric and his colleagues' entrance at Catterick on 18 June 1940, large numbers of British forces had been withdrawn from France. However, the Germans had also lost many pilots, aircrews and aircraft during the Blitzkrieg, and several weeks would now pass in relative quiet while the Luftwaffe established its authority at the Belgian, Dutch and French airfields they had occupied. They rebuilt damaged infrastructure and facilities, and moved many units forward to occupy new bases closer to the Channel coast. They also scrambled to replace their losses in preparation for their next big push: their planned assault on the British Isles.

Prime minister Winston Churchill was very much aware that to defeat and occupy Britain, Hitler would first need to achieve complete air superiority over the country. Although the lull enabled German forces to consolidate their position in western Europe, the interval also allowed Britain to prepare. The RAF was working at a feverish pace to build up strength in aircraft and aircrew, and replace their own losses of May and early June. Although the RAF had almost doubled its fighter strength to 640 aircraft by the beginning of July, it still looked weak in the face of the Luftwaffe's might, which was estimated to have encompassed around 2,500 bombers and fighters. The challenge that lay ahead was daunting to say the least.

Following a few days of kit issue, formalities, familiarisations, briefings and meeting fellow pilots and groundcrews, Eric and his three colleagues took to the air for the first time on 21 June. The weather was cloudy, but fair periods offered very good visibility in a light and variable wind. During the morning, Squadron Leader Hood made thirty-minute instrument flying practice sorties in the squadron's Miles Master with both Pilot Officer Langley and Sergeant Pilot Usmar; after lunch, all four new pilots made their first flights in a Spitfire; Langley and Lock at 14:30 hours, McAdam at 14:35, and Usmar at 15:30.

However, there was quite a procedure for them to learn in order to get the aircraft safely airborne. As the rigger dropped the top Sutton Harness straps over the pilot's shoulders, the pilot would turn on the petrol cock, prime the engine, put on his helmet, plug in his R/T lead and switch on the radio, check the airscrew pitch control and trimming tabs, lock his harness, switch on the ignition switches, signal the airman at the trolley-accumulator and press his button to start the engine. As the engine fired, the pilot signalled to the airmen to unplug the trolley-accumulator and remove the chocks in front of the wheels, whereupon the pilot would open his throttle and move forward. Picking up speed across the strip, the aircraft would finally lift off, but the work did not stop there. One of the biggest challenges for pilots on early model Spitfires was learning to coordinate between controlling with the right hand and working the throttle with the left, then changing to controlling with the left hand and pumping a lever up to thirty times with the right to lift the undercarriage manually. It required quite a bit of practice to get right, and many a pilot 'burped' his aircraft away from the airfield to the amusement of the groundcrew before he got the hang of the manoeuvre.

Once airborne and having climbed away with the wheels retracted, we can only imagine the thrill it must have been for Eric and his colleagues to fly the RAF's most modern and sleek aircraft for the first time, with all its horsepower. However, it was not straight into the action from this moment forward, and the quartet spent the ensuing weeks in training, getting comfortable with the aircraft and its manoeuvrability, speed, rate of climb and armament, and familiarising themselves with the area, including navigational landmarks, local conditions and night flying procedures, before they were allowed to fly operationally. In fact, it would not be until a full six weeks after his arrival on the squadron that Eric would be declared day and night operational and was released on an unsuspecting Luftwaffe. No one, perhaps Eric least of all, could have suspected how successful he would become in the air, but the time taken now in additional training on an active squadron proved to be a prudent investment.

Eric, Langley, McAdam and Usmar disappear from view in operational squadron documentation over the ensuing weeks as their non-operational training programme continued. For the rest of the squadron, however, it was a busy time as the Luftwaffe upped the ante in preparation for the aerial assault that would pave the way for Germany's planned invasion.

In late June and early July, the operational pilots spent a lot of their time on scrambles, responding to unidentified or hostile radar plots, which were generally on an inbound (westerly) course over the North Sea. Sections were also regularly sent up on more mundane business, tasked with flying along set patrol lines up and down the coast, to be ready in the air in case of a raid.

Shifts alternated between day operations from RAF Catterick and from their forward base at RAF Hartlepool, and night readiness from RAF Leeming and RAF Hartlepool. Pilot Officer Ted Shipman recalled that during night shifts, 'We were allowed to sleep in our flying kit, but conditions were far from comfortable lying on the stone floor of the watch office with only a straw paillasse to provide some degree of comfort.'[3]

Night-time engagements at this period of the war, prior to the introduction of efficient radar systems, were very much hit-and-miss affairs and it required an element of luck to make an interception in the darkness, particularly at sea without the assistance of any form of light. The vast majority of night-time scrambles were therefore fruitless and there was little reward for the effort and sleep deprivation. Even during the daytime, pilots would often return to Catterick having seen no sign of their quarry, or having established that the plot was friendly.

Sometimes, however, everything fell into place and a successful interception was made. One such occasion occurred just before lunch on 8 July 1940, when No. 41 Squadron's Blue Section shot down a Junkers Ju88 bomber, which crashed in flames at Aldbrough, East Yorkshire. Flying Officer Tony Lovell and Sergeant Pilot Jack Allison shared the victory, and no doubt Eric would have listened intently as the story was told and retold in the mess afterwards.

Following this brief excitement, the ensuing few weeks were relatively quiet, and the squadron's work comprised a mundane litany of uneventful patrols. In fact, it was so quiet at times that on 10 July 1940 – the day considered today as being the first day of the Battle of Britain – No. 41 Squadron undertook no operational flying whatsoever. During most of July 1940, the pilots' activity was confined to scrambles, patrols and practice flying, but the lull in activity was a distinct advantage for Eric, Langley, McAdam and Usmar, who were able continue their operational training in relative peace. On 22 and 24 July, Eric and John McAdam also flew to RAF Leeming to undertake dusk landing practice.

In late July, No. 41 Squadron received orders to fly south to participate in the quickly developing Luftwaffe offensive that would become the Battle of Britain. At 14:00 hours on 26 July, fourteen pilots took off for a thirteen-day deployment at RAF Hornchurch in Essex, and commenced their first of two tours during the campaign. They included Squadron Leader Hood, Flight Lieutenants Norman Ryder and Terry Webster, Flying Officers John Boyle, Tony Lovell and William Scott, Pilot Officers George Bennions, Guy Cory, John Mackenzie, Oliver Morrogh-Ryan, Ted Shipman and Ronald 'Wally' Wallens, and Sergeant Pilots Robert Carr-Lewty and Edward Darling.

Eric and his three colleagues were initially left behind at RAF Catterick, but McAdam headed down to Hornchurch the following day, accompanied by Flying Officer Douglas Gamblen and Sergeant Pilot Ted Howitt. Within days Langley and Usmar headed to Hornchurch, too.

Eric did not join them as he had other business to attend to. As No. 41 Squadron departed, he was granted leave to marry his sweetheart, 21-year-old former Shrewsbury beauty queen, 'Peggy' Meyers. The oldest child and only daughter of a Canadian First World War soldier and his British war bride, they were married on 27 July 1940 in a ceremony at St Julian's church in Shrewsbury.

Located on the north-eastern corner of the intersection of Fish Street, High Street, Milk Street and Wyle Cop, St Julian's had originally been built in 1195, but had undergone several transformations since then. Appearing in the Domesday Book as the church of Saint Juliana, the base of the bell tower dated from the 12th century, and comprised coursed and squared red sandstone, raised in white sandstone. A sandstone extension was added around 1485, and it was during this period that the tower above the original foundation was rebuilt. The main body of the church was replaced with a classical design between 1749 and 1750, which saw the original early English chancel demolished and replaced with a Georgian 'Preaching Box'. These works, undertaken by Shrewsbury architect and engineer Thomas Pritchard, were so thorough that he retained the tower as it stood, but rebuilt almost everything else. Further embellishments followed a century later, which included a five-bay nave, a Welsh slate roof, a lean-to Tuscan porch against the northern and southern walls of the tower, gargoyles and a parapet and pinnacles. Its stained-glass windows were replaced in 1861 and, during this period, a new Victorian façade was also added to the south side of the church.

Eric's best man was Peggy's younger brother, Peter, and Peggy's bridesmaid was Eric's younger sister, Joan. As her parents had already died, Peggy was given away by her uncle, Harley Beard, and the church's vicar, Reverend Leonard Newby, officiated. Peggy wore a 'dusky pink' wool georgette dress and matching hat, and 'wine-coloured' shoes and accessories, and carried an ivory prayer book. Eric was dressed in full RAF officer's dress uniform with pilot officer cuff insignia, Wings and VR lapel pins, peaked cap and gloves. Joan Lock wore a 'powder blue' georgette dress with matching headdress.

St Julian's church tower's six bells were cast by Mears and Stainbank of Whitechapel in 1868, having replaced an earlier set dating from 1706. Owing to the war, however, they remained silent as the freshly betrothed Mr and Mrs Eric Lock, and their families and friends, left the church. They exited through a guard of honour provided by uniformed ladies of the Auxiliary Territorial Service (ATS), of which Peggy was a member. It is believed the newlyweds enjoyed a brief honeymoon before Eric was required to report back for duty with No. 41 Squadron.

On account of his short stature at 5 feet 6 inches, and the 'dumpy' figure he made in his flying suit, Eric had quickly earned the nickname 'Sawn-off Lockie' from his fellow pilots on the squadron. Now married to a girl who was two inches taller than him, it comes as no surprise, perhaps, that she quickly earned the moniker 'Tacked-on'. It was not long, however, before Eric proved that what he may have lacked in height he more than compensated for in courage and skill in the cockpit.

In the early evening of their wedding day, as the newlyweds were still celebrating with their families, No. 41 Squadron's pilots were involved in their first combats of the Battle of Britain. Although only a little over 200 miles to their south-east, it seemed a world away.

Vectored on to a trio of Me109s flying up the coast towards Folkestone, six of the squadron's pilots found themselves in an advantageous position for a strike and dived on them. The pilots became split up as they chased individual targets, and while Flight Lieutenant Webster claimed one Me109 destroyed five miles off Dover, he almost became a victim himself when attacked by another enemy aircraft a short distance from the French coast. The squadron's other pilots were unable to make claims.

The following afternoon brought more action when the squadron was scrambled to intercept a large raid on Dover that arrived in several waves from 14:00 hours. The first wave was met by No. 74 Squadron with considerable success, and No. 41 Squadron was tasked with intercepting the second. Led by Squadron Leader Hood, eleven pilots approached Dover at 20,000 feet, only to sight around thirty Me109s above them. Initially, the squadron was not seen and attempted to get out to sea with the aim of wheeling about and catching the Luftwaffe on its way home, hopefully low on fuel and ammunition. However, the plan was foiled when three Me109s spotted them and dived straight for the rear of Squadron Leader Hood's section. Seeing the action unfolding before him and unable to raise his colleagues on his R/T system, Flight Lieutenant Webster raced to their aid alone. He opened fire on one of the Messerschmitts, but not before it had attacked and slightly wounded Flying Officer Tony Lovell, making him the squadron's first casualty of the Battle of Britain. When Webster opened fire on the Me109, it pulled up and then fell into a spin, out of sight. He subsequently claimed it probably destroyed.

Pilot Officer Bennions, flying with Webster, attacked the second Messerschmitt, which half rolled and dived almost vertically. He followed it down and opened fire again, ultimately sending the aircraft straight into the Channel, fifteen miles off Dover. A short while later, Webster spotted another Me109, which he attacked, but he was compelled to break off early as he sighted six enemy aircraft nearby, and was only able to claim it damaged. That afternoon's engagements were just a foretaste of what was to come.

On 29 July 1940, the squadron was involved in its first major battle of the campaign, in which it claimed four destroyed and one damaged enemy aircraft. However, it did not go all its own way, and its own losses amounted to one man killed in action, three aircraft destroyed and three damaged. The encounter began to give the airmen an appreciation of the formidable task that lay before them.

Airborne at around 07:20 hours to patrol Manston and continue on to Dover, the squadron was still climbing towards the Channel when they received a report of a large-scale inbound attack. It was unusually early for the Luftwaffe, and included around eighty Ju87 Stuka dive-bombers, whose target was the Port of Dover, closely escorted by a like number of Me109s. No. 41 Squadron approached Dover at 12,000 feet with some haste, feeling they had sufficient altitude as their customers were reported to be between 5,000 and 10,000 feet. Initially, Squadron Leader Hood spotted enemy aircraft approximately 1,000 feet below them and to starboard, and ordered the squadron into line astern. The pilots quickly brought themselves into position, but as they were about to attack them, a large formation of Me109s was sighted to port, just 1,000 feet above them. They were wheeling across the sun to strike the squadron from behind in a line astern formation, and even more Messerschmitts were seen above them.

An aggressive engagement then ensued, but No. 41 Squadron was not alone: within minutes, they were joined in the air by Hurricanes of Gravesend's No. 501 Squadron and North Weald's No. 56 Squadron, and Spitfires of Kenley's No. 64 Squadron. Although totalling some thirty-eight aircraft, they were still only half the strength of their aggressor's force. Nonetheless, they gave as hard as they took and headed home just after 08:00 hours claiming no less than seven Me109s and eight Ju87s destroyed, and one Me109 and six Ju87s damaged, for the loss of two RAF pilots.

For their part, No. 41 Squadron claimed four Me109s and one Ju87 destroyed, one Me109 probably destroyed and one Ju87 damaged. However, Flight Lieutenant Webster's, Flying Officer Scott's, Pilot Officer Bennions's and Pilot Officer Mackenzie's Spitfires all sustained combat damage, and Flying Officer Douglas Gamblen, who had been with the squadron since November 1937, was shot down into the Channel and killed. Being the first loss since the new pilots had joined the unit, this was no doubt a chilling lesson in the realities of war. Only around half of the eleven aircraft that had departed Hornchurch that morning returned unscathed.

RAF Hornchurch had begun to keep a tally of the victories claimed by squadrons based in the Wing since 3 September 1939. By the end of July 1940, No. 41 Squadron appeared on the list with fourteen destroyed and two probably destroyed, totalling sixteen victories to date. They were a long way behind some other units, such as No. 54 Squadron with sixty-eight victories, and No. 32 Squadron with sixty-one. However, it would not be long before No. 41 Squadron's successes climbed and surpassed them.

Over the ensuing six days, the squadron enjoyed a brief lull in activity despite being airborne operationally on a number of patrols. Weather conditions played a role in this, but the pilots were also deployed on convoy patrols between Luftwaffe raids, were unable to reach areas of activity in time, or simply saw nothing when scrambled to intercept hostile radar plots. This provided a welcome respite, and allowed the unit a little time to lick its wounds and replace or repair its aircraft.

This period also provided Sergeant Pilot Frank Usmar and Pilot Officer Gerald Langley the opportunity to make their first operational sorties with the squadron. Usmar's was undertaken on a ninety-five-minute morning convoy patrol with Flight Lieutenant Webster and Sergeant Pilot Darling on 1 August, while Langley participated in three squadron-strength patrols during the afternoon and early evening of 2 August.

It was not until 5 August that the Luftwaffe was seen again. On that occasion, a lone He111 bomber on reconnaissance work was sighted briefly during a series of convoy patrols off Dover when it dipped below a cloud layer at 21,500 feet. However, its crew spotted No. 41 Squadron simultaneously and immediately climbed again, out of sight. Flight Lieutenant Webster nonetheless made after the aircraft and chased it in and out of banks of cloud as they headed east, towards France. Closing to within 100 yards, Webster exchanged fire with the rear gunner, but avoided getting hit. While he saw his own fire enter the bomber's fuselage, he was unable to establish whether he had caused any specific damage. He banked around for a second attack, this time targeting the engines, and managed to knock one out. However, he was compelled to break off the engagement and make a strategic withdrawal when he saw a number of Me109s heading toward them. Webster arrived back at Hornchurch without further ado, claiming the He111 damaged.

No. 41 Squadron had almost reached the end of its brief deployment to Hornchurch and received orders to return to Catterick on 8 August, ostensibly for a short rest, before returning south for the remainder of the Battle of Britain and beyond. Before they did so, though, another major battle was fought on the morning of their departure. There were three major attacks by the Luftwaffe on shipping along No. 11 Group's section of the English coast on 8 August, and No. 41 Squadron was involved in repelling the second. The raid comprised a series of attacks on shipping in the Manston–Beachy Head area and on a convoy off the Isle of Wight between 09:00 and 13:00 hours. Thirteen of No. 41 Squadron's pilots took off in the direction of RAF Manston at 11:25 and, on approaching the airfield at 25,000 feet, sighted around a half-dozen aircraft 13,000 feet below them.

Flight Lieutenant Webster and Flying Officer Wallens dived down to establish their identity, and soon recognised the black crosses of seven Me109Es in two loose formations, which were cruising in level flight. Webster and Wallens swept down unseen behind them and opened fire on the more-or-less static targets as they came into range. The results were extraordinary and when the firing stopped, Webster and Wallens were credited with one Me109 destroyed each, one shared destroyed, plus three Me109s probably destroyed, two of which were credited to Webster and the third to Wallens. Webster's victories that day made him the squadron's first ace of the war and he was awarded the Distinguished Flying Cross as a result less than two weeks later. Although Eric had not even commenced operational flying by this time, he was nonetheless destined to become the squadron's second ace.

Following this operation, No. 41 Squadron spent the rest of the day preparing for its return to RAF Catterick, but needed to wait for No. 54 Squadron to arrive from the same airfield first, as it was replacing it at Hornchurch. It was not until mid-afternoon that the unit was finally able to depart for Catterick, and it arrived there at 16:30 hours, to find Eric waiting for the airmen, fresh from leave. One can well imagine there was a late session in the bar that evening as Webster and Wallens retold their story of the morning's excitement, and other pilots recounted their combats and victories as Eric caught up on news of the squadron's two-week deployment to Hornchurch.

The unit now rejoined No. 219 Squadron at Catterick to take up station and sector defences for the next few weeks. Returning to routine operations again, the first day's operational flying was confined to two uneventful patrols, one of the Saltburn–Whitby area by a section of three pilots at 09:00 hours, and another east of Saltburn at 13:30 in less than ideal conditions.

The latter patrol, comprising Pilot Officer 'Ben' Bennions, Eric and Sergeant Pilot Bob Carr-Lewty, constituted Eric's first ever operational sortie. The trio was airborne for an hour and twenty-five minutes, but they saw nothing and landed again at 14:55 with little to report. This concluded the day's operational flying. The following day was not dissimilar and operational flying encompassed just three uneventful patrols. The third and last of these, an early evening routine patrol by six pilots between 18:00 and 18:45 hours, provided Sergeant Pilot John McAdam with the opportunity finally to make his own first operational sortie with the unit; he had been on the squadron over seven weeks already.

The lull in activity off the front line gave Squadron Leader Hood the opportunity to rest his pilots before the coming onslaught and several were given six-day leave passes. These commenced on 10 August with Flight Lieutenant Terry Webster, followed by Flight Lieutenant Lord Gisborough (the intelligence officer) on 11 August, Squadron Leader Hood, Flying Officer William Scott and Pilot Officer Guy Cory on 12 August, Flying Officer Tony Lovell on 16 August, Pilot Officer Oliver Morrogh-Ryan on 18 August, and finally Flight Lieutenant Ryder on 19 August.

It was slowly but surely becoming clear, however, that the Luftwaffe was beginning to take more interest in the north of the country, as they probed a potential 'back door' to avoid the aerial defences of No. 11 Group. On 11 August, this was brought home to the squadron when a lone reconnaissance aircraft was intercepted over Helmsley, Yorkshire, by a trio of pilots – Flying Officers John Boyle and 'Wally' Wallens and Sergeant Pilot Darling – who were undertaking the day's only operational patrol.

Around half an hour into the operation, they sighted an aircraft 1,000 feet above them and climbed to investigate it. On drawing near, the pilots identified it as a Junkers Ju88 bomber on reconnaissance work, but realised they had also been seen as its pilot immediately commenced a steep dive toward a thick cloud bank. Giving chase, the trio quickly closed to 100 yards, Boyle taking the lead and firing as he did. This immediately elicited thick black smoke and caused the dorsal gunner to cease firing. Wallens then drew near to make his own attack, with slight deflection at ranges of only forty to fifty yards as they dodged in and out of cloud cover. He observed his incendiaries entering the fuselage and port engine, which subsequently feathered. The Ju88 then entered cloud again and Wallens lost it.

Darling remained above the cloud bank, hoping the aircraft might reappear and soon saw the enemy pilot had levelled his damaged aircraft out approximately fifty feet below the top of the cloud. In due course it emerged into a clear patch again, and this gave Darling the opportunity to fire a short burst at it from dead astern at a range of 250 yards, before cloud hid it anew. He dived after it, but soon emerged below the cloud base. About a minute later, however, he sighted the aircraft above him and made another attack on it from below, observing his tracer around its rudder.

The Ju88 had slowed up significantly by this time, but was lost in cloud again and was last seen in a gradual dive. Boyle, Wallens and Darling returned to Catterick unsure of its ultimate fate, but an observation post later reported as having seen it fly out over the North Sea to dump its camera, then turn back for the English coast. It subsequently made a belly-landing on Newton Moor, near Scaling. One of the crew had been killed, but three were captured. Boyle, Wallens and Darling were credited with a shared victory – No. 41 Squadron's nineteenth, and No. 13 Group's fifty-ninth since the outbreak of war.

The ensuing three days were quiet and comprised unsuccessful interceptions and uneventful routine patrols. These included a scramble to intercept Raid X20 on 14 August, which constituted Eric's second operational sortie. Airborne with Pilot Officers 'Ben' Bennions and John Mackenzie at 16:55 hours, the trio was back on the ground again at 17:30, having seen nothing. It had thus far been a subdued start to Eric's operational flying career.

However, the relative quiet of the past few days belied the truth, and everything was about to change. The Luftwaffe was on the eve of launching a major offensive on the north of the country, and the entire squadron would be heavily involved in repelling a veritable armada of bombers. Eric would also stand the ultimate test and undertake his first combats. He had not seen the Luftwaffe yet, let alone any action, and was therefore an unknown quantity. This battle was a watershed for him, and he would quickly become an essential part of No. 41 Squadron's defensive strategy. Little could anyone have imagined what was to come; a nonentity today, just one of hundreds of other young fighter pilots in the RAF, Eric was about embark on a journey that would see him decorated and become a household name within the space of just a few brief months. But it would not come without a price.

Chapter Four

Battle of Britain Ace

August – September 1940

Germany's plans for its invasion of the British Isles, 'Operation Seelöwe' (Sea Lion), foresaw landings along the English south-eastern coast between Portsmouth and Ramsgate, at Ventnor on the Isle of Wight and at Lyme Regis in Dorset, launched from points along the French and Belgian coasts. In order for the plan to succeed, however, there were several major conditions precedent. These included:

- the destruction of Royal Navy coastal units and facilities;
- the destruction or sufficient engagement in other theatres of the Royal Navy, including surface vessels, submarines and the Fleet Air Arm;
- the removal of all British sea mines in the English Channel;
- the blockade of both ends of the Channel with German sea mines;
- the domination by heavy artillery of coastal areas in the Straits of Dover;
- the destruction of morale in the RAF; and, above all else,
- the achievement of air superiority over the RAF.

If control over the proposed landing areas was not achieved, the RAF and Royal Navy could decimate the German invasion force before it even reached England. The most crucial element of the invasion, without which all else could not succeed, was therefore the last item on the above list – air superiority – and the campaign to achieve it quickly became known as the Battle of Britain.

Although the build-up to the campaign began soon after Dunkirk fell in early June 1940, the Battle itself is generally considered by Britain to have commenced on 10 July. It is also deemed to have taken place in four general phases:

   10 July–11 August 1940: the Channel battles;
   12–23 August 1940: attacks on coastal airfields;
   24 August–6 September 1940: attacks on inland airfields;
   7 September–31 October 1940: attacks on cities (the Blitz).

During the first phase, the Luftwaffe effectively probed British defences, seeking weaknesses, and methodically attacked Chain Home radar masts, coastal defences, convoys in the Channel and Channel ports. These early assaults were spearheaded by three divisions: the Third Air Fleet, which was based in France; the Second Air Fleet, which was located immediately north of the Third Air Fleet in northern France, Belgium and the Netherlands; and the Fifth Air Fleet, which was headquartered in Norway. All three were equipped with significant numbers of aircraft.

The RAF considered that, with the exception of about 400 aircraft sited elsewhere, the rest of the Luftwaffe was available to attack Britain on 1 August 1940. Their estimated strength included 1,200 single-engined fighters within 120 miles of the English coast, 500 heavy fighters, 2,000 long-range bombers, 940 short-range bombers and dive-bombers, 550 troop-carrying aircraft, 800 supply planes, 600 aircraft in training schools that could be used as reserves, and 15,000 paratroops.[1] While it was considered unlikely that any more than eighty per cent of this air power would be fully serviceable for operations against Britain at any given time, it was nonetheless a formidable force to be reckoned with.

The RAF's No. 11 (Fighter) Group, commanded by Air Vice-Marshal Keith Park, MC and Bar, DFC, was responsible for air defences in south-east England. The group was organised into sectors surrounding London, with its headquarters at RAF Uxbridge. Commands were passed from group to sector headquarters, each of which was in charge of several aerodromes, satellite airfields and fighter squadrons.

Encircling London, the sector airfields were, clockwise from three o'clock, RAF Hornchurch, RAF Biggin Hill, RAF Kenley, RAF Tangmere, RAF Northolt, RAF Debden and RAF North Weald. While under No. 11 Group's command, No. 41 Squadron was based at RAF Hornchurch, although its satellite, RAF Rochford, was often used as a forward base during daylight hours.

AVM Park had twelve Hurricane squadrons and seven Spitfire squadrons at his disposal in No. 11 Group on 14 July 1940, while No. 13 Group, where No. 41 Squadron was based on that date, boasted a further five squadrons of each type. No. 12 Group had respectively six and five squadrons at their disposal on 24 July 1940, while No. 10 Group had two of each. On 27 July, RAF Fighter Command reported an operational strength of 1,377 pilots.

Despite RAF numbers appearing to be significantly lower than Germany's in both manpower and aircraft, Britain still had noteworthy advantages. Being on the opposite side of the English Channel to the Luftwaffe was perhaps the greatest of all. Utilising the Chain Home radar stations, the RAF had advance warning of the Luftwaffe's pending arrival, with indications – though primitive by today's standards – of direction, numbers and altitude. Although only a brief forewarning, the Channel provided a buffer and bought the RAF some crucial time to get airborne squadrons to the area where the Luftwaffe was expected to arrive, and to scramble others and get them climbing before the Luftwaffe arrived.

Moreover, enemy pilots and aircrew shot down over English territory, wounded or not, were captured and taken out of circulation; German aircraft that were shot down in England, which might have otherwise been repairable or salvageable for parts, were lost from fleets; damaged aircraft had to fly back across the Channel to get home, but were often forced to ditch or return to England, such as the Ju88 shot up by the squadron on 11 August; and, perhaps most importantly, limits in fuel and range meant that Luftwaffe fighters could only operate over English territory for brief periods before being forced home, and could only penetrate so far into the country. The Luftwaffe had none of these problems during its offensives in Poland, the Low Countries or France, but they now presented daunting issues for the Luftwaffe's pilots and aircrews, that did not exist for the RAF's.

And, thus, the scene was set for a significant showdown between two of the world's largest air forces. The battle commenced on 13 August 1940 when the Luftwaffe launched 'Operation Adlerangriff' (Eagle Attack) against south-eastern England. The day it was initiated was named 'Adlertag' (Eagle Day) and was considered by the Luftwaffe to be their formal commencement of what we call the Battle of Britain.

At Catterick two days later, the morning dawned to thick cumulus cloud up to 5,000 feet. Haze rose above that altitude out to sea, and there was a light north-westerly wind with moderate to good visibility. The day started innocuously enough for No. 41 Squadron with an uneventful forty-five-minute patrol of Whitby at 10,000 feet by a trio of pilots from 08:00 hours. However, it would prove to be the squadron's greatest day of the war so far: within a few hours, the Luftwaffe would launch its largest daylight raid yet on England's northern counties.

German intelligence had inaccurately deduced that the might of the RAF was based in the south of the country, and that the north was therefore practically undefended. This day that error cost the Luftwaffe dearly, and their miscalculation of the RAF's strength sent the Luftwaffe back across the North Sea minus twenty-two of the aircraft that had made the outbound journey.

The Fifth Air Fleet sent 134 aircraft to attack a number of north-eastern airfields. Sixty-three Heinkel He111s from III/KG26, loaded with 500 kilogram and 250 kilogram high-explosive bombs, were assigned the targets of RAF Dishforth and RAF Linton-on-Ouse. They were escorted by twenty-one Me110s from I/ZG76, which were fitted with long-range belly tanks, plus jettison tanks under each wing. Fifty Junkers Ju88s from KG30 were also sent to attack RAF Driffield.

This was considerable bombing power to strike just three airfields, and was clearly designed to inflict the maximum possible infrastructure damage and render them inoperable for some time. However, on account of the substantial range at which they were operating, there was no single-engined fighter cover, and this left the force exposed to significant risk.

The attack commenced soon after midday when plots started to build in RAF control rooms, and a quick succession of movements ensued as alarms were sounded and the RAF prepared itself for the Luftwaffe's arrival. Raid 26 of twenty-plus aircraft was first plotted at 12:05 hours, 125 miles south-east of Fife Ness, travelling west, and Turnhouse's Nos 253 and 605 Squadrons, and Dyce's No. 603 Squadron, were brought to immediate readiness. At 12:10, Raid 50 of twenty-five-plus aircraft was plotted 100 miles east of Acklington, travelling at 240 mph, and No. 605 Squadron was ordered into the air to patrol Arbroath at 20,000 feet. At 12:13, Raid 46 turned south-west towards Acklington; No. 72 Squadron was ordered into the air to patrol the area at 10,000 feet, and subsequently at 25,000 feet. Three minutes later, No. 41 Squadron was called to readiness, and at 12:20 hours, No. 605 Squadron's orders changed and they were directed to May Island at 20,000 feet instead.

At 12:22, Raid 50 turned north and merged with Raid 46, eighty-five miles east of St Abb's Head, then split into three groups, continuing together on a south-westerly course towards Acklington. Meanwhile, No. 605 Squadron was ordered to St Abb's Head at 20,000 feet and thirteen pilots from No. 41 Squadron were ordered into the air at 12:34, to patrol Seaham Harbour at 20,000 feet; they were airborne within three minutes. Three squadrons were now in the air to greet the inbound Luftwaffe force, and another two – Nos 219 and 607 Squadrons – would soon reinforce their numbers. Approximately ninety enemy aircraft were about to enter No. 41 Squadron's airspace.

No. 41 Squadron was airborne in four sections under the command of Flight Lieutenant Norman Ryder. It was only Eric's third operational sortie since joining the squadron, but it proved to be his baptism of fire. His position (Red 3), and those of Pilot Officer Langley (Blue 3) and Sergeant Pilot Usmar (Green 3), were indicative of their current status within the squadron and their relative inexperience. They were there to watch, learn and strictly follow their section leaders' orders.

The first unit to make contact with the Luftwaffe was No. 72 Squadron, whose pilots intercepted a large formation of enemy aircraft at 18,000 feet, thirty miles east of the Farne Islands. They reported that the aircraft were:

Approx. 100 He.111s and Ju.88s in 3 waves of 10 close vics line abreast, each V of 3 to 10 aircraft, escorted by 36 Me.110s in 2 waves of 6 wide vics, each of 6 aircraft, fighter waves 1,000 feet above and astern of bombers. ....²

It must have made an impressive sight.

No. 72 Squadron circled the northern extremity of the formations, after which two sections attacked the bombers from above and behind, 'mostly [from] dead astern at point blank range',³ while the third section attacked the escorting Me110s. Both the bombers and heavy fighters employed limited evasive action, as the intention was clearly to continue directly to their planned targets. In fact, no sooner had No. 72 Squadron attacked, than the enemy formation divided into arrangements of thirty to forty aircraft, one turning north-west and another south-west, while the fighters generally remained off the coast.

Effectively ignoring No. 72 Squadron's presence, the bombers then proceeded to make landfall without their Me110 escort. Not surprisingly, No. 72 claimed several victories as a result. In a strike on a formation of Me110s off the coast, it also managed to shoot down the commanding officer of I/ZG76, Hauptmann Werner Restemeyer. His belly tank was hit and the aircraft exploded in mid-air; hardly had the attack begun than No. 72 Squadron removed the commander of the Me110 force from the battlefield.

Meanwhile, No. 79 Squadron had also become airborne and intercepted the raid twenty-five miles north-east of Blyth at 25,000 feet at 12:48 hours. It sighted about sixty aircraft flying southwards off Amble, towards Newcastle, in line astern vics, escorted by a large number of Me110s. These escorts were attacked by No. 79 Squadron, who found them 'timid [as they] turned away before reaching the coast, leaving [the] bombers unescorted'.⁴

When more aircraft were plotted twenty miles east of the Tyne at 12:56, No 41 Squadron was vectored to investigate and sweep around Blyth. A few minutes later, No. 219 Squadron was ordered into the air, too, to patrol Scarborough at 20,000 feet, while all the RAF's high-speed launches in the area were ordered to readiness. No. 41 Squadron approached the area, led by Pilot Officer 'Ben' Bennions, and soon sighted the inbound Luftwaffe formation approximately ten miles ahead of them. They were inbound towards Seaham Harbour at a bombing altitude of 13,000 feet, and received a dramatic reception from the coastal anti-aircraft batteries, which heralded their approach with energetic bursts of fire. Bennions observed that 'they were in a mass arrow head formation of 50 bombers massed in the arrow head, escorted by about 40 fighters, 500 yards astern and 400 feet above'.⁵ This was the first time that Eric had seen the Luftwaffe and the sight must have filled him with both awe and trepidation, as it would any man.

Bennions was ordered to attack the bombers and dispatched B Flight's Green Section, led by Pilot Officer Ted Shipman, and Blue Section, led by Flying Officer

Tony Lovell, to keep the large number of heavy escort fighters occupied. He then spearheaded A Flight's Yellow and Red Sections on to the bombers to make an initial dummy beam attack to break up their formation, and only three pilots fired. However, the tactic failed and B Flight was also unable to break up the Me110s; both the enemy bombers and their escorts maintained their tight formation. To avoid crossfire from the bombers and forward fire from the Me110s, Bennions therefore ordered A Flight to break away and climb behind the main formation of escorts instead.

The pilots attacked a rearguard of three Me110s, and then split up as they pursued individual fighters and straggling bombers. However, they were again surprised by the Luftwaffe's reaction: '[The] bombers maintained formation and [the] escort fighters made no attempt to attack our aircraft ... and even when attacked from astern, only [the] aircraft actually attacked made any attempt to engage our aircraft.'[6]

Bennions fired at one of a trio of rearguard fighters, expending a two-second burst, which immediately resulted in smoke emitting from its port engine. The Me110 broke to port, with Bennions following, and made for the cover of cloud. As it entered the cloud, Bennions broke off and returned to the squadron, still above and astern of the enemy fighters. He then sighted a lone Me110, which was climbing to join the rest of the formation. Positioning himself dead astern of it, Bennions opened up at 250 yards and after a short burst once again caused the port engine to smoke. This aircraft glided down towards Barnard Castle with petrol or glycol freely flowing out behind it as it went. Seeing it continue downwards, making no effort to recover, Bennions left it at approximately 2,000 feet and climbed again to find the squadron. Unable to do so, he returned to RAF Catterick and landed, to claim this aircraft destroyed and the first Me110 damaged.

Yellow 2, Flight Lieutenant Norman Ryder, held his fire until Bennions had led A Flight away from the dummy attack on the bombers to attack the fighters. However, picking out a Ju88 instead, he positioned himself slightly below its stern quarter at 13,000 feet and opened fire from 250 yards. Return fire from the dorsal gunner soon ceased and a large piece of the bomber's cowling detached itself, which just missed Ryder and passed over his port wing. He then observed 'a violent crimson explosion'[7] in the centre of the fuselage. Having expended all his ammunition on the aircraft, Ryder broke away six miles west of Seaham Harbour, considering the aircraft was probably destroyed: the Ju88 was losing height, its flaps or dive brakes appeared to be down and smoke was emitting from the fuselage.

Pilot Officer Oliver Morrogh-Ryan approached the fighter formations over Seaham Harbour with Yellow Section, and then spotted a Ju88 that had already been engaged by another of the squadron's Spitfires. The aircraft climbed and stalled just 100 yards in front of him. He fired a solid burst into it and saw pieces fly off the nose area, before it plummeted towards the ground. Looking about, he realised he had lost the main formation and returned to RAF Catterick to claim the Ju88 destroyed.

After the initial dummy attack on the bombers, Pilot Officer Robert Boret singled out a Ju88 at 14,000 feet and opened fire at a range of 300 yards. The aircraft broke to starboard, then commenced a slow downwards spiral in that direction. Boret followed it down and fired two more short bursts until it disappeared into cloud cover at 4,000 feet. He then returned to base, and although he submitted a Combat Report, does not appear to have made a claim: his report gives no indication of any damage he may have caused.

After Bennions had broken A Flight away from the dummy attack, Pilot Officer John Mackenzie separated from Yellow Section and climbed with Red Section above the bomber formation. He immediately picked out a Ju88 that was flying slightly to starboard of the main formation and opened fire, closing to eighty yards before he broke off. This resulted in the enemy aircraft turning sharply to starboard, with smoke pouring from its starboard engine. The plane then made for cloud cover and was lost. Mackenzie returned to Catterick and claimed the Ju88 probably destroyed. It was his first victory.

His No. 2, Sergeant Pilot Roy Ford, had followed him throughout his attacks, and then undertook a beam attack of his own on the formation. In doing so, he lost sight of the bombers, but soon noticed an Me110 making for the cover of cloud. Ford closed in on it and opened fire at 400 yards, but it reached cover before he could observe any effect of his fire. However, as it emerged from the cloud again, he saw the aircraft wheeling around on to his tail to attack him. Unable to turn inside the Me110, he took evasive action, dived for cloud himself and returned to base unscathed.

Following the initial dummy attack, Eric singled out an Me110 at 13,000 feet over Seaham Harbour. He checked his watch; it was 13:08 hours. He fired two short bursts at its starboard engine, which immediately emitted smoke and the enemy pilot thrust his aircraft into a steep dive to port to evade his fire. Eric later reported: 'I followed it down to 10,000 ft firing at the fusalage [sic], the machine gunner stopped firing, then continuing my dive, I fired at the port engine, which was then on fire. I left it at 5,000 feet still in a vertical dive, with both engines on fire.'[8] Eric then returned to RAF Catterick and claimed the Me110 destroyed.

Unfortunately, there is no further detail available on his victory, but it is clear that it was a remarkable achievement: he had claimed it in his first combat, on the first occasion that he had seen the Luftwaffe, and on his third-ever operational sortie. It was not uncommon for men to go through their entire careers without a victory, and yet Eric had managed to claim a decisive one with no combat experience but for mock dogfights during his training. Perhaps there was a little luck involved, and many targets to choose from within a small area, but it was a significant learning experience that stood him in good stead for his future combats.

While A Flight was thus occupied, B Flight was also in the thick of the action. When Bennions led A Flight towards the bombers, Flying Officer Tony Lovell broke B Flight away and guided them straight towards the escorting fighters. Lovell ordered his pilots to pick out one each and he chose the rearmost Me110 for himself. Making a textbook attack from dead astern, he fired a six-second burst from a range of 250 yards. Striking the belly tank, the Messerschmitt exploded and broke up in mid-air. Veering away, he sighted an Me110 that was attacking a Spitfire and closed to 250 yards where he fired the rest of his ammunition at it. Pieces detached themselves from the aircraft and the pilot appeared to lose control. However, by this time, another Me110 had successfully found its way on to Lovell's tail and he was forced to break off. Finding himself with no ammunition to defend himself, he evaded and returned to base to claim his first Me110 destroyed and his second probable.

When B Flight received its order to attack individual fighters, Pilot Officer Ted Shipman, leading Green Section, ordered his section to port to make a No. 3 attack on a section of Me110s. However, before the pilots could bring themselves into range to open fire, the Me110s turned sharply to port and headed straight for them. Shipman assumed the Me110s had not even seen them as they did not open fire. He later recalled: 'This was most unexpected, and our training did not prepare us for this tactic. They weren't supposed to do this!'[9] Taken unawares, he fired a two-second burst at one of the aircraft at 400 yards range. It broke to port at very close quarters, and he could not observe any effect of his fire. Looking around, he saw another Me110 and fired a number of deflection shots at it from varying ranges. The aircraft's pilot took wild evasive action and, once again, Shipman was unable to notice any effect of his fire upon it. Eventually, he succeeded in positioning himself on the Me110's tail, and delivered a stern attack, firing the remainder of his ammunition from 200 yards. This had the desired outcome and plumes of smoke billowed from its starboard engine, which feathered. However, although the Me110 appeared to be out of control, it then made an erratic turn to port and disappeared into cloud cover in the region of Barnard Castle. Unable to witness its ultimate fate, Shipman was compelled to return to Catterick to claim the Messerschmitt probably destroyed.

Later, when the sector intelligence officer confirmed that an Me110 had crashed near Streatlam Camp, around three miles east of Barnard Castle, both Shipman and Bennions thought the aircraft may have been theirs. Subsequent analysis of their claims and combat films could not determine whose victory it was. Ultimately, the Me110 was shared between them, as it was believed that Shipman had likely immobilised an engine and Bennions finished it off.[10]

When the three Me110s that Shipman had intended to attack turned towards Green Section and approached them head-on, Pilot Officer 'Wally' Wallens half rolled on to the tail of one of them as it passed him. He opened fire on it with a two-second burst from 100 yards, saw his rounds enter the aircraft, but then broke away and climbed before observing any effect. Moments later, he spotted another Me110 below him and dived on it to make a quarter attack with two rings deflection. Turning inside the aircraft, he raked it from stern to nose with a three-second burst, causing pieces of the fuselage to dislodge. The Messerschmitt then plunged into a steep uncontrolled dive, spewing smoke, and disappeared into the cloud layer below. As Wallens was unable to witness its ultimate fate, he claimed this Me110 probably destroyed, but made no claim for the first.

Finally, Sergeant Pilot Frank Usmar fired a brief deflection shot at an Me110 that passed just fifty yards ahead of him, but his attention was immediately drawn to a Heinkel He111, which was steadily approaching him. He swung his Spitfire around to face the aircraft, immediately fired a short burst at it, and climbed to starboard out of its way. However, Usmar had struck the Heinkel's fuselage fuel tank, and it exploded with such force at close range that his Spitfire was blown, uncontrolled, some distance by its upward current.

Though shaken, he managed to regain control of his aircraft and dived to 7,000 feet where he levelled out again. As he did so, he sighted a bomber emerging from cloud cover and fired a short burst from his beam, closing to full astern. Before he could observe any results of his attack, however, the aircraft disappeared back into cloud and was not seen again. Usmar then climbed to 10,000 feet but, seeing no more enemy aircraft, decided to head home. This was also his first victory, and was similarly as spectacular as Eric's, being both his first combat and first contact with the Luftwaffe: '[By 13:35 hours] … the attack on the north-east had virtually fizzled out and most of the raiders had fled: the few that remained scattered their bombs over County Durham, generally without strategic effect, before they too turned towards the sea. KG26 never found their original targets.'[11]

No. 41 Squadron's pilots all returned to RAF Catterick unscathed, and nine of the thirteen pilots on the operation compiled together their largest list of claims yet against the Luftwaffe on a single operation.

Victories, 15 August 1940	Destroyed	Probables	Damaged	Location
Bennions, George H.	–	–	Me110	Seaham Harbour, Durham
Bennions, George H. Shipman, Edward A.	Me110	–	–	West of Durham – Barnard Castle
Lock, Eric S.	Me110	–	–	Seaham Harbour, Durham
Lovell, Anthony D.J.	Me110	Me110	–	Barnard Castle, Durham
Mackenzie, John N.	–	Ju88	–	Seaham Harbour, Durham
Morrogh-Ryan, Oliver B.	Ju88	–	–	Seaham Harbour, Durham
Ryder, E. Norman	–	Ju88	–	6 miles west of Seaham Harbour, Durham
Usmar, Frank	He111	–	–	Durham area
Wallens, Ronald W.	–	Me110	–	Durham area

The Luftwaffe had been hit hard that day, and their raid was a major failure. In addition to No. 41 Squadron's ten claims, Nos 72 and 607 Squadrons each claimed eight enemy aircraft destroyed and three probably destroyed, No. 79 Squadron claimed six destroyed and three probably destroyed, No. 605 Squadron claimed four destroyed and three probably destroyed, and No. 219 Squadron claimed two probably destroyed and two damaged. The Tyne anti-aircraft batteries also claimed five aircraft destroyed and the Tees batteries another one. In all, No. 13 Group's units claimed a massive fifty-nine victories: thirty-one destroyed, nineteen probably destroyed and three damaged. No major military targets were harmed, and only four RAF fighters were damaged, one pilot wounded and one injured when landing.

Upon their return home, KG26 reported eight bombers lost, KG30 seven bombers and ZG76 seven Me110s. Although these numbers are significantly lower than the RAF's claims, they do not include statistics for damaged aircraft, and in any case indicate that the Luftwaffe lost approximately sixteen per cent of the planes it had dispatched and over eighty airmen in a single operation – a figure any air force could ill afford to lose in a single operation.

It was a bitter blow for the Luftwaffe, which had clearly underestimated the strength of the RAF in the north of Britain, and had hoped to enter the country unchecked. Clearly, Luftwaffe intelligence had no inkling of Dowding's policy of rotating squadrons between the north and south of the island to rest pilots. This simple procedure derailed a major offensive, as it provided battle-tested squadrons and combat-experienced pilots in the north of the country, too.

As the operation resulted in such unacceptably high losses, which would be unsustainable over an extended period, the Fifth Air Fleet took no further part in

BATTLE OF BRITAIN ACE 53

the Battle of Britain. This was the first significant victory of the campaign – one in which No. 41 Squadron had played a solid role – and it was now down to the Second and Third Air Fleets to achieve air superiority over the RAF without them.

As such, it was just as much actions such as those over northern England on 15 August 1940, as it was those in the skies over the south-east that prompted prime minister Winston Churchill to make one of his most famous speeches before the House of Commons five days later:

> The gratitude of every home in our Island, in our Empire, and indeed throughout the world, except in the abodes of the guilty, goes out to the British airmen who, undaunted by odds, unwearied in their constant challenge and mortal danger, are turning the tide of the world war by their prowess and by their devotion. Never in the field of human conflict was so much owed by so many to so few.[12]

Although just a brief sentence in a larger speech, the words 'Never in the field of human conflict was so much owed by so many to so few' have become some of the most famous that we associate with the Battle of Britain today. Considering the size of the Luftwaffe force attacked and driven off by the squadrons in No. 13 Group on 15 August 1940, No. 41 Squadron earned this accolade as much as any other unit fighting over Essex, Kent, Sussex and Surrey at this time. And this pertained to Eric as much as it did any other pilot on this squadron.

As the Luftwaffe recoiled after its beating in the north of England on 15 August, and rethought its strategies, the ensuing days were quiet and passed with little of interest to report. Patrols were flown and scrambles undertaken to intercept plots, but most were uneventful and it was six days before No. 41 Squadron saw the Luftwaffe again.

On the afternoon of 21 August, Pilot Officers Ted Shipman and Gerald Langley, and Sergeant Pilot Frank Usmar, were on a routine patrol of Whitby and Scarborough, when they were ordered fifteen miles off the coast to intercept a plot designated Raid X7. Shipman soon sighted a lone He111 bomber, two miles dead ahead of them in 5/10ths cloud at 9,000 feet, heading east. He ordered his section into line astern as they closed, and then opened fire from dead astern at a range of 300 yards, closing to 200, and expended one long burst of 1,440 rounds. The dorsal gunner immediately fired back at him and when the Heinkel dived, the ventral gunner opened up, too, but the tracers indicated their fire was wide and their efforts were in vain. Shipman had hit the Heinkel's starboard fuel tank and the engine emitted white smoke. As a result of the damage, the aircraft fell into a steep downwards spiral to starboard, which progressed to a vertical dive. The starboard wing tore off just before the aircraft hit the water and it sank immediately, ten to fifteen miles east of Flamborough Head. Shipman re-formed his section and returned to RAF Catterick, landing just after 17:00 hours to claim the Heinkel destroyed. Neither Langley nor Usmar had had an opportunity to fire.

Nominal Roll, 21 August 1940[13]

Flight A	Flight B
Flight Lieutenant E. Norman Ryder	Squadron Leader Hilary R.L. Hood
Flying Officer William J.M. Scott	Flight Lieutenant J. Terence Webster
Pilot Officer John. N. Mackenzie	Flying Officer Anthony D.J. Lovell
Pilot Officer Guy W. Cory	Pilot Officer John G. Boyle
Pilot Officer Oliver B. Morrogh-Ryan	Pilot Officer Ronald W. Wallens
Pilot Officer Robert J. Boret	Pilot Officer Edward A. Shipman
Pilot Officer George H. Bennions	Pilot Officer Gerald A. Langley
Pilot Officer Eric S. Lock	Sergeant Pilot I. Edward Howitt
Flight Sergeant James E. Sayers	Sergeant Pilot Edward V. Darling
Sergeant Pilot Robert A. Carr-Lewty	Sergeant Pilot Jack W. Allison
Sergeant Pilot Roy C. Ford	Sergeant Pilot Frank Usmar
Sergeant Pilot John McAdam	

The ensuing days were spent on routine patrols and flying training, but the night of 24/25 August 1940 was of particular note. This was not because of anything No. 41 Squadron was involved in, but rather because the Luftwaffe bombed central London for the first time. Hitler had banned attacks on civilian targets and this strike was actually an accident. However, fearing the Luftwaffe had changed its tactics, Bomber Command retaliated by bombing Berlin the following night.

Reichspropagandaminister Josef Goebbels expressed a 'kolossale Wut gegen die Engländer'[14] – a colossal rage against the English – for the attack, and planned his response. This heralded the beginning of the Blitz and resulted in the mass evacuation of London and other cities, as children, women and valuables were sent to the country. However, this had the ironic consequence of easing pressure on the airfields, enabling the RAF to repair and rebuild damaged infrastructure, and to re-equip, resupply and reinforce air and ground units. The events of these few days and nights are seen as a crucial turning point in the Battle of Britain.

After almost a month at RAF Catterick, No. 41 Squadron was sent back to RAF Hornchurch on the afternoon of 3 September 1940. An initial fifteen pilots departed Catterick in their Spitfires at 13:30 hours: Squadron Leader Hood, Flight Lieutenants

Ryder and Webster, Flying Officers Lovell, Scott and Wallens, Pilot Officers Bennions, Cory, Langley, Mackenzie and Morrogh-Ryan, and Sergeant Pilots Carr-Lewty, Ford, Howitt and Usmar. They were diverted to Debden en route as a result of a raid in progress in the Hornchurch sector when they were due to arrive, and therefore put down early at RAF Debden at 14:15. The pilots took off again at 16:00 and landed at Hornchurch in bright, almost cloudless skies just under thirty minutes later.

The Battle of Britain was now in full swing, and they found that the atmosphere at Hornchurch had changed completely since their last visit; there was now a 'powerful, but subdued, sense of urgency in the air'.[15] Significant improvements had been made at the airfield under the station commander, Wing Commander Cecil Bouchier, OBE, DFC, who, like the station commander at RAF Catterick, Wing Commander Guy Carter, was coincidentally also a former No. 41 Squadron pilot. It seems the pilots were in good hands wherever they were posted.

Station defence staff had been increased to approximately 1,800 army and RAF personnel, and the entire airfield had been surrounded with barbed wire. A series of trenches had been dug, additional pill boxes had been built at strategic locations outside the perimeter and, across the River Ingrebourne, the ridge that overlooked the aerodrome was now patrolled twenty-four hours a day by a detachment of the Glasgow Highlanders. This served to protect the airfield's RDF (radio direction finder) and VHF huts, but also provided some immediate defence if German forces landed and attempted to secure the high ground that dominated the airfield.

A searchlight had been erected on the western side of the airfield, illuminating areas where German forces might land, and a dispatch rider letter service was introduced in case telephone lines were cut. Two armoured cars manned by army personnel had also been deployed, and four Bofors guns were now in emplacements manned by a detachment from the Royal Artillery.

Emergency accommodation contingency arrangements were put in place for up to 1,000 people in the event of building damage, special evacuation routes were mapped out, and an emergency landing ground was identified at Hainault Farm, around six miles north of Hornchurch Station. Plans had also been prepared by the Royal Engineers for the destruction of ammunition, fuel and stores dumps in case the airfield was threatened with evacuation and capture, and this same unit was responsible for filling in and repairing bomb damage to the airfield.

No. 54 Squadron was eagerly awaiting No. 41 Squadron to relieve them at Hornchurch, so they could fly north to RAF Catterick for rest. Attesting to the level of action they had recently been involved in, they were leaving as the current top-scoring Hornchurch-based unit with claims of ninety-three destroyed and fifty-two and one shared probably destroyed, for losses of their own of twenty-eight aircraft and ten pilots.

No. 41 Squadron now joined Nos 222 and 603 Squadrons at Hornchurch. Taking up the accommodation and dispersals areas vacated by No. 54 Squadron, No. 41 Squadron's A and B Flights were allocated separate dispersals and huts on opposite sides of the airfield's grass strip, and the airmen spent the rest of the day settling in; there was no operational flying.

The following day, Eric, Flying Officer Boyle, and Sergeant Darling arrived from Catterick, and Sergeant Pilots McAdam and Allison turned up soon after them by ground transport. That day, the rest of the squadron was airborne on two patrols, but both were uneventful. It was the proverbial quiet before the storm.

Thursday 5 September 1940 dawned to almost cloudless skies and a light wind. It would develop into the squadron's most intensive day in its history, which saw it savaged and left it in tatters. By the end of the day, approximately one-third of the pilots had become casualties in one form or another. The battles of 15 August paled into insignificance in comparison.

The Luftwaffe mounted two major attacks on Kent and London on this day. The first of these comprised approximately 150 aircraft, made up of two groups of twenty Dornier Do17 bombers, which were protected on the flanks and rear by around fifty Me109s each. They made landfall between Dover and Dungeness at 09:40 hours and headed to the Croydon–Kenley–Biggin Hill area via Maidstone, although a few also penetrated as far as Brentwood.

No. 41 Squadron was one of ten units ordered to intercept the Luftwaffe, but only four – Nos 41, 111, 501 and 603 Squadrons – engaged them, assisted by B Flight of No. 79 Squadron, which was already airborne to patrol Biggin Hill. No. 41 Squadron was also airborne, having been in the air since 09:15 hours on a routine patrol to Manston, but Eric was not among them.

As the raid developed, the unit was vectored to Maidstone at 25,000 feet, and the Luftwaffe was soon sighted 9,000 feet below them. Squadron Leader Hood, leading B Flight, ordered the squadron into line astern, then told Flight Lieutenant Norman Ryder to detach A Flight and remain above them to cover B Flight's attack. Ryder should then choose his own objectives and pick his opportunity to attempt to break through to the bombers.

And then it was on. Flying Officer Boyle claimed a destroyed Me109; Squadron Leader Hood claimed a damaged Dornier Do17 but returned to base early as his engine was running roughly; Flying Officer Wallens claimed a damaged Do17 and a probable Me109; Flight Lieutenant Webster claimed an Me109 and an He113 destroyed, and an Me109 damaged; and Sergeant Pilot Darling may have damaged an Me109, but submitted no formal claim.

While they were in the midst of their combats, Flight Lieutenant Ryder led A Flight down on to the Me109s that were attempting to attack B Flight from the rear and flanks. The pilots picked out individual fighters and pounced on them, sending them in all directions. Ryder, Pilot Officer Bennions and Sergeant Pilot Carr-Lewty each claimed an Me109 probably destroyed, but Carr-Lewty ran out of fuel and force-landed his aircraft near Stanford-le-Hope. Although uninjured, he was the only casualty of the 09:15 patrol, but in return the squadron claimed three enemy aircraft destroyed, four probably destroyed and three damaged, for the total expenditure of 9,728 rounds of ammunition.

For its part on this morning, No. 79 Squadron claimed one Do215 probably destroyed, No. 111 Squadron claimed two Me109s destroyed, one Me109 probable and one Do17 damaged, and Nos 501 and 603 Squadrons each claimed one Me109 destroyed, one probable and one damaged. However, there were several casualties: No. 19 Squadron lost their officer commanding, who was killed, while No. 501 Squadron sustained one casualty who was shot down and wounded, and No. 603 recorded two: one pilot killed and a second wounded.

The day's second raid commenced at 14:15 hours, and comprised three separate attacks. The first targeted the Thames Estuary, the second Biggin Hill and the third Detling. No. 11 Group ordered thirteen fighter squadrons to intercept the inbound raid: Nos 1 (Canadian), 41, 43, 46, 66, 72, 111, 222, 249, 253, 501, 601 and 603. Of these units, Nos 41, 43, 46, 66, 72, 222, 249, 501 and 603 engaged the Luftwaffe, as did Nos 17, 73 and 303 Squadrons, who were not detailed to the raid, but were airborne, sighted the Luftwaffe, and attacked them anyway.

No. 41 Squadron took off at 14:59 in four sections of three pilots, led by Squadron Leader Hood, with an order to patrol base at 15,000 feet. However, as the pilots climbed away from Hornchurch, with Eric as No. 2 to Flight Lieutenant Ryder, the Luftwaffe was seen to their port, over Rochford, heading straight toward them. The enemy formation consisted of thirty Ju88s in tight vics, with He111s in the leading section and a large number of Me109s as escorts.

Pilots, 5 September 1940 15:00 hours	Serial No.	Section	Position
Hood, Hillary R.L.	P9428	Green	1
Wallens, Ronald W.[16]	X4021	Green	2
Boyle, John G.	R6697	Green	3
Webster, J. Terence[17]	R6635	Blue	1
Lovell, Anthony D.J.	R6885	Blue	2
Howitt, I. Edward	N3118	Blue	3
Ryder, E. Norman	R6887	Red	1

Lock, Eric S..	N3162	Red	2
Morrogh-Ryan, Oliver B.[17]	R6635	Red	3
Bennions, George H.	R6884	Yellow	1
Cory, Guy W.[16]	X4021	Yellow	2
Ford, Roy C.	R6756	Yellow	3

With no time to gain any height advantage, Hood initially ordered the squadron into line astern, but then directed B Flight to echelon port instead, for a head-on attack. A Flight, under Ryder, was instructed to act as rear protection. Hood swung in behind a section of three Do17s, and Flying Officers Wallens and Boyle followed him around. It is unknown today whether Hood and Boyle fired, but Wallens later reported that he opened fire on the starboard aircraft with a two-second burst from dead astern, causing the aircraft to emit thick blue smoke and dive out of the formation. However, they were unable to press home their attack as four to six Me109s of JG54 swept in behind them and they were forced to break away. From his position, Ryder saw the Luftwaffe formation turn north, while Hood and Wallens broke hard to port and dived. As they did, enemy fighters rapidly followed them and Hood appears to have been hit almost immediately. There is no firm evidence of what happened to him, but his aircraft is believed to have exploded and broken up over Nevendon, Essex. A parachute was found, and fragments of his aircraft, but his body was never recovered and he remains missing to this day.

After firing at the bombers, Wallens dived almost vertically to 10,000 feet to escape the fighters and then climbed up-sun to around 18,000 feet. Turning south-east, he headed out to sea with the sun behind him and went in search of enemy fighters. He soon sighted two Me109s below him, around ten miles south-east of Dover, on their way home in open formation. Sweeping down behind them, he closed to 300 yards and opened up on one from dead astern and slightly below with a two- to three-second burst, as he reduced his range to 200 yards. Large pieces dislodged from the rear of the Me109 and it emitted thick blue smoke, after which it turned on its side and made a steep dive towards the sea.

Wallens then slid across behind the second Me109, whose pilot was oblivious to the loss of his colleague, and lined up the aircraft in his sights. He was about to open fire, when he was attacked from behind. Cannon and machine-gun fire ripped holes in his rudder and wings, destroyed his instrument panel and radio, and scored the inside of his armoured glass windscreen. Hit in the leg by a cannon shell, which felt like a hammer blow, he later attested, it did some horrific damage. Seriously wounded, he turned back for the English coast, pleased to find his aircraft still flying, though labouring under the damage it had sustained. Recognising he would likely have to bale out sooner or later, Wallens decided to do so while the aircraft was flying straight and level. However, on trying to slide back his canopy, he found it would not budge and realised he would have to make a forced-landing on solid ground or he would drown.

In time he made landfall and steered towards Hornchurch, losing height as he went. He made it to within four miles of the airfield when the engine seized at low altitude and he glided down to make a heavy landing in a field near Orsett, Essex. The aircraft slid through a fence and over a ditch before it came to rest under a large tree.

Wallens was on the ground, but could not free himself and was immensely afraid of the aircraft catching fire. Although it seemed like an eternity to him, two men soon ran up and freed him. It was only now that he realised what a close shave he had had: a round of ammunition had removed the right earphone from his flying helmet and the face of his watch had been removed by another, or by a piece of shrapnel or flying debris. He was taken to hospital and did not return to flying until May 1941.

Having originally led Blue Section down after Squadron Leader Hood in the dive to escape the Me109s, Flight Lieutenant Terry Webster climbed again to seek a suitable target. By this time, other British squadrons had arrived on the scene and the sky was full of Spitfires and Hurricanes, all pitted against large numbers of Me109s, Ju88s and He111s.

One of No. 73 Squadron's flight commanders, Flight Lieutenant Reginald Lovett, was close by, attacking a Ju88, when return fire from the bomber hit his starboard wing. Breaking away to evade the fire, he collided with Webster, who was climbing towards the main enemy formation. Lovett's Hurricane lost a wing, but Webster's Spitfire disintegrated in mid-air. Nicknamed 'Unlucky Lovett' by his fellow pilots after a series of mishaps, he was perhaps actually fortunate on this occasion in that was able to parachute to safety, and landed at Rawreth uninjured. His aircraft crashed in farmland approximately a quarter of a mile south-east of Nevendon Hall.

It is believed that Webster also managed to take to his parachute, possibly injured, but eyewitnesses reported seeing a pilot's parachute became entangled in his tailplane. As no one else fits the circumstances, it is believed to have been Webster, who did not survive. Pieces of his Spitfire fell over a large area, from Bonvilles Farm on the A127 Southend arterial road, across fields, and in Nevendon, which is where the main portion of the fuselage was found. Fragments of the aircraft were discovered by numerous local people, including the tail section, the seat, the engine and a wing. Webster himself was recovered by the A127. The distribution of wreckage from Lovett's and Webster's aircraft implied a common point of origin over Bonvilles Farm at North Benfleet, Essex.

Little is known of the action that Webster's No. 2, Flying Officer Tony Lovell, was involved in, although it is known that he was shot down over the Thames Estuary and injured. Initially spinning down several thousand feet, he baled out at a suitable height and landed safely on Pitsea Marshes. His Spitfire plunged into a residential area in South Benfleet, striking two homes and setting their roofs on fire, but fortunately no one on the ground was hurt. Lovell came to the site to see the damage for himself, limping slightly from an ankle injury. Most of the aircraft had fallen on the road but the engine, which had probably detached itself on impact, finished up on a vacant piece of land between two houses.

It is possible that whoever shot down Lovell, or that pilot's wingman, went after the No. 3 in the section, Sergeant Pilot Ted Howitt. When Flight Lieutenant Ryder saw the mauling B Flight was taking, he led A Flight down to take on their attackers. He dived on to the Me109 on Sergeant Howitt's tail, firing five bursts as he chased it earthwards to 8,000 feet. The Messerschmitt started smoking, and then exploded at around 7,000 feet near the Isle of Sheppey, Kent. Ryder saved Howitt's life and claimed the Me109 destroyed.

Eric was flying his first operational sortie from Hornchurch and was Ryder's wingman. He witnessed his flight commander's victory, and then broke away to find a target of his own. Setting his sights on an He111, he attacked and seriously damaged the bomber, but provides no detail of the action in his Combat Report. He followed the aircraft down as it lost altitude and ditched in the Thames, its momentum suddenly arrested in a large splash and spray of water.

The victory thus confirmed, Eric climbed back to 8,000 feet, where he sighted another He111, which had become separated from the main formation and was flying alone. Firing initially at its starboard engine, which he set on fire, the bomber slowed and Eric quickly closed to just seventy-five yards. Opening fire again with two long bursts, smoke emitted from the fuselage and the pilot dropped the undercarriage to indicate he was giving up, and commenced a glide to bring his aircraft down safely. Eric understood the message, stopped firing and escorted the Heinkel down to confirm his second victory.

However successful Eric may have been thus far this day, he was still new to combat – it was only his fifth operational sortie and second engagement – and he made an error, which could have had a fatal outcome. In his concentration on the bomber, he had failed to see an approaching Me109. In fact, he was unaware of it until it opened fire on him from astern and below, and he was wounded in the left leg. The injury was only slight and damage to his aircraft minor, and Eric took violent evasive action and whipped around on his opponent. The Luftwaffe pilot climbed away and stall-turned, but the tactic failed and Eric was presented a perfect target. He opened fire, hit the Messerschmitt's fuel tank, and it exploded in mid-air. Looking about, he caught sight of the second Heinkel again, which was still gliding earthwards. He dived after it, and caught up with it in time to watch it hit the water at the mouth of the Thames, approximately ten miles from the first. Displaying humanity despite the job at hand, Eric circled a nearby boat and flashed his downward light until it headed toward the downed aircraft. He then joined up with Red 3, Flying Officer 'Buck' Morrogh-Ryan and returned to base.[18,19]

Morrogh-Ryan had also been in action, as the No. 3 in Flight Lieutenant Ryder's Red Section. Like Eric, he had also witnessed Ryder's destruction of the Me109 on the tail of Sergeant Howitt, but had then lost the main formation. However, he soon sighted a lone Me109 making for France down the Thames, and gave chase. Catching up with it over Margate, just before they reached open sea, Morrogh-Ryan fired all his ammunition into the aircraft, which was smoking by the time his last round was discharged. Unable to defend himself anymore, he broke off to return to Hornchurch, but looked back to see the Messerschmitt burst into flames. It then turned on to its back and dived into the sea. On his return up the Thames, Morrogh-Ryan witnessed Eric's victories, and joined up with him to fly home together. Eric had also used up all of his ammunition by this time and was just as determined to get back to Hornchurch as quickly as possible.

Independent of Ryder's Red Section, Pilot Officer 'Ben' Bennions had led Yellow Section directly towards the bombers. Approaching a trio of Ju88s from astern, he picked out one and fired two two-second bursts. By the time he stopped firing, the dorsal gunner had fallen silent and the port engine had begun to emit smoke. Bennions then spotted an Me109 diving towards him and swerved to port to evade it. Climbing again, he saw that the formation had turned to starboard, and this gave him a new opportunity to make an attack.

Diving anew, he picked out another Ju88 below him and fired several bursts at it, which resulted in its port engine exploding and port undercarriage dropping. He fired again, this time aiming for the starboard engine, and it, too, was soon smoking. The Junkers slowed markedly and started to fall below and behind the main formation. However, as Bennions had exhausted all his ammunition by this time, he broke off the engagement and did not witness its ultimate fate. He then returned to Hornchurch, where he claimed his first Ju88 damaged and his second probably destroyed.

Flying Officer Guy Cory and Sergeant Pilot Roy Ford had followed Bennions around in line astern for the initial attack on the Ju88s. Flying as Yellow 3, Ford watched as Bennions and Cory veered away after firing at them, then opened fire on one of the bombers himself, expending a two-second burst with one ring deflection. He then pulled away, too, as he was attacked by Me109s, and evaded by making a spin to escape them. Levelling out again, he found himself approximately 2,000 feet above a number of Hurricanes. He was about to join up with them when a lone Me109 dived across his line of flight. He fired a two-second burst, as he dived on to its tail, then fired another two bursts at it from a range of 200 yards as he followed it down. After a final burst of fire, Ford noticed what he thought was white vapour issuing from the aircraft, but he then lost sight of it. Ford now found himself alone, five miles out over the Channel and around five miles north of the Thames Estuary. He turned back for the coast and headed directly for Hornchurch where he claimed the Me109 damaged.

In the melee, Flying Officer Cory was shot up and slightly wounded in the leg. He force-landed his aircraft on the Isle of Sheppey, but few further details are available on the circumstances of the engagement in which he was involved.

Twelve Spitfires had departed Hornchurch at 15:00 hours, but only eight returned at 15:45, and two of them had also suffered combat damage. Within forty-five minutes that afternoon, No. 41 Squadron had been changed irrevocably, and the day would prove to be its most intensive of the war. By its end, two pilots were dead and three more wounded, four aircraft had been destroyed, and two damaged, and nineteen victories were credited to the unit. Never before and never again would No. 41 Squadron's tally of victories or casualties in a single day be so high.[20] The full list of victories for 5 September is shown below.

Victories, 5 September 1940	Destroyed	Probables	Damaged	Location
Bennions, George H.	–	Me109E	–	8 miles south of Maidstone, Kent (09.15)
Bennions, George H.	–	Ju88	Ju88	Isle of Sheppey, Kent (15.00)
Boyle, John G.	Me109E	–	–	Maidstone, Kent (09.15)
Carr-Lewty, Robert A.	–	Me109E	–	South-East of Canterbury, Kent (09.15)
Ford, Roy C.	–	–	Me109E	Isle of Sheppey, Kent-Channel (15.00)
Hood, Hilary R.L.	–	–	Do17	South of Gravesend Ashford, Kent (09.15)
Lock, Eric S.	Me109E	–	–	Isle of Sheppey, Thames-Estuary, Kent (15.00)
Lock, Eric S.	2 He111	–	–	Isle of Sheppey, Thames-Estuary, Kent (15.00)
Morrogh-Ryan, Oliver B.	Me109E	–	–	Margate, Kent–Channel (15.00)
Ryder, E. Norman	–	Me109E	–	Maidstone, Kent (09.15)

Bayston Hill Quarry, managed by Charles Lock, ca 1910. © *Tarmac Quarry.*

Bomere Farm, Bayston Hill, where Eric was born on 19 April 1919. © *Steve Brew; photographed with the kind permission of Tim and Sarah Adkins.*

Clockwise, from top: Charles Lock with Eric, aged about three, and Joan, around twelve months. © *Lock and Cornes families.*

Eric and Joan with their pet Collie, Bomere Farm, ca 1927.
© *Lock and Cornes families.*

Eric, aged about twelve months.
© *Lock and Cornes families.*

Eric, around seven years old, with Joan at Bomere Pool. © *Lock and Cornes families.*

Clivedon School, pictured a few years before Eric attended, with children playing in the adjacent field.
© *Henry Hand.*

Clivedon School, Church Stretton, which Eric attended in 1926-1928, is now a private home.
© *Mike Bradbury; photographed with the kind permission of Bill and Claire Hatfield.*

Above: The large schoolroom of the former Shrewsbury Boys' High School, where Eric would have had his lessons. © *Gerald Cock via Nigel Shuttleworth.* **Inset:** Eric, Joan, and his parents on holidays at Rhyl, Denbighshire, northern Wales, ca 1928.
© *Lock and Cornes families.*

The Lock family, ca 1929. © *Lock and Cornes families.*
Inset: Eric on 18th birthday in 1937 with his Singer 9 Le Mans. © *Lock and Cornes families.*

Peggy Meyers, aged about eighteen, around the time that Eric first met her.
© *Philip and Richard Meyers.*

Eric in a Sidcot Suit during flying training at Meir Aerodrome or RAF Little Rissington, 1939.
© *Melissa John via Greg Muddell.*

Eric with fellow RAFVR Sergeants undertaking pilot training at Meir, 1939. © *Lock and Cornes families*

Eric in uniform outside a hut during flying training at Meir or Little Rissington, 1939.
© *Melissa John via Greg Muddell*

The Metropole Hotel and De La Warr Pavilion, Bexhill-on-Sea, where Eric undertook his ITW course in late 1939. Drill was done in the carpark, and a number of lessons were taught on the flat rooftop of the pavilion. © *Bexhill Museum.*

Eric's class during its first term at 6 SFTS, Little Rissington, early 1940. © *Lock and Cornes families*

Eric during his SFTS training. Note the Harvard trainer in the background, 1940.
© *Melissa John via Greg Muddell.*

Eric's class at 6 SFTS, RAF Little Rissington, spring 1940. © *Lock and Cornes families.*

Eric as a Sergeant Pilot during his advanced term at 6 SFTS, prior to him being commissioned on 18 June 1940. © *Melissa John via Greg Muddell.*

Eric with Sgt Plt John McAdam, who joined 41 Squadron from 6 SFTS together on 18 June 1940. © *Lock and Cornes families.*

When Eric married Peggy Meyers on 27 July 1940, their Best Man was Peggy's brother Peter and their Maid of Honour was Eric's younger sister Joan. © *Philip and Richard Meyers.*

Eric with a 41 Squadron Spitfire, ca July-August 1940, possibly at RAF Catterick. © *Melissa John via Greg Muddell,*

Above: Eric at the door of the Lock family home, 'Eastington', on Lyth Hill Road, Bayston Hill, ca August 1940. © *Melissa John via Greg Muddell.*

Right: A portrait of Eric, photographed in the latter half of September 1940, probably during his few days leave at the end of the month.
Crown Copyright expired.

Lock

SECRET.   FORM "F"

A.
B.   46.
C.   15.8.40.
D.   A. Flight 41 Squadron.
E.   90.
F.   Ju.88, Me.110.
G.   1308.
H.   Seaham Harbour.
J.   15,000 feet
K.
L.   NIL.
M.   NIL.
N. (1) N/A.
N. (2) N/A.

Me110 Destroyed g. 9/6

GENERAL REPORT.

In formation with 41 Squadron we were ordered to patrol north of base 20,000 feet. After flying for a while, we saw formation of Ju.88 and Me.110. The Squadron then went into line astern, we made an attack, the second attack, I fired two short bursts into the starboard engine of a Me110. This started to smoke, it went down in a steep dive to Port. I followed it down to 10,000 ft firing at the fusalage, the machine gunner stopped firing, then continuing my dive, I fired at the port engine, which was then on fire. I left it at 5,000 feet still in a vertical dive, with both engines on fire.

                                    E. S. Lock.

                        Signed.   E.S. Lock. P/O.

Eric's first Combat Report, in which he claimed the destruction of a Messerschmitt Me110 on 15 August 1940. © *41 Squadron Archives.*

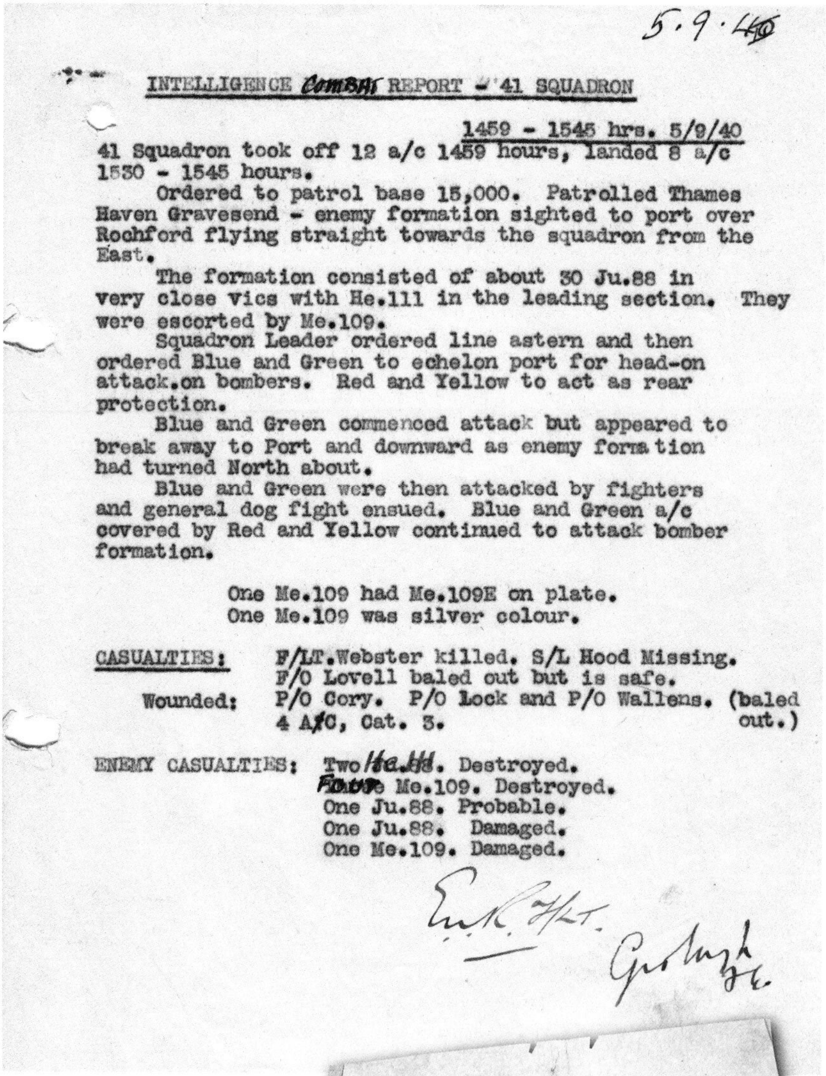

5.9.40

INTELLIGENCE COMBAT REPORT – 41 SQUADRON

1459 – 1545 hrs. 5/9/40

41 Squadron took off 12 a/c 1459 hours, landed 8 a/c 1530 – 1545 hours.

Ordered to patrol base 15,000. Patrolled Thames Haven Gravesend – enemy formation sighted to port over Rochford flying straight towards the squadron from the East.

The formation consisted of about 30 Ju.88 in very close vics with He.111 in the leading section. They were escorted by Me.109.

Squadron Leader ordered line astern and then ordered Blue and Green to echelon port for head-on attack on bombers. Red and Yellow to act as rear protection.

Blue and Green commenced attack but appeared to break away to Port and downward as enemy formation had turned North about.

Blue and Green were then attacked by fighters and general dog fight ensued. Blue and Green a/c covered by Red and Yellow continued to attack bomber formation.

One Me.109 had Me.109E on plate.
One Me.109 was silver colour.

CASUALTIES: F/LT. Webster killed. S/L Hood Missing.
F/O Lovell baled out but is safe.
Wounded: P/O Cory. P/O Lock and P/O Wallens. (baled out.)
4 A/C, Cat. 3.

ENEMY CASUALTIES: Two He.111. Destroyed.
Four Me.109. Destroyed.
One Ju.88. Probable.
One Ju.88. Damaged.
One Me.109. Damaged.

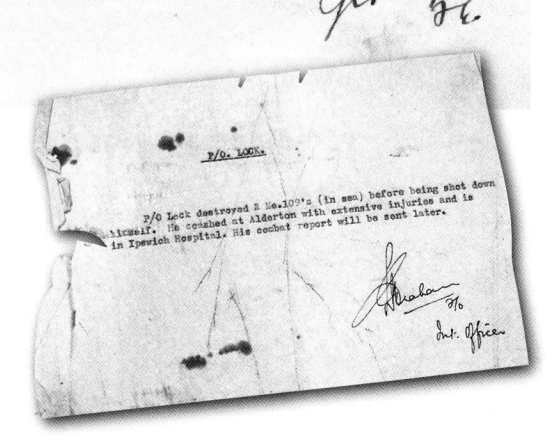

P/O. LOCK.

P/O Lock destroyed 2 Me.109's (in sea) before being shot down himself. He crashed at Alderton with extensive injuries and is in Ipswich Hospital. His combat report will be sent later.

Int. Officer

Above: An Intelligence Report for the deadly operation that overshadowed the afternoon of 5 September 1940. © *41 Squadron Archives*.

Right: Eric's initial Combat Report, submitted in his absence on 17 November 1940.
© *41 Squadron Archives*.

17.11.40
41 Sqn

Intelligence Patrol Report
41 Squadron (0800-0938 hours) 17/11/40.

12 aircraft 41 Squadron left Hornchurch 0800 hours for Maidstone Line at 15,000 feet. 603 Squadron led and they increased height to 30,000 feet, after forming up.

Between Clacton and Herne Bay they saw trails of some 40 E/A in pairs some in shallow VICS and some line abreast, at 20-25,000 feet.

The Squadron followed 603 in a diving attack in line astern out of the sun on the enemy, which included Me.109's and He.113's.

Enemy turned into sun and dived when attacked, making themselves difficult to see.

Dog fights ensued and 41 Squadron pilots were successful in destroying 5 Me.109's and damaging a sixth.

P/O MILEHAM, who damaged a Me.109, reported that it outclimbed him. He saw three which were all yellow with a black cross on their engine cowlings.

Cloud was patchy, 5/10th at 5 to 15,000 feet.
No assistance from A.A.
10 aircraft landed Hornchurch 0938 hours.
P/O ALDRIDGE landed, on his nose, at Matlask.
P/O LOCK, crashed at Alderton and is seriously wounded.

Our casualties 1 Spitfire Cat.3 (P/O Lock, wounded)
      1 Spitfire Cat.2 (P/O Aldridge, uninjured).

Enemy casualties 5 Me.109's destroyed (by F/Lt.Lovell,
              P/O Aldridge,
              P/O Lock 2 (all in sea)
           and P/O Mackenzie (inflames)
1 Me.109 damaged (by P/O Mileham, white smoke).

F/O
for Int. Officer
41 Sqn.

AIR MINISTRY (Dept.OA),
KING CHARLES STREET,
WHITEHALL, S.W.1.

17th September, 1940.

Dear Lock,

My very best congratulations on the award of the Distinguished Flying Cross.

Yours sincerely,

Pilot Officer E. S. Lock, D.F.C.,
No. 41 Squadron,
Royal Air Force,
Hornchurch,
ESSEX.

AIR MINISTRY (Dept.OA),
KING CHARLES STREET,
WHITEHALL, S.W.1.

1st October, 1940.

Dear Lock,

Well done again. Heartiest congratulations on the award of the bar to your Distinguished Flying Cross.

Yours sincerely,

Pilot Officer E. S. Lock, D.F.C.,
No. 41 Squadron,
Royal Air Force,
Hornchurch,
ESSEX.

Above: Official letters from the Air Ministry advising Eric he had been awarded the Distinguished Flying Cross and the bar to the Distinguished Flying Cross.
© *John & Jennifer Milner*

George R.I.

George the Sixth by the Grace of God of Great Britain, Ireland and the British Dominions beyond the Seas, King, Defender of the Faith, Emperor of India, Sovereign of the Distinguished Service Order, to our Trusty and Well beloved Eric Stanley Lock, Esquire, on whom has been conferred the Decoration of the Distinguished Flying Cross, Pilot Officer in Our Royal Air Force Volunteer Reserve. Greeting.

Whereas We have thought fit to Nominate and Appoint you to be a Member of Our Distinguished Service Order We do by these Presents Grant unto you the Dignity of a Companion of Our said Order And we do hereby authorize you to Have, Hold and Enjoy the said Dignity as a Member of Our said Order, together with all and singular the Privileges thereunto belonging or appertaining

Given at Our Court at St James's under Our Sign Manual this seventeenth day of December 1940 in the Fifth Year of Our Reign.

By The Sovereign's Command.

Anthony Eden
The Principal Secretary of State having the Department of War for the time being.

Pilot Officer E.S. Lock, D.F.C.
Royal Air Force Volunteer Reserve.

Left: The Royal Warrant for Eric's Distinguished Service Order, dated 17 December 1940.
© *Lock and Cornes families*

Ryder, E. Norman.	Me109E	–	–	Isle of Sheppey, Kent (15.00)
Wallens, Ronald W.	–	–	Do17	South of Gravesend. Kent (09.15)
Wallens, Ronald W.	–	Me109E	–	South of Gravesend. Kent Mid-Channel (09.15)
Wallens, Ronald W.	Me109E	–	–	10 miles south-east of Dover, Kent (15.00)
Webster, J. Terence	2 Me109E	–	Me109E	Gravesend–Ashford, Kent (09.15)

Three of the nine enemy aircraft destroyed by the squadron this day fell to Eric. The young man clearly had a talent for flying and aerial combat. He was only on his first operational sortie from Hornchurch, and his fifth overall of his career, and had an eighty per cent strike rate: four confirmed victories in five operational sorties. It would perhaps be presumptuous to claim that this was unprecedented, but pilots of this calibre were extremely rare; he was just one victory away from becoming an ace.

However, the squadron had also lost a significant element of its leadership, experience and knowledge in this battle. One of the RAF's promising career officers, Squadron Leader 'Robin' Hood, had been in the RAF for almost thirteen years and had graduated from Cranwell in 1929. Although he had been with No. 41 Squadron less than six months, his leadership was recognised with the award of a Distinguished Flying Cross on 11 August 1940.

Flight Lieutenant Terry Webster had been with the RAF since being granted a short service commission in August 1935. After Hood, he was the most senior pilot on the squadron and had been officer commanding (OC) B Flight since the beginning of the conflict. He, too, had already been awarded a DFC. Having claimed a number of victories over Dunkirk and in the early days of the Battle of Britain, he had become the squadron's first ace of the war.

Flying Officer 'Wally' Wallens had joined the Reserve of Air Force Officers (RAFO) in June 1937 and was commissioned two months later. He had been with No. 41 Squadron since March 1938, and had transferred to the RAFVR during that time. He claimed his first victories in early August 1940 and had significant combat experience under his belt by the time he was shot down on 5 September. Wallens remained in hospital and then on convalescence until April 1941 and was ultimately allowed to fly again, but only domestically.

Flying Officer Tony Lovell had fortunately only injured his ankle while landing in his parachute and was otherwise little the worse for wear for his experience; he was flying again the following morning. Although it would be approximately three weeks before Webster was replaced as OC B Flight, it was ultimately his wingman, Flying Officer Lovell, who was chosen to take over the role.

There was no respite for the squadron, however, and another busy day awaited them after a fitful night's rest. The Luftwaffe launched three major raids against London and the south-east on 6 September, the first of which involved an estimated 270–300 bombers and fighters in an attack on the Thames Estuary between 08:45 and 09:45 hours. The second took place between 12:30 and 13:40 and comprised approximately 250 aircraft whose objective appeared to be Chatham. The third occurred between 17:20 and 18:45 hours, when approximately 150 enemy aircraft crossed in over Dover, heading for Maidstone, followed by another wave of fifty aircraft a short while later.

No. 41 Squadron mounted three patrols during the day and intercepted the Luftwaffe's first and third raids, the latter with considerable success. When the first attack developed, fifteen squadrons were scrambled to intercept them. The enemy formations navigated in over Kent, flying in a north-westerly direction towards the Thames, and were met by fighters of Nos 1, 43, 73, 249, 303, 501 and 601 Squadrons, and elements of No. 66 Squadron. Fighters of Nos 79 and 111 Squadrons, both on aerodrome defence duties, and No. 41 Squadron, still under sector control, also engaged them. No. 41 Squadron's involvement was fairly limited, however. Twelve pilots were ordered to patrol base at 08:45 hours, led by Flight Lieutenant Norman Ryder. Despite their proximity to the action, and their altitude of 20,000 feet, they saw practically nothing, largely due to thick ground haze. However, there were two exceptions.

Flying Officer John Mackenzie fired at a Dornier Do17 without result, but Eric, who was sporting a slight wound from his last sortie, had a more hair-raising experience. Still on a steep learning curve, he passed out 'for some unknown reason'[21] and could well have lost his life for the second time in two days. He regained consciousness after a free fall of several thousand feet and regained control of his aircraft at 8,000 feet, but discovered he had strayed from the rest of the squadron in the process. Climbing to find them again, he sighted instead a lone Ju88 above him, at an altitude of approximately 18,000 feet. Giving chase, he followed it out over the Channel. Although his presence was not realised – the Junkers employed no evasive action – Eric did not gain a suitable position for an attack until the aircraft had commenced its descent towards the French coast. Eric opened up on the Ju88 from a range of 200 yards as he closed to 100, firing for four to five seconds as they crossed the French coast together. He expended around 2,400 rounds into the aircraft, and subsequently saw it crash in a location he believed was approximately twenty miles east of Calais. He then returned to Hornchurch where he claimed the Ju88 destroyed.[22]

In doing so, Eric had achieved something that few men ever did, and certainly not so early in their operational flying careers. This young man, who was still a long way from being a seasoned fighter pilot, had claimed five destroyed enemy aircraft and thereby achieved 'ace' status within a mere six operational sorties. He was the second pilot on the squadron to become an ace during this war, but the achievement was so unique that, of No. 41 Squadron's 325 Second World War pilots, only ten claimed five or more victories while on the unit.

By the time Eric re-crossed the English coast, the Luftwaffe's attack had petered out and it did not appear to have attained its objectives. The enemy formations left the mainland between Beachy Head and North Foreland, fighting rearguard actions against the RAF as they did so. Although No. 41 Squadron had had little involvement in the raid, other squadrons had experienced significant success, claiming no less than twenty-eight enemy aircraft destroyed, twelve probably destroyed and ten damaged, but sustained casualties of seven pilots killed and seven wounded.

No. 41 Squadron was airborne again at 12:50 hours, when eleven aircraft undertook an uneventful patrol of almost one hour, but Eric was not involved. Following a few hours' break, the unit was scrambled anew at 17:35 to intercept the Luftwaffe's third raid of the day. Having passed overhead near Dover at 17:30, 150 enemy aircraft flew towards Maidstone and the Thames, followed by another 50 aircraft that crossed in between Dover and Dungeness forty minutes later and flew to the same area.

No. 11 Group scrambled fourteen squadrons: Nos 1, 1 (Canadian), 17, 41, 46, 66, 72, 73, 111, 222, 249, 257, 501 and 603, but only Nos 41, 111 and 222 Squadrons engaged the Luftwaffe; the rest failed to make contact. No. 41 Squadron was led by Flight Lieutenant Ryder, but once again Eric was not among them, and he missed out on some significant action. The squadron encountered thirty to forty Me109s in small formations above them, flying on a reciprocal course, and caught them unawares. Climbing towards them, the pilots commenced their attack by choosing individual targets. In the ensuing combats, Pilot Officer Bennions claimed two Me109s destroyed, Flight Lieutenant Ryder and Flying Officer Tony Lovell each claimed one Me109 destroyed, Flying Officer Mackenzie claimed one Me109 destroyed and a second probably destroyed, and Flying Officer Scott and Sergeant Pilot Darling each claimed one Me109 probably destroyed. The last man was on the ground again at 18:45 hours, and this concluded the day's flying.

During this attack, No. 11 Group as a whole claimed eight destroyed, three probable and one damaged enemy aircraft. Of this total, No. 41 Squadron claimed five of the eight destroyed and all three probable. The remaining victories were claimed by 222 and 249 Squadrons; RAF casualties amounted to just two pilots shot down but uninjured.

Available records suggest that Eric did not fly operationally on 7 September. It was another big day for the RAF, however, despite the fact there was only one major raid late in the day. No. 41 Squadron was airborne on five patrols, and claimed two enemy aircraft destroyed, three probably destroyed and three damaged, and although one Spitfire was written off and two damaged, no one was hurt. In total on this day, the RAF claimed forty-two enemy aircraft destroyed, twenty-three probably destroyed and twenty-five damaged, all bar one during the afternoon's raid. However, they came at a significant cost and a dozen pilots were reported killed and eight wounded, while sixteen Hurricanes and eight Spitfires were written off.

Eric was airborne operationally again the following morning, when No. 41 Squadron was scrambled in response to the Luftwaffe's only raid of the day. The attack took place over Kent and the Thames Estuary between 11:10 and 13:00 hours and arrived in two phases consisting of approximately 100 aircraft. The first phase crossed in north-east of Dover, orbited between Dover and Dungeness, and then returned across the Channel. The second passed the homeward-bound first raid and bombed Dover. An element of this incursion then returned to France, while another continued on to the Thames Estuary and returned home over Kent via Dungeness. Ten RAF units were ordered to intercept them – Nos 41, 46, 72, 253, 257, 303, 501, 504, 603 and 605 Squadrons – but as a result of weather conditions only Nos 41, 46, 501 and 605 Squadrons succeeded in doing so.

No. 41 Squadron was airborne at 11:20 hours, led by Flight Lieutenant Ryder, and vectored to Dover at 15,000 feet, above 10/10ths cloud with a top of 10,000 feet. They did not see any bombers, but soon spotted at least thirty Me109s to both port and starboard, between 5,000 and 10,000 feet above them. Flying darkly camouflaged Spitfires against the white backdrop of the cloud below them, No. 41 Squadron was in a dangerous position, and Ryder needed to act fast. He ordered the pilots into line astern for a full boost climb to attack the Messerschmitts. The rearmost position was flown by Flying Officer William Scott.

Before long, Scott reported Me109s to the rear of the squadron, but moments later pilots towards the back of the unit formation saw Scott being dived upon by an Me109 and subsequently disappearing into the cloud cover in flames. They later reported seeing two large holes in the wing root of his Spitfire, from which flames were emitting. The offending Me109 followed Scott down into the cloud, and some of the pilots dived after it but were unable to engage it. Scott's Spitfire was seen from Dover Harbour to plunge into the Channel and a destroyer was redirected to the site, but to no avail.

The remaining ten pilots, thereunder Eric, were unable to make any claims of their own, and landed again at 12:50 hours. Other units enjoyed more success, claiming four enemy aircraft destroyed, three probably destroyed and three damaged. There was no further operational flying for No. 41 Squadron on the 8th.

During the day, Squadron Leader Robert Lister arrived at Hornchurch to take over command of the unit, following the loss of Squadron Leader 'Robin' Hood. In the wake of the disastrous events of 5 September, Flight Lieutenant Ryder had taken over interim command until an officer commanding could be appointed. Although nothing is stated in official records, it is quite clear from accounts provided by several pilots that they had hoped that Ryder would be promoted into the role. However, it was not to be, and 27-year-old Lister was appointed instead. The men were bitterly disappointed that 'their' man had not been given the job, and Sergeant Pilot Roy Ford later recalled: 'It is an understatement to say that the whole Squadron was dismayed when [Ryder] did not succeed Robin Hood in September 1940.'²³

Once again, on 9 September, the Luftwaffe only made a single, large attack on south-east England, which occurred mid- to late afternoon. This allowed Squadron Leader Lister to get airborne after lunch to carry out some local reconnaissance and familiarise himself with the area. At around 16:30 hours, approximately 200 enemy aircraft, comprising both combined and independent formations of Ju88 and He111 bombers with Me109 escorts, crossed in between Dungeness and North Foreland in two waves. One element of the raid was directed towards London, while the other appeared intent on attacking the Hawker factory at Kingston. Seventeen squadrons – Nos 1 (Canadian), 41, 46, 66, 92, 213, 222, 229, 249, 253, 303, 501, 504, 602, 603, 605 and 607 – were detailed to intercept them. Of these units, twelve – Nos 1 (Canadian), 41, 46, 92, 222, 253, 303, 501, 602, 603, 605 and 607 – succeeded in doing so, as did No. 72 Squadron, which was not detailed to attack but was in the air at the time on station defence.

No. 41 Squadron was airborne at 16:44, led by Flight Lieutenant Ryder, in sunny weather with 1/10th cloud at 8,000 feet, ordered to patrol Maidstone and the south of London. Ryder soon sighted two aircraft by themselves in the Maidstone area and broke away with Red Section to investigate them, leaving Pilot Officer Bennions in command of the remaining nine aircraft. Recognising them as Me109s, Ryder attacked one from astern, immediately resulting in smoke issuing from it. He continued firing as he closed to 100 yards, until the smoke developed into flame, which emanated from the engine cowling. The Messerschmitt subsequently rolled on to its back and fell vertically out of control until it disappeared from view in a cloud bank. Ryder then climbed to 25,000 feet to engage another two Me109s near Dover, accompanied by his No. 2, Flying Officer John Mackenzie. Ryder eventually managed to latch on to the tail of one, which immediately half-rolled and dived for cloud cover. Giving chase, he opened fire from 300 yards, closing slightly, and observed his fire striking the aircraft just before it entered cloud. Ryder followed it in, but did not see it again. He later claimed his first Me109 destroyed and his second damaged.

In the meantime, Mackenzie had attacked the second of the pair, and opened fire from 200 yards. Glycol immediately issued from the Me109 and he closed to 100 yards, where he opened fire again with a second, longer burst. When the glycol stream turned into smoke, Mackenzie closed in further and fired a third time, whereupon the Messerschmitt exploded. Smoke and flying pieces of debris enveloped him, and he broke away to starboard in an attempt to avoid it.

Meanwhile, continuing the patrol in command of the rest of the squadron, Bennions had attempted to zero his pip-squeak radio navigation system with the controller. However, when he received no reply, he ordered the pilots to climb with him to 31,500 feet. The squadron continued in this manner for approximately ten minutes, until Bennions sighted a large formation of enemy aircraft below and approximately ten miles to the north-west of them, between Dover and Deal.

He instructed the pilots to echelon starboard, with Eric as rearguard, then called on Blue Section to attack the highest section of Me109s from out of the sun, and the rest of the pilots to take on the next aircraft below them. Diving on to them, Bennions attacked the outermost Me109 in the formation from 200 yards, firing three three-second bursts as he closed to seventy-five yards. The aircraft burst into flames and black smoke, rolled over to port and fell into an uncontrolled dive. Bennions then headed home and claimed the Me109 destroyed.

Leading Green Section, Flying Officer John Boyle led his section down to attack aircraft lower in the formation. Descending slowly to get himself into the best position, he suddenly noticed an Me109 in his rear-view mirror and made a steep diving turn to starboard. His evasive action paid off as the enemy pilot was unable to get an accurate deflection shot, despite firing several bursts at him. Both aircraft were descending rapidly and the Me109 eventually broke off the engagement and veered away. However, Boyle now turned on his attacker and fired his own deflection shot, expending a four-second burst at a range of 200 yards. This resulted in smoke and flames issuing from the aircraft. Boyle then made a spiral dive to starboard but, as he did, noticed another large formation of enemy aircraft above him to the south, at about 10,000 feet. Climbing towards the sun in a gentle turn to port, he kept the formation in sight until he reached an altitude of 30,000 feet. Eventually diving out of the sun towards the enemy aircraft, he realised too late that his speed was too great and overshot them. Climbing anew, he picked out a suitably positioned He111 and attacked it from below, firing a long burst from 300 yards, closing to 150. Boyle observed his rounds entering the aircraft but could see no further effect of his attack. He subsequently claimed the Me109 destroyed and the He111 damaged, both off the south coast near Brighton.

Sergeant Pilot 'Birdie' Darling had also spotted the Me109s coming in from behind during the initial dive, but while Boyle had seen one, Darling had detected three. Boyle and Darling broke simultaneously, but Darling managed to manoeuvre his way around behind them. Choosing one, he attacked it, but was surprised with the ease with which he was able to do so. He opened fire at 200 yards, continuing to discharge rounds as he closed to 150. During this time, the enemy pilot took no evasive action and Darling therefore kept shooting at it until he ran out of ammunition. By the time he stopped, the Me109's engine had been knocked out, and Darling watched as it made a belly-landing twenty miles north-north-west of Shoreham. He circled the aircraft until a van drove into the field towards the pilot, and he then landed at nearby RAF Tangmere to refuel before returning to Hornchurch.

The last section down was Yellow, believed to have been led by Pilot Officer Guy Cory. After an initial ineffective dive, he found himself on his own at 18,000 feet, where he sighted a lone Ju88 flying south-east approximately 4,000 feet below him. It appeared to be making for the coast, descending slightly as it went. Ideally positioned, Cory gave chase and made four attacks on the bomber from astern at ranges of 300 yards down to 200. Its pilot took little evasive action and, as there were no other enemy aircraft in the vicinity, Cory was able to deliver his attacks without any interference. By the time he had completed his second strike, the Ju88's port engine had stopped, and after his fourth the starboard engine had also ceased.

During this time, however, Cory experienced return fire from the dorsal gunner and he was hit in the engine, resulting in his cockpit filling with heavy fumes. Nonetheless, the Junkers was fatally damaged and its wounded pilot force-landed his aircraft in a ploughed field one mile east of Nuthurst, near Horsham. Cory force-landed his own aircraft in a field, uninjured, approximately four miles from the Ju88. A short while later, a section of soldiers arrived in the field, picked Cory up and drove him to the aircraft he had shot down, where he met the wounded pilot. He returned to the squadron the following morning by train and Underground with his parachute draped over his shoulder!

Eric also saw action as the squadron's rearguard. When Bennions led the pilots down in the initial attack, he was surprised to be dived upon by three Spitfires, whose identities remain unclear. Positioned at the rear of the squadron formation, with no one to protect your tail, was a dangerous role that had cost Flying Officer William Scott his life only the day before. Eric now understood why: 'I half rolled and tried to formate [sic] on them but this made me suspicious. I got quite close to one and saw he had only one letter on the fuselage – of this I am quite certain.'[24] Having lost the rest of the section in doing so, however, Eric climbed to 20,000 feet and orbited a while by himself until a dozen Me109s passed approximately 6,000 feet below him. He watched and waited, taking his time to decide his next move, and noted that the Messerschmitts were not in any particular formation, but rather 'spread all over the place'.[25]

This was the first time he had flown as rearguard, having until now only operated in a subordinate role within a section, where his No. 1 called the shots. For the first time he was operating independently as his own master, and could decide his own strategies, movements and targets. He took on the role and made it his own, became skilled at it, turned it into his own specialty, and quickly developed into the lone hunter that he would become known for.

His strategy was counterintuitive in one respect; rather than seeking the safety of numbers, he began to shun the rigidity of structured formations, seeking freedom of movement, and preferring instead the element of surprise that was delivered by an unexpected individual operator. Surveying the skies from a superior altitude gave him the greatest possible view of the aerial battlefield below him. In a battle where every advantage counted against the vast number of enemy aircraft being thrust at the RAF, Eric was able to pick out his prey, like a hawk circling a field, and choose his target on his own terms – the loner, the straggler, the best positioned, the weakest link. He learned to play this card to his fullest advantage, and seldom failed. This sortie provided his first taste of this strategy and he would return to it repeatedly with significant success.

Eric now chose a lone, unsuspecting Me109, some distance from the rest of his colleagues and dived down behind it, then climbed slightly to strike it from below. He does not provide any further detail on the attack in his Combat Report, but confirms another definitive victory with a simple, brief, unequivocal statement: 'He exploded.'[26] Eric then made a similar attack on another Me109, firing several bursts at it from below. Before long, this aircraft burst into flames and plummeted towards the ground. He considered the aircraft came down approximately ten miles from Dover, and returned to Hornchurch to claim both Me109s destroyed, his sixth and seventh victories in eight operational sorties.

The last pilot was on the ground at 18:25 hours, at which time it was established that the squadron had claimed seven Me109s and one Ju88 destroyed, and one Me109 and one He111 damaged. A number of additional fighters and bombers had also been attacked, but the pilots had not had the time to observe any visible effects. These included an Me109 set upon by Sergeant Pilot Ted Howitt, which is recorded as damaged on his pilot service record, but for which he did not submit an official claim. The only casualty was Cory's force-landed Spitfire.

Other No. 11 Group squadrons also enjoyed significant success, and by the end of the raid a total of thirty-two enemy aircraft were claimed destroyed, eight probably destroyed and ten damaged. These included those of No. 41 Squadron, whose pilots claimed the greatest total of any unit that afternoon. Casualties were surprisingly light across the board, considering the damage done to the Luftwaffe.

Following a day's respite as a result of poor conditions on both sides of the Channel, unsuitable weather continued well into the morning of 11 September. As a consequence, only one major raid was mounted by the Luftwaffe all day, which did not take place until mid-afternoon. No. 41 Squadron was therefore not airborne operationally until after lunch, but they returned claiming three enemy aircraft destroyed and three damaged for the cost of two aircraft written off and one pilot sustaining light wounds from shell splinters.

The attack developed at 15:15 hours and involved an estimated 270 bombers and fighters, which targeted the London–Riverside–Woolwich area, and the Portsmouth–Southampton district. It lasted ninety minutes and was followed by a minor strike on Dover and shipping off the port. Bombs were dropped at Charlton, Deptford, Greenwich, King's Cross, Lewisham, London Bridge, Paddington, South Bromley, Surrey and Victoria Docks and Woolwich. The Cunliffe-Owen Aircraft Factory at Southampton was also damaged, as were houses and shops at Dover and Dover Priory Station.

As the raid came in, Nos 1 (Canadian), 17, 41, 46, 66, 72, 73, 92, 213, 222, 229, 249, 253, 257, 303, 501, 504, 602, 603, 605 and 607 Squadrons were scrambled and all but 257 and 607 Squadrons engaged the Luftwaffe. RAF claims by the end of the raid totalled a massive sixty-seven destroyed, twenty-one probably destroyed and thirty-nine damaged, while the coastal anti-aircraft batteries claimed another nine destroyed and nine damaged of their own. RAF losses reported in the immediate aftermath amounted to ten pilots missing and one killed, and sixteen Hurricanes and seven Spitfires written off.

No. 41 Squadron was scrambled as the first plots appeared at 15:15 hours, led by Flight Lieutenant Ryder, with an order to patrol from Maidstone to Southend. This was Squadron Leader Lister's first operational sortie with the squadron, but he is understood to have flown as No. 3 in Ryder's Red Section.

Sergeant Pilot Ted Howitt was assigned to a new role of 'spotter' and was vectored 125° to the Dover and Deal area to patrol and report any enemy raids he saw approaching the coast. He climbed to 17,000 feet west of Maidstone and immediately sighted twelve to fifteen Me109s flying in a northerly direction 2,000 feet below him. He reported their presence to the controller, then turned south and climbed steadily into the sun until he reached Dungeness at an altitude of 32,000 feet.

Looking about, it was only minutes before he observed a large formation of bombers crossing in south of Folkestone on a course of 320° at approximately 25,000 feet. He identified them as Ju88s and noted they were being escorted by both Me109s and Me110s. He reported his observation to the controller again, and had just turned to starboard when he noticed a second large formation, of similar composition, making landfall at Dungeness on a course of 330°. Once again, Howitt reported the sighting, but just as he had done so was attacked from the rear. A cannon shell burst near his port wing and splinters made a few holes in the wing, but no serious damage was done. He broke away violently, succeeded in escaping his attacker, and did not see him again even though he was at an altitude of around 30,000 feet with wide open skies around him.

A while later, feeling safe enough to look around again, Howitt viewed a third formation approaching Deal and Dover, and then a fourth proceeding in a westerly direction up the Thames towards London. Again, he reported his observations, amply fulfilling his brief, and was then ordered to rejoin the squadron over Southend at 25,000 feet. However, on account of the number of enemy aircraft now around him, and between him and his unit, he made a wide detour to port towards Tunbridge Wells instead. As he approached the area, he sighted a lone aircraft and dived to identify it. Just as he did, there was a loud bang in his engine, which was immediately followed by excessive vibration and dense clouds of steam. Howitt prepared to bale out of the aircraft, but when he realised it was not on fire and he could still maintain some control, he decided to make a forced landing as a preference. He glided from 20,000 feet to 5,000 and noticed an (unidentified) airfield at which he managed to land his damaged Spitfire without trouble. Subsequent examination of the aircraft indicated that the oil cooler had been punctured, which resulted in two connecting rods breaking and seizing solidly. Howitt was safe but had also experienced the extreme dangers of operating alone.

In the meantime, twelve pilots from No. 603 Squadron had also taken off from Rochford and joined up with the rest of No. 41 Squadron, at around 28,000 feet over Rochford Bay. Approximately fifteen miles south-east of Hornchurch, they sighted a large formation of Ju88s and He111s in vics of five and in line astern, heading north 5,000 feet below them, with an escort of Me110s and a number of Me109s higher up. Flight Lieutenant Ryder led Red and Blue Sections in a dive on to the formation out of the sun, in an effort to cut it in two, and was followed down in line astern by No. 603 Squadron. Ryder fired at a Ju88 as he passed through the formation, and caught a brief glimpse of smoke emanating from its port engine as the wing dipped slightly. Dogfights then ensued as the two squadrons successfully broke up the formation, and many of the bombers turned back south again, dropping their payloads on open country across Kent.

Ryder made an attack on another Ju88 by joining a defensive circle of orbiting aircraft, but experienced substantial return fire and good evasion tactics from that aircraft's pilot, and gave up on the attack. He soon found yet another Ju88 and had just begun to fire when he came under attack from astern himself, and a piece of his hood dislodged itself and flew off behind him. At this time, he received an order from the controller to patrol RAF Hornchurch to intercept fifty-plus enemy aircraft, but before he could do so received a new order to land. He subsequently claimed the first Ju88 damaged, but made no claims for the others.

Ryder's No. 2, Pilot Officer Gerald Langley, followed his leader down and fired a solid five-second burst at a Ju88, opening fire at 400 yards and closing to just 50 as he did so. He struck the bomber on its port side and possibly damaged its port engine. However, as he turned away from the attack, he saw tracers pass over his port wing and then lost control of his aircraft. His controls were rendered useless and he was forced to bale out north of Sevenoaks from an altitude of about 6,000 feet. He landed in a garden at Sevenoaks, fortunately none the worse for wear, and returned to Hornchurch that afternoon to claim the Ju88 damaged. This was his first victory.

Pilot Officer 'Ben' Bennions, who was leading Blue Section, had also dived with Ryder's Red Section in the initial attempt to break up the enemy formation. He attacked an Me110 in a section of six with a two-second burst, closing from 200 yards to 50, and the aircraft rolled over to port and dipped away. However, his speed was too great and he overshot the aircraft and was unable to see if he had inflicted any damage, or if this was merely the pilot's evasive action. He then released several short bursts of ammunition at another Me110 in front of him, climbed slightly and dived on to the next one following it. After his third such attack, he received a solid burst of fire down the starboard side of his Spitfire and felt a sharp pain in his left heel. He broke away but found he was no longer able to defend himself as his air bottle had been pierced, rendering his guns inoperable. He also found his wheel brakes and flaps were not working and realised his top petrol tank had been perforated by bullets. Left little choice, he exited the battle and returned to Hornchurch. His heel required a little attention, but he made a claim for one damaged Me110.

Pilot Officer John Mackenzie also dived on a formation of Ju88s but found his dive too steep and his speed too great to take an accurate aim at them. He then climbed to 30,000 feet and orbited awhile, looking for a new opportunity to strike out of the sun. In time, he spotted a straggling He111 heading for the coast at an altitude of 10,000 feet. He made a shallow dive towards it and attacked it from dead astern, opening up at 500 yards and closing to 100. The Heinkel took evasive action and Mackenzie came under fire from its dorsal gunner. Noting he was short of fuel, Mackenzie fired one more long burst and broke away. As he did, however, he saw smoke issue from the port engine, but then caught a glimpse of an aircraft behind him. He dived to ground level, fearing an Me109 was on his tail, but looked back to recognise Eric instead. While Mackenzie headed for RAF West Malling to refuel – he only had seven gallons left in his tank – Eric stayed airborne and watched the He111 glide down to force-land at Hildenborough, two miles north-west of Tonbridge. Mackenzie therefore claimed it destroyed.

Before joining up with Mackenzie, Eric had dived on to a formation of bombers, which he broke up. Picking out a Ju88 by itself, he fired several bursts from astern at ranges from 200 yards down to 100, which had no effect, perhaps indicating the aircraft was carrying armour plating. Changing tactics, he made a new assault from its stern quarter, but this also had no effect, but for its pilot diving to evade his fire. Determined not to lose the opportunity, Eric then attacked the Ju88 from below. On this occasion, he felt he must have seriously wounded or killed the pilot as the aircraft immediately dived and crashed in a field seventeen miles south of Maidstone. Eric circled the wreck briefly, which was on fire, until it exploded a few minutes later.

Climbing again, he had only reached 6,000 feet when he was attacked by an Me110 with black and white stripes on its tailfin. A twenty-minute dogfight ensued, during which Eric came under heavy fire from the dorsal gunner. Nonetheless, he managed to set the fighter's starboard engine on fire and this caused the aircraft to crash approximately ten miles south-east of the Ju88 that he had brought down earlier. Looking about again, he spotted one of the squadron's Spitfires and joined up with it, to find Pilot Officer Mackenzie finishing off his attack on a He111, and watched as it crash-landed to confirm his victory. However, realising he was out of both ammunition and fuel, Eric landed his aircraft at West Malling right behind Mackenzie, where he found he had received hits on his port wing from either the Ju88 or Me110, but they had only caused light damage.

The squadron had been hit hard in the day's battles and almost half the aircraft were damaged or destroyed, but thankfully injuries were only light. However, the pilots had also inflicted some damage on the Luftwaffe. Displaying rare talent in aerial fighting, Eric's two victories brought his tally to an astounding nine destroyed enemy aircraft over the course of nine operational sorties – a strike rate of 100 per cent. He had now surpassed the squadron's top scorer, Flight Lieutenant Terry Webster, who had been killed less than a week before.

No. 11 Group's claims for the day totalled some sixty-seven enemy aircraft destroyed, twenty-three probably destroyed and thirty-nine damaged, prompting the AOC No. 11 Group, AVM Keith Park, to send the following congratulatory message to all squadrons participating in the day's actions:

The Group Commander sends congratulations to all Squadrons on their magnificent fighting this afternoon resulting in the breaking up of [a] heavy attack on London and aircraft factories in the suburbs. Of 21 Squadrons despatched, 19 Squadrons intercepted and engaged the enemy inflicting heavy losses, thanks to the excellent team work between Squadrons working in pairs and to the efficient work of Sector operations staff, most of whom are working under very difficult conditions.[27]

No. 41 Squadron was not called upon operationally during the ensuing two days, primarily as a result of reduced Luftwaffe operations that were caused, in part at least, by unsuitable weather conditions. A few bombers got through, nonetheless, and both Buckingham Palace and RAF Hornchurch were targeted. A stick of bombs was dropped on the south-south-westerly edge of No. 41 Squadron's airfield, one bomb falling on the perimeter track and another on a small-arms dump, but no major damage was done and Hornchurch remained fully operational throughout.

Continuing poor weather kept Luftwaffe activity to a minimum again during the morning of 14 September, and confined it to individual nuisance raids on seaside resorts. No. 41 Squadron undertook two local reconnaissances in the morning, but when the weather cleared after lunch, the Luftwaffe was back in business and undertook two major raids before the day was over. The first of these targeted London between 15:40 and 16:20 hours, while the second was directed towards Kent and the Thames Estuary between 17:55 and 19:00.

The first attack comprised approximately 200 bombers and fighters, which crossed in on a north-westerly bearing towards west London at altitudes of between 15,000 and 20,000 feet. Seventeen squadrons were ordered to intercept them, but only five – Nos. 41, 222, 253, 501 and 603 Squadrons – succeeded, plus No. 73 Squadron, although not actually detailed to do so.

No. 41 Squadron was airborne at 15:50 hours with ten pilots led by Flight Lieutenant Ryder, but little information is available on their activity. In fact, the only details appear on a Composite Combat Report in No. 41 Squadron's archives, which states in handwriting, 'S/L Lister Slightly Wounded 1 Spitfire Cat 3', below which appears the following statement in typewritten text: 'Blue 1 reports that Blue 2 (S/Ldr. Lister) did not assume a line astern formation and did not get into it when called up. His R/T may have been bad. He was straggling and was not known to have been shot down until an Army Officer telephoned.'[28]

It is apparent that the squadron did not sight the Luftwaffe, but they were themselves seen, as Squadron Leader Lister was picked out as a straggler, shot down and wounded in the arm. He baled out, but his injuries were considered serious enough that he did not return to the unit and was replaced as officer commanding that evening by Squadron Leader Donald Finlay, a pre-war Olympic hurdler. Once again, to the pilots' disappointment, Ryder was passed over.

The Luftwaffe's second raid developed at 17:55 hours when three consecutive formations, totalling approximately 200 aircraft, flew in between Dover and Dungeness, on a generally westerly course. One formation of around sixty aircraft entered the Inner Artillery Zone (IAZ), while a second of about ninety stayed in the East Kent area. The remaining formation split into two groups, one heading for Maidstone and the other Gravesend. The RAF sent up nineteen units to meet them: Nos 1 (Canadian), 17, 41, 46, 66, 72, 73, 92, 213, 222, 229, 249, 253, 257, 303, 501, 504, 603 and 607 Squadrons, but only eight succeeded in doing so: Nos 41, 46, 66, 72, 92, 222, 249 and 504 Squadrons.

Nine pilots of No. 41 Squadron were scrambled at 18:10, led by Flight Lieutenant Ryder once again, while Eric was sent up ten minutes ahead of them 'acting as a reconnaissance machine'[29] in a repeat of the spotting exercise successfully executed by Sergeant Pilot Ted Howitt three days earlier. As Eric headed alone to the Gravesend area, the rest of the squadron climbed to 25,000 feet where they were ordered to patrol.

While still climbing, Ryder spotted seven Me109s on a westerly course some distance above them, at 31,000 feet. He led the squadron up to 30,000 feet to attack the planes from below and, on reaching that altitude, turned towards them. However, the aircraft were then lost to sight, and Ryder considered they had probably taken cover in or above thin cloud in the area. They were not seen again and in time he guided the pilots back to Hornchurch where they landed at 19:00 hours, empty-handed.

Eric, on the other hand, was elsewhere, confidently carrying on the war by himself. Patrolling the south-eastern coast from Ramsgate to Dungeness between 31,000 and 33,000 feet, he sighted twelve Me109s in a diamond formation, flying in an easterly direction between Dover and Deal. He prepared to attack the last section of the formation, and was just closing in on a suitable target when he caught sight of seven Me109s diving on him from above. Having learned from his error of 5 September, he was now keeping a lookout around him, developing sharp eyes and a honed awareness. The Messerschmitts peeled off around 3,000 feet above Eric and made an 'S' dive towards him to position themselves for a head-on attack from the same altitude. Boldly holding his ground, he waited until the leading Me109 was in range and fired a long burst. The aircraft passed over him with just a few feet clearance, and Eric made a sharp turn to starboard and looked back in time to see it going down in flames. He was then attacked head-on by another Me109. With nerves of steel, Eric tried the same tactic again: 'I waited until he was at point blank range. I saw my bullets go into the enemy aircraft, and as he went past underneath me, I gave him a very long burst.'[30] However, seeing more Me109s diving towards him, he decided not to push the odds, half rolled, dived for cloud cover, and made a strategic withdrawal.

As he dropped below the cloud base, Eric spotted a man descending by parachute and followed him down to near ground level. He felt, 'pretty certain it was an Me109 pilot, as [he] saw him wearing a tin hat'.[31] The German pilot had no opportunity to flee as troops approached him as soon as he landed, and he put his hands in the air. In fact, when Lock made a low pass over the field, the pilot looked up and waved back to him.[32]

Eric then returned to Hornchurch where he claimed two Me109s destroyed between Dungeness and Ramsgate, thereby making him a double ace. He had expended just 960 rounds of ammunition in bursts fired at ranges of three hundred yards down to just twenty. It appears that Eric's aircraft also sustained light combat damage in the action, as Category 1 damage is recorded in the 'Our Casualties' section of his Combat Report. With eleven victories now under his belt in as many operational sorties, he was maintaining an average of one victory for every operational sortie he had flown.

The climax of the Battle of Britain is considered to have been 15 September 1940. The Luftwaffe launched two major raids against London on this day, at 11:00 and 14:00 hours, followed by a smaller raid against Portsmouth at 17:45. Although the day came at a cost to No. 41 Squadron, and indeed to the RAF as a whole, it was a crushing one for the Luftwaffe, upon which it 'suffered the heaviest casualties in any one day since the beginning of the War. [...] An outstanding feature of the [day's] results shows that enemy bombers and fighters were destroyed at the ratio of 2 to 1.'[33]

No. 11 Group's squadrons claimed 115 enemy aircraft destroyed, 38 probably destroyed and 64 damaged. Other groups' victories raised the RAF's overall claims for 15 September to a massive 177 destroyed, 42 probables and 72 damaged. In addition, coastal anti-aircraft batteries claimed another 14 destroyed.[34]

No. 41 Squadron intercepted both London raids and played a significant role in this historical day, claiming five and two shared destroyed, three probably destroyed and three damaged enemy aircraft, but sadly at the cost of one pilot killed in action. Eric was involved in both operations, and while he did not engage the Luftwaffe on the first, another two victories followed during the second, which preserved his incredible record.

The day's first attack crossed in between Dungeness and North Foreland at 11:00 hours, comprising approximately 120 bombers and fighters. After making landfall, the formation split into two, one group proceeding to west London and the other to the Docklands. No. 11 Group scrambled sixteen squadrons to intercept them – Nos 1 (Canadian), 41, 46, 66, 72, 92, 222, 229, 249, 253, 257, 303, 501, 504, 603 and 605 – of which all but 222 Squadron were engaged. No. 73 Squadron, which was not detailed to engage but was already airborne, also intercepted the Luftwaffe.

For its part, No. 41 Squadron scrambled ten pilots at 11:40 hours, led by Flight Lieutenant Ryder, with an order to patrol Gravesend at 20,000 feet. However, they had only reached an altitude of 13,000 feet when the controller vectored them on to an interception. Within minutes, Ryder sighted a formation of thirty Dorniers with a strong fighter escort ahead and to port. He ordered the pilots into line astern to prepare for an attack on the bombers out of the sun, but they were jumped by several Me109s before they could do so. The squadron immediately broke up and took violent evasive action, but Pilot Officer Gerald Langley was unable to escape the assault and was shot down over Thurrock, Essex, and killed.

The squadron's strike on the bombers was thereby thwarted, but three successes were nonetheless claimed. Pilot Officer 'Ben' Bennions broke hard as the Me109s attacked, then made a steep climbing turn to starboard with an Me109 on his tail. When the Messerschmitt fell out of the turn, Bennions banked around, turned the tables and got behind it. The German pilot rolled his aircraft on to its back and dived vertically to evade him, but he was followed down, and when he flattened out Bennions closed to 250 yards and fired three bursts of two seconds as he reduced his range to just seventy-five yards. The Me109 burst into flames, and the pilot jettisoned his hood and baled out. The aircraft hit the ground south-west of Dering Wood, and just north of the Tonbridge–Ashford railway line at Biddenden Green. Unable to find further customers, Bennions then returned to Hornchurch to claim the Messerschmitt destroyed.

As a result of the initial attack, Flying Officer Tony Lovell veered away, but then sighted a lone Me109 turning east and descending. Giving chase, Lovell dived after it and pursued it unseen for around fifteen miles. Closing to 250 yards, he fired a burst of five seconds, which resulted in white fumes issuing from the enemy plane's port wing root. When the pilot kept on flying and refused to give up, Lovell fired additional bursts of five and six seconds each, until the Me109 caught fire. The pilot baled out south-east of Canterbury, and, although he had sustained burns in the attack, was still able to return a salute from Lovell as he was descending in his parachute.

Having broken away during the initial attack, Sergeant Pilot 'Birdie' Darling climbed alone to 20,000 feet and patrolled off Dover. Seeing nothing, he was returning to base when he sighted sixteen Dornier Do215 bombers crossing the coast on a southerly bearing. Picking out a straggler five miles off Dover, Darling dived on it but overshot, and turned about to try again. This time, he opened fire at 250 yards and expended two four-second bursts as he closed to seventy-five yards. The Dornier's port engine emitted smoke, but he was unable to press home his attack as an Me109 approached him from astern. Darling disengaged, turned for home again, and claimed the Dornier damaged.

The last man was on the ground at 12:45 hours, but there was little time for the pilots and groundcrews to rest or think about lunch. The latter busied themselves re-arming and refuelling the aircraft, while the former were debriefed and submitted reports for the operation; it was not long before the pilots were airborne again to intercept the next large raid.

Eric and Sergeant Pilots Frank Usmar and John McAdam would also have been troubled by the failure to return from the operation of their good friend Gerald Langley, with whom they had trained and spent most of the past year. They may not have known yet that he had been killed, but sightings by the pilots at the time they were bounced may have been sufficient enough to raise serious concern for his life. He had served less than three months on the squadron and lasted for just six weeks of operational flying.

But there was little time to dwell on it, as around 240 enemy aircraft crossed in between Dover and Hastings at 14:00 hours and headed for London. The formations comprised Do17, Do215, He111 and Ju88 bombers, with the usual Me109 and Me110 fighter escorts. Every single-seater fighter squadron in No. 11 Group was scrambled to meet them – Nos 1 (Canadian), 17, 41, 46, 66, 72, 73, 92, 213, 222, 229, 249, 253, 257, 303, 501, 504, 602, 603, 605 and 607 – and all twenty-one succeeded in doing so, as did a lone pilot of Northolt's Station Defence Flight.

No. 41 Squadron received the order to take off at 14:10 and ten pilots were quickly airborne, led once again by Flight Lieutenant Ryder, with an order to patrol base at 25,000 feet and join up with No. 92 Squadron. As they climbed, they could already see aircraft contrails to the east. No. 92 Squadron was not seen, but as they reached 25,000 feet alone the pilots sighted twenty to thirty Do17s around 6,000 feet below them and to the east, heading in the direction of London, with a substantial scattered Me109 escort, ranging from that altitude up to 30,000 feet.

The unit moved into a line astern formation and tried to weave through the fighter escort to the bombers, but were split up by the fighters, and individual combats quickly ensued. However, they soon had back-up as anti-aircraft fire took on the lower levels of aircraft and, in short order, a number of other RAF squadrons joined the fray. Having ordered the squadron to attack, Ryder led the pilots towards the bombers, through the fighter escort, expecting to be attacked at any time. When this did not occur, he picked out a Dornier to pounce on, but it was engaged by friendly fighters before he could bring himself into firing range. He circled the bomber, without attacking it, and waited his turn to make his own strike. Then positioning himself astern of the aircraft, Ryder closed in and fired a five- to six-second burst from 250 yards, as he closed to 200. Judging by his tracer, he was certain his fire was hitting the aircraft, but he was unable to ascertain the damage he caused as the Dornier entered cloud cover and was lost to view.

Meanwhile, Flying Officer John Boyle had seen Me109s dive on the squadron during their initial line astern attack, and had turned and climbed to meet them. He flew head-on towards one Messerschmitt in a vic of three and opened fire at 500 yards. Closing to just 20 yards before breaking to avoid a collision, he looked back to see smoke and flames emitting from the fighter as it spun downwards. Looking about, he saw a bomber formation 1,000 feet below him and dived straight towards it. He opened fire on one aircraft with full deflection and broke off to escape a collision, but was unable to see any damage he may have caused. Then noticing a lone Do17 making for cloud cover, he fired a short burst at it as he closed from 250 to 100 yards, and saw Flight Lieutenant Ryder shooting at the same plane. Aircraft of other squadrons also fired at the Dornier, after which Boyle made two more attacks on it. He and Ryder followed the aircraft down below the cloud base and were ultimately able to witness it force-landing at Lower Stoke on the Isle of Grain. Ryder was awarded one-fifth of a victory, while Boyle was awarded his Me109 destroyed and a one-fifth share in destroying the Do17.

Sergeant Pilot 'Birdie' Darling had also seen the Me109s diving on the squadron during the unit's initial line astern attack. When one attempted to get on his tail, he spun down until he felt it was safe, and then levelled out again. On doing so, he sighted twenty Heinkel He111s approximately 8,000 feet below him, about five miles east of Hornchurch. He dived again, aiming to position himself behind the formation, so that he could make a stern attack on the last Heinkel in the group. Although he fired a good five-second burst at his chosen bomber, his speed was too great and he overshot. He broke away and looked back to see the bomber break formation and lose height.

Darling then made a second strike on it, expending his remaining ammunition at ranges of 250 yards down to 75, while the Heinkel continued to descend before disappearing into cloud. Dropping below the cloud base, he eventually saw it again at 6,000 feet, with its wheels down and both propellers feathered. However, he lost sight of it anew in scattered cloud approximately six miles north-east of Hornchurch. Unable to find it again, he returned to base, where the ground staff also attested to having seen a bomber descend in a slow glide. Despite their testimony, though, Darling was only awarded a 'probable' victory as he had not witnessed the aircraft's ultimate fate.

Pilot Officer Harry Baker was in the original line astern formation when he saw fighters above the squadron, heading in their direction. He climbed to meet them and eventually managed to position himself behind the rearmost Me109 in one formation. Yet as he closed, his aircraft went into a spin and he had to fight to recover it. On regaining control, he noticed he was heading straight for a large formation of He111s over Southend. Easing back on his stick, he fired at each bomber that came into his sights as he dived towards them. He briefly saw his rounds enter the bow of the rearmost Heinkel, and then passed under the aircraft and into cloud cover.

A short while later, Baker spotted two Hurricanes attacking another He111 and joined them. He emptied his remaining ammunition into the bomber in a single six-second burst at ranges of 200 yards down to 20. This resulted in smoke issuing from the port engine, followed by the pilot dropping his undercarriage. In time, the bomber landed below the high-water line on mud flats at Asplens Head, Foulness, and the crew were captured. Baker claimed his first He111 damaged, and the second shared destroyed.

Pilot Officer 'Ben' Bennions engaged several Me109s, and was finally able to put a short burst into one, which immediately climbed, made a stall turn and then spun down into the cloud below. However, he was unable to observe any physical effect of his attack, or see smoke or flame. Deciding not to give chase, he looked around and soon spotted a large formation of Me110s diving towards cloud cover over Ashford. He attempted to attack one, but was forced to break off when he was engaged by an Me109. Evading the Messerschmitt, Bennions then sighted a lone Do17 and followed it as it crossed out near Dungeness, bound for France. He closed to around 300 yards and fired three four-second bursts at the bomber as he reduced his range to 100 yards. He saw his first burst enter the port side of the fuselage, while his second struck its starboard engine, which started smoking. He saw no further result from his third burst, but could do no more as his ammunition was exhausted, and so turned back for Hornchurch where he claimed the Do17 damaged at 2,000 feet, four miles south of Dungeness.

When the initial order into line astern was given, Pilot Officer John Mackenzie picked out a Dornier below him at 10,000 feet, ignoring the Me109s that were diving towards them from above. As he closed on the bomber he was unfortunately seen and its pilot dived for cloud cover. In a hurry to attack it before it reached the cloud, he opened fire on it at a range of 500 yards and fired a long burst as he closed to 50. The port engine caught fire, but then the aircraft disappeared into cloud south of London and was not seen again. Mackenzie subsequently returned to Hornchurch and claimed the Do17 destroyed. But the claim was disallowed as he had not seen it on the ground and his Combat Report was amended to read 'probable'.

When the initial line astern attack took place, Eric peeled off to port and dived towards the Dorniers, but was unable to find a suitable target. He climbed again and soon sighted a formation of three Do17s, escorted by three Me109s, just above cloud. Before he could reach them, he saw a Hurricane attack the fighters and decided to join him and provide some assistance. The Hurricane pilot, who would subsequently be revealed to be Pilot Officer Tom Neil of North Weald's No. 249 Squadron,[35] shot down two of the Messerschmitts in flames, and Eric closed in and attacked the other. Approaching from astern and slightly below, he fired 'rather a long burst',[36] which sent the aircraft into a vertical dive into the sea on fire.

Neil had initially thought that Eric was another Me109 joining the battle, but realised he was an RAF pilot when he shot the Me109 down. Then recognising the code EB on the fuselage of Eric's aircraft, thereby indicating he was a pilot of No. 41 Squadron, Neil proceeded to strike one of the Dorniers, which he shot down with visible effect: the aircraft did at least one somersault, and pieces of its wings detached as it fell to earth.

Eric joined up with Neil after this attack, and saw him point to the remaining two Dorniers about a mile ahead of them. The latter beckoned Eric to make a combined assault on them, and they opened their throttles and selected one aircraft each. The two men made initial stern attacks to silence the rear gunners, and then carried out half-attacks. Eric's second strike on 'his' Do17 caused its starboard engine to burst into flames, whereupon it plunged straight into the sea. By now, the other Dornier had dived to sea level with the Hurricane in pursuit. Eric explained: 'We carried out half- and beam attack[s] on the remainder. After a while the starboard engine caught fire and he also landed in the sea by a convoy, but this was shot down by [the] Hurricane 30 to 40 miles south east of Clacton.'[37]

By this time, Eric had run out of ammunition and left Neil to it, who he last saw still chasing the remaining Dornier. He returned to Hornchurch and claimed one Me109 and one Do17 destroyed.[38] Eric had done it again, and was maintaining his 100 per cent strike rate with thirteen victories claimed over the course of thirteen operational sorties.

The squadron's final victory of the operation fell to Flying Officer Tony Lovell. He had also broken away to evade the Me109s attacking the squadron's original line astern formation, and peeled off only to see a nearby He111. He made a quarter-attack on the bomber, but when he saw no results of his fire, he made a steep climbing turn to return to the unit. As he did, a large number of Me109s passed him at 8,000 feet and he picked out a yellow-nosed fighter and attacked it from astern at a range of 300 yards. Lovell fired consecutive bursts of five, four and seven seconds as he closed to 200 yards, and this resulted in a significant amount of white smoke issuing from the aircraft. A few seconds later, the aircraft made a violent skid, flipped over and dived into the clouds on its back, approximately three miles south-west of RAF Hornchurch. Lovell then returned to base, where he claimed the Messerschmitt probably destroyed.

The day had dealt a heavy blow to the Luftwaffe, whose commanders had told them the RAF was practically defeated. However, it was now very clear to every Luftwaffe airman in dogfights over England that this was far from the truth, and Hitler was consequently forced to rethink his strategy. 'Operation Sea Lion', the invasion of Britain, was indefinitely postponed, and this signified a major watershed in the war. It was far from over, but this climax in the Battle of Britain is widely seen as the turning point: Hitler had been stopped for the first time since 1938.

No. 41 Squadron had played a significant role, claiming four Me109s, one Do17, a shared Do17 and a shared He111 destroyed, one Me109, one Do17 and one He111 probably destroyed, and one Do17, one Do215 and one He111 damaged, for the loss of Pilot Officer Gerald Langley, who was killed in action.

Following this frenzied day, 16 September's increasingly rainy and gusty conditions offered the squadron a brief respite from the Luftwaffe's onslaught, and activity reduced significantly after an initial morning raid. That attack, comprising between 200 and 240 aircraft, crossed in between Dungeness and North Foreland just after 07:00 hours, and headed for London and the Docklands. Twelve squadrons were scrambled – Nos 41, 46, 66, 72, 92, 222, 249, 257, 501, 504, 603 and 605.

However, the cloudy conditions prevented most units from making contact and ultimately only Nos 17 and 222 Squadrons succeeded. Even then, they were unable to claim any victories as enemy aircraft escaped into cloud cover before any damage could be inflicted. No. 41 Squadron scrambled eight pilots at 07:30, which included Eric, and they were led by Flight Lieutenant Ryder. They saw nothing of the Luftwaffe, as the weather was so poor that it forced them to land at Tangmere at 08:45 hours; they remained there until an improvement in the weather allowed them to return to Hornchurch.

After the morning's raid was over, the rest of the day's sorties were conducted by lone Luftwaffe aircraft using cloud for cover, which dropped bombs indiscriminately on targets of opportunity in Kent and south-east London. Several No. 11 Group squadrons were sent up to intercept them, but no further contacts were made. It was not until 18:45 that No. 41 Squadron was airborne again for a patrol, when nine pilots, again including Eric, took off, led once more by Ryder. However, no enemy were seen and the pilots returned to Hornchurch with nothing to report, concluding the day's operational flying.

Luftwaffe activity remained light throughout the morning of 17 September, and the only hostile plots proved to be individual reconnaissance aircraft. The controller scrambled pilots singly, in pairs, or in sections to intercept them. Among them was Eric, who was ordered to patrol below the cloud base at 07:45 hours. However, neither he nor most others enjoyed any success, and a section from No. 602 Squadron made the only claim before lunch: a damaged Ju88.

At around 14:30, however, a number of formations of enemy aircraft were plotted off Cap Gris Nez, which orbited for about thirty minutes before heading for England. The attack consisted of approximately 260 aircraft, and over two-thirds of them crossed in on a course for London; the remaining eighty aircraft stayed in readiness over the Channel. In response, No. 11 Group scrambled No. 1 (Canadian), 17, 41, 46, 66, 72, 73, 92, 222, 229, 249, 253, 257, 303, 501, 504, 603 and 605 Squadrons, but only Nos 41, 303, 501 and 603 Squadrons engaged them, along with Nos 213 and 607 Squadrons, who were not detailed to intercept but were airborne at the time.

No. 41 Squadron took off at 14:50 hours with eleven pilots, which included Eric, and was led by Pilot Officer 'Ben' Bennions. They were ordered to join up with No. 603 Squadron over Manston, and Flying Officer John Boyle was designated as the spotter. The planes were heading in a south-westerly direction, with Boyle shadowing them from above, when the controller ordered the unit on to a bearing of 270°. As they turned to starboard on to this vector, five to ten miles south-east of Dover, Boyle noticed two formations of enemy fighters above them at around 26,000–27,000 feet. He warned the squadron and then boldly climbed alone towards the first formation of seven Me109s. He drew to within 350 yards of them before opening fire with a five-to six-second burst as he closed to 250 yards. The fighters reacted in an unexpected way, though, and all seven simply banked away and headed for France. Although Boyle had observed no effect from his attack, in banking away to evade him one of the Me109s collided with another and they both spun down out of control. Boyle then attempted to approach a second formation of fighters, but was himself attacked and forced to beat a hasty withdrawal. His aircraft sustained combat damage, but he was able to return to Hornchurch safely to claim the two Me109s destroyed as a result of his actions.

Meanwhile, a formation of thirty to forty Me109s attacked the rest of the squadron out of the sun from 1,000 feet above them, when they were approximately 25,000 feet over Chatham. However, Bennions saw them coming and was able to turn the pilots towards them. A number of combats then ensued, which scattered the squadron over a wide area.

Bennions evaded an attack from a group of five Me109s and then climbed to 15,000 feet where he sighted a loose formation of another four orbiting Maidstone. Able to close without being seen, he attacked the rearmost aircraft from the inside of their turn to port. He fired a two-second burst from 200 yards as he reduced his range to just 75, and this resulted in pieces flying off the aircraft, after which it rolled over, spun down, and plummeted straight into the ground at Bishopden Wood.

Like Bennions, Sergeant Pilot 'Jock' Norwell initially dived away to evade the Me109s, and then climbed again. Then, seeing a lone Me109 south of Chatham at 28,000 feet, he fired a three-second burst at it from 300 yards and damaged it, but it succeeded in evading him. Shortly thereafter, he approached another Me109 and fired a four-second burst as he closed to 100 yards. Glycol issued from the aircraft, but Norwell could do no further damage and he ultimately claimed both Me109s damaged.

Several of the squadron's Spitfires sustained varying degrees of combat damage that afternoon, but the pilots were all unhurt. They included Flying Officer Harry Baker, who force-landed his aircraft at Stelling Minnis, badly shot up, Flying Officer John Mackenzie, who crash-landed near Dover, and Pilot Officer Harry Chalder, who received combat damage off Dover. Unfortunately, little information appears to have survived on the circumstances relating to each, but one intelligence report lists one aircraft sustaining Category 3 damage (only repairable to ground instructional airframe status), two Category 2 damage (repairable at a maintenance unit or contractor off site), and several aircraft Category 1 damage (repairable on site).

Although Eric was an active participant on the operation, he could not bring the Luftwaffe into a successful engagement and returned to Hornchurch unable to make any claim for the second day in a row. However, there was some consolation for the brief fall in his stellar strike rate, as it was announced that both he and Pilot Officer Bennions had been bestowed the Distinguished Flying Cross. Although not officially awarded until 1 October 1940, Bennions had won his for destroying 'seven enemy aircraft and possibly several others',[39] while Eric's citation recognised nine victories: 'This officer has destroyed nine enemy aircraft, eight of these within a period of one week. He has displayed great vigour and determination in pressing home his attacks.'[40] The mention of eight enemy aircraft within a week suggests they are referring to the victories achieved by him between 5 and 11 September 1940. The announcement of the award appeared in the No. 11 Group operations record book (ORB), and was reported in *The Times* on 28 September.

The Luftwaffe mounted four major attacks on the south-east on 18 September, and No. 41 Squadron's pilots intercepted those commencing at 09:00, 12:15 and 15:40 hours. The unit enjoyed another successful day, claiming a total of three enemy aircraft destroyed, five probably destroyed and seven damaged, for the cost of no more than light combat damage to several aircraft.

The first raid lasted just an hour from 09:00 and comprised around 100 aircraft in two formations, which crossed in near Dover and headed directly for London.

Thirteen units were ordered to intercept them, of which Nos 41, 72, 92, 501 and 603 Squadrons – and Wing Commander Victor Beamish, who was operating independently – succeeded in engaging them. Despite being outnumbered, the RAF's attacks were sufficient to stop the Luftwaffe from penetrating beyond Biggin Hill.

For their part, eleven pilots of No. 41 Squadron took off at 09:10 hours, led by Pilot Officer Bennions, ordered to patrol Maidstone at 20,000 feet with fellow Hornchurch-based No. 603 Squadron. Once airborne, however, they were given a vector of 130°, told to climb to 25,000 feet and then ordered to orbit. They did not do so for long as several formations of Me109s, totalling approximately fifty aircraft, were soon sighted 5,000–7,000 feet above them. Bennions ordered the pilots into a line astern formation, and led the climb towards the fighters, eager to eliminate the Luftwaffe's height advantage as quickly as possible. However, they were seen and the Messerschmitts split into smaller formations of no more than five aircraft and dived toward them. The squadron's pilots immediately took evasive action, but were pursued and several aircraft were damaged, although no one was injured.

After some effort, Bennions brought an Me109 into his sights at 33,000 feet over Maidstone, and gave it a two-second burst from 250 yards. He fired another burst of the same length as he closed to 100 yards, and pieces of the aircraft flew past him as the Messerschmitt commenced a descent in a flat spin, with white streams of petrol or glycol issuing from each side of its fuselage and black smoke from its tail. At that time, though, he was approached by five Me109s and had to break off his attack. He successfully evaded them and returned to Hornchurch unscathed, but was unable to witness the ultimate fate of his target. As such, he was left with little choice but to claim it only probably destroyed south of Maidstone.

During the initial climb towards the Me109s, Eric, who was flying as rearguard again, noticed what he thought were another three pairs of Me109s climbing towards them from below. He informed Bennions and broke away to make sure, but before he could get close to them, the last pair had already passed him at a range making it fruitless to give chase. However, he then spotted a large formation of what he believed were friendly fighters ahead of them. A moment later, the aircraft gave away their allegiance when they saw them, too, and immediately turned away to avoid them; Eric now knew they were Me109s and this gave him a new opportunity.

Lining himself up for an attack out of the sun on the rearmost Me109 in a pair, he fired from a range of 200 yards with a burst of two to three seconds. The Messerschmitt immediately side-slipped and fell into a vertical dive with smoke and glycol pouring from its engine. Eric then turned his attention to the second of the pair and opened fire but could not observe any result before it disappeared into cloud cover. He descended through the cloud, but could not locate either aircraft. He then returned to Hornchurch, claiming the first Me109 probably destroyed, justifying his claim with the explanation that 'it could not have got home'.[41] This was his first unconfirmed victory.

The third and last pilot to claim victories on this operation was Sergeant Pilot Frank Usmar. Left behind in the initial ascent, he climbed independently to 28,000 feet where he saw an aircraft flying along the coast. Upon investigation it proved to be a Spitfire, so he turned away. On doing so he sighted five Me109s heading towards Maidstone at 25,000 feet. He dived down behind them in the Charing area to deliver a stern attack on one of the aircraft, and fired a four-second burst at a range of 200 yards. Then closing to just 50 yards, he released a second burst of the same length, which resulted in a blue flame emitting from the Messerschmitt's port side. The plane then turned over and went down in the direction of Dungeness.

As the other Me109s had not reacted, Usmar did not follow the aircraft down, but rather slid across behind its wingman. To his surprise, the aircraft continued on its course, apparently aware of neither Usmar's presence nor the fact he had just lost his colleague. Attacking this aircraft, too, he fired two four-second bursts, one from dead astern and one with slight deflection from starboard. This aircraft similarly rolled over and went down in the vicinity of Romney Marsh. Not wanting to push his luck any further, Usmar now broke to starboard and dived away. Before he left the area, he observed that both the Me109s he had attacked were still losing height. He then returned to base, where he was granted one Me109 probably destroyed and one damaged.

The day's second raid commenced just an hour and forty-five minutes later and involved approximately 250 enemy aircraft, which made landfall near Dover. They split into multiple formations and headed for London, employing 'tip and run' tactics as they went. Random bombing took place at a wide range of locations from Gillingham, Kent, to Worthing, Sussex, and there were even isolated attacks on places such as Harwich in Essex. Seventeen squadrons were ordered to intercept them, but only Nos 41, 46, 222, 249, 303, 501 and 603 succeeded in doing so. Between them, these units claimed eight destroyed, four probably destroyed and six damaged for the reported casualties of two RAF pilots missing.

No. 41 Squadron was airborne at 12:35 hours, when ten pilots took off, led by Pilot Officer Bennions once again. Following orders similar to the morning's, the unit was directed to join up with No. 603 Squadron and patrol Maidstone at 20,000 feet. While orbiting to await No. 603's arrival, however, Bennions sighted a loose formation of forty to fifty Me109s off their port beam, ranging between

500 feet and 5,000 feet above them. In scenes reminiscent of the morning's operation, Bennions ordered the squadron into line astern and started climbing towards them. However, when the Messerschmitts dived on them, Bennions swiftly instructed the pilots to take evasive action instead, owing to their clear disadvantage, and the squadron scattered.

Bennions himself succeeded in climbing to 32,000 feet, where he attacked a formation of five Me109s orbiting west of Gravesend. He closed in on the rearmost fighter and fired two two-second bursts of ammunition, whereupon the aircraft exploded and his forward vision was obscured. Bennions tried to pull up and over the debris, but then sighted another Me109 in his rear-view mirror, firing at him from astern. He felt several rounds strike the port side of his Spitfire but managed to turn about and attack the offending aircraft. He fired two short bursts at it, and this resulted in pieces dislodging themselves from the Messerschmitt's starboard wing, while black smoke poured from what he believed was the oil cooler under the same wing.

The Me109 half-rolled away, at which time Bennions's attention was drawn to another small formation of Me109s approaching him from his port rear quarter. He banked towards them and fired at the No. 4 in the formation, which reacted as if it had been hit and half-turned away. Bennions rolled after him and when the pilot levelled out, he fired a long burst at the aircraft, causing it to emit large quantities of white smoke from the port wing, about three feet from the fuselage. At this point, Bennions ran out of ammunition and, leaving the Messerschmitt descending towards Dover trailing a long stream of white smoke, he took stock of the damage to his own aircraft and decided it was time to return to Hornchurch. He re-formed the squadron over Gravesend and landed safely with Category 1 damage, claiming one enemy aircraft destroyed, one probably destroyed and one damaged.

As the Me109s made their original dive on the squadron, Eric took a full deflection shot at one Me109, 'and it was seen to go down in smoke'.[42] The unit broke up as a result of Bennions's order to take evasive action, and when the command came to re-form, he climbed to 28,000 feet but was unable to see anyone from the squadron. He decided, therefore, to climb further. On reaching 31,000 feet, he sighted a lone Me109 and gave chase, rapidly closing to a range of 200 yards, where he fired a short burst. Seeing no visible effect on the aircraft, he closed to 100 yards and attacked it from slightly below. He had released only two short bursts of ammunition when the Messerschmitt exploded and fell into the Channel just off Margate. On returning to Hornchurch, Eric claimed the first Me109 probably destroyed and the second destroyed.

Sergeant Pilot 'Birdie' Darling broke away to evade the original group of Me109s diving on the squadron, then climbed to 25,000 feet. He sighted a loose formation of twenty Me109s and stalked them for a time, until he could close in on a straggler five miles inland from Dover. However, when he opened fire, the Me109 dived for the nearest cloud cover and made a beeline for the Channel. Not to be outmanoeuvred, Darling climbed over the cloud and waited for the Messerschmitt to reappear, which it did a short while later, just over the coast. He closed anew and fired two long bursts from 250 yards as he reduced his range to just 30, resulting in smoke emitting from its starboard side. The Me109 immediately started losing height in a steady glide towards France, but did not have enough altitude to make it all the way and it eventually ditched in the Channel. Darling then returned to RAF Hornchurch where he claimed it destroyed.

The last pilot to declare a victory on this operation was Sergeant Pilot 'Jock' Norwell who, after the initial attack and evasion, sighted three Me109s heading home in line astern, ten miles west of Manston at 25,000 feet. He dived almost vertically on to the rearmost aircraft and fired a four-second burst from 500 yards as he closed to 250. He hit the Me109's fuselage between the cockpit and the tail, but two of his guns failed and he could ultimately only claim the aircraft as damaged.

The third and last major attack on 18 September was undertaken by around 250 He111s and Ju88s, escorted by fighters, between 15:40 and 18:00 hours. No. 11 Group scrambled seventeen fighter squadrons in response but only four were successful: Nos 41, 66, 92 and 213. Between them, they managed to claim seven destroyed, three probably destroyed and six damaged. No. 41 Squadron was off the deck at 16:12, comprising nine pilots led by Flying Officer John Mackenzie, but Eric was not among them. However, the unit enjoyed limited success and could only take credit for one Ju88 and three Me109s damaged.

This concluded a long and tiring operational flying day, in which the pilots claimed three destroyed, five probably destroyed and seven damaged enemy aircraft for no loss of their own. As a whole, No. 11 Group declared its casualties as one pilot killed in action and two missing, and seven Hurricanes and six Spitfires written off. They also maintain that seventeen enemy aircraft were destroyed, thirteen probably destroyed and seventeen damaged, a total of forty-six victories against approximately 600 aircraft that entered the area.

No. 41 Squadron had certainly made its presence felt, having punched above its weight and claimed approximately one-third of the whole group's victories. This proved to be the Luftwaffe's last significant daylight bomber raid, and this is also borne out in Eric's rate of victories. Between 18 September and 5 October, he could only make two more claims, and both of these occurred on 20 September.

The weather on 19 September confined Luftwaffe activity to individual reconnaissance aircraft, which made landfall along the Kent coast and patrolled areas of Kent and Sussex. A few penetrated as far as East London and indiscriminate bombs were dropped on targets of opportunity on docks along the Thames. A large number of individual aircraft also patrolled the Channel, where three were intercepted by the RAF.

Consequently, it was a very quiet day for No. 41 Squadron, and no interceptions were made. Individual pilots undertook patrols at 09:25, 11:20 and 13:10 hours, followed by a trio at 15:30 and a final pair at 16:10. The 15:30 patrol included Flight Lieutenant Ryder, Eric and Sergeant Pilot Beardsley, who were airborne for a full hour, but they saw no sign of the Luftwaffe and returned to Hornchurch with nothing to report.

All operational flying ceased at 17:35, but it was not a restful night as the squadron was woken in the early hours of the following morning when the Luftwaffe visited RAF Hornchurch and dropped a single bomb on the south-east corner of the airfield. It exploded, but fortunately no damage was done.

On 20 September 1940, Luftwaffe activity was once again generally confined to reconnaissance flights by individual aircraft on account of the weather conditions. The one exception came in a raid of 100 enemy aircraft between 10:50 and 12:00 hours, consisting almost entirely of fighters. These aircraft crossed in between Dungeness and East Bay, and then split in two. One formation headed northwest towards the Thames Estuary and reached the Isle of Sheppey before turning for home; the other made for the Biggin Hill and Kenley areas before it turned back across the Channel. Eleven units were scrambled to intercept them but only six units – Nos 41, 72, 92, 222, 253 and 603 Squadrons – succeeded in doing so. No. 11 Group's total claims for the day were four enemy aircraft destroyed, one probably destroyed and two damaged.

For their part, No. 41 Squadron was airborne with ten pilots to patrol Manston at 11:20, led by Flight Lieutenant Ryder, who assigned Eric as spotter. The unit rendezvoused with fellow Hornchurch-based No. 603 Squadron over the airfield, and commenced a climb together to their patrol height. However, they had not yet reached that altitude when they were dived upon by a large number of Me109s, and both squadrons were hit hard.

It is apparent that they were taken by surprise, as one of No. 603 Squadron's pilots was killed, a second baled out and a third crashed on landing, though uninjured, for the claims of only two Me109s damaged. No. 41 Squadron came out of the fight little better, having had two pilots shot down, although unhurt, for two enemy aircraft destroyed. Those shot down were Flying Officer John Mackenzie – who had attempted to attack some He111s but was shot down by Me109s and force-landed near West Malling – and Pilot Officer 'Ben' Bennions, who force-landed at Lympne due to having sustained return fire from a Ju88.

While this was happening, Eric was over Maidstone by himself, involved in combats of his own. Having climbed to 33,000 feet, he did not have to wait long before he sighted a number of bombers crossing in near Dover at 15,000 feet, and reported them to the controller. A short while later, he spotted three 'He113s' with orange noses 'going round in a circle between Maidstone and Canterbury'[43] just 3,000 feet below him.[44] Eric set off in pursuit but was spotted, and the three aircraft 'split up in all directions'.[45] He picked out one that was diving towards Dover, and fired several one-second bursts from ranges of 250 yards down to 100. He had no trouble overhauling the aircraft, owing to his height and speed, and his adversary did not attempt to attack him. White vapour emanated from under the aircraft's starboard wing after three bursts, and then flame issued from its engine. Moments later, they passed over the Dover balloon barrage 'with only a few feet to spare',[46] and the enemy aircraft continued in a shallow dive until it crashed into the Channel approximately fifteen to twenty miles north-west of Boulogne.

Eric then climbed back to the cloud base at 2,000 feet and orbited the area awhile. A short time later, a Henschel Hs126 reconnaissance aircraft 'appeared from nowhere'[47] and circled the downed aircraft at an altitude of no more than fifty feet. Grasping the opportunity offered, Eric pounced on it and fired a two-second burst from seventy-five yards down to point-blank range. The Henschel went straight into the Channel, tail first. Seeing several more enemy aircraft flying up and down the Channel below the cloud base, Eric climbed back into cloud cover and headed home to claim the He113 (Me109E) and the Hs126 destroyed.

Minimal operational flying was undertaken during the afternoon and comprised just two patrols, one by a trio of pilots at 12:55 hours and another by Flight Lieutenant Ryder and Eric at 14:30. However, both were uneventful and this concluded the day's operational flying.

Eric had now claimed eighteen victories to his credit – sixteen destroyed and two probably destroyed – over the course of twenty-two operational sorties. This still equated to an impressive strike rate of over 80 per cent. However, he was about to commence an unprecedented lull, and was unable to claim another victory for two weeks, no doubt in part as a result of the fact he only flew nine sorties in that time.

During the night, the peace was broken by the Luftwaffe again – accompanied by air-raid sirens, spotlights and anti-aircraft fire – and two parachute mines were dropped on RAF Hornchurch. One fell just outside the camp and the second on the perimeter track near the aircraft stop butts on the south-west corner of the airfield; both failed to explode. The unexploded parachute mine was defused at around 12:30 hours by two officers of HMS *Vernon*, after which they stayed for lunch in the mess. They then left Hornchurch for nearby Dagenham to defuse another two parachute mines, but a large explosion was heard at 16:30 and it was later established that both men had been killed.

That evening, No. 41 Squadron scrambled a dozen pilots at 18:00, which included Eric, but they saw nothing and were on the ground again at 19:10. This was repeated on 23 and 25 September, when Eric was airborne with the squadron to intercept inbound raids, but nothing was seen on either occasion.

Eric then undertook no further operational flying for the rest of the month, and is presumed to have been granted leave. In his absence, the squadron was involved in some heavy fighting, claiming two enemy aircraft destroyed, five probably destroyed, and three damaged, but they were hard-fought and came at a great cost to the unit. Six pilots were shot down, one of whom was killed, while four were wounded, one of whom subsequently died. A further five aircraft sustained combat damage.

The month as a whole had constituted the squadron's most intensive of its almost twenty-five-year existence, and it had consequently taken a bitter toll. The unit had lost several men killed and wounded, and now had its third officer commanding within those short few weeks. The pilots were also tired and the squadron desperately needed fresh, but experienced, pilots.

However, especially on account of Dowding's policy of rotating squadrons in and out of active areas for rest, a continuous flow of pilots was available to bolster depleted squadrons, a fact particularly obvious on No. 41 Squadron during the last few days of September and first few days of October 1940. In the space of four days, no less than eleven new pilots – approximately one-half of the squadron's pilot strength – were posted in, marking the first major influx of pilots since Eric, Langley, McAdam and Usmar had arrived on 18 June. Six of the pilots were sourced from No. 610 Squadron, four from No. 611 and one from No. 266. The new men added a fresh dynamic to the unit, brought new energy to the ranks and delivered some respite for the squadron's battle-weary pilots. It was, therefore, in many respects a very different squadron to which Eric returned on 1 October.

Chapter Five

Great Courage
October 1940

The day that Eric returned to operations, the Luftwaffe delivered five major attacks: the first on Southampton and the others on Kent and the south-east. Owing to its distance from Hornchurch, No. 41 Squadron was not called upon to intercept the Southampton attack, and the unit consequently remained on the ground until just after lunch.

The day's second raid, of a 'tip and run' nature, commenced at 13:00 hours when fifty fighters crossed in at 20,000 feet and made for mid-Kent. There were no reports of bombers among them, so when Lympne and the Romney area were bombed it was assumed that many of the fighters had been fitted with bombs. Eleven squadrons were scrambled to intercept them, but only No. 41 Squadron succeeded. Twelve pilots, including Eric, took off at 13:05, with an order to patrol Hornchurch and Rochford at 28,000 feet. When nothing was seen for over an hour, it seemed that the unit was going to have an uneventful patrol. However, at 14:15, a few Me109s were seen slightly above the squadron, at around 30,000 feet over Epsom.

Squadron Leader Don Finlay climbed to attack one of the aircraft, opening fire from below at a range of 250 yards. Smoke poured out of the Messerschmitt as it dived away steeply, closely followed by Finlay and Flying Officer Dennis Adams, who was on his second operational sortie with the squadron.

Finding himself in an advantageous position, Adams also opened fire on the aircraft from a range of 350 yards. He let fly with three short bursts as he closed to 150 yards, but appears to have thwarted Finlay's attack, as the squadron leader was compelled to break off when Adams almost collided with him. However, Finlay's own assault was handicapped by four of his eight guns failing. The pair continued to follow the Me109 down until it disappeared into cloud at 4,000 feet trailing black smoke and glycol, with no sign of it pulling out. They descended below the cloud base but could see no sign of the Messerschmitt and subsequently claimed it as shared damaged. Yet when an unclaimed Me109 was later found on the ground at Falmer, the victory was elevated to destroyed, a fifty per cent share going to each pilot. This constituted both pilots' first victories with the squadron.

The airmen then turned for home but, having been in the air for some time, descended to conserve oxygen, as many of the pilots were beginning to get low supplies. On the way down, Pilot Officer 'Ben' Bennions sighted a formation of Hurricanes and, to the east over Henfield, a larger formation of Me109s. As he still had half a bottle of oxygen, he decided to break away from the squadron and attack them. He chose the aircraft nearest to him in what he thought was the last of a series of echelons.

Closing in on the Messerschmitt, he fired two short bursts at its starboard quarter, quickly resulting in the plane catching fire and the pilot opening his hood. At that moment, though, Bennions was hit by cannon fire; shells entered his cockpit and he was seriously wounded. He lost consciousness and the aircraft fell several thousand feet uncontrolled until he came to, arrested the dive, and managed to slide back his shattered hood and bale out. Losing consciousness several times again as he descended under his canopy, he ultimately landed in a field on Dunstalls Farm at Henfield, Sussex, with severe injuries to his right arm and leg; more seriously, he had been blinded in one eye. He was initially admitted to Horsham Cottage Hospital but was subsequently transferred to Queen Victoria Hospital at East Grinstead, where he underwent plastic surgery performed by pioneering plastic surgeon, Dr Archibald McIndoe.

By then one of the unit's longest-serving members, Bennions survived the ordeal but did not return to the squadron. With ten and one shared destroyed enemy aircraft, seven probables and five damaged under his belt by the time he was shot down, he was the next highest scoring pilot on the unit after Eric, and would ultimately remain its second-highest-scoring pilot of the war, behind Eric.

The Luftwaffe made three subsequent raids on 1 October 1940, and No. 41 Squadron was airborne again during the last of these, albeit without Eric. Comprising fifty bombers and fighters, No. 11 Group dispatched nine squadrons to intercept them, but only Nos 41 and 222 succeeded in doing so. However, there was only a single claim, which fell to Flight Lieutenant Tony Lovell who destroyed an Me109.

The night of 1/2 October was one of the quietest Hornchurch had experienced since the beginning of the Blitz, but it was merely the proverbial quiet before the storm. The Luftwaffe kept the RAF extremely busy on 2 October with nigh on continuous attacks throughout the day. Consisting almost entirely of fighters, which made bearings for London via Kent, they came in five phases: between 08:50 and 09:30 hours (thirty aircraft); 09:30 and 10:30 (eighty aircraft); 11:55 and 13:00 (forty fighters and ten bombers); 13:00 and 14:15 (twenty-five aircraft); and

14:15 and 18:00 (two attacks of approximately twenty-five aircraft each).

Numbers of squadrons were airborne all day in response to the raids, which is also evident from entries in No. 41 Squadron's ORB, where the following five patrols are recorded: between 08:40 and 09:45 hours (eleven pilots); 12:10 and 12:40 (eleven pilots); 13:30 and 13:50 (twelve pilots); 15:10 and 16:00 (thirteen pilots); and 16:35 and 17:05 (eleven pilots).

The 08:40 patrol constituted the first time that Squadron Leader Finlay led the unit on an operation, but he was ultimately airborne on all five patrols on the 2nd. For his part, Eric participated in the third, fourth and fifth of these, but the Luftwaffe could not be engaged and the unit ended the day empty-handed. It was felt this was because the enemy fighters were able to operate at greater speeds than when protecting bomber formations, and RAF squadrons therefore had too little time to reach sufficient altitudes to intercept them. There was therefore a lot of work for No. 41 Squadron's pilots and groundcrew for no reward. Eric now had two days off operational flying and returned on 5 October ready for more action; it would prove to be another good day for him.

The Luftwaffe was very active on 5 October, on account of favourable weather conditions, and made six attacks during daylight hours: four over the south-east and towards London, one on the Poole area and one on the Portsmouth district. No. 41 Squadron was airborne four times, and Eric twice, and he claimed victories during both sorties. As a whole, the unit ended the day with claims of four enemy aircraft destroyed, two probably destroyed and three damaged for no loss.

The day's first raid was of the 'tip and run' nature, in which approximately two dozen fighters and bombers made landfall at Dover at 10:00 hours and then headed for Maidstone. The entire raid was over within thirty minutes. Four squadrons were scrambled, thereunder No. 41 Squadron, and the unit had twelve pilots airborne at 10:10. However, nothing was seen and they landed again twenty minutes later.

The second raid commenced only thirty minutes after the squadron landed from the first. Two formations of twenty-five enemy aircraft crossed in at 25,000 feet over Dungeness and headed for the Biggin Hill–Kenley area, although a few penetrated as far as London. They were followed by a second wave of approximately fifty aircraft, which flew to Chatham via Maidstone. The majority of the aircraft were fighters, but at least two bomber formations were also involved.

No. 11 Group scrambled eleven squadrons in response, which claimed a combined twenty destroyed, three probably destroyed and thirteen damaged for the loss of one pilot of No. 303 Squadron. No. 41 Squadron was airborne at 11:05 with twelve pilots and ordered to patrol Hornchurch at 30,000 feet. They were three-quarters of an hour into the operation when six yellow-nosed Me109s were sighted passing on a perpendicular course between Chatham and Dungeness, 4,000 feet below them. The squadron dived on them and in the ensuing combats, Pilot Officer Denys Mileham claimed one Me109 destroyed and one damaged, Sergeant Pilot 'Bam' Bamberger an Me109 destroyed, and Pilot Officers Robert Boret and John Lecky each an Me109 damaged. Flight Lieutenant Tony Lovell sustained combat damage to a wing but was not hurt, and the pilots were all back on the ground by 12:20 hours. Once again, they had little time to rest, eat, rearm and refuel, as the Luftwaffe commenced its third raid a little over an hour later.

At 13:30, a diversionary formation of twenty-five enemy fighters came in at 20,000 feet on a sweep to Maidstone and the Isle of Sheppey, and left again via North Foreland. They were closely followed by a second wave of approximately 100 aircraft, comprising around two-thirds fighters and one-third bombers, which made landfall near Dover. Half of the aircraft flew to central London and then turned south-east to rejoin the rest of the formation, which had remained over central Kent. They then crossed out together at numerous places along the south-eastern coast. Strangely, for the size and boldness of the attack, bombs were only reported to have been dropped at Forest Hill and Rotherhithe.

No. 11 Group scrambled sixteen units in response to the raid, but only Nos 41 and 74 Squadrons successfully intercepted the enemy formations and claimed victories. Led by Squadron Leader Finlay, nine of the unit's pilots took off to patrol Maidstone at 13:30 hours, just as the first fighters were flying in. Finding cloud layers at 27,000 feet, and between 31,000 and 32,000 feet, they initially patrolled above the cloud, but after seeing nothing, descended again, through both layers, to 25,000 feet. The pilots became separated as they did so, however, and on emerging again, Eric, leading Yellow Section, found himself alone, some distance from the rest of the squadron, and about 2,000 feet above and behind them. He saw the squadron turn north-east, but then sighted seven Me109s above him, flying in line abreast formation between him and the unit.

Climbing into the sun to gain height, Eric positioned himself for an attack and 'joined one of the last formations of Me.109s'.[1] With the experience and patience borne of many combats in the past four weeks, Eric 'waited for quite a while'[2] and observed the formation as he shadowed it. He noted that 'The 7 Me.109's ... adopted the following patrol tactics. The centre a/c just dropped behind and patrolled the rear of the formation, and then regained its position. The two a/c on his flanks then dropped back, and were in turn replaced by the next pair of flanking a/c, and so on.'[3]

It is clear they were oblivious to Eric's presence. Having watched long enough, he lined himself up behind the Messerschmitt to the extreme port of the formation and fired a one-second burst of gunfire from 200 yards. The aircraft immediately

GREAT COURAGE

dived, with smoke and glycol emitting from its engine. Seeing the remaining Messerschmitts continue on, unaware their colleague had just been shot down, Eric let it go and moved in behind the next one. He fired a one-second burst from the same range and the aircraft started to side-slip. He therefore fired two more one-second bursts as he closed to 100 yards, and the plane fell into a steep dive, with flames flowing from the engine and pieces flying off as it descended. The Messerschmitt crashed between West Malling and Ashford, and Eric returned to Hornchurch to claim the first Me109 probably destroyed and the second destroyed.

Meanwhile, the rest of the squadron had also sighted and chased small scattered formations of Me109s with little luck. Two enemy aircraft were spotted by Flying Officer John Mackenzie some distance below him at 7,000 feet, and he dived on them. But they saw him coming and one swerved to starboard, while the other shot off in the direction of the Channel. Chasing the latter, Mackenzie slowly overhauled it and was surprised to note that it bore tail fin markings similar to British fighters, with red, white and blue vertical stripes. He opened fire from 200 yards with a two-second burst astern, and then discharged a second burst at its starboard quarter. It was not until he fired a third time, with deflection, that the first results of his attack became evident and the Messerschmitt started smoking heavily. Closing to just eighty yards, Mackenzie fired the rest of his ammunition into it, causing flames to issue from the starboard side of the fuselage, near the wing. Then seeing another three Me109s above him, and realising he was unable to defend himself, he decided to head home and left his opponent to his fate. As he turned, however, he saw the Me109's pilot discard his hood, intending to bale out, and returned to base to claim the Me109 destroyed and in the Channel.

The last pilot was on the ground at around 14:55 hours, but the Luftwaffe again left little time for the groundcrews to rearm and refuel the squadron's aircraft, and the pilots had no time to rest. The day's fourth attack had been launched on the Poole area while the unit was airborne on the third attack, but the day's fifth commenced at 15:30, and the pilots were airborne again five minutes after it commenced. On this occasion, fifty enemy bombers and fighters made landfall in two formations simultaneously, one over Dungeness and the other over Hastings. The Dungeness formation then flew due west over Ashford and Tunbridge Wells, where they rendezvoused with the Hastings formation. The attack penetrated no further than the Kenley area and sought out targets of opportunity in Kent, east Sussex and east Surrey.

No. 11 Group scrambled thirteen squadrons in response, but No. 41 Squadron was the only unit that succeeded in engaging them. Eight pilots were airborne at 15:35 to patrol the Maidstone–Hornchurch area, but they were soon vectored on to a like number of bombers reported to be flying in a north-westerly direction from Gravesend. They climbed through 8/10ths cloud at 5,000 feet, then another 8/10ths band with a top of 30,000 feet, above which they levelled out.

Eric, who was flying as Yellow 1 in his preferred position as rearguard, spotted a dozen Me109s climbing towards the rear of the squadron to attack them. His report did not reach the rest of the unit, as they did not react to his call, but then an unidentified voice was heard over the R/T saying that they were Hurricanes. Eric knew otherwise but could not raise the other pilots and therefore took them on himself. He dived on them from above and behind, singled out an aircraft, and attacked it from astern and slightly above with two one-second bursts from 250 yards, closing to 150. The aircraft climbed almost vertically, then 'fell forward into a vertical dive',[4] streaming glycol from under its right wing. Eric watched it spin down through cloud to approximately 7,000 feet, where he left it to its fate. It made no attempt to recover and Eric assumed it would crash somewhere in the Tonbridge– Maidstone–Sevenoaks area.

Before he returned to base to claim the Me109 probably destroyed, he noted several pairs of Me109s arriving on the coast from the Channel, which he felt were intended to escort home bombers or fighters in distress and keep the RAF from taking advantage of the situation. Seven of the squadron's pilots landed back at Hornchurch at 16:42 hours and the eighth returned at 17:00 via a stop at Rochford, presumably to refuel.

This ended a long day's operational flying, upon which forty-one operational sorties were flown by the unit in four operations. Eric's tally of victories had climbed again and now totalled seventeen destroyed and four probably destroyed over thirty-one operational sorties – a success rate of over two victories for every three operations.

Eric was in action again two days later, on 7 October, when the Luftwaffe launched three major attacks on London and the south-east. No. 41 Squadron operated against all of them, and although Eric was only involved in the first, and fired his guns, he could not make a claim.

The day's initial raid began at 09:30 hours and involved around 100 enemy aircraft, mostly fighters, which crossed in near Dungeness. The raid began with a sweep by approximately thirty Me109s, which were closely followed by more fighters between 20,000 and 30,000 feet, and a number of bombers between 15,000 and 20,000 feet. Several aircraft crossed the IAZ, but little bombing took place and the only apparently concentrated attack was directed at the balloon defences at Dover.

No. 11 Group sent up eighteen squadrons in response, which together claimed two destroyed and three damaged for the loss of two pilots killed. Hornchurch's

Nos 222 and 603 Squadrons were dispatched immediately, but No. 41 Squadron, at Rochford, was not called upon until around an hour into the raid. No. 222 sighted a large formation of bombers but could not engage them on account of their altitude and returned empty-handed. No. 603 Squadron managed to climb to 29,000 feet but were still bounced from above by a formation of Me109s, and lost one pilot killed in action and another shot down who baled out into the Channel and was rescued unhurt. They were also unable to make any claims.

No. 41 Squadron also found it difficult to claim any victories. Eleven pilots were ordered into the air at 10:40 to patrol at 25,000 feet and await enemy aircraft returning to France, hopefully low on fuel and ammunition. At approximately 11:10, Squadron Leader Finlay sighted a lone Do215 around ten miles south-west of Maidstone at 25,000 feet, travelling in an easterly direction. Considering the 09:30 attack was considered to have ended at 11:00, this aircraft was either a straggler or, more likely, thought Flying Officer John Mackenzie, an independent, heavily armoured reconnaissance aircraft. Seeing no protective escort, Finlay ordered Green Section to attack it, but when they did not react, he presumed he had R/T problems and set upon the aircraft himself.

Firing a burst from astern at 250 yards, he broke to port and came around again. Making a second attack from astern, on this occasion he caused the port engine to smoke. Closing to 150 yards just off Dover, he fired a third time, and then broke off when he saw another of the squadron's aircraft slide in above him; the squadron had got the message! This appears to have been Flying Officer John Mackenzie, who later recorded in his logbook:

> S/LDR Finlay opened attack followed by self, F/O Adams & P/O Wells. 'A' Flight then went in, F/LT Ryder, P/O Lock & P/O Leckie [sic]. D.O.215 eventually crashed in Channel, P/O Lock and P/O Leckie [sic] being last two to attack. F/O Adams' machine was set on fire and he baled out. [...] This machine was heavily armoured and carried heavy rear gun armament.[5]

Mackenzie fired deflection shots at the bomber, first from port, and then starboard, and saw his ammunition entering the fuselage. However, the dorsal gunner's aim was also straight: Mackenzie's aircraft was hit and glycol poured over his windshield, forcing him to break off the attack. He returned to Rochford safely, but his aircraft was considered to have sustained damage that could only be repaired off site.

Flying Officer Dennis Adams then took his own shot at the bomber, but the dorsal gunner was quicker. Few details are available, but Adams managed to make landfall again before baling out. He was unhurt and landed at Postling, near Folkestone.

It is understood that Pilot Officer Edward Wells then made his own attack,[6] as did Flight Lieutenant Norman Ryder, Eric and finally Pilot Officer John Lecky. Despite all their attacks, only Finlay and Mackenzie submitted claims for damaging the aircraft, but the last man to fire, Lecky, was granted the aircraft destroyed. However, no Combat Report appears to have survived for him in either the National Archives or No. 41 Squadron collections, and the only information is provided in the squadron ORB and, in more detail, on Flying Officer Mackenzie's Pilot Service Record, which states: 'P/O Lock and Lecky went in later and Lecky shot it down into cloud. Lock waiting below saw it into sea.'[7]

With the exception of Adams and Mackenzie, the remaining pilots were back on the ground at 11:30 hours, but they only had ninety minutes' respite before they faced the Luftwaffe again. No. 41 Squadron was airborne twice more, in response to the Luftwaffe's second and third raids, but Eric was not involved. During the former operation, the squadron only made a single claim when Flying Officer James Walker shot down an Me109, but the Luftwaffe was not seen at all during the latter.

This ended the operational flying day for the unit, but the Luftwaffe visited RAF Hornchurch again during the night and dropped a number of incendiaries and high-explosive bombs on the station. Fortunately there were no casualties, but one road was damaged and a mains water pipe was also severed.

Eric was airborne again the following day, when the Luftwaffe launched three major attacks in quick succession during the morning, but confined itself to individual reconnaissance sorties during the afternoon. The first raid began at 08:30 hours, when a wave of fighter-bombers made landfall in the Winchelsea Bay area of Sussex, and headed straight for central London, where they split up and dropped several bombs. A second wave then arrived in the Dungeness area and proceeded towards London, but separated beforehand, and few aircraft penetrated as far as the capital.

No more than about fifty aircraft were involved, but No. 11 Group scrambled sixteen squadrons in response. However, owing to the fighters splitting up rather than remaining in formation, they proved a difficult adversary, and only one could be claimed destroyed and two damaged. RAF Hornchurch had all three of its resident squadrons in the air on the operation, but none sighted the Luftwaffe.

The second raid began at 10:30 when thirty enemy aircraft crossed in over Dymchurch and flew straight to London. There were no reports of bombs being dropped by this formation, which was likely intended as a fighter sweep, and they crossed out again at Hythe at 11:00. Simultaneously, though, large numbers of fighters milled in the Channel, and individual aircraft flew along the coast between Dungeness and South Foreland. One small group of aircraft also made a third attack in two days on the Dover balloon barrage, but a lone audacious Luftwaffe pilot flew all the way to Kenley via Bexhill-on-Sea and dropped bombs near Lingfield.

This time, No. 11 Group ordered seven squadrons to intercept the fighters, easily outnumbering their foe, but once again victories were hard to come by. Hornchurch's three squadrons were airborne, but only No. 222 Squadron could make any claim, when it shared the destruction of a Ju88 with No. 605 Squadron. For their part, No. 41 Squadron sent up five pilots at 10:55 hours, which included Eric, but they saw nothing and returned empty-handed.

The third attack, comprising in total around forty-five aircraft, commenced at 11:30. No. 11 Group sent up three squadrons in response, and these appear to have all been from Hornchurch. No. 603 Squadron was attacked by half a dozen Me109s and claimed one probably destroyed, but Nos 41 and 222 Squadrons returned without success. On account of deteriorating weather, this concluded the day's operational flying.

Aside from a number of reconnaissance flights by individual aircraft, only two major attacks were launched on the south-east by the Luftwaffe on 9 October. In all, the RAF made nine claims during these raids, six alone falling to No. 41 Squadron, which reported two destroyed, two probably destroyed and two damaged. Half of the unit's claims were credited to Eric.

The first attack comprised three phases: one between 11:00 and 11:40 hours, the second from 11:50 to 12:30, and the third 12:30 to 13:15. The first phase saw twenty-four fighters come in at 20,000 feet over Dover and head in the direction of London over the north of Maidstone. Eight of these aircraft detached themselves at Maidstone and flew to Chatham, while the remaining sixteen aircraft flew to Hornchurch. However, the aircraft reached no closer to London than Woolwich and Romford, and a few bombs were dropped at the latter location, before they returned to France down the Thames Estuary.

The second phase comprised another twenty-four aircraft, which crossed in at 20,000–25,000 feet over Dungeness and flew toward Hornchurch, before turning east at the Thames. They then followed the estuary towards the Channel and flew out again over Deal. Even as this sweep was under way, several smaller raids were made on the coast between Dover and Hastings, and one of approximately fifteen aircraft made landfall at Rye, but made no deep penetration and crossed out at Hastings again after dropping bombs at West Malling and Hastings. The third phase involved sixty enemy aircraft, which arrived between Dover and Dungeness, infiltrated as far as east Kent and Maidstone, and left again between Dungeness and South Foreland. No bombs were reported to have been dropped at all on this raid.

In response to the three phases, No. 11 Group ordered a total of ten squadrons into the air. All three of Hornchurch's squadrons were involved, Nos 41 and 222 being sent up during the first and second phases and No. 603 from Rochford in the last, but all three were unsuccessful. No. 41 Squadron had ten pilots airborne from 11:15 to 12:50 hours, which included Eric, but they saw no sign of the Luftwaffe and returned to base for a late lunch, with nothing to report.

The Luftwaffe's second attack began at 14:40, and comprised two phases, the first lasting until 15:35 and the second from 15:35 to 16:15. The former consisted of fifty fighters in two formations, which made landfall between Dover and Dungeness at 20,000 feet and headed towards Maidstone. One formation split up just north of Maidstone and eight aircraft flew to the Isle of Sheppey, then on to Hornchurch, Tilbury and Gravesend; the remainder proceeded towards the docklands and central London. Twenty aircraft from the second formation flew into London, and bombs were reported to have been dropped at Eltham, Poplar, along the Thames Estuary and at Wanstead. All aircraft returned to the Channel on reciprocal courses, and No. 11 Group responded by ordering up twelve squadrons to intercept them.

The second phase commenced as the first ended, when sixty fighters appeared in two formations between 25,000 and 30,000 feet, and headed for Maidstone. The first formation split into two at Rochester, one group flying to Biggin Hill and the other, comprising approximately fifteen aircraft, to central London. The second formation advanced towards Hornchurch, but turned south-east just south of the area and flew over the docklands, providing significant activity in a triangular area between Hornchurch, Maidstone and Kenley. Bombs were dropped at Blackheath, near Manston, at New Cross and Ramsgate and along the Thames Estuary. On this occasion, No. 11 Group detailed ten squadrons to intercept the Luftwaffe, some of which were already airborne in response to the first phase.

In total, the group's fighters claimed three Me109s destroyed, two probably destroyed and two damaged aircraft from this attack, all of them the work of the Hornchurch Wing. Nos 41 and 222 Squadrons were ordered up together at 14:50 hours to patrol Hornchurch, with No. 41 leading and comprising ten pilots led by Squadron Leader Finlay. The two squadrons climbed to 25,000 feet, and were on a course of 270° in the Maidstone area when Finlay first sighted a number of fighters. He ordered the pilots into line astern in preparation for a strike but it soon became clear that they were friendly aircraft. The wing then climbed further, and a short while later three Me109s were spotted below them, travelling on an easterly course in loose formation. A number of Spitfires were also seen approaching them from their far side, clearly intent on attacking them. Finlay banked hard to starboard and dived on the Messerschmitts, closing on the tail of one, and immediately fired a three-second burst from 150 yards down to 100. This caused smoke and sparks to emit from beneath the cockpit area of the enemy aircraft, but Finlay could not press his attack home as he was himself pounced on from above.

Just as Finlay was confronting the trio of Me109s, a further twenty to twenty-five Messerschmitts appeared out of cloud at 30,000 feet and immediately dived toward No. 41 Squadron. Seeing this, No. 222 Squadron in turn spun on them and a dogfight ensued, in which they claimed one Me109 destroyed and saved No. 41 Squadron from a potential disaster.

As it was, Squadron Leader Finlay was hit by fire from above by an Me109, although it had no immediate effect. He broke off sharply and blacked out for a time. When he regained consciousness and control of his aircraft, he found himself alone and patrolled the Ashford area by himself for approximately twenty minutes, in the hope of finding a lone straggler. Unable to do so, he returned to Hornchurch where he found he could not lower his undercarriage and belly-landed, but fortunately was not injured and claimed the Me109 damaged.

Pilot Officer Robert Boret was also attacked by an aircraft, which he believed was an Me110, but sustained no damage. Sergeant Pilot Leslie Carter received hits in his radiator and oil cooler, and his cockpit filled with fumes. He fell into a dive, but finally flattened out and made a forced landing at Rochford. However, No. 41 Squadron also inflicted their own damage.

Sergeant Pilot John McAdam became separated from the rest of the pilots and patrolled alone in the Ashford area at 12,000 feet, hoping to catch a lone returning aircraft. In time, he sighted an Me109 ahead and 2,000 feet below him, flying on a south-easterly course. He immediately dived and closed to just fifty yards, where he opened fire with a burst of two seconds. The Messerschmitt's pilot dived sharply for cloud cover, and as McAdam overshot him he clearly saw some holes in the rudder, which he assumed he had caused, although the aircraft did not appear to be in any trouble. McAdam was unable to locate the aircraft again and returned to base to claim the Me109 damaged in the Ashford area.

Considerably more success was enjoyed by Flying Officer James Walker. Having sighted the Me109s diving on them from above, cloud cover initially confused matters and he lost both the enemy aircraft and the squadron. He climbed towards 21,000 feet in an attempt to find the unit but only sighted a single Me109 at approximately 17,000 feet around four miles away, heading for France. He accelerated after it, out over the Channel, and was within ten miles of the French coast when he finally caught up with it.

Clearly confident that he was almost home and well out of danger, the Messerschmitt's pilot did not see Walker approaching, and he was able to close to 100 yards before he opened fire with a three-second burst from astern. He saw his tracer enter the fuselage and wings, and black and white smoke immediately issued from the engine. Its pilot banked hard to port and applied boost to evade him, but Walker fired a deflection shot at the aircraft lasting five seconds, from ranges of 250 yards down to 200. The pilot then tried the opposite tack and climbed steeply to starboard. However, Walker was on him again, firing another deflection shot from 250 yards closing to 150. The Me109's engine then seized and the propeller stopped rotating. The pilot ditched his aircraft in the Channel around two miles off the French coast, and Walker headed home to claim the Me109 destroyed.

Meanwhile, Eric, who was once again flying as rearguard, had also been busy. He had remained about 2,000 feet above the rest of the pilots to cover them when they dived on the original trio of Me109s, and the precaution was soon justified. Within minutes, he spotted another small formation of Me109s pass beneath him in line abreast formation, apparently intent on attacking the squadron. Pouncing on them, Eric chose the aircraft to port of the formation and fired two short bursts from astern. The Messerschmitt tried to evade his fire, but immediately emitted glycol from beneath its starboard wing. Eric followed it down, firing as he went, until the pilot changed tactics and made a steep climbing turn out to sea instead. In doing so, though, he showed the aircraft's vulnerable underside and Eric fired another burst straight into it. The engine started smoking, then seized, and the aircraft plunged into the Channel around ten miles off Dover.

As Eric was returning to the English coast, he sighted a formation of five Me109s crossing out south of Dungeness on their return to France. Banking around to come in behind and slightly below them, he targeted one that was lagging a little to the rear of the rest. He fired three bursts at it from astern, and the aircraft immediately spun down towards the sea. Taking the opportunity offered, he fired at another Me109 in the same formation, and was able to get in two bursts before his ammunition ran out. However, even with this brief attack, the aircraft started smoking and commenced a shallow dive towards the Channel. Unable to do any more, Eric turned for home, convinced that 'these two Me.109's would not get home'.[8] He returned to base to claim the first Me109 destroyed and the latter two probably destroyed.[9]

The last pilot was on the ground at Hornchurch again at 16:37 hours, where it was realised that No. 222 Squadron, and very likely Eric as well, had saved the unit from a potential disaster. The practice of deploying a rearguard was certainly paying dividends.

Thursday 10 October saw three attacks on east Kent and the Thames Estuary, and one on Weymouth, which resulted in No. 41 Squadron being airborne in unit

GREAT COURAGE

strength four times, without result. Eric was airborne for the first two of these.

The first raid commenced at 08:30 when nineteen fighters and six bombers crossed in over Deal, Kent. They had come from the direction of Calais and had passed over a convoy off Dover, which they were clearly not interested in. The aircraft then proceeded across the Thames Estuary to Shoeburyness, where they split in two. Six aircraft wheeled around to Southend and the rest swept the Isle of Sheppey and left the country again at Dover. No. 11 Group scrambled six squadrons in response, three of which were from the Hornchurch Wing. For their part, No. 41 Squadron sent up ten pilots at 08:40, which included Eric, but they returned at 09:40 having seen nothing of the Luftwaffe. Nos 222 and 603 Squadrons were equally as unsuccessful.

The second raid began less than fifteen minutes after No. 41 Squadron had landed from the first, and totalled around eighty-five aircraft. No. 11 Group dispatched eight squadrons to intercept the enemy, but No. 41 Squadron was not called upon until 10:45, a good fifteen minutes after the raid was considered to have ended. Consequently, the eleven pilots, who were led by Flight Lieutenant Tony Lovell and included Eric, once again saw no sign of the Luftwaffe and returned at 12:15 with nothing to report.

No. 41 Squadron was airborne twice again, once during the Luftwaffe's third raid and once during the early evening, but both were as uneventful as the first two patrols; the Luftwaffe was not seen all day.

The Luftwaffe mounted four attacks on the south-east of England on 11 October. They were primarily fighter sweeps by high-altitude Me109s, and a few penetrated as far as London. It was, however, a black day for No. 41 Squadron. Although the pilots were only airborne twice, they lost two pilots killed and three aircraft destroyed. Only Eric could uphold the squadron pride, by claiming the unit's only victory of the day.

The initial attack took place between 10:40 and 11:35 hours, when the first of several small raids made landfall between Hastings and Ramsgate. Eleven squadrons were scrambled to intercept their adversaries, but there was little success and only a single Me109 could be claimed destroyed by No. 72 Squadron. The Hornchurch Wing was airborne, but No. 41 Squadron did not sight the Luftwaffe at all.

The day's second raid started at 11:50 when thirty to fifty enemy aircraft crossed in at 25,000 feet over Hastings, swept over Biggin Hill and Kenley, then split up and made their way out over Hastings again by 12:15. The third attack commenced at 14:15 when a Luftwaffe formation made landfall at Deal, two came in at Dungeness, and a fourth flew up the Thames Estuary. Seven squadrons were dispatched in response to the second strike and fifteen for the third, but No. 41

Squadron was not called upon to participate in either.

The fourth and last raid of the day commenced at 16:00 when two enemy formations, totalling approximately sixty aircraft, made landfall between Dymchurch and Dover, passed over Maidstone and Tonbridge, and headed toward London. They reached as far as the Beckenham–Dartford area before a number turned back toward Dymchurch, and the remainder swept over Kenley, Biggin Hill and Tunbridge Wells before departing over Dungeness. Bombs were reported to have been dropped at Beckenham, south of Dartford, at Margate and near Ramsgate. No. 11 Group dispatched eleven squadrons to intercept them, which together claimed a total of just two Me109s destroyed. One of these fell to a pilot of No. 92 Squadron, the other to Eric. All three of Hornchurch's resident squadrons were scrambled during the raid, but only No. 41 Squadron succeeded in engaging the Luftwaffe. However, even though Eric claimed a victory, it was bittersweet.

The squadron took off with eleven pilots at 15:45, a quarter of an hour in advance of the raid crossing in, and were ordered to patrol base at 30,000 feet. But the lead time was still insufficient to climb to this altitude before the Luftwaffe arrived – a Spitfire Mark I required a full twenty-seven minutes – and this proved to be their undoing.

Once airborne, the squadron was directed to rendezvous with Biggin Hill's Nos 66 and 92 Squadrons over Maidstone, but this instruction was subsequently amended and they were vectored on to Raid 32J before they could join up. A short while later, having reached the Maidstone area at 27,000 feet, the unit sighted approximately fifty Me109s in several small formations, another 4,000 feet above them. They were 'mainly in echelons of five and seven but vics of three were seen, and also four in line astern. One pilot [saw] a wide vic of six with [a] small vic of three inside it. One formation of five in echelon were camouflaged with black and orange stripes like a tiger, with yellow undersurfaces [sic].'[10]

The squadron climbed hard in an effort to eliminate their height disadvantage as quickly as possible, but were seen. A leading group of eight Me109s sent three aircraft down to dive through the squadron as apparent decoys while the remaining five attempted to get behind the unit. This strategy yielded immediate success against Yellow Section, which was once again designated as rearguard, and Pilot Officer John Lecky was promptly hit from astern and shot down in flames over Maidstone. The nineteen-year-old was seen to bale out but was later found dead near West Kingsdown, Kent; he had been with No. 41 Squadron only nine days.

Eric, who was leading the section, saw the Me109s diving towards them and made a steep climbing turn into the sun as they opened fire. Turning downwards again with the sun behind him, he tried to locate his unit but instead sighted five Me109s around 3,000 feet below him, flying away from him off his port bow. He dived after them and closed unseen on the last aircraft in the formation. When he had brought himself into a range of approximately 250 yards, he opened fire with two two-second bursts from astern and slightly below. The Messerschmitt immediately 'did a flick roll'[11] and fell away with smoke and glycol streaming from its engine. Eric followed it down and fired another two-second burst, which hit the engine again and caused it to catch fire. He broke off the engagement at 20,000 feet, leaving the aircraft in a steep dive with its engine 'a mass of flames'[12] approximately five miles off Dungeness. Eric claimed the Me109 destroyed for the expenditure of 960 rounds and was 'able to add one more to his already impressive total'.[13] He had now been credited with nineteen enemy aircraft destroyed and another six probably destroyed.

In the initial confusion, as Lecky was shot down and the squadron continued climbing towards the Me109s to gain critical height, Flying Officer Desmond O'Neill and Sergeant Pilot Leslie Carter collided with one another. Carter baled out unhurt but O'Neill, trapped in his aircraft, was killed. Carter's Spitfire crashed and burned out at South Ash Manor, West Kingsdown, and O'Neill's machine hit the ground nearby.

Eight pilots were back on the ground at 16:40 hours, and this concluded the day's operational flying. Three Spitfires had been written off and the squadron was left with only twelve serviceable aircraft for over twice the number of pilots. The peak of the Battle of Britain may have passed, but that fact was probably still imperceptible for the average pilot, who likely thought the RAF would not be out of the woods for some time yet.

Although already announced on 30 September, Eric was officially awarded a Bar to his Distinguished Flying Cross on 11 October, in recognition of having shot down fifteen enemy aircraft in nineteen days. His citation read:

> In September, 1940, whilst engaged on a patrol over the Dover area, Pilot Officer Lock engaged three Heinkel 113s one of which he shot down into the sea. Immediately afterwards he engaged a Henschel 126 and destroyed it. He has displayed great courage in the face of heavy odds, and his skill and coolness in combat have enabled him to destroy fifteen enemy aircraft within a period of nineteen days.[14]

Good weather on 12 October resulted in almost continuous attacks by the Luftwaffe between 09:00 and 14:30 hours, which the RAF considered one long raid in five phases. These were followed by an hour's break before a further hour-long raid from 15:30. No. 41 Squadron was airborne twice, but they could make no claims, and although they sustained no casualties, an aircraft was written off in a flying accident.

No. 41 Squadron was among six units scrambled to intercept the fourth phase of the first attack, and eleven pilots, including Eric, took off at 12:10. However, they did not sight the Luftwaffe at all and returned to base at 13:15 with nothing to report. The Luftwaffe was back at 15:30 with approximately eighty aircraft bound for London, which were closely followed by four further small formations. No. 11 Group sent up eleven squadrons to repel them, which claimed a combined three Me109s destroyed, six probably destroyed and four damaged, but No. 41 Squadron was not called upon until approximately ten minutes before the attack was considered over.

Twelve pilots, thereunder Eric, were airborne at 16:20, led by Flight Lieutenant Ryder, but Sergeant John McAdam's engine failed during his initial climb away from Hornchurch. He crash-landed near Romford, and was not injured, but the engine was seriously damaged and the airframe had to be written off. As the Luftwaffe left the country within minutes of the squadron becoming airborne, nothing was seen and the pilots were back on the ground at 18:00.

The following morning, overcast skies kept Luftwaffe activity to a minimum before lunch and their operations consisted of only armed reconnaissances by individual aircraft. It was not until a weather improvement just after lunch that the Luftwaffe arrived in any force, and three attacks were delivered within four hours between 12:30 and 13:35, 13:40 and 14:45, and 15:40 and 16:10. Eric was airborne with No. 41 Squadron during the second and third raids, but the Luftwaffe was not seen at all and the squadron ended the day empty-handed.

The unit spent the following day on the ground on account of unsuitable weather, but improved conditions on 15 October brought the Luftwaffe back again. The south-east was subjected to six daylight raids, five of which took place before 13:15 hours, and the last between 15:50 and 16:30. An additional attack was also made on the Southampton area between 12:00 and 13:00. In each case, the targets appeared to be railway lines. No. 41 Squadron was airborne twice operationally; once during the first attack, and once in the afternoon, between raids. They were unable to achieve any victories, but lost one pilot killed in action.

The Luftwaffe commenced its first attack at 08:05 hours, when twenty-five Me109s crossed in over Dungeness and headed towards the Thames docklands, where they split up. Ten minutes behind them, a formation of fifteen Me109s passed in over Dungeness at the same altitude on their way to Maidstone and Biggin Hill, and back out the same way. At the same time as the second formation made landfall, a third came in over Ramsgate, comprising ten Me109s. These aircraft flew to Whitstable, turned south to Dungeness, and then flew back up to the Isle

GREAT COURAGE

of Sheppey, where they crossed out again.

No. 11 Group scrambled eight squadrons in response, which included No. 41 Squadron, and Eric was one of eleven pilots who took off at 08:25, led by Squadron Leader Finlay. They were vectored off the coast to catch returning raiders, and although the pilots attempted to engage a large number of scattered aircraft, they were unable to make any claims. However, when they landed again at 09:45, it was without 23-year-old Sergeant Pilot Philip Lloyd, who had been shot down off the north Kent coast and killed; he had only been with the squadron a few days. His body was washed ashore near King's Hall, in Herne Bay, Kent, twelve days later.

Thursday 17 October was another busy day upon which the Luftwaffe mounted four attacks on Kent and London before 17:00 hours. No bombers were involved, and all sorties were undertaken by Me109s carrying single bombs slung under their fuselages. No. 41 Squadron was airborne three times, but Eric only once. He participated in the last patrol, and saw some action, but for no reward.

The first attack did not commence until 09:15, but in anticipation of a busy day, No. 41 Squadron was airborne early when twelve pilots undertook a patrol between 07:35 and 08:10. However, as the Luftwaffe had not yet begun their offensive operations, nothing was seen. Following the morning's raid, during which the squadron was not called upon to participate, there was relative quiet until 13:30, and it was during this next period that the unit was airborne for the second time. The pilots sighted a Luftwaffe formation, which one man fired at, but it was lost in the sun before any damage could be done.

The third attack commenced at 15:00 and arrived in four waves. The first comprised thirty aircraft, which was closely followed by a second of the same size. A third, of only eight aircraft, then crossed in and shadowed the first formation on a parallel course, soon to be joined by a fourth, consisting of fifteen to twenty aircraft. No. 11 Group dispatched fourteen squadrons in response to the raid, and together they claimed one destroyed, one probable and two damaged for no loss.

It was not until 15:40 hours – approximately fifteen minutes before the raid was considered over – that No. 41 Squadron was finally called upon. At that time, the ten pilots, which included Eric and were led by Flying Officer Guy Cory, were sent up on to the Maidstone line at 15,000 feet, and subsequently ordered to 30,000 feet. They remained airborne until 17:10, around fifteen minutes after the day's fourth attack ended, and ultimately claimed two more victories for no loss. The fourth and last attack commenced at 16:25, when twenty aircraft crossed in over Dungeness and flew to Benenden, where they split up, and around fifteen aircraft subsequently penetrated the IAZ. These aircraft flew back over the Biggin Hill–Kenley area and also Maidstone, and crossed out at Deal. The remaining aircraft orbited Biggin Hill, then flew east over Rochester and the Isle of Sheppey and followed the first fifteen aircraft out at Deal.

A second formation of fifteen aircraft crossed in 18,000 feet over Deal at the same time as the first came in, and made for Maidstone where it split up. Some of these machines orbited Sevenoaks and then crossed out at South Foreland, while the remainder flew to a point south-east of Maidstone before leaving the country at Folkestone. No. 11 Group ordered five squadrons to intercept the two formations but they could not hinder bombs being dropped at Dover and New Romney.

Already airborne in the Maidstone area since before the end of the third attack, No. 41 Squadron climbed to 31,500 feet, but Yellow Section – Eric and Pilot Officer Frederick Aldridge – became separated in haze. Eric continued on a vector of 280° for several minutes, his view restricted on account of conditions, but then spotted nine Me109s below him in a line astern formation. He dived after them and fired on the last in line, but was unable to close sufficiently to make a claim.

However, he found Aldridge again and the two pilots flew toward Chatham, where they saw scattered Me109s. Eric dived on one but was again unsuccessful. Aldridge, however, noticed an Me109 above them at 35,000 feet and climbed towards it. Managing to close to just 100 yards without being seen, he fired a one-second burst as he reduced his range to fifty yards and immediately sent the aircraft down through the haze, passing Eric on his port side. Eric later confirmed that the aircraft came 'hurtling past him, spinning and smoking, and still out of control at 2,000 feet',[15] ten miles south of Chatham. Unable to establish its ultimate fate, however, Aldridge was only able to claim the fighter probably destroyed.

Meanwhile, the rest of the squadron had also spotted Me109s over the Kent coast and split up as pilots sought out individual aircraft. Flying Officer Cory ended up in a defensive circle for a time, sharing the tail-chase with a number of enemy aircraft and four other Spitfires over the Isle of Sheppey. He subsequently sighted fifteen Me109s flying south-east in a loose formation, but they were difficult to see in the hazy conditions and ultimately too far away to engage.

Pilot Officer Edward Wells sighted a group of six to nine Me109s, and fired at one without result. He then spotted a lone Me109 returning from the London area at 15,000 feet, heading towards the Channel, and immediately set off in pursuit. The aircraft was about 2,000 feet below him and it took some time before he could overhaul it. However, he managed to approach the fighter without the pilot becoming aware of his presence, and was able to close to a range of 250 yards before he opened fire. Discharging a preliminary burst of two seconds as he closed to 200 yards, glycol vapour immediately billowed from the aircraft. The Me109 commenced a shallow dive, but at approximately 7,000 feet, it unexpectedly fell into a steep descent and plunged straight into the sea off the Kent coast. Most of the pilots had arrived back at Hornchurch by 17:20 hours, but Wells landed at

GREAT COURAGE   111

Manston to refuel before returning to Hornchurch, where he claimed the Me109 destroyed. This ended the day's flying.

Continuing poor weather conditions prevented large-scale attacks by the Luftwaffe on 19 October, and the squadron's activity was generally confined to individual raiders. A number of raids also orbited over the Channel without making landfall, and it was perhaps in response to these that No. 41 Squadron was ordered on patrol at 13:05. Eleven pilots, thereunder Eric, took off at that time, led by Squadron Leader Finlay, and they were still airborne when a raid of about seventy Me109s made landfall at 14:25. However, having already been airborne eighty minutes, they were in no position to become embroiled in combats and were ordered to land. The patrol constituted the unit's only operational flying for the day.

Improved conditions brought the Luftwaffe back in force on 20 October, and the south-east was subjected to five attacks, which took place between 09:45 and 10:30 hours, 11:10 and 11:45, 13:25 and 14:00, 14:20 and 15:00, and between 15:15 and 15:40. No. 41 Squadron was airborne three times, and Eric twice, which provided him the opportunity to add another victory to his tally after a nine-day break.

The day's first attack began when two dozen Me109s crossed in near Hythe at 19,000 feet and flew to London via Maidstone and Biggin Hill, continued to Northolt and Harrow, and then left the country again via Maidstone and Dover. At the same time, several enemy formations orbited over the Channel but did not make landfall.

No. 11 Group dispatched eight squadrons in response, which included Nos 41 and 603 Squadrons, which were directed to patrol Rochford and Hornchurch. No. 41 Squadron's contingent comprised twelve pilots, including Eric, who were airborne at 09:50, led by Squadron Leader Finlay. Despite the fact that No. 603 Squadron sighted and engaged a number of Me109s without result, No. 41 Squadron did not see the Luftwaffe at all and returned to Hornchurch at 11:20 with nothing to report.

The second attack commenced at 11:10 when two formations totalling around seventy fighters crossed in near Dungeness. No. 11 Group sent up eight squadrons to intercept them, but as No. 41 Squadron had just landed, the groundcrews were busy refuelling and servicing the aircraft during most of the raid and the unit was therefore not called upon. There ensued a ninety-five-minute lull in Luftwaffe operations, during which time No. 41 Squadron's pilots were able to have some lunch and get back in the air.

At 12:25, Nos 41 and 603 Squadrons took off as a wing to patrol the Maidstone line, with No. 41 comprising twelve pilots led by Flight Lieutenant Tony Lovell. After an uneventful hour in the air together, the squadrons were ordered to land

and, in preparation, descended to 20,000 feet. However, while doing so, Lovell sighted anti-aircraft bursts at around 25,000 feet and heard over the R/T that enemy aircraft were approaching from the south-east. This was the commencement of the day's third attack.

Approximately thirty Me109s had crossed in over Ramsgate at 23,000 feet and were flying towards London. Another formation of fifteen Me109s followed them in on the same course, but did not fly any further than Dartford; some of these aircraft orbited over south-east Kent, apparently awaiting the return of their colleagues. No. 11 Group ordered five squadrons to intercept them, but the Luftwaffe still managed to drop bombs at Old Street in London, at Greenwich, and Tatsfield in Surrey.

As they were the only two squadrons in the air at that time, the controller immediately commanded Nos 41 and 603 Squadrons to climb again and proceed north-west, which put them on a parallel course to the inbound enemy fighters. At 30,000 feet, Lovell turned the wing northwards to intercept the Luftwaffe, and at around 13:45 they passed over large numbers of Me109s in the Biggin Hill area, which were in the process of banking around to head out again, 5,000 feet below them. The aircraft were flying 'in two closely packed bunches, without any particular formation',[16] but varying in altitude by as much as 1,500 feet. Lovell ordered the wing into line astern, and they dived together on to the Me109s, No. 41 Squadron immediately attacking the rearmost group, 'each Spitfire engaging his most suitable opponent'.[17]

Lovell was the first man down and attacked an Me109 in the rear centre of the formation, opening up with a two-second burst from 250 yards and closing. It was obvious that the pilot did not realise he was there until he opened fire, and he managed to get in a second burst, of three seconds at 200 yards, before the pilot reacted. The Messerschmitt fell into a spin and then burst into flames. Lovell turned away to port and came under fire from five Me109s at once. Taking violent evasive action, he managed to escape them, but in doing so lost the rest of the wing. The controller instructed him to land and he returned to Hornchurch to claim the Me109 destroyed.

Squadron Leader Don Finlay dived until he was just below a vic of five Me109s flying level at 25,000 feet, then he climbed astern of one of them and fired a one-second burst from 200 yards, closing to 150. Glycol immediately emitted from the aircraft, but it turned sharply and flew into the sun, and Finlay was unable to see it anymore. He chased a number of other Messerschmitts but had no further success, and could ultimately only claim the first Me109 damaged.

Flying Officer Peter Brown singled out an Me109 at 25,000 feet, to the rear of the formation, and fired a one-and-a-half second burst at 150 yards from astern and slightly below. This immediately resulted in glycol streaming from the enemy aircraft, but he followed it up with a second burst of the same length with slight deflection from just 100 yards, and the Messerschmitt commenced what appeared to be an uncontrolled dive. The aircraft fell several thousand feet, but it was only a ruse and the pilot soon recovered his machine and started to climb again. However, Brown had followed him down, and quickly closed again to just 100 yards where he fired another two bursts. The aircraft half rolled and Brown set off in pursuit again, but the pilot then baled out. The Me109 crashed in woods north-west of West Malling airfield, and the pilot landed a short while later near Wrotham.

Sergeant Pilot Aubrey Baker spotted an Me109 that had escaped the wing's initial attack, and was now detached from the main formation and diving southwards by itself. Giving chase, he closed rapidly from astern, but when the Messerschmitt reached 15,000 feet, its pilot spotted him, hauled his aircraft out of its descent, and attempted to make a half-roll to port. As he did so, Baker fired two short bursts from 200 yards, closing to just 100, and the aircraft fell into a vertical dive with glycol streaming from it. He followed the Me109 down to where it was lost from view at 5,000 feet in the Orpington area. By the time Baker last saw it, the pilot had made no attempt to pull out of his high speed descent, and although he initially claimed it as damaged, he was granted a probable victory.

Eric also enjoyed some success. As usual, his section was flying as rearguard: his speciality. When the wing made its initial dive on the Me109s below them, he singled one out and commenced his attack with a burst of three seconds from its rear quarter at 250 yards. As he swung in behind it and closed to 100 yards, pieces flew off the aircraft, prompting Eric to fire another three-second burst. This sent the Messerschmitt into a steep climbing turn to starboard, but it stalled at the top of the climb and spun down in flames north of Biggin Hill. Eric claimed it destroyed for the expenditure of 960 rounds.

No. 603 Squadron, which had followed No. 41 down into the attack, had also done some damage, but the whole fight was over within twenty minutes. The two units landed straight afterwards, but it was not until they were on the ground that the extent of their success was realised. No. 41 Squadron had claimed three destroyed, one probably destroyed and one damaged, while No. 603 Squadron claimed another two destroyed, two probably destroyed and two damaged. The sortie brought Eric's tally to twenty: he had become a quadruple ace in the space of just over nine weeks.

The Luftwaffe was back again at 14:20 hours to launch its fourth attack of the day. No. 11 Group scrambled seven squadrons but Nos 41 and 222 Squadrons were not among them as they were busy refuelling, rearming, and reporting. A fifth and final raid developed at 15:15 but once again No. 41 Squadron was not one of the seven units scrambled to meet it. The unit became airborne once more, but on a routine patrol from 17:10, in which Eric did not participate.

This concluded the day's operational flying, but Hornchurch was again the target of a night-time raid. During the hours of darkness, a lone bomber orbited Hornchurch for some time, presumably as a result of visibility issues stemming from low cloud and haze, and finally dropped two 100kg bombs on the airfield. One fell on a road behind the hangars and the other on the landing ground itself. However, they caused no damage or casualties.

Eric did not fly operationally for the ensuing three days, but took to the air twice on 24 October. Weather once again reduced Luftwaffe activity, and although there was a fair amount of action over the Channel, almost all of the enemy aircraft that approached the coast turned back out to sea again. Only a few made landfall, one of which was shot down by No. 17 Squadron and another damaged by No. 229 Squadron. No. 92 Squadron also ventured out into the Channel where it intercepted and damaged a bomber. Bombs were reported at Brentford, Hayes and Willesden, but it was an otherwise relatively quiet day.

Presumably expecting bigger things on account of activity in the Channel and raids approaching the coast, Hornchurch's squadrons maintained standing patrols all day. For their part, No. 41 Squadron was airborne on three uneventful patrols: 08:05–09:10 hours (eleven pilots), 12:45–14:30 (twelve pilots) and 16:40–18:05 (nine pilots). Eric participated in the first two of these patrols, but the squadron ended the day having not seen the Luftwaffe once.

Nonetheless, the day was noteworthy for No. 41 Squadron as it was equipped with new aircraft. During the early evening, No. 611 Squadron flew in to pick up fourteen of the unit's Mark Ia Spitfires, and left behind a like number of their own Mark IIas. No. 41 Squadron had been flying Mark Is since they had replaced the unit's Hawker Furies in late December 1938. The aircraft that the squadron received were a part of the first order for 1,000 Mark IIs, which were built by Vickers-Armstrong (Castle Bromwich) Ltd as Mark IIas from June 1940 onwards. No. 611 Squadron had been the first unit to be issued with the Mark II, in late August 1940, but was ordered to give them up to No. 41 Squadron and revert to Mark Is again when the decision was made to start re-equipping front-line units with the new version. No. 611 subsequently kept No. 41 Squadron's Mark Ias until February 1941, when they moved south to Rochford and were once again issued with Mark IIs.

Although the general dimensions and armament of the Spitfire IIa were the same as those of the Spitfire Ia, the main improvements in the Mark IIa were better armour protection for the pilot and a Rolls-Royce Merlin XII engine, which provided 1,175 horsepower on take-off, a greater rate of climb and a higher ceiling.

With little time to familiarise themselves with their new aircraft, No. 41 Squadron was called on three times on 25 October in response to four attacks by the Luftwaffe on London and the south-east. These took place between 08:45 and 10:30 hours in three waves, 11:50 and 12:45 in two formations, 13:10 and 13:55 in one formation that split into smaller groups, and between 14:40 and 15:40 in three waves. The squadron intercepted the first and last of these raids and ended the day with claims of three destroyed, two probably destroyed and nine damaged – no small achievement in new aircraft.

When the day's first attack commenced, an initial wave of seventy-five aircraft crossed in between Dungeness and Hastings in three formations, comprising Me109s and about a dozen Do17 bombers. These aircraft flew north-west toward London, but only thirty penetrated as far as the capital, while the rest flew no further than the Kenley–Biggin Hill area. A second wave, of three formations totalling around fifty Me109s, then made landfall between Dungeness and Folkestone and headed for London via Tonbridge and Biggin Hill. Fifteen aircraft turned back at Sevenoaks and the remainder continued on to the capital, before leaving the country over Rye or down the Thames Estuary via Hornchurch. The third wave consisted of only twenty aircraft, which crossed the coast at Dungeness but penetrated no further than Ashford.

During this attack, bombs were reported to have been dropped at Battersea, Bermondsey, Camberwell, East Ham, Lambeth, Poplar, Southwark, Wandsworth and Westminster. In one of the biggest scrambles in some time, No. 11 Group sent up seventeen squadrons in response, among whom were Hornchurch's three resident units. Nos 41 and 603 Squadrons flew as a wing, while No. 222 Squadron joined up with Biggin Hill's No. 92 Squadron to form a composite wing.

Having received an order to patrol Hornchurch and Rochford, and join No. 603 Squadron over Rochford at 23,000 feet, No. 41 Squadron was airborne at 08:55 hours, comprising a dozen pilots led by Flight Lieutenant Norman Ryder. Once the units had rendezvoused, they were vectored south and instructed to climb to 31,000 feet, but sighted anti-aircraft fire over Tilbury before they could do so. The wing was then given a new vector, taking them to the Maidstone area, and at 09:50 they sighted approximately thirty yellow-nosed Me109s to the south of them, flying west at 27,000–28,000 feet. The aircraft were in two formations of around a dozen aircraft each, with another four Me109s stepped up and behind each of them, just south-west of Maidstone.

Flight Lieutenant Ryder took A Flight down out of the sun to attack the four rearguard Me109s in the rearmost formation, leaving B Flight above for cover, under the charge of Flying Officer John Mackenzie. Picking out a particular

Me109 for himself, Ryder fired a long burst from 250 yards, which resulted in a small amount of smoke issuing from the aircraft. Realising he was under attack, the Messerschmitt's pilot half-rolled his aircraft and then made a series of vertical turns to evade him. Nonetheless, Ryder was able to follow the enemy aircraft until he could close to 150 yards, and released another long burst. His gunfire struck the Me109 again, causing heavy, dense black smoke and glycol to billow from it. Ryder fired a third long burst, but by now the smoke had intensified and the pilot was no longer undertaking any evasive action.

The Messerschmitt entered cloud in a steep dive on an east-north-easterly course and was not seen again. Ryder searched for it below the cloud base but could not locate it and assumed it must have come down somewhere north of Maidstone. His No. 2, Pilot Officer Frederick Aldridge, confirmed Ryder's report, but without the aircraft's ultimate fate established, he was only granted the aircraft as probably destroyed, which he claimed with seven guns as one was inoperable.

Pilot Officer Aldridge had followed Ryder down, and attacked the Me109 adjacent to the one Ryder had engaged. Opening fire from its rear quarter at 300 yards, he swung around until fully astern of the aircraft and closed to 200 yards. Having fired two short bursts from seven guns – like Ryder, one was also inoperable – the Messerschmitt's cockpit canopy flew off and hit his radiator. In attempting to dodge it, however, Aldridge lost sight of the aircraft and did not see it again. He patrolled a further fifteen minutes but saw nothing else of interest and returned to Hornchurch to claim the Me109 damaged.

Flying Officer Peter Brown, believed to be Ryder's No. 3, followed Ryder and Aldridge down and attacked an Me109 from 200 yards without effect. In doing so, however, he lost the squadron and therefore climbed again, alone. At 25,000 feet, he sighted nine Me109s off his starboard beam and boldly turned to attack them. Vastly outnumbered, he was soon involved in a frenzied dogfight but managed to get himself on to the tail of one the Messerschmitts, and fired two short bursts from as near as fifty yards. When glycol flowed from the aircraft, he discharged two more two-second bursts at it with slight deflection, which resulted in it rolling on to its side and diving straight down into cloud. Losing sight of it, he chased another Me109 out to sea and attacked it, but ran out of ammunition after his first burst. This was earlier than he had expected and it later transpired that two of his guns had failed to fire due to cold, while two had misfired.

Brown then returned to base, making no claims for the first and third Me109s, but claimed the second probably destroyed, stating in his report that he believed it would have crashed within the vicinity of Rye. When it was subsequently established that an Me109 had force-landed at Broom Hill, near Lydd, and the pilot captured, his claim was raised to destroyed.

Hot on the heels of Red Section in the initial dive was Yellow Section, led by Eric. Singling out his own Me109 to Red Section's port side, he attacked it from astern and slightly above at a range of 250 yards. Firing just a single one-second burst as he closed to 200 yards, the aircraft reacted immediately by climbing almost vertically. Eric followed it upwards, but the Messerschmitt stalled and 'fell forward into a vertical dive'[18] with glycol streaming from beneath its starboard wing. He watched it fall from 28,000 feet to approximately 7,000, where he left it, noting the pilot had made no attempt by that altitude to recover his aircraft. He assumed the machine would crash in a triangular area bounded by Sevenoaks, Maidstone and Tonbridge, and claimed the aircraft probably destroyed. The victory had required just 140 rounds from seven guns, as one was inoperable, and this constituted his last victory of the Battle of Britain.

Sergeant Pilot Terence Healy followed Eric down in his dive and subsequent climb after the Me109, but when the ascent became too steep, he broke away to starboard and searched for his own target. He was unsuccessful, but after a while he sighted a lone Spitfire and decided to join up with it. As he closed, he realised it was in fact Eric, and they subsequently patrolled together awhile.

Without warning, Eric suddenly turned sharply to starboard and dived under Healy, who lifted his nose slightly to allow him to do so. He then tried to follow Eric around but was unable to see him. However, he sighted an Me109 ahead of him and gave chase. Approaching from its starboard beam, Healy closed to 180 yards where he opened fire with a two-to-three-second burst with deflection. He recognised no immediate result but the pilot realised he was under attack and made a steep climbing turn to port. Healy followed him around, slightly below, then lined up and fired a second burst of ammunition of equal length as he closed to just sixty yards. This resulted in pieces flying off the Me109, although he could not confirm their origin. The aircraft dived away again and Healy was unable to catch up with it and therefore broke off his attack. He then returned to base and claimed it as damaged.

Having initially remained above A Flight as cover, orbiting for a short while, B Flight soon sighted yet another formation of twelve Me109s just below them at 28,000 feet. Flying Officer Mackenzie led the flight down and picked out an Me109 for himself, opening fire with an eighty-round burst from 150 yards, closing to 100. The Me109 emitted a little smoke, rolled over and veered away, and although Mackenzie tried to follow the fighter, he lost it, and was only able to claim it as damaged.

Pilot Officer Edward Wells dived on to the rearmost aircraft in a section of four Me109s at 28,000 feet, and attacked it from its rear quarter at 250 yards, closing to 100. He fired a one-and-a-half-second burst, but was unable to fire any further as his air system failed. Nonetheless, his brief burst was sufficient to cause glycol to stream from the aircraft and send it into a steep diving turn to starboard. Wells was unable to follow it down to establish its ultimate fate as several Me109s were closing on him and, as all his guns were inoperable, he broke off and made a hasty exit. On landing, he claimed the Messerschmitt probably destroyed.

Finally, Sergeant Pilot John McAdam sighted two Me109s flying south-east at 25,000 feet, approximately 3,000–4,000 feet below him. He tried to attract Flying Officer Mackenzie's attention but was unable to do so and therefore dived down after them alone and followed them out over the coastline. As he approached, one of the Me109s pulled away from the other and McAdam concentrated on the straggler of the pair, whose pilot was clearly not aware of his presence. Closing to 150 yards, he opened fire and kept his finger on the firing button for several seconds as he followed the Me109 into a descent to 10,000 feet. Five guns failed to operate and he was only able to release a total of 720 rounds, but as he had reduced his range to between seventy-five and fifty feet, he hit the aircraft numerous times. The Me109 soon steepened his dive and hit the water without attempting to recover, approximately seven to eight miles south-east of Dungeness. McAdam returned to Hornchurch and claimed the aircraft destroyed.

By the time the last pilot was on the ground at 10:30 hours, the squadron had claimed one Me109 destroyed, three probably destroyed and four damaged, although Brown's probable victory was subsequently raised to destroyed. The one unfortunate common feature of the patrol, however, was the significant number of gun failures on the 'new' Mark II Spitfires, which were experienced by at least six of the pilots. This cannot have instilled much confidence in the new mark for the pilots.

For their part, No. 603 Squadron, which had been with No. 41 at the beginning of the engagement, had become split up and, although they had attacked a number of formations, were unable to make any claims. However, two pilots were shot down and baled out, one of whom was wounded, while a third crash-landed and was injured.

The squadron then enjoyed an almost ninety-minute break before the Luftwaffe returned for its second attack. At 11:50, two formations totalling eighty aircraft crossed in between Dover and Dungeness, and headed toward Chatham and Hornchurch, but did not attempt to reach London. Bombs were dropped at Addington, East Farleigh, Erith and on the Isle of Sheppey, after which the aircraft headed down the Thames Estuary and exited the country between Dover and Hastings.

In response to the attack, No. 11 Group sent up ten squadrons and No. 12 Group dispatched a 'Big Wing' of three squadrons to assist them. Among those scram-

GREAT COURAGE   119

bled from No. 11 Group were Nos 41 and 603 Squadrons, which were once again sent up together, between 11:55 and 13:00. No. 41's contingent comprised nine pilots, including Eric, and were led by Flight Lieutenant Ryder. The two squadrons were ordered to patrol the Rochford line, and subsequently the Mayfield line, but the patrol was uneventful and the Luftwaffe was not seen.

Ten minutes after they landed, the Luftwaffe mounted its third raid of the day, when a single formation of around seventy Me109s made landfall in the Winchelsea area. No. 11 Group ordered up ten squadrons, but as Nos 41 and 603 were busy refuelling and rearming, they were not called upon. At 14:40, the Luftwaffe launched its fourth and last attack of the day when four waves crossed the coast at Folkestone, comprising in total 100 enemy aircraft. Some penetrated as far as London, but the rest spread out over Kent.

No. 41 Squadron was scrambled to the Maidstone line with No. 603 Squadron once again, and were airborne at 14:46, led by Squadron Leader Finlay. Initially unsuccessful, the wing was in the Dungeness area when instructed to land at 16:00, but then spotted twenty to thirty inbound Me109s, carrying bombs slung under their fuselages. Finlay immediately ordered a diving line astern attack and, in the subsequent combats, Flying Officer Guy Cory claimed two Me109s damaged, Flying Officer John Mackenzie and Pilot Officer Edward Wells each claimed one damaged, and Sergeant Pilot Bob Beardsley initially damaged an Me109, but subsequently attacked a second, which he claimed destroyed. This concluded the day's operational flying for No. 41 Squadron on one of its most successful days in some time.

Sunday 27 October was a busy day for the Luftwaffe, which had units airborne continuously in the Channel and over south-eastern England from 07:30 to 12:00 hours, followed by several small patrols during the afternoon, which culminated in a large-scale attack at 16:30. No. 41 Squadron was airborne on three occasions as a result, but Eric only participated in the first of these.

The day's attacks commenced when a number of formations were plotted in the Channel at 07:30. Some of these made landfall and headed for London, but one He111 consciously separated itself from one formation and bombed Folkestone Harbour. Numbers of Me109s from this raid penetrated as far as the Kenley–Biggin Hill area. While this was ongoing, a smaller formation approached Beachy Head from the south-east, then turned south and flew down the coast, machine-gunned Newhaven, and dropped bombs near Seaford.

A lone Do215 also crossed in and flew north-west to London on a reconnaissance sortie, then turned east and flew down the Thames Estuary before being intercepted and probably destroyed by No. 249 Squadron. Soon afterwards, five more enemy formations arrived, and several of these aircraft, thereunder a Ju88, reached the IAZ and bombed Lewisham, Stepney and Tottenham. Before 11:30, bombs were also reported to have been dropped at Banstead Downs, Carshalton, Crockham Hill, north of RAF Croydon, north-west of Ford, Hawkhurst, Streatham Common and Thames Ditton, while troops were machine-gunned near Shoreham.

No. 11 Group scrambled fourteen squadrons throughout this four-hour period, which claimed six enemy aircraft destroyed, four probably destroyed and five damaged. No. 41 Squadron was among those called upon, and was up with six pilots at 07:30, including Eric, and were led by Flight Lieutenant Tony Lovell. Unfortunately, they did not sight the Luftwaffe at all and returned with nothing to report at 09:15. Another six pilots were scrambled at 10:25, but they were equally unsuccessful and landed again at 11:50.

Further Luftwaffe activity continued into the afternoon, but No. 41 Squadron was not called upon again until 16:20 when nine pilots were airborne for a routine patrol ten minutes before the start of the day's only large-scale attack. Comprising three simultaneous waves of enemy aircraft, each had its own target: Martlesham Heath, London and Southampton. No. 11 Group sent up fifteen squadrons to intercept them, and units from both Nos 10 and 12 Groups were also active, but they had little success between them. However, one of the few victories during this attack was recorded by No. 41 Squadron when Flying Officer Dennis Adams claimed a damaged Me109. It was later reported to have gone into the sea off Folkestone, and was therefore elevated to destroyed.

Following a quiet day due to unsuitable weather, improved conditions on 29 October brought increased Luftwaffe activity again and five large-scale attacks were executed during daylight hours. Three of these were directed over Kent towards London, one on Southampton and one on Essex and Kent airfields. No. 41 Squadron was airborne three times as a result, and Eric participated in them all.

The first attack was launched at 10:40 hours when thirty Me109s crossed in at 25,000 feet over Dungeness and flew towards the capital. They were engaged by two RAF squadrons in the Biggin Hill area and split up, but in the event only one enemy aircraft was claimed as damaged. A few of these fighters nonetheless managed to reach London, and bombs were dropped on Brompton Road and at Wanstead. No. 41 Squadron was among those scrambled to intercept the attack, and was airborne with eleven pilots under Flight Lieutenant Ryder at 10:45. However, they did not sight the Luftwaffe once and returned to base at midday with nothing to report.

The Luftwaffe's second raid commenced ten minutes after No. 41 Squadron landed, and as they were rearming and refuelling the unit was not involved. The

GREAT COURAGE   121

pilots were also not called upon when the third raid was launched at 13:15, and were next airborne at 14:35, approximately twenty minutes into the Southampton attack, when Flight Lieutenant Tony Lovell led a dozen pilots into the air. On account of the attack's distance from Hornchurch, though, the squadron was consequently not ordered to intercept and landed again at 16:10, having seen nothing worthy of reporting.

The last attack of the day was also its largest, lasting for an hour from 16:20 hours, and involving between 150 and 200 enemy aircraft. Two formations headed for Essex via North Foreland, and dive-bombed RAF North Weald, while another nine separate formations approached from the south-east, but did not attempt to reach London. A formation of Italian bombers and fighters was also seen near Dover, and bombs were reported near Deal, west of Dover, and in the Selsey Bill area.

No. 11 Group scrambled eighteen squadrons in response and together these units claimed thirteen destroyed, ten probably destroyed and four damaged enemy aircraft. As No. 41 Squadron had only landed ten minutes before the attack commenced, they were not called upon immediately as they needed time to rearm and refuel. It was therefore not until 17:25 – around five minutes after the raid was considered over – that twelve pilots were ordered to undertake a patrol for stragglers, led by Flying Officer John Mackenzie. However, nothing was seen and they landed again thirty minutes later, with nothing to report. This concluded the day's operational flying.

Eric undertook no further operational flying during the last two days of October, and his 17:25 patrol on 29 October constituted his last operational sortie of the Battle of Britain. As far as can be established, he had flown fifty-five operational sorties throughout the campaign, during which he had claimed twenty destroyed and seven probably destroyed enemy aircraft.

No. 41 Squadron as a whole claimed eighty-nine destroyed, forty-three probably destroyed and fifty-four damaged enemy aircraft, and Eric's contribution toward this total accounted for an astonishing twenty-three-and-a-half per cent of all destroyed aircraft and just over sixteen per cent of probably destroyed aircraft. His next closest rival was Pilot Officer George 'Ben' Bennions, who had claimed ten and one shared destroyed, seven probably destroyed and five damaged before he was shot down and wounded on 1 October 1940.

Considering only victories between 10 July and 31 October 1940, various analyses declare Eric as either the highest-scoring pilot, or the highest-scoring British pilot of the Battle of Britain.

Chapter Six

Shot Down and Wounded

November 1940 – June 1941

Despite continued offensive operations by the Luftwaffe over south-eastern England, November 1940 began quietly for No. 41 Squadron. Following two days off operational flying, Eric was airborne on uneventful patrols on 1 and 2 November in his regular Spitfire IIa, P7314, and then flew no operations for the ensuing three days.

Nominal Roll, 4 November 1940[1]

Flight A	Flight B
Squadron Leader Donald O. Finlay	Flight Lieutenant Anthony D.J. Lovell
Flight Lieutenant E. Norman Ryder	Flying Officer John N. Mackenzie
Flying Officer M. Peter Brown	Pilot Officer Denys E. Mileham
Flying Officer Guy W. Cory	Pilot Officer Edward P. Wells
Pilot Officer Eric S. Lock	Pilot Officer Norman M. Brown
Pilot Officer Frederick J. Aldridge	Pilot Officer Michael F. Briggs
Sergeant Pilot Robert A. Beardsley	Sergeant Pilot I. Edward Howitt
Sergeant Pilot Aubrey C. Baker	Sergeant Pilot John McAdam
Sergeant Pilot Terence W.R. Healy	Sergeant Pilot Leslie R. Carter
Sergeant Pilot Roy C. Ford	Sergeant Pilot Robert A. Angus
	Sergeant Pilot Ralph V. Hogg

On 6 November, Eric undertook another uneventful patrol in his usual aircraft. Although he participated in three operations the following day, they were just as quiet, as the Luftwaffe was either not seen or was too far away to intercept. The Battle of Britain campaign was clearly over and opportunities to engage the Luftwaffe were becoming fewer and further between. It was 8 November before Eric saw any further action, except on this occasion he was on the receiving end.

The Luftwaffe made three attacks on south-east England that day, the first on Kent and Sussex at 10:00 hours, and two on shipping on the Thames Estuary, at 13:20 and at 16:15. No. 41 Squadron was only called on to participate in the first

SHOT DOWN AND WOUNDED 123

Thames Estuary attack, and was airborne in unit strength between 12:40 and 14:20, led by Squadron Leader Finlay. The Luftwaffe's 13:20 attack comprised three separate raids, designated 17, 21 and 27. Raid 17 was first plotted at Étaples at 13:05 as six-plus aircraft, Raid 21 near St Omer at 13:21 as twelve-plus, and Raid 27 ten miles north of Calais at 13:37 as six-plus. These raids subsequently arrived over the south-east as a total of forty Ju87 Stukas and Me109 escorts, and made their main attack on shipping east of Clacton, while diversionary attacks were made on Croydon and Woolwich.

Nos. 41 and 222 Squadrons were patrolling the Maidstone line at the time and were ordered to intercept Raid 17. No. 222 Squadron succeeded in doing so, and was able to claim one enemy aircraft destroyed over the Channel. For No. 41 Squadron's part, Eric was the only pilot to engage the formation.

He was flying in his favourite position as rearguard in his usual aircraft, P7314, and set his sights on a suitable target near Dungeness. However, he was attacked and hit by another enemy aircraft before he could do any damage himself. He was forced to break off his engagement to evade his adversary, but was unhurt. Eric attempted to limp his seriously damaged aircraft home to Hornchurch, but it would not carry him all the way and he was compelled to force-land his Spitfire near Manston.[2] The aircraft was subsequently salvaged and repaired, and ultimately returned to service in late February 1941, albeit with No. 611 Squadron.

Sergeant Pilot Terence Healy's aircraft, P7544, which had only been delivered to the squadron brand new three days prior to this operation, and was on its maiden operational flight, also received slight damage. The circumstances are not recorded, but it is known that Healy was not injured in the incident. No. 41 Squadron was back on the ground at 14:20 hours and the unit was not called upon again that day.

Meanwhile, Kenley's Nos 501 and 605 Squadrons were initially ordered to patrol the Croydon line at 15,000 feet, but then directed to climb to 30,000 feet to patrol the Biggin Hill line. They were also instructed to intercept Raid 17, and chased the Luftwaffe back to the coast. They were unable to make any claims, but No. 501 Squadron lost one of their own killed. Northolt's Nos 302 and 615 Squadrons were moved on to the Croydon line at 15,000 feet to replace the Kenley Wing, and engaged the diversionary attack on Croydon at 13:46. They claimed one destroyed and two damaged, for the loss of a pilot of No. 302 Squadron, who was killed in action.

A similar pattern of uneventful patrols resumed over the ensuing days, and Eric was airborne once each on 9 and 10 November, and twice on 11, 13 and 14 November, but he undertook no operational flying on 12, 15 and 16 November. All eight sorties were undertaken in P7544. This was the same aircraft that Sergeant Pilot Healy had taken on its maiden operational flight on 8 November and had sustained combat damage. That damage cannot have been serious, though, as Eric flew her operationally only the following day, and retained her as his personal aircraft from 9 November onwards.

When 17 November 1940 dawned, Eric could not have imagined how the day would end. The events that unfolded were a watershed for him, a turning point that would drastically alter his life, and irrevocably change the positive, happy-go-lucky person he had always been. He would no longer be the invincible young man of the day before, and the experience deeply affected him.

Initially cloudy skies improved to fine conditions with 4/10ths cloud at 11,000 feet, and another layer at 18,000 feet; visibility was considered good in a light southwesterly wind. The Luftwaffe launched three attacks on England's south-east today, the first of which targeted convoys in the Thames Estuary at 08:45 hours, and included diversionary attacks on Felixstowe and Ipswich. The second arrived over Kent at 15:10, and the third over Beachy Head only forty minutes later, when bombs were dropped at Newhaven. The Hornchurch Wing intercepted the first of these, and a spectacular series of dogfights ensued.

The attack came in three main formations, which were designated Raids 44, 47 and 48. The first was plotted at 08:33, around fifteen miles east of Boulogne as two-plus aircraft, and was later upgraded to thirty-plus. The second plot appeared at 08:38, eight miles east of Boulogne as twenty-plus aircraft at 20,000 feet, and was subsequently upgraded to sixty-plus. The third was plotted at 08:45, fifteen miles east of Cap Gris Nez as eighteen-plus aircraft at 17,000 feet.

Having taken off together for a routine patrol at 08:00, Nos 41 and 603 Squadrons were already airborne on the Maidstone line when the attack began. No. 603 Squadron was leading, having climbed to 30,000 feet, with No. 41 Squadron close behind. No. 41's contingent comprised twelve pilots in three sections, which were led by Squadron Leader Finlay and both flight commanders.

A minute after the first plot appeared, the controller ordered Debden's No. 257 Squadron into the air to protect the convoy 'Adapt', and the unit was airborne at 08:45. As they took off, Biggin Hill's Nos 66 and 74 Squadrons received the order to take over the Maidstone patrol line from the Hornchurch Wing, and were airborne at 08:53. At 08:46, Kenley's Nos 253 and 501 Squadrons were also scrambled with an instruction to patrol the Biggin Hill line, and were airborne within four minutes. At 08:55, No. 17 Squadron was ordered to join No. 257 Squadron over 'Adapt', and were airborne at 09:00 hours.

As No. 17 Squadron took off, Nos 41 and 603 were sent to the Thames Estuary to patrol over the convoys. Meanwhile, Nos 66, 74, 253 and 501 Squadrons had also been ordered to sweep along the coastline between Dungeness and Manston and, at 09:02, North Weald's Nos 46 and 249 Squadrons received the order to take off and patrol between Rochford and Burnham-on-Crouch. Ten squadrons were now airborne to meet the inbound attack.

A short while later, the Hornchurch Wing sighted the vapour trails of at least forty aircraft[3] over the Thames Estuary, between Clacton and Herne Bay. They were flying 'in pairs, some in shallow vics, and some line abreast'[4] between 20,000 and 25,000 feet, and proved to be Me109Es of JG54. The Messerschmitts were approximately 2,000–5,000 feet below them, off their port bow, coming from the south-east. The wing was immediately ordered to engage them and, approaching them from their rear, 'were fortunate enough to be able to dive on them out of the sun in line astern'.[5] No. 603 Squadron went down first, and were followed by No. 41 Squadron. However, they were seen and the enemy formations broke up, turning into the sun and diving, consciously trying to make themselves difficult to see.

Nonetheless, on account of their altitude and speed, the wing was on them in no time and a series of aggressive dogfights ensued in which both sides claimed victories and counted losses. No. 603 Squadron quickly claimed three Me109s destroyed and a fourth probably destroyed, for no loss. No. 41 Squadron's pilots split up as they sought out individual targets: Flight Lieutenant Tony Lovell, leading B Flight, claimed the first victory, followed by Pilot Officers Denys Mileham and Frederick Aldridge, Flying Officer John Mackenzie and, lastly, Eric.[6]

Lovell dived on to an Me109 approximately seven miles north of Herne Bay, but the pilot saw him coming and turned towards the sun. Matching his turn, Lovell closed and fired, opening with a two-second burst at 200 yards. In an attempt to escape his fire, the pilot turned away from the sun, but this gave Lovell a new opportunity and he fired anew, this time at a range of just 100 yards for a full four seconds. His aim was straight and pieces flew off the Messerschmitt, accompanied by white smoke. The aircraft then turned over on to its back, diving and turning as it went. Lovell closed in to fire a final burst, but the Me109 performed a half-roll and dived straight into the sea. He had expended 960 rounds for his seventh confirmed victory.

Pilot Officer Mileham sighted an Me109 positioning itself to attack another Spitfire over the Thames Estuary. He swept in from quarter astern and opened fire at 100 yards, but the aircraft turned away and easily out-climbed him into the sun. Fearing its escape, Mileham fired one long burst of 800 rounds over a span of five seconds, as the Me109 drew away to 300 yards' range. His fire resulted in white smoke emanating from the Messerschmitt's underside, but he was unable to press home his attack as he was engaged by another Me109. He broke off, successfully evaded his aggressor, and subsequently engaged two more Messerschmitts.

However, on each occasion he was himself attacked by other enemy aircraft and forced to break off.

Pilot Officer Frederick Aldridge picked out an Me109 that had become separated from the rest. He chased the aircraft for some time but was unable to close and eventually gave up, finding himself now some distance from the location of the original attack. Seeking instructions from the controller, he was vectored towards Chatham at 20,000 feet where he sighted a lone Me109 flying on an easterly course out to sea, parallel to the Thames. Giving chase, he followed it for a while, but the Luftwaffe pilot suddenly altered his course to a north-westerly direction, having probably lost his way, Aldridge surmised. Intercepting him quickly on this course, Aldridge positioned himself astern of the aircraft and was about to open fire when the pilot spotted him for the first time. The German attempted an escape by making a stall turn, but it was the wrong tactic under the circumstances and Aldridge caught him at the top of the stall. Opening fire at an altitude of 7,000 feet and a range of 200 yards, he expended 320 rounds in a two-second burst, as he closed to 100 yards. Having been struck by a stream of solid fire, the aircraft fell from the sky and plunged straight into the Channel, approximately ten miles off Felixstowe. Aldridge orbited long enough to see a boat heading to the scene, 'but it was a waste of time their going, so [he] turned them back'.[7]

However, what remains unexplained is that Aldridge subsequently force-landed his aircraft at Matlaske, Norfolk, 'owing to his aircraft [having] been damaged by the enemy'.[8] He provides no explanation for the damage on his Combat Report, but after shooting down the Me109, he was presumably attacked by another.

Meanwhile, Flying Officer John Mackenzie had settled on a trio of Me109s at 15,000 feet. Coming in from astern, he followed them around as they made a wide sweeping turn northwards from Herne Bay to Clacton. Closing to within a suitable range, approximately ten miles east of Clacton, Mackenzie picked out an Me109 on the port side of the formation. Opening up from slightly below the aircraft at a range of 100 yards, he fired a burst of three seconds as he closed to just fifty yards. Considering his proximity, Mackenzie felt he might also take a shot at the leading Me109, but its pilot broke away sharply on realising his wingman was under fire. Having to satisfy himself with his original choice, he therefore fired a second burst at the port Messerschmitt, which then burst into flames and rolled over. Recognising the horrific situation the Luftwaffe pilot now found himself in, he fired a third burst into the Messerschmitt 'in an effort to kill [the] pilot so he would not burn to death'.[9] The aircraft then fell vertically into the sea.

Eric (P7544), who was flying at the rear of the squadron formation, was also in action. However, little information was available immediately following his attack as he was shot down and seriously wounded. A Combat Report written for him in his absence states that he destroyed two Me109s at 25,000 feet, north of the Thames Estuary, expending two two-second bursts on each at a range of 100 yards, and explains:

> P/O Lock destroyed 2 Me.109s (in sea) before being shot down himself. He crashed at Alderton with extensive injuries and is in Ipswich Hospital. His combat report will be sent later.[10]

He subsequently provided the promised account of his actions from his hospital bed in an undated, likely dictated, report that stated:

> Being at the rear of the Squadron I picked out an E.A. and gave two two-second bursts from below and behind, the E.A. emitted smoke and flame and went into a steep dive and I followed and watched him hit the sea.
> I climbed back to 20,000 feet [and] did another astern attack on another Me.109 firing two two-second bursts which set the E.A. on fire and he dived into the sea.
> I was then about 20 miles off the coast and the next thing I remember was diving towards the sea. I tried to open the hood but could not do so and crash landed near Martlesham Heath.[11]

Eric had sustained serious wounds in his left arm and both legs in the attack, but was in a sufficient state of mind to withdraw from the battlefield and make for the English coast as quickly as he could. Weighing up his options, he realised he was in serious trouble. He was unable to move his arm, and was bleeding profusely from multiple wounds. These were no superficial injuries; he was going to require some serious treatment.

Eric may have considered baling out of his damaged aircraft, but winter was nearing and the air and water temperatures were probably not conducive to his survival for the length of time it may have required to locate him. His wounds were also requiring treatment that might not allow so long a wait. However, taking into consideration that he may not get any choice in the matter, he tried to open his cockpit hood to prepare for that eventuality. He found he was unable to do so, but whether this was on account of damage to the hood or his injuries he does not say. The sobering implication, therefore, was that if he did come down in the sea, he would drown. As such, his paramount objective immediately became getting himself back to solid ground as quickly as possible.

Eric's only option now was to force-land his aircraft once he crossed the English coast. Ideally, he hoped to reach RAF Martlesham Heath, which lay approximately eight miles inland, but he could not make it and crashed-landed his Spitfire in a field on Buckenay Farm, near Alderton. It was a close shave; he came down less than a mile from the coast.

Although considered 'in all, a very successful action'[12], No. 41 Squadron did not come out of the fight without their own nose bloodied, and lost their prize pilot in the process. As formality and regulation would have it, Eric was posted from No. 41 Squadron to the 'non-effective' strength of RAF Hornchurch. However, No. 41 certainly claimed a good share of the wing's victories, which are shown below.[13]

Sqn	Pilot	Destroyed	Probable	Damaged	Location
41	Aldridge, Frederick J.	Me109E	–	–	Off Felixstowe
41	Lock, Eric S.	2 Me109E	–	–	Thames Estuary – Channel
41	Lovell, Anthony D.J.	Me109E	–	–	7 miles north of Herne Bay
41	Mackenzie, John N.	Me109E	–	–	Off Clacton
41	Mileham, Denys E.	–	–	Me109E	Thames Estuary
603	Boulter, John C.	Me109E	–	–	Thames Estuary
603	Berry, Ronald	Me109E	–	–	North of Thames Estuary
603	Stokoe, Jack	Me109E	–	–	30 miles east of Rochford
603	Pinckney, D.J. Colin	–	Me109E	–	East of Herne Bay

During the same raid, Nos 17 and 257 Squadrons also engaged a formation of approximately sixty aircraft south-east of Harwich, consisting of Me110s escorted by Me109s of JG26; their target was RAF Wattisham. While No. 257 Squadron attacked the Me109s, No. 17 Squadron went after the Me110s. The former unit returned to base to report one man wounded and another killed in action, but claimed two Me109s destroyed and one damaged. For their part, No. 17 Squadron claimed two Me110s destroyed and one probable, for the loss of one aircraft shot down, although its pilot baled out and was unhurt. Nos 66 and 74 Squadrons undertook their designated sweeps, but failed to rendezvous with Nos 253 and 501 Squadrons. Although the former two squadrons conducted an independent sweep of the coastline, and the latter pair a patrol of the Biggin Hill line, no enemy aircraft were seen by any of them and they returned to base with nothing to report.

Meanwhile, in a field near Alderton, Suffolk, Eric's ordeal was still a long way from over. Trapped inside his aircraft, he was unable to free himself as a result of both his injuries and the damage to his cockpit hood. However, two soldiers soon discovered him, prised open the hood and carefully pulled him out of the cockpit.[14,15] When they found him, there is no doubt he would have been in a state of shock. This is caused by any condition that reduces blood flow, such as significant blood loss and nerve damage, both of which Eric is likely to have been suffering. Often described as a state of physical shutdown, a body can enter shock when there is not enough blood circulating, and this can cause the failure of multiple organs. More specifically, 'traumatic hypovolemic shock' is brought on by severe blood loss, where there is no longer enough blood to supply the vital organs, and this can lead to heart failure.

The soldiers who freed Eric from his cockpit would have been trained in at least the basics of first aid and, aside from obvious large amounts of blood, may have recognised the tell-tale signs that Eric was in shock. The symptoms include dizziness, light-headedness, faintness, nausea, confusion, anxiety, low blood pressure, pale, cool and clammy skin, profuse sweating, chest pain, and bluish lips and fingernails; Eric may have been displaying several of these signs.

Realising the seriousness of his wounds, they built an improvised stretcher with their rifles in the sleeves of a buttoned-up greatcoat. It is unknown what immediate first aid may have been rendered but if they were carrying standard-issue field dressings, they would no doubt have sought to stem the blood flow, perhaps applying sulfa powder and bandages, and making him as comfortable as possible, likely keeping him warm with a second greatcoat.[16] However, they are unlikely to have been carrying any form of pain killers, such as morphine, as these types of drugs were only issued to trained medics.

With great effort, the pair then carried Eric some distance across fields, and into the village of Alderton to obtain some professional help for him. This trek must have seemed to take an eternity for Eric, who would have been in excruciating pain and likely barely conscious. Once in the village, the soldiers were able to arrange transportation and Eric was driven fifteen miles to the East Suffolk and Ipswich Hospital, in Ipswich. As a clear emergency case, Eric would have received immediate treatment.

Some accounts suggest that Eric lay in his cockpit for an hour or two before he was rescued but the period of time is unlikely to have been so long on account of his serious wounds and blood loss, which, untreated, could well have cost him his life before he was found. Indeed, considering the lapse of time between his initial wounding twenty miles off Clacton and his arrival in hospital, it is a wonder he survived at all. His injuries were ultimately dryly summarised in his service record as 'G.S.W. Lft forearm, Lft leg and Rt. Knee'[17] but this brief statement belies the horrific scale of the damage.[18]

It is apparent that Eric had been attacked by an unseen Me109. These aircraft were armed with two MG17 machine guns over the engine, with 1,000 rounds per gun, and an Ikaria MG FF cannon mounted on each wing, with 60 rounds per gun. Having been hit in the left arm and both legs might suggest an attack from his port beam. However, no available documentation indicates whether the ammunition that struck Eric was presumed to have been machine gun or cannon, or both. In the least, the lack of burns would suggest that neither was armed with incendiary rounds. The two weapons had the following specifications:

Weapon	Calibre	Length	Weight	Standard Types	Rate of Fire	Muzzle Velocity
MG17	7.92mm	57mm	10.8g	Steel core, tracer	1,200rpm	775m/sec
Cannon	20mm	80mm	134g	HE, AP, incendiary	520rpm	600m/sec

Based on this information, the kinetic energy of the machine-gun rounds would have been 2,392 foot-pounds (3,342 joules) at the point of impact, while the cannon rounds applied 17,790 foot-pounds (24,120 joules). Although the rounds would first have had to have passed through the metal skin of the Spitfire, or its Perspex hood, which would have slowed the projectiles slightly, the seemingly simultaneous impact in both legs and an arm would nonetheless have felt like being hit by a sledgehammer on these limbs.

In fact, the force was great enough to break Eric's left forearm in two places. The projectile appears to have entered his arm below the elbow and travelled down his sleeve to his fingertips, causing tissue damage and a gaping wound all the way. This type of high-velocity penetrating ballistic trauma likely caused what we would refer to today as a Grade III compound fracture. Such fractures result in extensive damage to skin, muscles and nerves, and are characterised by a high degree of contamination from foreign bodies, in Eric's case probably shell splinters, uniform fragments, Spitfire skin slivers and Perspex shards. As a result, such wounds attract up to a fifty per cent risk of infection and an immediate application of antibiotics is necessary even before surgery.

This is, of course, where sulfa powder became invaluable during the early years of the war, and it is worth emphasising that it had barely been in regular use for two years by the time of Eric's injuries. Although gunshot wounds to limbs that resulted in fractures were not necessarily fatal in themselves, the complications created by them were generally treated with immediate amputation during the 19th century and into the early years of the 20th. However, on account of the susceptibility to infection, even after amputation the death rate stood at forty-one per cent as recently as the Franco-Prussian War of 1870–71.

Following Eric's admission to hospital, the medical staff's priority would have been to stabilise his vital organs. He would also have been given blood, if it was available, as transfusions were well established by this time. Blood would have been preferable to plasma as it was not just a volume of blood that he would have required, but also its oxygen-carrying capacity. Unfortunately, the transfusion of blood cannot stabilise a patient with immediate 100 per cent effectiveness and, therefore, despite such a procedure, some patients may still die or remain seriously ill until blood oxygen levels reach their normal concentration, usually after about two to three days. More antibiotics would no doubt have been administered, as well as morphine for the pain, as this period was critical for Eric's survival.

As soon as his wife and parents were informed, they drove 200 miles from Bayston Hill to see him. Charles, Dora, Peggy and Joan stayed in a nearby hotel and visited Eric when they were permitted, but he was in a very serious condition and barely able to speak with them. One can but imagine how distraught they would have been at seeing him in such a serious condition.

On 24 November, approximately a week after he was shot down, Eric was considered stable enough to be transferred 120 miles to Princess Mary's Hospital at RAF Halton, near Wendover, Buckinghamshire, for specialist treatment. Opened in 1927, the hospital catered predominantly for air force personnel and, in 1940, became the first hospital in the world to use penicillin on a large scale; Eric could not have been in better care.

Out of necessity, the work on irrigating his wounds would have commenced at Ipswich, but his arm trauma – clearly the worst of his injuries – became badly infected, and his sister Joan still remembered decades later that the smell was appalling. With penicillin now available to him in sufficient quantities, it was applied with good result and over his month at Halton, he underwent multiple operations to remove shrapnel and other foreign bodies, to reset his broken arm, and to mend the damage done to his legs. Although impossible to corroborate with official records, newspaper reports at the time suggested that Eric underwent operations to fifteen leg wounds, in addition to his broken arm.

The existence of so many leg wounds may be suggestive of fragmentation of the shells that struck him, or a high-explosive shell striking the lower confines of the cockpit. They may also indicate injuries sustained from secondary objects, such as metal, glass, plastic or Perspex splinters from the cockpit skin, hood, instruments and control panel. As a high-velocity projectile passes through tissue, it rapidly decelerates and transfers its kinetic energy into it. This creates a pressure wave that forces tissue out of the way, creating a temporary cavity that can be much larger than the projectile itself. Therefore, in addition to a visible surface injury caused directly by the object entering the body, penetration often causes deeper secondary injuries. Although tissue generally moves back into place and fills the cavity that was created, the cavitation frequently does considerable damage first.

As such, assessment of such injuries can be difficult because the damage is internal and often not immediately obvious. A patient with those kinds of injuries is thoroughly examined, and X-rays are made both above and below the external wounds to identify the type and location of otherwise invisible foreign bodies, the nature of broken bones and indications of damaged organs. Foreign bodies are then removed, where it is considered safe to do so, but they may also be left in situ if the surgery required to extract them could cause more damage than leaving them or could endanger vital organs. In such cases, scar tissue will eventually form around the objects and generally do not cause lasting issues. At the same time, dead, damaged or infected tissue is also removed from in and around wounds to improve the chances of healthy tissue regenerating and healing damaged tissue.

Although the details of Eric's surgery are not available, we can certainly imagine the treatment he underwent, based on general high-velocity trauma medicine. It requires no guesswork, however, to appreciate that such wounds and the resulting invasive surgery on multiple injuries would have led to excessive bruising, and a painful and lengthy recovery. No doubt, he would have made good use of the hospital's penicillin and morphine supplies.

It was while Eric was undergoing these treatments at Halton that he was advised that he had been awarded the Distinguished Service Order. Although not officially gazetted until 17 December 1940, news of the DSO was released from at least 28 November, when the RAF Hornchurch ORB recorded:

> It was announced [today] that P/O Lock, of 41 Squadron, was awarded the D.S.O. P/O Lock was shot down and seriously wounded on 17th November, after having shot down two Me.109s and brought his total bag to 21 e/a destroyed and 7 probably destroyed. Reports on his condition have doubts as to whether he will fly again. Even if this should prove correct, he has made his full contribution towards the winning of the War.[19]

One newspaper reported at the time that the message was delivered to Eric by his officer commanding (Squadron Leader Don Finlay), who flew to RAF Halton to advise him personally. He brought with him a case of champagne and a congratulatory telegram, which read:

> AIR OFFICER COMMANDING GROUP AND ALL RANKS THIS STATION SEND THEIR HEARTIEST CONGRATULATIONS ON THE D.S.O. AWARDED YOU YESTERDAY BY

THE KING. NEWS OF PROGRESS YOU ARE MAKING AND THE AWARD OF THIS WELL-WON DECORATION HAVE MADE THE WHOLE STATION HAPPY.[20]

By the time he was shot down, Eric had twenty-two confirmed victories and seven probables to his credit, all of which had been achieved on No. 41 Squadron. The official citation stated:

> This officer has shown exceptional keenness and courage in his attacks against the enemy. In November, 1940, whilst engaged with his squadron in attacking a superior number of enemy forces, he destroyed two Messerschmitt 109s, thus bringing his total to at least twenty-two. His magnificent fighting spirit and personal example have been in the highest traditions of the service.[21]

Established in 1886 to reward officers of all services for meritorious or distinguished service in action, the order is generally awarded to officers in command, although awards to lower officer ranks could be made for a high degree of gallantry just short of deserving the Victoria Cross. This underscores the high regard in which Eric was held by the RAF, particularly when one considers he was the youngest pilot in the RAF at that time to have received the DSO. Ultimately, his was one of only three bestowed upon No. 41 Squadron's pilots during the Second World War. The other two were awarded to Squadron Leader Petrus Hugo in 1942 and Flight Lieutenant Thomas Burne in 1945.

The award was heralded widely in the newspapers, both in the Shrewsbury area and nationally, under headings such as,

>WOUNDED D.F.C. PILOT GETS D.S.O.
>He Has Shot Down 22 Germans

>Salop Pilot Gets D.S.O. While in Hospital
>Colleagues Send Him Champagne

>Pocket Pilot, 21, is R.A.F.'s Ace

>Shrewsbury Air Hero
>Three Decorations in Three Months

>D.S.O. for Young Shropshire Pilot
>Shot Down 22 Enemy Planes

'Five Bob Flyer' is Now a Fighting Ace
Pocket-sized Pilot Who Married a Beauty Queen.

The *Daily Mail* also reported that the pupils of Prestfelde School in Shrewsbury, where Eric had completed his education, had been given a day's holiday when he was awarded the Distinguished Flying Cross, and were now 'planning to ask for a whole week'![22]

Congratulatory messages flowed in from all quarters, even from local government. At Shrewsbury Town Council's meeting on 9 December 1940, the mayor, Captain Harry Steward, OBE, MC, spoke of Eric's award and wounding. He was acutely aware of the dangers he had faced as his own son was a pilot in the RAF.[23] On the mayor's suggestion, the council unanimously agreed to send Eric a message of congratulations, 'coupled with best wishes for his speedy recovery from his wounds'.[24] Acknowledging that many Shropshire men had been decorated for acts of bravery during the war, he felt it unfair to name individuals, lest some failed to be mentioned. However, in noting that Eric had won three decorations in the space of three months, he felt an exception should be made as this achievement was 'worthy of special mention'.[25]

Following a month's treatment at Halton, during which time Eric's wounds had all been cleaned and stitched, and his arm splinted to heal its break, he was transferred to the Queen Victoria Hospital (QVH) in East Grinstead, Sussex, on 23 December. His injuries, especially that on his arm, had left deep and unsightly scars, and he was now to undergo skin grafting by pioneering plastic surgeon, Dr Archibald McIndoe.

Initially founded as a small cottage hospital in 1863, QVH had grown significantly and moved three times, and was now at its fourth location, in a purpose-built facility in East Grinstead that had been opened in 1936. The hospital began to specialise in burns treatment, employing the relatively unknown innovation of skin grafting, often referred to as plastic surgery, to repair the disfigurement caused by burns and other injuries, and to reconstruct facial features.

The field was still very much in its infancy in the country, a reality underscored by the fact that there were only four full-time plastic surgeons in England immediately before the outbreak of war in September 1939: Tommy Kilner, Rainsford Mowlem, Harold Gillies – considered the father of modern plastic surgery – and his cousin, Archibald McIndoe. With grim foresight, the War Office anticipated the need for their skills and one of the four surgeons, 38-year-old New Zealander Dr Archibald McIndoe was appointed to the RAF as a consultant in plastic surgery. The following year, he was sent to QVH with a team of anaesthetists and nurses to found an RAF centre for plastic surgery. They arrived in East Grinstead on 1 September 1939, just two days before the declaration of war, to prepare for its ominous consequences.

Although skin grafting had been practised with varying levels of success since Roman times, such surgery was associated with great pain during both the removal of skin and its reattachment, until the development of anaesthetic. This advance led to approximately 11,000 skin grafts being performed in the United Kingdom on over 5,000 wounded First World War servicemen from 1917 onwards, mainly by Harold Gillies and Tommy Kilner. Most of these operations were undertaken to reconstruct facial injuries caused by gunshot wounds.

However, as infection was also a significant issue, the discovery and availability of antibiotics such as sulphanilamide (sulfa powder and tablets) and penicillin made surgery and recovery more bearable and, particularly, more survivable. Prior to that time, many patients died of secondary, rather than primary, issues.

It is a grim fact that McIndoe had no shortage of customers, but on account of the unique nature of his work, and practically free reign to experiment, he was able to develop and refine many new immediate treatments, surgical techniques and rehabilitation regimes. He also debunked and eliminated some existing procedures.

For example, noting that airmen who ended their flights in the sea recovered better than those who had not, he pioneered the use of saline baths prior to commencing any surgical procedures. He also removed the use of tannic acid from burns treatment, as he discovered it did more harm than good in the long run. McIndoe was also a keen supporter of the so-called 'walking-stalk skin flap' technique, in which skin grafts were created by taking a flap of skin, which was still attached to the body, forming it into a tubular shape to reduce infection, and attaching it to the location where skin needed to be grown. Although having the skin attached at both ends created some grotesque facial features in the immediate term, the procedure promoted blood circulation and growth, and the flap was detached once a graft began growth of its own. Most importantly, however, it was extremely successful.

Lastly, McIndoe recognised that physical recuperation and healing was only half the battle, and that a patient could not fully recover from his injuries without additional psychological convalescence. He believed in holistic rehabilitation, designed to reintegrate men into society once their treatment was complete. This saw many liberties afforded that were not otherwise permitted for patients. For instance, patients were allowed to wear their RAF uniforms or civilian clothes instead of the traditional 'hospital blue' suit, and only the prettiest nurses were allowed to care for them. The wards were decorated with chintz curtains, equipped with a piano, a wireless and a barrel of beer, and McIndoe often joined them for social evenings.

On some occasions, entertainers were brought into the hospital to put on private shows. One such star was British forces sweetheart Celia Lipton. Known as the 'British Judy Garland', she had been singing and dancing since the age of ten, and went on to entertain troops at the Royal Albert Hall in London, in RAF hangars throughout Britain, and across the Western Front.

Moreover, McIndoe appealed to the people of East Grinstead to invite his patients to their homes as guests and, for those who could not do so, to treat them as normally as possible. This, too, was a success, and East Grinstead soon became known as 'the town that did not stare'. It was felt that this community support was instrumental in enabling many men to reintegrate into public life and lead more or less normal lives. Many former patients returned to service, albeit often in lesser capacities, such as in Operations Control Rooms, but they took with them invaluable experience from their former roles in the air.

On account of the severity of their wounds, some men were unable to return to service, but received full pay until their treatments were completed and were then invalided out of the RAF. Once again, McIndoe came to their aid and he loaned money to several men to enable them to get back on their feet. It is little wonder so many men felt a strong personal gratitude and loyalty toward McIndoe. He also built a strong personal relationship with his patients, who he always referred to as 'my boys'.

It was into this 'fraternity', this close-knit community, that Eric was delivered two days before Christmas 1940. His wounds had healed significantly by this time, but unlike many of his ward-mates, his scars were not outwardly obvious: when fully clothed, there was no sign of the hidden scars on his arms and legs. Having not suffered burns or facial disfiguration like many of his fellow patients, one can well imagine that he felt somewhat out of place when he arrived.

However, even though we have no images or detailed descriptions of his injuries to go by, and cannot therefore evaluate the seriousness of them for ourselves, given the limited availability of resources we can safely assume that he would not have been sent to QVH if it were not necessary. In fact, the only real hint we have of the damage is an unusual comment by his sister Joan, who stated many years later, without further explanation, that his arm 'looked like wooden jam spoon'.[26]

The main reason that Eric's plastic surgery was not undertaken earlier is that, in order for a graft to be successful, it is imperative that the recipient area is healthy and in a state capable of accepting and feeding with blood. So considered, it is clear why Eric's treatment took place in three distinct steps: (i) stabilisation in Ipswich Hospital; (ii) cleaning, stitching and dressing his wounds, and setting his broken arm in Princess Mary's Hospital at RAF Halton; and finally (iii) skin grafting at Queen Victoria Hospital.

Considering Eric had not sustained burns, it is presumed his treatment did not include a saline bath, but available records do confirm that he underwent three operations for grafts to gunshot wounds to his left arm and both legs by the time of his release from QVH almost exactly four months later. While details of his operations are once again not available to us, we can perhaps surmise what kinds of procedures may have been included in his treatment, based on the practice at the time.

One of Eric's fellow patients was Flying Officer Richard Hillary, who was exactly a day younger than him, and although born in Sydney, Australia, was educated in Shrewsbury around the same time as Eric, albeit at a different school. He was serving with No. 603 Squadron, which arrived at Hornchurch on 27 August 1940, exactly a week before No. 41 Squadron's own arrival at the station for the Battle of Britain. Hillary claimed five victories in that week, thereby achieving ace status, but was shot down in flames and seriously injured the day that No. 41 Squadron arrived. Although the two men had a significant amount in common, it is doubtful whether they would have met each other prior to QVH.

Hillary had sustained significant damage to his face and hands. The burns were so extensive that bone protruded from his knuckles, his mouth was missing its top lip, and his eyes were devoid of eyelids. However, he was to make a remarkable recovery at the hands of McIndoe and returned to flying. He also wrote an autobiography, *The Last Enemy*,[27] which provides us with an extraordinary insight into QVH, the operations that were undertaken and the patients he shared his ward with.

In order to replace Hillary's eyelids, an area was chosen on the inside of his left arm to take a paper-thin section of skin, and his arm was shaved and sterilised prior to the procedure. Another pilot being operated on that same day, No. 600 Squadron's Flying Officer Tony Tollemache, needed a graft for his hand, but his 'new' skin was taken from his leg, which was prepared in the same way. Both were denied food prior to their operations and were given a full anaesthetic for their procedures.

This leaves us to consider the locations targeted for the source of Eric's grafts. Requiring grafts to both legs and one arm, his undamaged right arm and the backs of his legs may not have provided enough skin for all three. It is possible, therefore, that skin may also have been taken from his back, his neck, or his buttocks; records do not specify.

A light top layer of skin, such as that used for Richard Hillary, is usually left to heal by itself, but Eric's damaged arm may have required a full thickness graft. Such a graft would have necessitated stitching of the donor area afterwards. The area from which a top layer is removed is covered in sterile dressings, and requires approximately two weeks to heal, as it is effectively an open wound; the area from which a full thickness graft is taken usually requires five to ten days to heal, a slightly lesser time, as it is usually smaller and closed with stitches.

The other option was what we call today 'flap surgery', which is where the principles of the 'walking-stalk skin flap' technique were applied. In such cases, the point is to keep the skin alive and allow it to grow and merge with the recipient area, using the blood vessels contained within it. As this allows the blood supply to be maintained, there is a lower risk of a skin graft being unsuccessful, or 'failing to take', as there is with a detached graft. Such surgery is still used today for open fractures, so this is quite likely what McIndoe used in Eric's case, even though the source area is unknown. It is entirely plausible, therefore, that McIndoe utilised flap surgery for Eric's arm, but applied regular, detached grafts for his legs.

Flap grafts took all manner of forms, and many pictures survive of patients during such procedures. For example, jaws were attached by tubes of skin to the neck, and the nose to the forehead, to the neck, the shoulder, and even the wrist. However, this brought other complications with it that are perhaps not immediately obvious. Hillary explains in his book about how one unnamed squadron leader spent some time 'rubbing his eye with pieces of cotton-wool. The hair from his scalp was making it acutely uncomfortable. This is not so odd as it sounds, for during a flap graft on the nose the scalp is brought down to the top of one's eyebrow where it is neatly rolled and feeds the new nose. It is of course shaved but the hair tends to grow again.'[28]

A graft was fastened in place with sutures, and would generally take on a reddish-purple colour immediately after surgery. This would subsequently fade, but it could take a year or two to fully settle. Even then, the final colour may differ somewhat from surrounding skin, and the area may be slightly indented. Considering the recuperation period for both the skin source and the area grafted, and moreover the amount of skin Eric needed to fully graft his wounds, it is likely his three grafts were not undertaken at the same time.

Although somewhat tongue-in-cheek, Hillary's description of preparation for his surgery gives us a bit of an idea as to what Eric may have experienced when he underwent his own skin grafting operations. In the context of his account, Hillary is referring both to Tony Tollemache's and his own experiences, as they both underwent operations on the same morning. Following shaving and sterilisation of the area of skin being removed,

> The Charge Nurse then trundled in a stretcher on wheels, parked it beside Tony's bed, pushed his feet into an enormous pair of bed socks, and whipped out a hypodermic needle. This contained an injection to make one drowsy half an hour before being wheeled into the operating theatre. [...]

He then climbed onto the trolley, which was screened off, and after about half an hour he was wheeled away. […]

[After Tony returned from surgery…] it was time for me to go. Two nurses appeared at either end of the trolley and I was off. … I was welcomed by the anaesthetist, vast and genial, with his apparatus that resembled a petrol station on wheels. As he was tying up my arm with a piece of rubber tubing, McIndoe came in sharpening his knife and wearing a skull-cap and a multi-coloured gown, for all the world like some Bedouin chieftain. The anaesthetist took my arm and pushed the needle in gently. 'Well, good-bye,' he said. A green film rose swiftly up my throat and I lost consciousness.[29]

Unfortunately, however, not every operation was a success. Some grafts simply 'did not take' and died. Survival of a graft depended entirely on the wound forming a new blood supply to it. Where blood supply to the area was affected, for example where the initial wound was not yet healthy enough, or oxygen was restricted to the area ('tissue hypoxia'), a graft would die. In such a case, it was necessary to completely remove it and start again.

Hillary speaks of Hampden pilot Godfrey Edmonds, who had a similar operation to himself, in which both eyelids were grafted. Three days after surgery, it was clear his right eyelid had not taken, but the reason was infection, rather than specifically blood and oxygen supply. This was the other culprit when it came to graft failure, in Edmonds's case streptococcus, and his eyelid was removed. We know that Eric had similar issues. Aside from his sister Joan relating many years later that some of his grafts did not take and became infected, causing an 'appalling' smell, this is one of few occasions when Hillary mentions Eric by name.

He describes how a bug started in the ward and eight men, including Eric, were wheeled into another building to be isolated until they were well again. They were treated by nurses wearing masks, aprons and rubber gloves, and were not allowed visitors. Hillary explains who was included in the select group:

Opposite me was Squadron Leader Gleave with a flap graft on his nose and an exposed nerve on his forehead. … Next to him was Eric Lock, a tough little Shropshireman [… who …] had cannon-shell wounds in the arms and legs. On my left was Mark Mounsdon who trained with me in Scotland and was awaiting an operation on his eyelids. Beyond the partition was Joseph [Josef Koukal], the Czech sergeant pilot, also with a nose graft; Yorky Law, a bombardier, blown up twice and burned at Dunkirk, with a complete new face taken in bacon strips from his legs, and no hands; and Neft, a clever young Jew (disliked for it by the others), with a broken leg from a motorcycle accident.[30]

Despite isolation and special treatment, the infection initially grew and spread. Neft's face began to fester, and streptococcus soon appeared on Squadron Leader Gleave's nose. No one enjoys being sick, but Neft had a tendency to repeatedly complain about it and this began to test Eric's tolerance. As patiently as he could under the circumstances, Eric pointed out to Neft that, 'some of us had been fighting the war with real bullets and would be infinitely grateful for his silence'![31]

As the infection spread among the men, the smell became almost unbearable. Hillary took to dabbing a bandage on his face with aftershave to try to dispel the stench, but with little success. In an effort to eradicate the infection, the eight patients' heads were shaved, scrubbed with an anti-bacterial soap, and covered with sulfa powder. 'We submitted to this with a varying amount of protestation: the Squadron Leader was too ill to complain, but Eric Lock was vociferous and the rest of us sullen.'[32]

In time, the infection abated and the men were returned to the wards.[33] Despite Eric's sister's comment that his grafts did not take, no details are available to confirm this, although it is of course possible that one of his three operations was to replace a failed or infected graft. Considering that evidence suggests that Eric's third operation was not undertaken until April 1941, it is likely that if this did occur it was his first graft that failed, and the second was the replacement operation.

Aside from the ups and downs of Eric's physical healing, one piece of news that he received during his stay at QVH hit him particularly hard. When Eric had joined No. 41 Squadron from No. 6 SFTS in June 1940, he had done so with Sergeant Pilots John McAdam and Frank Usmar, and Pilot Officer Gerald Langley. Langley had been killed in action on 15 September 1940; Usmar was shot down and seriously wounded on 27 September 1940 and was out of action until June 1941; Eric had, of course, been shot down on 17 November 1940. Only McAdam had remained practically unscathed throughout, despite being shot down and slightly wounded on 24 September 1940. That all changed in February 1941 when Eric was informed that McAdam had been killed. That, in itself, was bad enough, but the way it had happened angered him to the core.

No. 41 Squadron had suffered no casualties in combat or flying accidents for over two months, but during an afternoon patrol on 20 February 1941 two pilots were killed, both claimed by Oberstleutnant Werner Mölders of JG51. The Luftwaffe ace had claimed twenty-eight victories during the Battle of Britain and fifty-five in total, earning him both the Spanish Cross in Gold with Diamonds and the Knight's Cross with Oak Leaves. He was the fourth-highest-claiming Luftwaffe pilot of the Battle of Britain.

Five of No. 41 Squadron's pilots took off at 15:10 hours to patrol the Canterbury line at 30,000 feet or below the condensation level, led by Flying Officer Peter Brown. They flew in a vic of three aircraft, with two weavers as rearguard, the latter pair comprising Sergeant Pilots John McAdam and Robert Angus. Ultimately, however, the patrol was undertaken between 19,000 and 24,000 feet as the pilots were experiencing extreme icing conditions, resulting in a ⅛-inch-thick coating of ice inside the cockpit and on all dashboard instruments.

At 15:54, while over Dover, the pilots were ordered to intercept Raid 36, which was reported in their immediate vicinity, but at 6,000 feet, some 19,000 feet below them. This proved incorrect, though, as the controller soon called up the pilots again and advised a new altitude of 18,500 feet. But this was also inaccurate, a fact realised just seconds later when Flying Officer Peter Brown looked up to see six Me109s in pairs approximately 1,000–1,500 feet above them, diving in their direction. Meanwhile, the rest of the pilots were looking downwards, searching the sky below them.

On Brown's shout, the men took immediate evasive action and broke away, while Brown himself commenced a steep climbing turn towards the Messerschmitts and opened fire. However, he was promptly hit in the tail by return fire, blacked out while evading, and fell 5,000 feet in a spiral dive before regaining consciousness. Finding his control column not responding, he opened his canopy and prepared to bale out but then managed to arrest both his spin and dive. Realising he still had sufficient height to pull out of his dive, he decided against abandoning his aircraft, closed his hood and climbed again.

As he ascended, he sighted a Spitfire going down in flames, and subsequently a pilot descending by parachute, and immediately called for air-sea rescue (ASR) assistance. Recognising the man as Sergeant Pilot McAdam, he followed him down below cloud, and noticed there was a hole in the front of his flying suit with smoke emanating from it. As he watched, McAdam suddenly 'burst into flames'[34] but all Brown could do was helplessly orbit him until he landed in the water off Dover.

At that point, the Luftwaffe appeared again, Brown's attention being drawn to their presence only when tracers passed over his wing. He turned to attack them but they took evasive action and he was unable to close. He fired a burst at them at long range without visible effect, then climbed into cloud cover. When he emerged above the cloud a few minutes later, he saw four Me109s heading back across the Channel to France. Soon after this, the remaining pair of Me109s was also seen flying home.

Sergeant Pilot Angus was shot down during the attack as well, but details of his loss are scant, and he was only seen to bale out into the Channel. Unable to do much else, the remaining pilots landed at Hornchurch again at 17:05 hours to report Angus and McAdam's losses. A search was undertaken for them by ASR patrol boat in very rough seas, and by a Lysander below an 8/10ths cloud base, in an area around ten miles north-east of Dover. Against the odds, McAdam's body was located, and it was subsequently ascertained that the reason Brown had seen him catch fire was that he had been shot in the back with an incendiary round, presumably while descending.

Angus, though, could not be found and still remains 'missing, presumed dead'. Considering the day's wintery conditions and likely water temperature, it is doubtful whether he would have survived for long before succumbing to the effects of hypothermia.

A few weeks after this event, Eric received a letter from Sir Walter Monkton, KCVO, KC, MC, director-general of the Ministry of Information in London, enclosing a white eagle feather from the Society of American Indians. Eric was taken aback at first, as white feathers had originally been distributed to men who had not signed up for service during the First World War, as they were considered cowardly. Despite deluded idealism with often misjudged targets, the symbolism stuck and even during the Second World War the receipt of a white feather was regarded as an accusation of cowardice. However, for the American Indians, eagle feathers had quite the opposite meaning. We have all seen Indians in Westerns wearing feathers on the back of their heads or chiefs wearing a full headdress of feathers. Those feathers are the equivalent of our medals and ribbons. They symbolise trust, honour, strength and power, and the battles a warrior has fought. To be given an eagle feather is to be recognised for bravery in much the same way as the Western world decorates members of its armed forces.

The reason Eric was now receiving one is that Chief Whirling Thunder of the 'Indian Council Fire', a society of American Indians headquartered in Chicago, had sent eleven feathers to the British Embassy in Washington DC for the RAF. They were delivered with a request for them to be presented to members of the air force who had 'specially distinguished themselves in operations against the enemy as marks of esteem from their Indian admirers across the Atlantic'.[35] It was in fact a great honour that the American Indians were bestowing on Eric.

Only days later, he was notified of yet another accolade. On 17 March 1941, Eric was Mentioned in Dispatches, and the *London Gazette* recorded his name as deserving particular mention for distinguished service. He ultimately received a certificate to this effect, which was executed by the Secretary of State for Air, Archibald Sinclair.

By the end of March, Eric was considered well enough to attend an investiture for his Distinguished Service Order and both Distinguished Flying Crosses at Buckingham Palace. He was formally released from QVH on the evening before and travelled to London for the occasion, which took place on 1 April 1941. It is not clear who Eric's witnesses were, but we may assume they were his wife, Peggy, and his parents, Charles and Dora. The medals were conferred by the King himself and the event was reported widely in the newspapers. Most carried a story along the lines that he was being awarded three decorations for shooting down twenty-two enemy aircraft, 'one more than his age'.

It is apparent from Richard Hillary's accounts that patients were allowed out of hospital for brief periods while their grafts healed and were permitted to travel home, and to attend events such as Eric's investiture at Buckingham Palace. With the exception of that particular occasion, we have no records of when Eric travelled home, but we know he did so as his sister, Joan, had a clear recollection of them. The wounds and surgery had taken a toll on him, she recalled, feeling that he 'looked awful, very pale and like an old man. He was obviously worn out both physically and mentally.'[36] She also remembered 'seeing him asleep, slumped in a chair at home looking terrible'.[37] The image she paints is clearly portrayed in two different photographs of Eric at Buckingham Palace that appeared in the newspapers at the time. He looks drawn and exhausted, just a shadow of his old self, and there is no excitement in his face despite the auspicious occasion.

According to the newspapers, Eric returned to QVH from the investiture for one further operation. Considering the seriousness of his arm wound, it is likely it was the first to be grafted, and he may have been given a second graft if the infection referred to by Richard Hillary and Eric's sister Joan did in fact result in partial or complete graft failure. If that was the case, then his third operation would have probably concentrated on one or both legs.

It was therefore likely that it was a relatively quiet twenty-second birthday that Eric celebrated at QVH on 19 April. However, this last procedure appears to have been successful and without complication as he was discharged from the care of Dr McIndoe to Dutton Homestall Convalescent Home a week after his birthday. A Red Cross facility near Ashurst Wood, and two miles east-south-east of East Grinstead, the convalescent home was a restored and modernised stately mansion. It comprised two main buildings, a courtyard, tennis lawns, a croquet lawn, a swimming pool, a summer house, a terrace walk and a kitchen garden, which were surrounded by parklands, woods and countryside. Eric remained in care here until 28 May 1941.

The south-western wing was a two-storey timber structure dating from the 15th and 16th centuries, which included an attic, casement windows and a tiled roof, and was known as Homestall. The eastern wing was a 16th-century timber-framed building with a two-storey porch and gable. Having originally been built in Dutton, Cheshire, around 1562, but moved to this location in the early 1930s, it was called Dutton Hall. The two buildings together were known as Dutton Homestall.

The Dewar family, of whisky fame, had owned the property since 1907, and had more recently become great benefactors of the Queen Victoria Hospital. The family supported Dr Archibald McIndoe's work and knew him well. After the outbreak of war in 1939, the Dewars allowed the buildings to be converted into a Red Cross evacuation hospital, but the property was transformed into a convalescent home the following year, initially housing wounded army officers. However, considering the Dewars' relationship with McIndoe, it comes as little surprise, perhaps, that as a result of the growing number of burns victims among airmen, particularly in the aftermath of the Battle of Britain, it was adapted anew to accommodate pilots of Fighter Command who were recuperating from skin grafts.

McIndoe believed that the success of a patient's convalescence relied on getting out of the hospital itself, and being able to recuperate in a more conducive atmosphere, with outdoor activity and interaction with family and friends. It was here, therefore, that Eric was sent immediately after being discharged from QVH. It was the perfect location, not only for its peaceful surroundings, but also for its proximity to the hospital for the patients. The environs would no doubt have been pleasantly reminiscent of Eric's recent – and yet strangely distant – childhood on Bomere Farm.

Unfortunately, nothing is known about his time here, but as there is no mention anywhere in Eric's service record or in other literature about physiotherapy, it was presumably here that he undertook remedial exercise to build muscle strength and regain full use of his left arm and legs – at least to as good a level as possible. The point of the stay appears to have been to regain mobility and function of his limbs, although such treatment during the 1940s was nothing like we know today, and consisted primarily of exercise, massage and traction.

Eric would doubtless have made good use of Dutton Homestall's facilities, played tennis and croquet, and walked, but May 1941 was a particularly cold month – the mean temperature was less than 50°F – and this may have precluded swimming in the home's pool. Despite the cooler than average conditions, rainfall was light and many dry days would have enabled Eric to enjoy the outdoors and get some exercise. The stay appears to have done him some good, as he improved considerably during his month here.

Following a check-up and overnight stay at QVH on 23/24 May, McIndoe decided that it was time to send Eric to RAF Hospital Halton for the RAF's own diagnosis on his progress. Arriving there straight from Dutton Homestall on 28 May, he was given an A2B2 status – fit for limited flying duties and limited ground duties – but was sent home on sick leave and told to report again on 25 June.

Eric now returned to Bayston Hill and stayed with Peggy in Eric's parents' house, 'Eastington', on Lyth Hill Road. He arrived home to a hero's welcome but it is understood that as much as he was pleased to be home, he was privately uncomfortable with the attention he received from strangers and the general public, as well meant as it was. Following numerous newspaper reports in both local and national media, Eric's exploits, gallantry medals and wounding were well known, and he could not go far from the family home or into Shrewsbury without being recognised.

He was a different man since being shot down and was quiet and reserved, shunning the attention he was getting, and shying away from the back-slapping, hand-shaking, congratulatory greetings he was receiving everywhere he went. However, he felt obliged to accept invitations to a number of civic engagements during May, June and July 1941 as the guest of honour. These included the local Rotary Club, the Masonic Lodge and the Salop Licenced Victuallers' Association. He also made a visit to the offices of the Shropshire Journal and to Shrewsbury's Sentinel factory, which produced steam locomotives and rail wagons. As Eric's father Charles was a member of the Shrewsbury general committee of the National Farmers' Union, the branch decided to honour Eric with an honorary life membership, 'in appreciation of his services to King and country'. Finally, the Bayston Hill Women's Institute also presented Eric with a silver box from the residents of Bayston Hill 'in recognition of his gallantry and skill'. He did not enjoy the attention and questions, and despite the fact it was warming up toward summer, he always wore full uniform with gloves to cover his scars and avoid discussing them.

In time, Eric's thoughts turned to flying again, and on 18 June, exactly a year since he was commissioned, he was confirmed in his appointment and promoted to the war substantive rank of flying officer. Even if undoubtedly expected – it was a more or less automatic promotion – there was probably no formal advice to him while he was on sick leave, although it appeared in the *London Gazette* a month later. On 25 June, Eric travelled 135 miles to RAF Hospital Halton for a re-evaluation of his fitness to return to duties. On this occasion, he was reclassed A1B, which implied he was now considered fit for full flying duties and all ground duties.

However, while cleared to return to duty, he was not sent on a flying refresher course as one might expect for someone having sustained such wounds and undergone an extended period of recuperation. He was also not posted to a non-operational unit in a role such as a flying instructor, for example, or to an operational unit off 'the front line' in No. 9 Group (Wales and the Isle of Man), No. 12 Group (Midlands), or No. 13 Group (Northern England and Scotland), to ease him back into operations.

Instead, he was promoted to acting flight lieutenant and posted directly to No. 11 Group's No. 611 Squadron as a flight commander. The unit was based at RAF Hornchurch, at the forefront of offensive operations, and Eric arrived there just two days later, after a further 180-mile journey. It barely left him, Peggy and his family time for goodbyes.

One could also be forgiven for wondering why he was not posted back to No. 41 Squadron. The unit was resting by then at RAF Catterick, in Yorkshire, which provided a perfect situation for easing someone such as Eric back into operations. The unit was kept busy flying operational patrols, but only experienced intermittent spats with the Luftwaffe. Indeed, this is exactly what was done for Flight Sergeant Frank Usmar, who had joined No. 41 Squadron with Eric from No. 6 SFTS in June 1940. He had been wounded in action on 27 September 1940 and had sustained facial burns and injuries to his right leg. Having been recuperating since then, he was posted back to No. 41 on 10 June 1941.

Another instance is Flying Officer 'Wally' Wallens, who had sustained a serious leg wound in action on No. 41 Squadron on 5 September 1940. He returned to the unit at Catterick in April 1941, but was rejected by the medical officer and sent away for a further period of convalescence. When his flying status was reinstated a month later, he was posted to No. 24 (Communications) Squadron at Hendon, and spent the rest of the war with an air-sea rescue squadron. Pilot Officer 'Ben' Bennions is yet another example. Following treatment with McIndoe at QVH, he was sent to RAF Catterick in February 1941 to serve in the Operations Room before his operational flying status was reinstated.

A return to No. 41 Squadron at RAF Catterick would have made sense for Eric, too. Even though there had been significant turnover since November 1940, he knew the unit and its aircraft, had already served under its officer commanding, and had previously been based at Catterick. Although No. 41 was moved back south to RAF Tangmere at the end of July 1941, a return to the unit on 27 June would have given him at least four weeks to find his feet again before being thrust back into the action in No. 11 Group.

Why was Eric sent directly to the front line instead, from convalescence to offensive operations with a new unit and new aircraft mark, within the space of just a few days? Although a posting to a front-line squadron may have been at Eric's own personal request – indeed, we shall never know – one must surely question the wisdom of such a posting, or the acquiescence to such a request. Having been so seriously wounded that it necessitated approximately seven months' treatment, multiple operations, skin grafts, recuperation and physiotherapy, surely it would have been prudent to ease him back into flying via a quieter initial posting elsewhere first, even if only for a short period until the RAF knew, and indeed Eric knew himself, how he would cope with returning to operations? Peggy also recognised that although he had recovered physically, he was never quite the same, and was left wondering if he could tolerate more fighting.

Eric was also returning to a very different war, one in which the operational tactics had changed, both as an outcome of the Battle of Britain and as a result of Hitler's new Eastern Front, which had only been launched days before his posting. Many of the Luftwaffe's fighter and bomber units had either already been withdrawn or were in the process of being moved from France to new deployments on the Eastern Front; the vastly depleted German fighter force gradually transformed its strategy to one of a largely defensive disposition. Offensive attacks on England were now fewer and farther between and more of a harassing nature than one of targeted strategy.

As much as this was a positive development for the British populace as a whole, this change in the nature of aerial activity had significant consequences for the RAF. Rather than the Luftwaffe having a short air-time over southern England amid British defences, as had been the case throughout the Battle of Britain, the RAF's fighters now had a short air-time over France, Belgium and the Netherlands. Furthermore, during the Battle of Britain, Luftwaffe pilots shot down over England were captured, but British pilots returned to their units to fly again. This situation was also now reversed as the RAF ventured across the Channel on offensive operations and the rate of perfectly fit pilots and aircrew being captured had consequently begun to rise dramatically.

The Channel was also an obstacle in itself. A wounded man or the pilot of a damaged aircraft over England could force-land or bale out. However, damage or injuries sustained over France had to be nursed back across the Channel to the safety of English shores. Some men reached the general proximity of the English coast and were rescued from the Channel by British amphibious aircraft or watercraft; for others it was a journey too far and they were never seen again.

The change to offensive operations also presented entirely new challenges for fighter pilots themselves. Their work shifted increasingly to bomber escort duties, and while their chief aim was to protect the aircraft in their care from German fighters, tight formations often eliminated the ability to fight independently as the Battle of Britain had regularly offered. Moreover, when the work was not bomber protection, it concentrated on low-altitude attacks on road, rail and sea targets, which brought their own inherent dangers: flak, small-arms fire, masts, aerials, overhead wires, trees and other obstructions, all of which took their toll on men and machines.

Low altitude was also a distinct disadvantage when enemy fighters were about.

An analysis of Eric's successes during the Battle of Britain shows that high-altitude independent fighting had always been his strategy. Often operating alone in the skies, his only friend was altitude and he exploited the advantage at every opportunity. Post-Battle of Britain offensive operations and combat at mid-range altitudes and below were completely new to him as he returned to operations with No. 611 Squadron. This was an entirely new way of fighting that Eric had much to learn about.

Chapter Seven

Back to Work

June – July 1941

Following his arrival at RAF Hornchurch on 27 June 1941, pending disposal, Eric was formally posted to No. 611 (West Lancashire) Squadron. A relatively young unit compared to his former one, it had been established as an Auxiliary Air Force day-time bomber unit at RAF Hendon in February 1936. The squadron did not receive its first aircraft – Hawker Harts – until June that year, but had by then moved to RAF Speke. Relocating to RAF Duxford two months later, the unit continued to fly its Harts until April 1938 when they were replaced with Hawker Hinds.

The unit underwent a major transformation on 1 January 1939, when it was converted to a fighter squadron, but it did not receive its first fighters – the Spitfire Mark I – until May, but then became one of the first units in the RAF to receive the new aircraft. Following the outbreak of war, No. 611 Squadron was moved to RAF Digby in Lincolnshire, where it was declared fully operational in May 1940. Participating in the withdrawal from Dunkirk, the squadron subsequently acquitted itself well throughout the Battle of Britain while stationed at RAF Ternhill and Digby. The unit was posted to the Hornchurch satellite airfield, RAF Rochford, in mid-December 1940 and had moved between there and RAF Hornchurch itself twice by the time Eric joined them at the latter airfield in late June 1941.

Eric was, of course, familiar with RAF Hornchurch as this was the last airfield at which he had been stationed with No. 41 Squadron when he was shot down in November 1940. Having operated out of the airfield for a few months during the Battle of Britain, he was comfortable in the surroundings, and this would have no doubt helped him to settle in.

Having been equipped with Spitfires Ia and IIa throughout 1940 and early 1941, and latterly with Spitfires Va, No. 611 Squadron was in the process of re-equipping with the Mark Vb as Eric arrived. Six were delivered on 25 June 1941, five on 29 June, three on 1 July, three on 9 July and five on 14 July, to reach and maintain an immediate establishment. The final Mark Va did not leave the squadron until 22 July. It is believed that Eric had not yet flown the Mark V, as he had only piloted Marks Ia and IIa during his five-month tenure with No. 41 Squadron.

Hornchurch's other resident units at this time were No. 54 Squadron, commanded by Squadron Leader Robert F. Boyd, DFC and Bar, and No. 603 Squadron, headed by Squadron Leader Forgrave M. Smith, both equipped with Spitfires Va and Vb. The station commander was Group Captain Harry Broadhurst, DFC, AFC, who, like Eric, had formerly served as an officer pilot on No. 41 Squadron. Eric's arrival on No. 611 Squadron was announced in the ORB at the end of the rest of the day's activity, and records, 'POSTING: F/Lt. ERIC STANLEY LOCK, D.S.O., D.F.C. (23 victories) posted to the Squadron from HORNCHURCH as Flight Commander "A" Flight.'[1, 2]

Approximately five weeks later, No. 11 Group issued a list of the pilots with twelve or more confirmed victories up to and including 30 June 1941. As he arrived on No. 611 Squadron, therefore, Eric was considered the equal fourth-highest-scoring pilot of Fighter Command with twenty-two victories, despite him having been out of action for the previous seven months:[3]

No.	Name	Sqn	Day	Night	Total
1	Wing Commander Adolph G. Malan, DSO*, DFC*	–	27	2	29
2	Squadron Leader R. Robert Stanford Tuck, DSO, DFC**	257	24	2	26
3	Flying Officer James H. Lacey, DFM*	501	23	–	23
4	Squadron Leader Michael N. Crossley, DSO, DFC	32	22	–	22
4	Flight Lieutenant Eric S. Lock, DSO, DFC*	41	22	–	22
5	Flight Lieutenant Harbourne M. Stephen, DSO, DFC*	130	21	–	21

On 28 June, as Eric was settling in, No. 611 Squadron's officer commanding, Squadron Leader Frederick S. Stapleton, was promoted to become RAF Hornchurch's wing commander flying, replacing Wing Commander Joseph R. Kayll, DSO, DFC, who had been shot down and captured two days before. Stapleton was in turn replaced on No. 611 Squadron by 24-year-old Squadron Leader Eric H. Thomas, who arrived from No. 222 Squadron. A flying instructor at Cranwell at the outbreak of war, Thomas served briefly with Nos 222, 19 and 266 Squadrons before settling in with No. 222 for a second tour, where he spent most of the Battle of Britain.

No. 611 Squadron was released all the following day as RAF Hornchurch hosted AOC-in-C Fighter Command, Air Marshal William Sholto Douglas, CB, MC, DFC. He stayed for lunch and Squadron Leader Thomas, the flight commanders

– Eric and Flight Lieutenant Stanley Meares – and some of No. 611 Squadron's pilots 'were presented to him'.[4]

Back to work on 30 June, the squadron provided an element of a Target Support Wing for bombers attacking Lens Power Station, but Eric did not participate. It did, however, provide Squadron Leader Thomas with his first opportunity to fly operationally with the unit.

Eric likely spent the day refamiliarising himself with the local area and conditions, and particularly getting to know the Spitfire Vb, an aircraft in which he had not yet had any combat experience. With the exception of approximately three weeks' flying the Spitfire IIa with No. 41 Squadron the previous October and November, most of Eric's flying had hitherto been on the Spitfire Ia and, as such, the Vb presented a new experience altogether. It had a greater speed, a higher ceiling, and most significantly perhaps, four of the eight .303-inch machine guns were replaced with two 20mm cannons. Although this effectively constituted two less weapons, the cannons packed a far greater punch than the machine guns.

The day also saw the departure of Flight Lieutenant Meares, who was promoted to squadron leader and posted to No. 74 Squadron to take command of that unit. He was replaced on No. 611 Squadron by 24-year-old New Zealander Flight Lieutenant James Hayter, who arrived from No. 92 Squadron to take over B Flight. As such, within the space of just three days, the top three positions on No. 611 had been filled by new pilots – Squadron Leader Thomas, Eric and Flight Lieutenant Hayter – constituting a complete change in command for the unit.

Tuesday 1 July 1941 saw Eric's first operational sortie with No. 611 Squadron, but it was fairly low-key and no action was seen. It was a hot day, and despite six uneventful 'Barrow Deep' patrols[5] being flown between 05:25 and 09:10 hours, thick haze led to the postponement of a wing operation planned for that morning. The operation was rescheduled to the early evening, and entailed No. 611 Squadron providing target support with the Hornchurch Wing for Blenheims attacking targets at Chocques.

Date	1 July 1941
Operation	Circus 28
Targets	Établissements Kuhlmann et Cie Chemical Factory and Power Station, Chocques, Nord-Pas-de-Calais
Bombers	No. 2 Group: twelve Blenheim IVs – aborted
Escort	Northolt: Nos 303, 306 and 308 Squadrons (Spitfire IIa/b) – aborted
Target Support	Hornchurch: Nos 54, 603 and 611 Squadrons (Spitfire Va/b)
	Tangmere: Nos 145, 610 and 616 Squadrons (Spitfire IIa/b)
Rear Support	Kenley: Nos 1, 258 and 312 Squadrons (Hurricane IIa/b)

The bombers and Northolt's Escort Wing rendezvoused over Canterbury at 18:05 hours and headed out over the Channel via North Foreland. However, haze up to 10,000 feet made flying conditions difficult, and the bombers aborted the operation and turned for home at 18:16, when only around seven miles east of Deal. Northolt's fighters escorted the bombers back to the coast, where Nos 306 and 308 Squadrons separated from them, proceeded to Northolt and landed. No. 303 Squadron remained airborne and headed back out over the Channel to sweep the Calais area. The Luftwaffe was not seen, but a significant amount of fairly accurate flak was encountered. However, there were no casualties and the pilots returned to Northolt with little to report.

The Hornchurch Wing was airborne at 17:40, 'in poor visibility and with considerable misgiving',[6] and proceeded to Canterbury, led by Wing Commander Stapleton. Arriving at the rendezvous at 17:57 at altitudes of between 13,000 and 16,000 feet, No. 603 Squadron spotted the bombers through the haze but lost them again almost immediately. A few minutes later they were sighted again, and the wing headed after them, endeavouring to overhaul them and take up their allotted position. Meanwhile, No. 611 Squadron's Pilot Officer John Reeves turned for home, presumably as a result of a problem with his aircraft, and landed at Hornchurch at 18:10.

Finally catching up with the bombers ten miles off North Foreland, the wing was thrown into confusion when they were seen to turn away. It was finally realised that the bombers 'had decided to call it a day but neglected to tell anyone about it. Meanwhile, some convincing-looking plots on the board made [the] Controller think the show was still on, and considerable misunderstandings resulted on the R/T.'[7]

The wing followed the bombers almost to Clacton, then gave up and headed out over the Channel at 18:30 to make an orbit off Gravelines and Dunkirk. Nothing was seen and the pilots returned to Hornchurch where they landed between 19:25 and 19:30 hours. This concluded the day's operational flying. For their part, No. 611 Squadron had deployed twelve pilots, including Eric. The uneventful nature of the operation provided perhaps the best conditions for him to have made his first operational sortie in almost eight months.

Unaware of the bombers' return, the Tangmere and Kenley Wings operated normally. Tangmere's squadrons made landfall on the French coast and proceeded towards Chocques, but were broken up under way. A section of No. 616 Squadron was unsuccessfully attacked by a pair of Me109s, but Nos 145 and 610 Squadrons orbited the target area for twenty-five minutes and saw no sign of the Luftwaffe. When the bombers failed to appear, they headed back out, but on the way No. 145 Squadron sighted six Me109s, which were fired at without claim, while No. 610 Squadron experienced very accurate flak over Le Touquet but sustained no damage.

BACK TO WORK   153

The Kenley Wing swept Le Touquet and Montreuil, but only saw a single Me109 that dived away inland before it could be attacked. The pilots then patrolled briefly off the coast before returning home to report the operation as uneventful.

Eric was airborne operationally again the following day, when he participated in a Hornchurch Wing sweep to St Omer during the evening. The wing was airborne between 17:40 and 17:45 hours, led by Wing Commander Stapleton, and followed twenty minutes behind a similar sweep by the Kenley Wing. For their part, No. 611 Squadron deployed twelve pilots under Squadron Leader Thomas. Kenley's sweep drew a few enemy aircraft into the air, which were seen by the Hornchurch Wing, but they were too far away to engage and there were no combats. The pilots all returned 'without adventure'[8] between 19:00 and 19:10, and this concluded the day's flying.

The third day of the month brought fine and hot weather, and two Circuses were undertaken to Hazebrouck Marshalling Yards. As the bombers failed to find their target on the morning operation, a repeat operation was mounted in the afternoon. While No. 611 Squadron participated in both, Eric was only deployed on the second.

The failure to achieve the objective on the morning's operation made the loss of No. 611 Squadron's Sergeant Pilot Martin McHugh, RNZAF, who was killed, all the more senseless. The pilots were also unable to make any claims of their own, but the Circus did give Flight Lieutenant Hayter the opportunity to make his first operational sortie with the squadron. Following lunch, No. 611 was airborne once again, to provide an escort for the second attempt to find the rail yards. The operation is summarised below.

Date	3 July 1941
Operation	Circus 31
Targets	Hazebrouck Marshalling Yards, Nord-Pas-de-Calais
Bombers	No. 2 Group: six Blenheim IVs
Escort	Kenley: Nos 258 and 312 Squadrons (Hurricane IIa/b) and No. 485 Squadron (Spitfire IIa)
Escort Cover	Hornchurch: Nos 54, 603 and 611 Squadrons (Spitfire Va/b)
Target Support	Tangmere: Nos 145, 610 and 616 Squadrons (Spitfire IIa/b) Biggin Hill: Nos 74, 92 and 609 Squadrons (Spitfire Vb)
Rear Support	No. 12 Group, Coltishall: No. 257 Squadron (Hurricane IIb) No. 12 Group, Wittering: No. 266 Squadron (Spitfire IIa) No. 12 Group, Digby: No. 401 Squadron (Hurricane IIb)
Independent Role	Northolt: Nos 303 and 308 Squadrons (Spitfire IIa/b)

The Blenheims and Kenley Wing rendezvoused on schedule and crossed out, with the fighters above the bombers. The Hornchurch Wing, which had taken off at

14:40 hours and rendezvoused over Southend, joined the formation off North Foreland. They made landfall together on the French coast at Gravelines at 15:20 and, although Me109s were seen at a distance, they reached Hazebrouck unhindered. Tangmere and Biggin Hill's Target Support Wings followed them in, the former wing crossing in over Hardelot and the latter over Gravelines.

On this occasion, the target was found without problem and the Blenheims bombed the marshalling yards from 10,000 feet. However, their payloads fell wide of the mark and bursts were seen in the town, south-west of the target area. The Luftwaffe took its opportunity as the formations were withdrawing and made several strikes on the formation. A lone Me109 attacked the bombers from astern near Cassel but several dorsal gunners opened up on the aircraft, which was hit and last seen in a dive. The bombers all returned safely.

Another Me109 attacked No. 258 Squadron, which caused no damage, and was in turn attacked by three of the unit's pilots without effect. No. 312 Squadron had a brief skirmish with approximately twenty Me109s, during which one Messerschmitt was destroyed for no loss, and No. 485 Squadron fired at an Me109 at extreme range but could make no claim. The wing crossed out with the bombers at 15:46 and struck the English coast at Shoeburyness.

The Hornchurch Wing was kept busy on its way back to the coast as a number of enemy aircraft were encountered. Group Captain Broadhurst claimed one Me109F destroyed and one Me109E probably destroyed, but No. 603 Squadron spent much of its time evading repeated attacks from above. Ultimately, however, one Me109E was claimed probably destroyed, for no loss. Two pilots of No. 54 Squadron broke away from the formation to engage an Me109 that had just shot down a Spitfire. They succeeded in returning the favour and claimed the offending enemy aircraft destroyed. The pair then fought their way back to the coast, but returned safely. No. 611 Squadron was not engaged and, once again, the pilots, which included Eric, came away empty-handed. They returned individually and in pairs and were on the ground at Hornchurch again between 16:15 and 16:30 hours.

Tangmere's Target Support Wing orbited the Hazebrouck–St Omer area during the bombing and saw several Me109s. No. 616 Squadron fired at six aircraft without claim, while No. 610 attempted to attack a few that managed to evade them; No. 145 Squadron saw one Me109, but it was too far away. The Biggin Hill Wing sighted thirty to forty enemy aircraft above them, but they showed little inclination to fight. Nonetheless, No. 609 Squadron claimed one Me109 destroyed and a second damaged, and No. 74 Squadron claimed one damaged, too. It did not go all their way, however, and No. 92 Squadron lost a flight commander who was shot down near Hazebrouck and captured.

No. 12 Group's Rear Support Wing swept the area from Gravelines to St Omer to cover the bombers' withdrawal, but No. 266 Squadron became separated from them and Nos 257 and 401 Squadrons undertook the sweep without them. These two units returned with nothing to report, but No. 266 Squadron met a dozen Me109s in the Hazebrouck area. There was considerable chaos when the enemy aircraft dived through the unit formation as the squadron came under simultaneous fire from flak, which was accurate in altitude and burst among them. In the ensuing combats, No. 266 Squadron claimed one Me109 destroyed, two probably destroyed and three damaged, but lost one pilot killed and another captured.

Finally, Northolt's free-ranging independent wing arrived off the French coast east of Dunkirk at 15:43 hours and split up to patrol the St Omer–Hazebrouck area. Between Bergues and Cassel, around a dozen Me109s were seen 10,000 feet below them but they were not attacked. A pilot of No. 303 Squadron broke off to chase a lone Me109 that was seen diving away east of Berck. He fired at it but could not make a claim. A short while later, the same pilot spotted an Me109 preparing to land. Taking advantage of the aircraft's vulnerable position he fired a short burst, whereupon it crashed and was claimed destroyed. Northolt's wing commander also claimed an Me109F destroyed.

Although clear over the Channel, 9/10ths cloud between 4,000 and 5,000 feet over France resulted in only one Circus being undertaken by No. 11 Group on 4 July 1941, but it was a large operation with three separate concurrent targets. The Hornchurch Wing participated in an attack on the Kuhlmann Chemical Factory and Power Station at Chocques by providing target support in unison with Wing Commander Douglas Bader's Tangmere Wing. It was a successful operation for No. 611 Squadron, but while some pilots were able to make claims, Eric was left above them with his section to provide high-cover protection for the rest of the squadron.

The Blenheims bound for Chocques rendezvoused with their Close Escort and Escort Wings over Southend at 14:30 hours, and then proceeded across the Channel. The formation was immediately attacked by enemy aircraft on making landfall at Gravelines, and continued to be attacked all the way to the target area. Despite repeated attempts to break through to the bombers, however, the Blenheims managed to make their bombing run unscathed. Eleven bombers struck the target and the twelfth bombed a rail junction at Aire. On account of cloud cover, however, no results were observed.

The North Weald and Biggin Hill Wings fended off further attacks on the bombers on the way back out, and succeeded in claiming six enemy aircraft destroyed, three probably destroyed and ten damaged. Despite their efforts, how-

Date	4 July 1941
Operation	Circus 32
Target 1 (Z.220)	Établissements Kuhlmann et Cie Chemical Factory and Power Station, Chocques, Nord-Pas-de-Calais
Target 2 (Z.440)	Abbeville Marshalling Yards, Picardie
Bombers (Z.220)	No. 2 Group: twelve Blenheim IVs
Bombers (Z.440)	No. 16 Group: twelve Blenheim IVs – aborted
Close Escort (Z.220) Escort Target Support Rear Support	North Weald: Nos 71 and 242 Squadrons (Hurricane IIa/b) Biggin Hill: Nos 74, 92 and 609 Squadrons (Spitfire Vb) Hornchurch: Nos 54, 603 and 611 Squadrons (Spitfire Va/b) Tangmere: Nos 145, 610 and 616 Squadrons (Spitfire IIa/b) No. 12 Group, Duxford: No. 56 Squadron (Hurricane IIb) No. 12 Group, Kirton-in-Lindsey: No. 65 Squadron (Spitfire IIa) No. 12 Group, Matlaske: No. 601 Squadron (Hurricane IIb)
Escort (Z.440)	Kenley: Nos 258 and 312 Squadrons (Hurricane IIa/b) and No. 485 Squadron (Spitfire IIa) Northolt: No. 308 Squadron (Spitfire IIa)

ever, one bomber was struck by a direct hit from flak in the Dunkirk area and was forced to ditch in the sea off Gravelines. One of the crew was rescued and captured, but the other two were killed. The escorts also paid a price: No. 74 Squadron lost one pilot killed and No. 609 Squadron lost another, who was shot down and captured.

The Hornchurch Wing was airborne at 14:15, with No. 611 Squadron led by Wing Commander Stapleton, Eric and Flight Lieutenant Hayter; the wing was directed by Hornchurch's station commander, Group Captain Harry Broadhurst. Nos 54 and 611 Squadrons reached the rendezvous over Southend at 14:27, but did not see the Blenheims or No. 603 Squadron and consequently orbited until 14:35, when Broadhurst decided to head across the Channel without them. They arrived over the target area ninety seconds before the scheduled bombing time, with No. 54 Squadron at 12,000 feet and No. 611 Squadron 1,000 feet above them.

At this time, numerous enemy aircraft dived on to them from above and, in the ensuing combats, No. 54 claimed five Me109s destroyed and one probably destroyed, and Group Captain Broadhurst shot down two more. However, he sustained injuries when his aircraft was struck in the wing and shell splinters entered the cockpit and hit his leg.[9] He subsequently made 'a classic belly-landing on the 'drome'[10] on returning to Hornchurch and was able to climb out of his Spitfire unassisted. The same day, he was awarded the Distinguished Service Order.

Wing Commander Stapleton led two sections of No. 611 Squadron's pilots down after the enemy aircraft, but ordered Eric to keep his section above them for protection. In the following dogfights, Stapleton claimed one Me109 damaged, Sergeant Pilot Arthur Leigh claimed one probably destroyed and another damaged, and Sergeant Pilot William Gilmour claimed one Me109 destroyed.

Stapleton spotted eight Me109s just after the bombers had completed their bombing run, which were climbing again after attacking another Spitfire. Being in an advantageous position, he turned towards them and fired a three-second burst with his machine guns at the leading aircraft, at a range of about 350 yards with a half ring deflection. He saw a small piece dislodge itself from the aircraft's tail, but this did not seem to hinder its flying and the pilot quickly climbed away.

Stapleton's No. 4, Sergeant Pilot Leigh, spotted a pair of Me109Fs with orange spinners, which passed over him towards the coast barely 200 feet above him. Climbing a little, he quickly brought himself astern of the port aircraft and opened fire with both his cannons and machine guns at a range of only 150 yards. He observed strikes from both types of ammunition on its port wing, but the Messerschmitt rapidly climbed away into the sun and Leigh lost him. Now finding himself alone, he turned towards the coast and sighted the bombers homeward bound, approximately five miles ahead of him.

He opened his throttle to catch them up but when still around two miles from them spotted a pair of Me109Es flying line abreast at 12,000 feet, heading straight for the bombers from the north. He turned towards them, but they saw him coming and veered away from their course. Leigh initially thought this provided him with an opportunity to make an attack on them from astern, but they then broke in opposite directions to evade him. Despite this, the port aircraft remained in a good position for an attack and Leigh opened fire on it with his cannons and machine guns from its port stern quarter. He observed strikes on the fuselage and centre section, and the Messerschmitt commenced a diving turn with smoke billowing behind it. Leigh then lost sight of the aircraft as he swung towards the second Me109, which was above him and to starboard of his position. However, the fighter was not sticking around; it climbed rapidly away and was not seen again.

Hurrying to catch up with the bombers once more, Leigh crossed out just behind them. Soon after doing so, he spotted yet another pair of Me109Es, above the bombers, and climbed towards them. However, they showed no desire to fight and turned back for France. As they did so, Leigh fired a parting shot at the starboard of the pair, but did not observe any result. He then continued across the Channel with the bombers, escorting them as far as North Foreland before breaking away and heading for Hornchurch.

While Leigh was occupied with his first pair of Me109s in the St Omer area, Sergeant Pilot Gilmour had spotted another two. Flying as the No. 4 on the port side of Eric's Charlie Section, he was on the outside of the formation as it wheeled around the target to head home. He was a little astern and slightly above Charlie 3 – Flying Officer Tom Williams – when he saw two Me109Es diving towards them.

Evading them and advising Williams, Gilmour turned to attack the pair and opened up on one of the Me109s with his cannons from 400 to 500 yards. Making a quarter attack, coming round to beam as the Me109 banked to port, Gilmour added his machine guns to the confrontation and closed to 250–300 yards.

He saw a large flash in the Messerschmitt's tail unit, and then pieces of the aircraft began to dislodge and fly off. Having commenced his attack at 10,000 feet, the pair had dived to 6,000 feet in the pursuit before Gilmour broke off, leaving the Me109 to its fate. At that time, it was falling vertically, its yellow nose against its grey fuselage clearly visible until it disappeared into cloud at 3,000 feet. Eric also saw the Me109 in this position and subsequently confirmed Gilmour's claim.

Meanwhile, No. 603 Squadron had successfully rendezvoused with the Blenheims and followed them across the Channel. Shortly after making landfall at Gravelines, however, they were 'dived upon from all directions'[11] by large numbers of Me109s. This scattered the squadron and ultimately very few pilots made it through to the target area, but one Me109 was claimed destroyed for the loss of one pilot, who was shot down and captured.

The Tangmere Wing made landfall near Le Touquet and proceeded to the target area unopposed. After orbiting Chocques awhile, the wing headed back out and, during their return, No. 616 Squadron attacked six Me109s in the St Omer–Gravelines area, claiming one destroyed and two damaged. Nos 145 and 610 Squadrons patrolled inland from the coast on their way home, but did not see any enemy aircraft.

Finally, No. 12 Group's Rear Support Wing patrolled from the coast near Gravelines to approximately ten miles inland to cover the withdrawal from Chocques. They saw no sign of the Luftwaffe and returned home with nothing to report.

The second part of the Circus, to Abbeville, stood in stark contrast to the success of the first. The Blenheims failed to rendezvous with their fighter escort, aborted the operation and returned to base. Kenley and Northolt's escort squadrons rendezvoused as planned, but when they were unable to locate the bombers they proceeded to France alone. However, no enemy aircraft were seen throughout and they returned to base with nothing to report.

Eric did not fly on 5 July, but the following day was a significant one for him. No. 611 Squadron was involved in another Circus, on this occasion escorting Short Stirling heavy bombers to Fives-Lille as an element of RAF Hornchurch's Target Support Wing. It was particularly successful for Eric as he made his first claim against the Luftwaffe since he was wounded in November 1940.

The Stirlings rendezvoused with their escorts and Hornchurch's Target Support

Date	6 July 1941
Operation	Circus 35
Target	Fives-Lille Engineering Works, Nord-Pas-de-Calais
Bombers	No. 3 Group: six Stirling Is
Close Escort	Northolt: No. 306 Squadron (Spitfire IIa)
Escort	North Weald: Nos 71 and 242 Squadrons (Hurricane IIa/b)
	Hornchurch: No. 222 Squadron (Spitfire IIa/b)
Escort Cover	Biggin Hill: Nos 74, 92 and 609 Squadrons (Spitfire Vb)
Target Support	Hornchurch: Nos 54, 603 and 611 Squadrons (Spitfire Va/b)
	Tangmere: Nos 145, 610 and 616 Squadrons (Spitfire IIa/b)
	Northolt: Nos 303 and 308 Squadrons (Spitfire IIa/b)
Rear Support	No. 12 Group, Duxford: No. 56 Squadron (Hurricane IIb)
	No. 12 Group, Kirton-in-Lindsey: No. 65 Squadron (Spitfire IIa)
	No. 12 Group, Matlaske: No. 601 Squadron (Hurricane IIb)
Low Support	Kenley: Nos 258 and 312 Squadrons (Hurricane IIa/b) and No. 485 Squadron (Spitfire IIa)

Wing over Manston at 14:00 hours, and headed out with the bombers leading, in two vics of three. Landfall was made on the French coast at Gravelines, and Lille was reached only twenty-eight minutes after the initial rendezvous.

The Stirlings found the target without difficulty and dropped twenty-four 1,000lb bombs and fifty-six 500lb bombs from an altitude of 14,000 feet. Two or three sticks were considered direct hits on the target, resulting in large fires and plumes of brownish-yellow smoke. Sticks were also seen to register on a small building to the east of the complex, on the marshalling yards, on a large building to the north-west of the marshalling yards and on a railway junction to the south of the target.

Northolt's No. 306 Squadron spotted approximately twenty-five Me109s during the operation but only one attempted to reach the bombers as they were leaving the Lille area. At the time, the Stirlings were flying in their two vics, approximately half a mile apart, leaving the rear of the first vic unprotected, which is precisely what the Me109's pilot sought to take advantage of. A bomber was damaged in the attack, but returned safely, while the Me109 was claimed probably destroyed.

The Escort Wing was also busy. Its squadrons were engaged by enemy aircraft on reaching Lille and combats continued all the way back to the French coast, resulting in claims by No. 71 Squadron of one Me109 destroyed, one probably destroyed and one probably destroyed that was shared with No. 306 Squadron. No. 242 Squadron also claimed one Me109 probably destroyed and one damaged, while No. 222 Squadron claimed one damaged.

Biggin's Escort Cover Wing rendezvoused with the bombers as planned and accompanied them to Lille. As they approached the target, approximately twenty

Me109s were sighted, which attempted to entice the wing away from the bombers. The ensuing combats continued all the way back to the French coast, with some zealous Luftwaffe pilots following them across the Channel, almost as far as Manston. The wing ultimately claimed three of their assailants destroyed, but at a cost of three of their own: No. 74 Squadron lost two pilots, one of whom was captured and the other killed in action, and No. 92 Squadron also lost one pilot killed in action. The pilot on No. 74 who died was Sergeant Pilot Leslie Carter, who had served with Eric on No. 41 Squadron during the Battle of Britain.

For their part, the Hornchurch Wing was airborne at 13:35 hours, with No. 611 Squadron deploying eleven pilots plus Wing Commander Stapleton. Other positions in the unit formation were filled by Squadron Leader Thomas, Flight Lieutenant Bruinier, Flight Lieutenant Hayter and, following a day's break from operations, also Eric. The wing rendezvoused with the Stirlings over Manston and crossed the Channel between 21,000 and 25,000 feet.

No. 54 Squadron descended to 17,000 feet over the target area to afford the bombers greater protection. It proved a prudent move as six Me109s were soon seen orbiting the area and four made an almost head-on attack on the unit. On their way back out, three Me109s passed them in the opposite direction, but their pilots clearly had other business on their minds as they flew past without attempting to take on the squadron.

After observing the bombing, Nos 603 and 611 Squadrons split up and descended, too, to escort the Stirlings back to North Foreland. No. 603 Squadron was briefly engaged and claimed one Me109 probably destroyed. A dozen Me109s then approached No. 611 threateningly near Ypres, but were spooked by something and suddenly dived away without attacking. A short while later, near St Omer, another twelve Me109s approached No. 611 Squadron head-on at the same altitude, but they avoided the fight when No. 611's pilots attempted to engage them.

Having by now descended to just 12,000 feet, Eric split his Charlie Section into two pairs, which allowed him the freedom to hunt almost independently, unfettered by the confines of the larger squadron formation. Still a little rusty in combat, however, he was initially caught unawares when an Me109F passed behind him and he 'suddenly saw him flash past in [his] mirror'.[12] Eric's instinct and reflexes were nonetheless still intact and he reacted immediately, making a steep climbing turn to port. Having come around approximately 100° in his turn, he found the Messerschmitt dead ahead of him at a range of approximately 250–300 yards and an altitude of around 14,000 feet.

He fired a brief burst with his cannons for the first time, totalling no more than 21 rounds, and immediately elicited the desired result; perhaps one better than he had dared hope for. Approximately a quarter of the Messerschmitt's starboard wing flew off, and another piece, 'about as large as a suitcase',[13] detached itself from the aircraft, too. Eric could not determine what it was in the brief second he glimpsed it, but felt it may have been the cockpit canopy. Regardless, the Me109 then side-slipped into a slow roll and went down. Eric 're-opened his score',[14] claiming the aircraft destroyed, thus constituting his first victory since 17 November 1940. It was only his fifth operational sortie since returning to operations.

His wingman, Sergeant Pilot William Gilmour, who had been awarded a Distinguished Flying Medal the previous day, was also in action. Having lost Eric in the melee, he linked up with another squadron's Spitfires for safety and headed out with them until he noticed 'a strange aircraft'[15] off to starboard. He flew in that direction to investigate it, but soon found himself alone in the sky. Without the safety of numbers, he felt it prudent to change course for home and avoid any trouble, and turned back on to that heading with the intention of flying parallel to the coast to get his bearings, and then cross out between Dunkirk and Mardyck to avoid flak.

However, as he made towards the coast, he noticed an aircraft diving on his starboard side, but was not immediately concerned as its spinner was the same colour as the RAF's. Then he saw 'little darts of flame and smoke coming from its leading edges',[16] and realised all was not as it had initially appeared. Gilmour made a steep turning climb to port, but then saw an Me109 coming straight towards him, its guns blazing. In an effort to evade the fire, he sent himself into a spin and did not recover his aircraft until between 3,000 and 4,000 feet over Dunkirk. On doing so, he made a beeline for the coast.

Before he knew it, though, he was attacked by another Me109 from his starboard side. Evading the assault, Gilmour managed to turn in behind the aircraft and 'opened fire with everything'[17] from approximately 200–250 yards dead astern. He observed strikes on the Messerschmitt's tail and saw pieces of its port wing dislodge and fly off. Its wing then stalled in a turn to port and the aircraft entered a spin. Gilmour broke away to starboard just in time to see yet another Me109 diving towards him. In an instant, he saw tracers and smoke trails all around him, and broke again, each pilot trying to manoeuvre around and out-turn the other.

Ultimately gaining the upper hand, Gilmour positioned himself behind the Messerschmitt but held his fire until he could bring himself down to a range of 150–200 yards. At this time, he opened up and immediately saw strikes on the tail. The pilot reacted by making a steep climbing turn, but Gilmour fired again and saw his rounds hit the cowling before his ammunition ran out. As soon as he realised his ammunition was spent, Gilmour dived for the coast at top speed, and did not see his adversary again. He landed at Manston at 14:30 hours with just two gallons of fuel left in his tank, and topped up before continuing the last brief leg home to

Hornchurch to make claims for one destroyed and one probably destroyed Me109E.

However, it did not all go No. 611 Squadron's way on the operation, and when the pilots returned it was established that Sergeant Pilot Norman J. 'Mushroom' Smith was not among them. Last seen attacking an Me109, the 'cheerful little farmer from the West Country'[18] failed to return from the operation and was later reported as a prisoner of war.

Reaching the Lille area ahead of the main formation, Tangmere's Target Support Wing orbited the Lille–Lens area and awaited the bombers' arrival. They observed the bombing, then followed the formation back out over Gravelines. The wing came under attack from enemy aircraft all the way to the coast but fought back and claimed four Me109s destroyed, one probably destroyed and one damaged. But these victories came at the expense of two airmen: No. 145 Squadron lost one pilot who was shot down and killed, and No. 616 Squadron lost another who was also unfortunate to have had engine trouble on the wrong side of the Channel and was captured.

The Northolt Wing operated independently over the target area but saw very few enemy aircraft. The squadrons remained high and followed the bombers out, but were involved in a number of scuffles on the way. Three victories were claimed – one destroyed, one probably destroyed and one damaged – but all three fell to the wing commander flying. No. 12 Group's Rear Support Wing patrolled from Dungeness to Le Touquet, St Omer and Gravelines, and then back across the Channel to Dover, but saw no enemy aircraft and returned to base with nothing to report. Lastly, Kenley's Low Support Wing was held in readiness throughout the operation, but was not called upon and did not become airborne. This concluded the Circus.

Eric was airborne twice operationally on 7 July. With summer at its height, it was 'another scorching day',[19] which included three Circus operations for No. 11 Group's

Date	7 July 1941
Operation	Circus 36
Target	Hazebrouck Marshalling Yards, Nord-Pas-de-Calais
Bombers	No. 3 Group: one Stirling I
Escort	North Weald: Nos 71 and 242 Squadrons (Hurricane IIa/b)
	Hornchurch: No. 222 Squadron (Spitfire IIa/b)
Escort Cover	Northolt: Nos 303 and 308 Squadrons (Spitfire IIa/b)
Target Support	Hornchurch: Nos 54, 603 and 611 Squadrons (Spitfire Va/b)
Rear Support	No. 12 Group, Fowlmere: No. 19 Squadron (Spitfire IIa)
	No. 12 Group, Coltishall: No. 257 Squadron (Hurricane IIb)
	No. 12 Group, Digby: No. 401 Squadron (Hurricane IIb)

fighter squadrons. No. 611 Squadron was involved in two of these. In the first, the pilots provided an element of the Hornchurch Wing's target support for a minor attack on Hazebrouck Marshalling Yards, and in the second they assisted with a Mopping-Up Wing for an operation to the Kuhlmann Chemical Factory and Power Station at Chocques.

No. 611 Squadron was airborne with the Hornchurch Wing at 08:55 hours, with the squadron led by Wing Commander Stapleton and the wing by Group Captain Broadhurst. No. 611's formation was rather 'top heavy' and included, besides Stapleton, also Squadron Leader Thomas and Flight Lieutenants Bruinier, Hayter and Lock; only three of the twelve pilots were not officers. Eric was no doubt geared up, and feeling encouraged by his success of the day before.

The sole bomber deployed in the attack succeeded in making rendezvous with the Escort Wing, Hornchurch's Target Support Wing and No. 12 Group's Rear Support Wing over North Foreland at 09:20. However, Northolt's Escort Cover Wing arrived at the rendezvous late, to find the main formation had moved off without them. Hurrying to catch up, they took up their allotted positions approximately ten miles off the coast.

The Stirling and her large escort made landfall at Gravelines where a little flak was encountered, and the Hornchurch Wing opened their throttles to move ahead and arrive over Hazebrouck before the main formation. However, no enemy aircraft were sighted all the way to the target by either group and, consequently, the bomber proceeded directly to the target unhindered. Twenty-four 500lb bombs were dropped from 8,000 feet, but, despite the ideal conditions, one bomb struck a building south of the goods yard and the remainder fell harmlessly in a field beyond it.

On the way back out, the Northolt Wing as a whole only sighted a single Me109 in the distance, but a pilot of No. 308 Squadron, who was returning across the Channel alone, encountered a section of four Me109s at 1,000 feet. Not passing up such an opportunity, the enemy aircraft attacked him, but were unsuccessful and No. 308 Squadron's pilot arrived home safely, if a little shaken.

Having arrived over Hazebrouck between 18,000 and 23,000 feet at 09:39, the Hornchurch Wing split into sections after the bombing and escorted the Stirling back to North Foreland. On the way, three enemy decoy aircraft dived on the wing from slightly above, then climbed again and repeated the tactic a few times, to no avail; the pilots did not take the bait. In time, a vic of three Me109s was seen above and behind No. 611 Squadron, and Red Section was compelled to dive away to avoid the threat they posed.

Five miles inland from Gravelines, No. 54 Squadron was attacked by a dozen Me109s, which were orbiting between 17,000 and 18,000 feet. One Spitfire sustained combat damage when its pilot was forced to dive to 6,000 feet and chased to approximately three miles off Gravelines by six Me109s. No. 603 Squadron was also in action. As they crossed out over Gravelines at 16,000 feet, they were pounced upon out of the sun by ten Me109s. The pilots succeeded in evading them, but were attacked again later, 10,000 feet over the Channel, by another pair of Me109s. Their strike was also foiled and the tables turned; one of the two aircraft was claimed probably destroyed.

Group Captain Broadhurst saw the most action of the operation, claiming two Me109s destroyed and one probably destroyed, the latter victory achieved in a damaged aircraft that could only turn in one direction as the rudder control and an elevator control had been damaged by a shell from an Me109. In stark contrast, although No. 611 Squadron sighted and evaded attacks by a number of Me109s, 'nobody had a chance to get in a scrap'[20] and the pilots all landed safely at 10:25 hours.

Having rendezvoused with the main formation over North Foreland, No. 12 Group's Rear Support Wing proceeded to the French coast at 20,000–24,000 feet. On reaching Gravelines, the wing split up into sections of four and patrolled between St Omer and the coast to cover the withdrawal. Once they had seen the Stirling cross out safely, they returned across the Channel themselves. Only four or five enemy aircraft were seen through the entire operation, but none were close enough to make an attack.

No. 611 Squadron was airborne again after lunch to participate in Circus 38, providing Eric with his second opportunity of the day to fly operationally. However, between the operations, an official Air Ministry photograph was taken of him, alongside Pilot Officer Wilfred Duncan Smith, Flying Officer Peter Dexter and Sergeant Pilot William Gilmour, who were captured walking towards the camera in front of one of the squadron's Spitfire Vbs.

The afternoon's target was once again the Kuhlmann Chemical Factory and Power Station at Chocques, in which No. 611 Squadron participated in Hornchurch's Mopping-Up Wing. The operation comprised the elements in the table opposite.

The bombers rendezvoused 9,000 feet over Rye at 15:00 hours with the Escort, Escort Cover and Target Support Wings, and proceeded to Chocques via Hardelot. Although the Luftwaffe was not seen by the bombers on the inbound leg, accurate and heavy flak greeted the formation on crossing in and followed it all the way to Chocques, which was reached at 15:26.

The Stirlings made their run in to the target at 9,600 feet and dropped fifteen 1,000lb bombs and forty-two 500lb bombs. Seven were seen to undershoot the target but the remainder were precise, and strikes were seen across the power station, on one of the cooling towers, on an ammonia tank and on nearby buildings. Indicating the success of the attack, the target was obscured by large plumes of

Date	7 July 1941
Operation	Circus 38
Target	Établissements Kuhlmann et Cie Chemical Factory and Power Station, Chocques, Nord-Pas-de-Calais
Bombers	No. 3 Group: three Stirling Is
Escort	Kenley: 258 and 312 Squadrons (Hurricane IIa/b) and No. 485 Squadron (Spitfire IIa)
Escort Cover	Tangmere: Nos 145, 610 and 616 Squadrons (Spitfire IIa/b and Va/b)
Target Support	Northolt: Nos 303 and 308 Squadrons (Spitfire IIa/b) Biggin Hill: Nos 74, 92 and 609 Squadrons (Spitfire Vb)
Mopping-up	Hornchurch: Nos 54, 603 and 611 Squadrons (Spitfire Va/b)

brown smoke as the formation left the area. As they did so, a handful of Me109s dived steeply out of the sun on to the bombers from their forward quarter. However, they continued down and were diving much too fast for Kenley's Escort Wing to attempt an interception. Several small formations of enemy aircraft also were seen, but all were too far away to engage, and the rest of the operation was quiet insofar as the Kenley Wing was concerned. They escorted the bombers back across the Channel and as far as Sittingbourne, before parting company and heading back to base.

Having rendezvoused with the bombers over Rye, the Tangmere Wing proceeded to France with the main formation, except for a section of No. 145 Squadron that became separated over the Channel and did not reach the target. This section sighted four Me109s above them and climbed to engage them, but were attacked from astern by other enemy aircraft.

Another of the squadron's sections had a similar experience a short while later, while patrolling the Boulogne–St Omer–Desvres region. Having sighted Me109s, they turned to engage them, but were attacked from astern by another pair. The attacks were relatively unsuccessful, however, and while all of the squadron's pilots and aircraft returned safely, one pilot was wounded. Nos 610 and 616 Squadrons reported accurate and heavy flak over the target area but returned with little further to report.

Northolt's Target Support Wing drew ahead on nearing the target. No. 303 Squadron then orbited Chocques twice, observing 'excellent' results of the bombing, but was dived upon by a trio of Me109s that attacked the rearmost section from their forward quarter. Reacting quickly, one pilot fired his guns at one of the Messerschmitts at point-blank range, but was unable to see any result. Another pair of Me109s was subsequently attacked, but once again no claim could be made.

No. 308 Squadron was set upon by one formation of six Me109s, and three formations of three, resulting in multiple combats, and three enemy aircraft were claimed destroyed and one probably destroyed for no loss. Two Spitfires were slightly damaged by flak, but all pilots returned, escorting the bombers back to England via Hardelot.

Biggin Hill's Target Support Wing crossed the Channel independently, making landfall over Gravelines. On the way to the target area, a large number of Me109s were seen above them, which made no attempt to take attack them. Remaining over the objective long enough to see the Stirlings complete their bombing run, they headed back out, chasing Me109s from the vicinity of the bombers on several occasions. No. 74 Squadron was bounced by a number of Messerschmitts, and one pilot was shot down, but No. 92 Squadron avenged his loss, claiming one Me109 destroyed and one damaged. The wing reached the coast at Hardelot a few minutes ahead of the bombers and slowed to let them pass, allowing them to cross out before doing so themselves. They escorted the bombers to mid-Channel, then parted company and headed for home.

The Hornchurch Wing was assigned the task of Mopping-Up Wing for the operation, and was therefore not airborne until 14:55 hours. No. 611 Squadron's formation comprised twelve pilots led by Wing Commander Stapleton and assisted by Flight Lieutenants Hayter and Lock. Proceeding to North Foreland and on to Gravelines between 28,000 and 30,000 feet, the wing then undertook a sweep to Merville, and crossed back out over Hardelot, having by that time descended over 11,000 feet.

The Luftwaffe was not sighted until approaching Hardelot, when a lone pair of Me109s were seen diving away from 17,000 feet. Soon afterwards another six Me109s were seen but not engaged, and finally a trio of Messerschmitts managed to separate one of the wing's pilots from the formation and chased him inland at altitudes down to 1,000 feet. Their pursuit ultimately proved unsuccessful, and all of the pilots returned to base between 16:10 and 16:25. This concluded the operation and No. 611 Squadron made no further operational flying that day.

Tuesday 8 July 1941 was considered 'probably the hottest, or at any rate the most stifling'[21] day of summer 1941 thus far and, as such, 'the idea of keeping the Hun on the hop and forcing him to maintain a state of readiness from dawn to dusk was not much appreciated by the pilots'.[22] However, operations did not let up and the Hornchurch Wing was allocated roles in two Circus operations during the day.

The flying day started early and the wing's pilots gathered at dispersals at 05:00 to be briefed for the first operation, in which they were to provide target support with Bader's Tangmere Wing for an attack on two power stations near Lens. It was another successful operation for Eric, and he was able to claim his second victory in three days.

Date	8 July 1941
Operation	Circus 39
Target	Works and power station, three miles east-north-east of Lens, and Mazingarbe Power Station, Nord-Pas-de-Calais
Bombers	No. 3 Group: three Stirling Is
Escort	Kenley: 258 and 312 Squadrons (Hurricane IIa/b) and No. 485 Squadron (Spitfire IIa)
Escort Cover	Biggin Hill: Nos 92 and 609 Squadrons (Spitfire Vb)
Target Support	Hornchurch: Nos 54, 603 and 611 Squadrons (Spitfire Va/b) Tangmere: Nos 145, 610 and 616 Squadrons (Spitfire IIa/b and Va/b)
Rear Support	Hornchurch: No. 222 Squadron (Spitfire IIa/b) Northolt: No. 306 Squadron (Spitfire IIa)

The bombers and the Escort and Escort Cover Wings rendezvoused 8,000 feet over Rye at 06:00 hours and set course for Boulogne. As landfall was made, accurate heavy flak opened up on the formation, which diverted from its course and made landfall anew over Hardelot. The remaining approach to the Lens area was undertaken without further interruption and two of the Stirlings attacked the power station near Lens, while the third attacked the power station at Mazingarbe.

Ten 1,000lb bombs and twenty 500lb bombs were dropped on the former objective from 7,800 feet, and accurate bursts were seen across the power station, resulting in 'dense smoke edged with red flames'.[23] Mazingarbe was targeted with five bombs of 1,000lb and ten of 500lb from an altitude of 8,000 feet. All bar one bomb overshot their mark, the exception striking the gasometer, which burst into flames and caused a plume of grey smoke that reached up to 2,000 feet. One of the two bombers that attacked the power station at Lens was hit by an accurate flak burst on leaving the area and crashed, killing five of the crew. The remaining two aircraft fortunately returned safely.

On reaching the target area, a number of Me109s approached the Escort Wing at the same altitude, and one was shot down by No. 312 Squadron. However, no direct attacks were made on the bombers. Shortly before the formation crossed back out at Gravelines, the Luftwaffe reappeared and engaged the Escort Wing, resulting in two enemy aircraft damaged, but three pilots lost to the wing – one killed and two who evaded capture and returned home via Spain.

Biggin's Escort Cover Wing rendezvoused with the main formation over Rye and accompanied them to the French coast where they were attacked by a lone Me109. It dived out of the sun, through the formation, then half-rolled and fired two white Verey lights, suggesting it was signalling to other enemy aircraft in the region. However, although Luftwaffe formations were subsequently sighted on the way to Lens, none made serious attacks. Three Me109s also approached to within 1,000 yards astern of the wing, positioning themselves to attack, but when some of the pilots turned and dived towards them, they broke away and did not return. On the way back to the coast, the Luftwaffe was encountered again and in the ensuing combats one Me109 was claimed destroyed, one probably destroyed and one damaged, but one pilot was shot down and baled out into the Channel.

The Hornchurch Wing was airborne between 05:35 and 05:40 hours to provide target support. As Squadron Leader Thomas did not participate, both No. 611 Squadron and the wing were led by Wing Commander Stapleton; the other two sections were led by Flight Lieutenants Lock and Hayter. The wing made landfall 18,500 feet over Gravelines and headed towards the south of St Omer, where they encountered approximately fifteen Me109Es above them at 20,000 feet. A 'general dog-fight'[24] ensued, which split up the wing, but the pilots were also compelled to keep an eye on several additional pairs of Me109s circling above the melee looking for an opportunity to pounce.

Stapleton chased a pair of Me109s and closed rapidly on one, until reaching a range of 300 yards where he opened fire with a two-second burst with his cannons and machine guns with a quarter ring deflection. When he saw no result of his fire, but recognised that the second aircraft was now in a better position for an attack than the first, he moved his attention to it instead. He fired a four-second burst at the latter from dead astern with his cannons and machine guns, and closed from 350 yards to 300 as he did, causing the Messerschmitt to flip over on its back and spin out of the combat. Stapleton banked and followed the aircraft down, but it continued earthwards at speed until it exploded on impact with the ground.

Pilot Officer Wilfred Duncan Smith, who was the No. 3 in Eric's Charlie Section, was separated from the section during this initial dogfight south of St Omer, and therefore linked up with Wing Commander Stapleton. He shadowed the wing commander during his attack on the first of two Me109s, but when Stapleton moved his attention to his second target, Duncan Smith took up the attack on the first. Firing a long burst with both his cannons and machine guns in a diving beam attack, he struck the Messerschmitt's starboard wing and saw a large piece dislodge and fly off. As the aircraft was in a turn to port at this moment, the loss of a portion of its starboard wing caused it to flip over and spin down out of control. He claimed the Me109 destroyed and subsequently witnessed Stapleton shooting down the other.

The wing partly re-formed a few miles north of Lens and orbited for about five minutes before it was split up again when set upon from above by more Messerschmitts at around 06:30 hours. This was when Eric spotted five Me109Es up-sun, at a higher altitude. He manoeuvred his depleted section in an effort to get behind them, but they were attacked by another small group of Messerschmitts. Evading them, Eric turned the tables, chose the last Me109 in the group, and fired a short burst of cannon 'but missed'.[25] Realising he was now alone and boxed in by a number of Messerschmitts, he applied the skills honed over many combats and spiralled down and away in a steep diving turn. He continued down to approximately 4,000 feet before arresting his dive and, upon levelling out, spotted a lone Me109 on a converging course.

Turning towards it, he executed a beam attack on the aircraft, opening with a brief burst of cannon fire from 300 yards, closing to 200. Immediately belching smoke, the Me109 took swift evasive action but Eric followed it down. However, the Messerschmitt was mortally damaged and he watched from approximately 2,000 feet as the aircraft continued its dive until it hit the ground near a wood. Seeing some troops nearby, Eric resumed his dive and sprayed them with a quick burst of machine-gun fire, before climbing again to find the squadron.

As he did, he was attacked by a trio of Me109s and was compelled to take immediate evasive action once again. Deciding it was time he 'pulled the plug',[26] he quickly withdrew and headed home alone at zero feet. Eric claimed the Me109 destroyed for the expenditure of just forty-four rounds of 20mm cannon ammunition, and had fired only another forty rounds of .303-inch machine-gun ammunition at the troops.

Charlie 4, Sergeant Pilot Norman 'Tubby' Townsend, had become separated from his No. 1, but remained within the squadron formation, seeking a suitable target. After several turns at approximately 15,000 feet, he spotted an Me109E diving away northwards and gave chase. Bringing himself to within 300 yards range, he fired a short, ineffective burst at the aircraft. He dived after the Messerschmitt and quickly closed to 150 yards where he opened up again with a solid five-second burst. This had the desired effect and the aircraft burst into flames. Smoke billowed from it and oil sprayed back and covered Townsend's windscreen. He watched as the damaged Me109 'fell away with pieces flying off',[27] but it passed underneath his aircraft as he overshot the position and ultimately did not see the aircraft crash. Finding himself alone between 3,000 and 4,000 feet, Townsend dived as low as possible and made a beeline for the coast and home. He arrived back at Hornchurch to find his spinner and wings smeared with oil, and claimed the Messerschmitt destroyed.

Flight Lieutenant Jan Bruinier had other problems to contend with, as his seat collapsed while he was manoeuvring for combat, and this sent him into a spin. He was eventually able to pull out of it and returned home at zero feet, sitting low in the cockpit, his sight hindered and unable to properly operate the controls. He crash-landed his aircraft at Hornchurch, without flaps or brakes, and wrote off both the aircraft and a small brick storage hut, but luckily sustained no personal injury. The wing was back on the ground between 07:15 and 07:30 hours. The other squadrons had also enjoyed some success, claiming three Me109s destroyed and four damaged.

Meanwhile, the Tangmere Wing had crossed in over Hardelot and proceeded to the target area without hindrance. A handful of Me109s were seen in the distance, but they were too far away to engage. Having circled Lens for the allotted time, the wing followed the bombers back out, leaving the coast over Gravelines. A few Messerschmitts shadowed them but did not bother them and the pilots returned safely, reporting the operation as uneventful.

Hornchurch and Northolt's Rear Support Wing both patrolled mid-Channel at low altitude, but were not engaged. No. 306 Squadron saw two Spitfires go into the Channel and circled one pilot until ordered to land. They had nothing else to report.

There was no further operational flying until after lunch, when Wing Commander Stapleton led the wing on a second Circus, on this occasion to Lille as Target Support Wing. It was a very hot afternoon, during which temperatures reached around 100°F (c. 38°C).

Date	8 July 1941
Operation	Circus 40
Target	Établissements Kuhlmann et Cie Chemical Factory and Power Station, Chocques, and Lille Power Station, Nord-Pas-de-Calais
Bombers	No. 3 Group: three Stirling Is
Escort	North Weald: Nos 71 and 242 Squadrons (Hurricane IIa/b)
	Hornchurch: No. 222 Squadron (Spitfire IIa/b)
Escort Cover	Northolt: Nos 303 and 308 Squadrons (Spitfire IIa/b)
Target Support	Hornchurch: Nos 54, 603 and 611 Squadrons (Spitfire Va/b)
	Tangmere: Nos 145, 610 and 616 Squadrons (Spitfire IIa/b and Va/b)
Diversion	No. 12 Group, Duxford: No. 56 Squadron (Hurricane IIb)
	No. 12 Group, Kirton-in-Lindsey: No. 65 Squadron (Spitfire IIa)
	No. 12 Group, Matlaske: No. 601 Squadron (Hurricane IIb)
Rear Support	Kenley: Nos 258 and 312 Squadrons (Hurricane IIa/b) and No. 485 Squadron (Spitfire IIa)
Mopping-up	Biggin Hill: Nos 92 and 609 Squadrons (Spitfire Vb)

The Stirlings rendezvoused with the Escort, Escort Cover and Target Support Wings over Manston at 15:00 and subsequently made landfall on the French coast east of Dunkirk. They were greeted by inaccurate light flak but remained unmolested for the rest of the journey to Lille, where accurate heavy flak opened up on the formation.

Two of the bombers successfully attacked the Kuhlmann works, and the third attacked Lille Power Station, dropping between them a total of fifteen 1,000lb bombs and thirty 500lb bombs from an altitude of 14,000 feet. However, on account

BACK TO WORK   171

of the flak barrage, all three were forced to take 'extreme' evasive action and no clear results of their bombing were observed. Nonetheless, as the formation headed out, clouds of dust and smoke were seen rising over the target area.

As the formation headed for the coast, three red-nosed Me109s made ineffective head-on strikes on the bombers. They were closely followed by two more Me109s, which made attacks from the bombers' forward port quarter. No. 242 Squadron dived after the latter aircraft and one pilot fired at them, claiming one of the Messerschmitts damaged. A sixth Me109 also attacked one of the Stirlings from astern, but was chased off by No. 222 Squadron. No. 71 Squadron was pounced on by a group of nine Messerschmitts shortly after leaving Lille, and while four pilots fired, none made claims and no casualties were sustained. The French coast was re-crossed at Gravelines and all three bombers returned safely, albeit with varying degrees of flak damage.

Northolt's Escort Cover Wing observed the bombing, which they reported to have been accurate. No. 308 Squadron was then attacked by a number of Me109s in response to which several pilots fired and one Me109 was claimed destroyed. One pilot also failed to return from the operation and was later reported to be a prisoner of war. No. 303 Squadron was heavily attacked by three formations of four Me109s, which simultaneously dived on the unit from their starboard and stern port quarter. Two pilots were killed and one wounded, but they claimed one Me109 destroyed.

Airborne at 14:40 hours, the Hornchurch Wing rendezvoused with the main formation over Manston between 24,000 and 26,000 feet. They moved forward after crossing the French coast and arrived over the target area ahead of the main formation at 15:27. At this time, the wing descended to 20,000 feet and orbited while it awaited the arrival of the bombers, only to look up to see fourteen Me109s cross above them from east to west at approximately the same altitude from which they had descended only minutes before. Caught at a distinct disadvantage, it was no surprise when the enemy aircraft turned and dived on to the wing, making a beeline for a section of No. 603 Squadron in the middle of the configuration. However, the wing hastily split up, and managed to evade their strike. Their attack foiled, several small formations of Messerschmitts circled above the wing awaiting a new opportunity, and just one section of three descended in an effort to fly through them, towards the approaching bombers.

Shortly thereafter, a formation of four Me109s dived on to the rearguard of No. 611 Squadron, and it was possibly in this attack that the unit sustained the wing's only casualty of the operation, Sergeant Pilot Brian Feeley, who failed to return. No one saw what happened to him, but Wing Commander Stapleton later reported seeing a parachute descending in the region of the battle, which was thought to have been Feeley. He was, however, killed.

The wing also exacted its own damage on the Luftwaffe and claimed several victories. No. 611 Squadron claimed two Me109s destroyed and two probably destroyed, while Nos 54 and 603 Squadrons each claimed two Me109s destroyed. Eric was unable to make a claim, but his Nos 2 and 3, Sergeant Pilot William Gilmour and Flying Officer Peter Dexter, both returned victorious.

Charlie 2, Sergeant Pilot William Gilmour, suddenly spotted an Me109E in close proximity, about to attack him from astern. Executing violent evasive action, he half-turned to port, throttled back, and allowed his Spitfire to side-slip. The tactic worked well and the Messerschmitt overshot him to starboard. Taking the upper hand, Gilmour turned back after it and expended a four- to five-second burst of cannon and machine-gun fire at its rear port quarter. His attack resulted in a flash under the cowling in the Messerschmitt's bow, and the engine burst into flames and emitted black smoke. Its pilot broke to port to evade further fire from Gilmour and dived away. Gilmour went to follow him but thought better of it, considering this would make him an easy mark for other enemy aircraft milling around. He climbed instead to 20,000 feet and followed the bombers on a parallel course to their heading, on their starboard side. He was soon joined by No. 611 Squadron's Sergeant Pilots Summers and Townsend, and the trio headed out together, crossing the French coast west of Dunkirk. Gilmour claimed the Me109 probably destroyed.

Flying as Charlie 3, Flying Officer Peter Dexter became separated from his section during the initial evasive action south of Lille, but managed to join up with another (unidentified) squadron over Lille, and headed back out with them. On the way, he spotted Eric diving in pursuit of an Me109, and left the safety of the formation to go to his aid and followed him down. As he dived after Eric, however, he was attacked from astern by an Me109 and compelled to scrap his plan and take evasive action instead. Shaking off the Messerschmitt, but thereby losing Eric, he climbed again to rejoin the bombers. While doing so, he sighted another Me109 and, being in an advantageous position, gave chase. He had fired a burst of just half a second when the enemy aircraft dived vertically. Dexter followed him down, only a short distance behind him, but pulled out of his dive below 1,000 feet. Although he did not see the Me109 crash, he last saw the aircraft at 500 feet, still diving vertically, and felt that, 'at the speed he was travelling there was very little probability of him being able to pull out'.[28]

While climbing again, Dexter was caught at low altitude by three Me109s and forced to drop to ground level to evade them. He was pursued all the way to the coast above the treetops and was only able to lose them when he entered sea mist over the Channel. Climbing once again, he turned back for the French coast and sighted a quartet of Me109s orbiting at just 500 feet over a beach south of Gravelines. Attacking one of the aircraft, he saw it 'spin into the ground with Glycol pouring out',[29] before he broke away and quickly headed home, pursued partway across the Channel by the other three. Dexter landed safely back at Hornchurch to claim his first Me109 probably destroyed and his second destroyed.

Sergeant Pilot Donald Fair, RNZAF, also claimed an Me109E destroyed, but details of his combat have not survived. The prolonged series of combats and evasive actions split the wing up considerably and pilots returned across the Channel individually or in small groups, some with fuel issues, others with navigational problems, 'landing as far apart as Coltishall, Stradishall, and Detling'.[30]

Tangmere's Target Support Wing headed to France independently and made landfall at Hardelot. On reaching Lille, the squadrons orbited the target area for fifteen minutes and then headed home. While circling, No. 616 saw a number of enemy aircraft, some of which were attacked without success. No. 610 Squadron sighted several Me109s above them, which resulted in a number of combats and evasive actions. These concluded with the claim of one Me109 destroyed for the loss of one pilot, who was shot down and captured, and another wounded. No. 145 Squadron also saw action. They were unable to make any claims, but lost one pilot killed and a second shot down and captured.

No. 12 Group's Diversion Wing rendezvoused over West Malling, crossed out over Dungeness and proceeded across the Channel until striking the French coast at Berck-sur-Mer. Descending 4,000–5,000 feet, the three squadrons then patrolled an area from Gravelines to west of St Omer and back. Two Me109Fs were sighted in the St Omer area, which were attacked, and one was claimed destroyed by No. 56 Squadron. Splitting into individual squadrons, the wing descended further and maintained a patrol off Gravelines to cover the withdrawal of the main formation. While doing so, an estimated fifty Messerschmitts were seen, and in the resulting combats No. 65 Squadron claimed two destroyed and one probably destroyed. Despite the large number of enemy aircraft encountered, the wing reported no casualties.

Kenley's Rear Support Wing patrolled the Goodwin Sands area between 15:15 and 16:35 hours. Only three enemy aircraft were seen when they approached a pilot of No. 485 Squadron head-on. They passed beneath him and he turned round after them, attacked one and claimed it destroyed. The final element of the Circus, Biggin's Mopping-Up Wing, swept from Gravelines, across the return route of the main formation, and then turned above it to follow the bombers out. They saw no enemy aircraft and returned with nothing to report.

Eric undertook no operational flying for the following three days, and made his next operational sortie on 12 July. That day, the wing was only called upon for one operation, which took place ahead of a break in the weather and heavy thunderstorms in the evening that cut power lines and left the station isolated for a few hours.

Date	12 July 1941
Operation	Circus 46
Target	St Omer Ship Lift, Arques, Pas-de-Calais
Bombers	No. 3 Group: three Stirling Is
Escort	Kenley: Nos 258 and 312 Squadrons (Hurricane IIa/b) and No. 485 Squadron (Spitfire IIa)
Escort Cover	Hornchurch: Nos 54, 603 and 611 Squadrons (Spitfire Va/b)
Target Support	Northolt: Nos 303 and 308 Squadrons (Spitfire IIa/b) Tangmere: Nos 145, 610 and 616 Squadrons (Spitfire IIa/b and Va/b)
Forward Support	No. 12 Group, Fowlmere: No. 19 Squadron (Spitfire IIa) No. 12 Group, Duxford: No. 56 Squadron (Hurricane IIb) No. 12 Group, Coltishall: No. 257 Squadron (Hurricane IIb)
Rear Support	Northolt: No. 306 Squadron (Spitfire IIa) North Weald: No. 242 Squadron (Hurricane IIa/b)

The Stirlings rendezvoused with their Escort and Escort Cover Wings over Manston at 10:00 hours and headed out together via North Foreland. Landfall was made at Gravelines seventeen minutes later, and the coast was crossed again near Hardelot at 10:35. As the formation travelled southwards, they attracted the attention of heavy flak, which was accurate in both height and position, and all three bombers sustained light damage. However, the target was reached without interference from the Luftwaffe and no flak was encountered in the St Omer area.

On reaching Arques, two Stirlings dropped their payloads, totalling forty-three 500lb bombs, from 12,000 feet. The third Stirling had difficulties with the release mechanism and was unable to bomb the ship lift, but succeeded in fixing the problem and bombed the railway line at Remilly-Wirquin, where a direct hit was observed. Only one enemy aircraft was seen by the bombers, which caused them no trouble, and although Kenley's Escort Wing sighted several more, none made any serious attempt to attack the formation.

It was a different matter for Hornchurch's Escort Cover Wing, however. Airborne at 09:30, the squadrons crossed the Channel with the main formation between 18,000 and 21,000 feet. No. 611 Squadron was led by Wing Commander Stapleton, and all the other positions in the squadron formation, bar two, were flown by officer pilots, thereunder Squadron Leader Thomas and Flight Lieutenants Bruinier, Hayter and Lock. Notwithstanding the attention they were given by the coastal flak batteries, the wing proceeded to the St Omer area without trouble, breaking into fours on arrival in the region.

No. 603 Squadron was intercepted by eight enemy aircraft just as they were about to turn west over the target to head out at 21,000 feet. These aircraft approached from the south at the same altitude, but five of them spotted a better prey and turned west to dive on No. 54 Squadron. The remaining three flew due north and climbed to give them a better advantage over No. 603 Squadron, but were chased by pilots of that unit as they did. No. 603 ultimately succeeded in damaging two of them.

At the same time as this engagement was taking place, the rest of the unit was attacked from astern by a further six Me109s. The squadron's pilots saw them coming, turned to meet them, and a dogfight ensued in which one enemy aircraft was destroyed, one probably destroyed and two damaged for no loss. The squadron re-formed and attempted to catch up with the bombers, which were now a significant distance ahead. They were unable to do so and ultimately returned independently via Calais.

No. 54 Squadron was engaged by a further seven Me109s. One was claimed damaged by Stapleton, but one of the unit's pilots was shot down and captured. No. 611 Squadron was not engaged throughout the operation, and escorted the main formation out over Hardelot and as far as Dungeness, where they parted company and headed for Hornchurch. The pilots landed at 11:00 with nothing to report, and were kept on readiness through the afternoon of this 'scorching hot day',[31] while Nos 54 and 603 Squadrons were released off camp until the following morning.

Meanwhile, Northolt and Tangmere's Target Support Wings were also completing their own roles in the operation. Nos 303 and 308 Squadrons operated on the same route as the main formation, but arrived in the target area ahead of it. Descending a few thousand feet on account of haze over the St Omer area, No. 303 Squadron was attacked repeatedly by enemy aircraft in formations of two and four. In the ensuing combats, one Me109 was claimed destroyed for no loss. No. 308 Squadron was engaged in a similar way on leaving the target, claiming two Me109s destroyed for the loss of one pilot who was killed.

Operating independently as usual, the Tangmere Wing reached the St Omer area at 10:15 hours. They proceeded to orbit the target area, but had only done so once when twenty Me109s were seen climbing in line astern formation from south of Dunkirk. No. 616 Squadron attacked them while they still had the advantage of height and claimed one destroyed, one probably destroyed and four damaged without loss. The wing then headed home over Gravelines, without further issue.

No. 12 Group's Forward Support Wing crossed out over Dungeness, traversed the Channel, and patrolled between Hardelot and Le Touquet. Two full patrols were made up and down the coast, but only five enemy aircraft were sighted, which avoided any engagement. In a similar vein, Northolt's No. 306 Squadron, acting as rear support, patrolled ten miles south-east of Dungeness. They sighted a further three enemy aircraft, which also made no attempt to engage them, and these two components of the operation both returned with little to report.

Following a day on the ground as a result of continuing stormy weather, the squadron was airborne at 09:45 hours on 14 July to provide an escort for Circus 48 to Hazebrouck Marshalling Yards. Eric had another successful day, and managed to claim his third victory in two weeks.

Date	14 July 1941
Operation	Circus 48
Target	Hazebrouck Marshalling Yards, Nord-Pas-de-Calais
Bombers	No. 2 Group: six Blenheim IVs
Escort	North Weald: Nos 71 and 242 Squadrons (Hurricane IIa/b)
	Hornchurch: No. 222 Squadron (Spitfire IIa/b)
Escort Cover	Hornchurch: Nos 54, 603 and 611 Squadrons (Spitfire Va/b)
Target Support	Biggin Hill: Nos 72, 92 and 609 Squadrons (Spitfire Vb)
	Tangmere: Nos 145, 610 and 616 Squadrons (Spitfire IIa/b and Va/b)
Forward Support	Kenley: Nos 485 and 602 Squadrons (Spitfire IIa)
Rear Support	Debden: No. 258 Squadron (Hurricane IIa)
	Kenley: No. 312 Squadron (Hurricane IIb)

The Escort and Escort Cover Wings rendezvoused with the Blenheims 12,000 feet over Southend at 10:00. The formation then headed across the Channel to make landfall just east of Gravelines at 10:22, and Hazebrouck Marshalling Yards were reached twelve minutes later. The Blenheims made their attack without hindrance from flak or the Luftwaffe, and dropped a total of twenty-four 250lb bombs and twenty-four 40lb bombs from an altitude of 10,000 feet. Some were seen to undershoot the target, while a few overshot, but the vast majority accurately straddled the rail yards. On the way home, enemy aircraft were seen that did not attempt to attack them, but accurate flak was encountered over Hardelot, which damaged three bombers, although they returned safely to base.

North Weald and Hornchurch's Escort Wing encountered a little flak on making landfall near Gravelines, but reached the target area before the Luftwaffe was seen for the first time. No. 242 Squadron sighted two Me109s attempting to attack a Spitfire, which evaded. They fired two short bursts at the offending aircraft, but were unable to make any claims. No. 71 Squadron only spotted half a dozen aircraft during the entire operation, but they were too far away to engage. No. 222 Squadron could only report a routine operation in which they escorted the bombers back out over Hardelot and as far as Dungeness.

BACK TO WORK

Airborne between 09:40 and 09:45 hours, the Hornchurch Wing rendezvoused with the bombers over Southend according to plan, and remained with them throughout the operation. Owing to pilot shortages, however, No. 611 Squadron could only muster ten pilots. Wing Commander Stapleton therefore flew with the unit as an eleventh man but, in a first for Eric, he led both a flight and the squadron with Stapleton as his No. 2, while Squadron Leader Thomas led the second flight. Soon after crossing the French coast at Gravelines, and thereafter all the way to Hazebrouck, small formations of enemy aircraft were seen high above the wing in the sun.

Despite this advantage, only a single Me109 made any attempt to attack the wing. This aircraft dived on a section of No. 603 Squadron, which was the top squadron in the wing formation, and shot down Sergeant Pilot Hunter who went down smoking and was subsequently captured. The attacker then became the prey but the best the squadron could do was to claim the Messerschmitt damaged. The unit was shadowed above and behind by a pair of enemy aircraft on the way back out to the coast at Hardelot, which made a few unsuccessful 'darting attacks' on stragglers.

However, larger numbers of enemy fighters in varying formations appeared just inland from Hardelot, which were engaged by both Nos 54 and 611 Squadrons. Diving to attack some of these aircraft near Boulogne, No. 611 Squadron's Flying Officer Peter Dexter collided with No. 54 Squadron's Sergeant Pilot John Panter, and only one parachute was seen after the incident. It was subsequently established that Panter had been captured but Dexter had been killed. Despite this setback, the wing achieved two victories against the Luftwaffe, with one Me109 claimed destroyed by No. 54 Squadron and a second claimed destroyed by Eric.

No Combat Report has survived for Eric's victory, but the squadron ORB records that he returned to base at 11:10 hours, 'talking nineteen to the dozen having had his "arse" chased off him by immeasurable Jerries but as he had fired at one 109 and saw 3 disintegrate at the same moment one can hardly blame him'.[32] This statement implies that Eric destroyed three aircraft, but no other source or evidence supports this suggestion. It is generally accepted that Eric claimed one Me109F destroyed near Boulogne on this occasion, and this is also supported by entries in the RAF Hornchurch and No. 11 Group ORBs. It would, however, also be his last.

Meanwhile, Biggin's Target Support Wing crossed the French Coast over Le Touquet and immediately sighted large formations of Me109s just inland waiting. Several engagements ensued, which resulted in one Me109F being destroyed by No. 609 Squadron for the loss of one pilot of No. 72 Squadron, who was shot down and captured. The number of enemy aircraft concentrated in the area prohibited the wing from reaching the target and they were unable to fulfil their brief.

The Tangmere Wing entered France over Boulogne and No. 616 Squadron flew straight to the target area, where it orbited in sections of four. One pilot broke away to attack a formation of three Me109s and shot one of them down, blowing off its tail with cannon fire. Few further enemy aircraft were seen, but one was subsequently claimed damaged.

No. 145 Squadron broke away from the wing formation shortly after crossing in to intercept a number of enemy aircraft. However, their intended targets evaded and climbed away, which resulted in the squadron becoming broken up. One section of four proceeded independently to the target area but when returning to the coast was unsuccessfully attacked at long range by a trio of Me109s. The section fired back, and one Me109 was claimed damaged before they continued to the coast and safely home. The remainder of the squadron had meanwhile patrolled the Calais–Boulogne–Cap Gris Nez area where a number of enemy aircraft were sighted but not engaged. They waited for the bombers to pass by and then followed them out over Hardelot.

After crossing in, No. 610 Squadron followed No. 145 Squadron's lead, going after enemy aircraft in the vicinity but, after a brief unsuccessful chase, regrouped and headed inland towards the south of St Omer. Around ten enemy aircraft approached the squadron in the Dunkirk area, passing them down their port side before turning about in an attempt to attack them from astern. However, after a complete orbit as the enemy aircraft came around and the squadron followed them around to hinder the move, the Luftwaffe gave up and dived away to the south. The squadron orbited the target area during which several Me109s were seen, and one formation of four made an unsuccessful head-on assault on the unit. The French coast was left at Hardelot and the unit returned home, reporting no victories or casualties despite several engagements.

Kenley's Forward Support Wing made landfall over Le Touquet and patrolled a line six miles inland between Le Touquet and Boulogne. No. 485 Squadron only spotted two Me109s throughout the operation, but they climbed away and avoided an engagement. No. 602 Squadron sighted large numbers of aircraft, but most were Spitfires. A few Me109s were also seen, and one was engaged and destroyed five miles south-west of Boulogne. Finally, Debden and Kenley's Rear Support Wing rendezvoused with each other over Dungeness, then proceeded to patrol the Channel ten miles south-east of Dungeness. They saw no sign of the Luftwaffe and returned to base with nothing to report.

Following Flying Officer Dexter's loss on the 14th, No. 611 Squadron's shortage of pilots and aircraft was now considered 'acute', and the squadron could only muster thirteen operational pilots. A fourteenth was not yet cleared to fly over

BACK TO WORK   179

France, and although three new pilots arrived on that date, two were fresh from a Hurricane OTU and had never flown a Spitfire, while the third had been rested as an instructor at an OTU for the previous twelve months. The latter man was the only one considered 'anything like operational'.[33]

No. 611 Squadron's pilots spent most of 15 July on the ground on account of poor weather, but conditions had improved sufficiently by the evening for seven uneventful Barrow Deep patrols to be undertaken between 18:05 and 22:55 hours. Eric participated in two of these with Sergeant Pilot William Gilmour, the first taking place between 18:45 and 19:45, and the second from 21:50 to 22:55. The latter constituted the last operational patrol of the evening.

The squadron was woken early the following morning for a Circus operation, which was due to commence at 07:00. However, when it was cancelled at 06:15, the pilots were redeployed on further Barrow Deep patrols, which were undertaken between 07:30 and 10:50. Eric only took part in one of these, paired up once again with Gilmour, from 09:50 to 10:50. As the weather was fairly cloudy, with intermittent rain, no further operational flying was undertaken for the rest of the day.

Two new pilots arrived from No. 124 Squadron at Castletown on the 15th, but one pilot had flown no operational hours and the other had only logged five operational hours on convoy patrols. As neither was considered 'fit to take on offensive sweeps',[34] their arrivals did nothing to alleviate the squadron's pilot shortage.

It was another very early start for the pilots on 17 July. They were woken at 03:30 and gathered in the mess at 06:00 for coffee and a briefing. However, at 06:15 the operation was postponed and the squadron was ultimately not airborne at all until 16:10. At that time, twelve pilots, including Eric, undertook a fighter sweep of the Gravelines–St Omer–Le Touquet area. 'A few rather timid 109Fs'[35] were sighted, but avoided contact and climbed out of range. Eric's No. 4, Pilot Officer Michael Gardner, made the only claim of the afternoon when he attacked an Me109F near Le Touquet.

The squadron was flying on a south-westerly course when four Me109Fs cautiously approached them at a slightly higher altitude. Gardner turned to port and climbed towards them but they were out of his range. The Messerschmitts turned north and continued around into the sun where he lost them. Giving up on them, Gardner turned to port at 25,000 feet to return to the squadron when a cannon shell struck his fuselage and smoke emitted from underneath his seat. Immediately throttling back and applying a hard left rudder, he forced his attacker to overshoot, and an Me109F passed down his port side. Turning after the aircraft, Gardner quickly positioned himself on its tail and opened fire with his cannons and machine guns at a range of just 150 yards. His attack caused the Messerschmitt's entire tail unit to break off and the aircraft half-rolled and went straight down, with pieces dislodging themselves as it went. Gardner followed the fatally damaged aircraft down to 10,000 feet before leaving it to its inevitable fate, noting that the pilot did not bale out during the descent.

Gardner then headed for home but was hit by flak, which damaged a wingtip and punctured the skin of his fuselage, but fortunately did not injure him. He therefore dropped to ground level, made for the coast as quickly as he could, and crossed out near Le Touquet. He arrived at Hornchurch to claim the Messerschmitt destroyed, and the rest of the squadron was back on the ground by 17:35 hours.

During the day, four more pilots arrived on the unit, one from No. 123 Squadron who had flown no operational hours, one from No. 124 Squadron with little experience, and, at last, two experienced pilots, who arrived from No. 66 Squadron.

Eric was not airborne operationally for the ensuing thirty-six hours and was next up with the squadron in the late afternoon of 20 July. During this period, he sat for a portrait by Captain Cuthbert Orde, a gifted artist and First World War pilot, who had been commissioned by Air Commodore Harald Peake to sketch approximately 160 Battle of Britain fighter pilots. Some of Eric's contemporaries from his time on No. 41 Squadron had already posed for their own portraits earlier in the year – Flight Lieutenants Norman Ryder and Tony Lovell and Squadron Leader Don Finlay – but Eric's was presumably delayed until 19 July as a result of his wounding and hospitalisation.

Cloudy conditions with intermittent rain delayed operational flying until shortly before midday on 20 July when No. 611 Squadron was airborne to provide target support for an abortive attack on Hazebrouck in Circus 52. However, 10/10ths cloud to 10,000 feet over France prohibited the bombers from dropping their payloads and they jettisoned their bombs into the Barrow Deep Channel. On account of the cloud cover, No. 611 Squadron saw nothing and was back on the ground shortly after 13:00 hours.

Flying practice was undertaken by the squadron after lunch, but the pilots were airborne again operationally during the late afternoon, this time including Eric. Working in unison with No. 54 Squadron, the pilots were tasked with determining the success of one of two Roadstead (anti-shipping) operations that had taken place earlier in the day.

The first Roadstead comprised six Blenheim bombers, escorted by Nos 222 and 242 Squadrons, which were targeting a tanker off Dunkirk. While No. 242 Squadron took on a guardian flak ship, the Blenheims went after the tanker but missed. Another Roadstead took place later, in which a second tanker was attacked off Le Touquet by another six Blenheims, escorted once again by Nos 222 and 242 Squadrons. On this occasion, the bombers' efforts were more successful and the tanker was hit and beached itself near Berck-sur-Mer.

It was now Nos 54 and 611 Squadrons' job to establish the damage inflicted in the latter attack. Airborne at 17:45, the wing and No. 611 Squadron were led by Wing Commander Stapleton. The pilots made their way to Le Touquet without opposition, were able to locate the tanker, and observed that it was being closely guarded by a number of Me109s. No. 54 Squadron attacked the enemy aircraft and Flight Lieutenant 'Jack' Charles, DFC, shot one of them into the sea. With the Luftwaffe occupied by No. 54 Squadron, No. 611 Squadron was able to make a closer inspection of the tanker, and it was seen to have been considerably holed.

The wing returned to Hornchurch between 18:45 and 19:00 hours without casualties, and, for their part, No. 611 Squadron reported the operation as uneventful. No. 611 then spent the rest of the evening on readiness and were finally released at 22:30.

The Guinea Pig Club

At Queen Victoria Hospital at East Grinstead, where Eric had undergone skin grafting operations for the wounds he sustained in November 1940, perhaps the most exclusive society in the world was founded on this day. Initially intended as a drinking club, the so-called 'Guinea Pig Club' originally comprised thirty-nine of Dr Archibald McIndoe's current and former patients. The name represented their role in the pioneering nature of the surgery McIndoe was undertaking at the hospital.

With the exception of a few honorary members, such as McIndoe himself, membership could only be gained by a member of the RAF or Allied air forces who had undergone at least two reconstructive skin grafting procedures at QVH. The latter criterion was one that none could possibly aspire to, making it the only exclusive club that no one wanted to be a member of.

However, embedded in the black humour that had inevitably become a defence mechanism around the terrible injuries and wounds being treated, the club was formed on 20 July 1941 with three membership levels:

1. The Guinea Pigs (the patients themselves)
2. The Scientists (the surgeons and medical staff)
3. The Royal Society for the Prevention of Cruelty to Guinea Pigs (friends and benefactors)

In keeping with this theme, QVH was called 'The Sty' and, naturally, the Guinea

Pigs' children were called 'the Piglets'. They refrained from extending the analogies to wives and significant others, perhaps out of respect, or perhaps recognising that they had survived thus far and it was not worth pushing their luck!

While the Guinea Pigs, or 'Pigs' as they informally referred to themselves, nominated Archibald McIndoe as the president and Squadron Leader Tom Gleave as vice-president, the appointments of the secretary and treasurer were carried with the same style of black humour that came to embody the formation of the club. Flying Officer Bill Towers-Perkins was elected as club secretary as his hands were so badly burned that he was unable to write letters and keep minutes, and Pilot Officer Peter Weeks became the treasurer as his legs were so seriously burned that he was unable to walk and members would be reassured that he could not abscond with the funds. These were initially levied at 2s 6d per annum.

Apparently not present for the actual inaugural event, a number of other former patients were proposed and seconded as members of the club. They included Eric and No. 41 Squadron's Flying Officer 'Ben' Bennions, who had been shot down and seriously wounded approximately six weeks before Eric, on 1 October 1940. They had flown together extensively on operations with No. 41 Squadron during the Battle of Britain and were the unit's two highest-scoring aces. Eric himself had undergone three procedures, Bennions several more.

Considering that Eric had flown operationally from Hornchurch during the afternoon, it is understandable that he would not have been in attendance. At the time, Bennions was also an operations officer at RAF Catterick in the north of the country, and was therefore also some distance from East Grinstead.

In time, the Guinea Pig Club grew to become a support network for its members and their families as they came to terms and dealt with the marked changes in their lives that were caused by their severe injuries. It also aimed to assist with the rehabilitation of its members during their long reconstructive treatments. By the end of the war, the club had 649 members from all across the Allied forces. Most were British (sixty-two per cent), but members included airmen from Canada (twenty per cent), Australia (six per cent) and New Zealand (six per cent), while men from Czechoslovakia, France, Poland, Russia and the United States made up the remaining six per cent.

Not unexpectedly, perhaps, throughout the early stages of the war and the Battle of Britain most members were fighter pilots. As the war progressed, however, the number of airmen of Bomber Command grew steadily until, by the cessation of hostilities in 1945, some eighty per cent of Guinea Pigs were derived from the ranks of that Command.

Despite its humble beginnings, and its formation more for socialising than any other reason, the Guinea Pig Club has survived until today, and has become a vital part of rehabilitation for burns patients and their families. The club still meets at East Grinstead and its president, at the time of writing, is the Duke of Edinburgh. The hospital itself is still renowned for its burns treatment. Although a member for only a very brief period, Eric was one of its founding members.

It was a relatively early start for No. 611 Squadron on 21 July on account of better weather than recently, and the wing attended a briefing for a Circus operation at 07:15 hours. They were assigned to the target support role for an attack on a factory in Lille in Circus 54.

Date	21 July 1941
Operation	Circus 54
Target	Atelier d'Hellemes Accumulator Factory, Lille, Nord-Pas-de-Calais
Bombers	No. 3 Group: three Stirling Is
Escort	Kenley: Nos 485 and 602 Squadrons (Spitfire IIa)
	North Weald: No. 71 Squadron (Hurricane IIa/b)
Escort Cover	Biggin Hill: Nos 72, 92 and 609 Squadrons (Spitfire Vb)
Target Support	Hornchurch: Nos 54, 603 and 611 Squadrons (Spitfire Va/b)
	Tangmere: Nos 145, 610 and 616 Squadrons (Spitfire IIa/b and Va/b)
Forward Support	Northolt: Nos 303 and 308 Squadrons (Spitfire IIa/b)
Rear Support	North Weald: No. 3 Squadron (Hurricane IIb/c)

The Stirlings and their Escort and Escort Cover Wings rendezvoused according to plan, stepped up from 15,000 feet over Clacton at 08:00, and set course for Lille. Immediately after they made landfall around seven miles east of Dunkirk, No. 602 Squadron sighted a number of Me109s high above them, flying towards the Escort Cover Wing in line abreast formation. The enemy aircraft soon swung around and dived straight through the squadron, and then pulled out of their descent and climbed again. No. 602 Squadron's pilots opened fire on them as they climbed but no results were seen.

The remainder of the formation continued to Lille without interference from the Luftwaffe. Their arrival over the target area drew the unwanted attention of accurate flak and all three Stirlings were slightly damaged. However, their payloads were dropped as planned and a total of fifteen 1,000lb bombs and thirty-six 500lb bombs were released on the accumulator factory. Some bursts were seen just south-west of the target, while others were observed on one large and two small buildings within the factory complex.

As the formation left the Lille area en route for home, two Me109s tried to attack the bombers, but No. 71 Squadron chased them off and claimed one destroyed. Another pair of the unit's pilots fired at a formation of four

Messerschmitts, but was unable to make a claim. No. 602 Squadron was attacked by enemy aircraft from above after leaving the target area and one pilot was seen to go down in a steep dive and was killed. The formation crossed out near Gravelines and made landfall on the English coast near North Foreland.

Biggin Hill's Escort Cover Wing arrived in the Lille region shadowed from astern by two or three small formations of enemy aircraft. They did not attack, but the wing was surprised to be accosted by accurate flak at 25,000 feet. This is believed to have been the cause of the loss of one of No. 609 Squadron's pilots, who was killed. In return, four Me109s were claimed damaged.

The Hornchurch Wing was airborne at 07:55 hours and proceeded to France independently of the main formation. No. 611 Squadron was led by Wing Commander Stapleton, and was supported by Flight Lieutenants Bruinier, Hayter and Lock, and also Squadron Leader Brenus Morris, who was attached from No. 403 Squadron. However, it was a less than auspicious operation for the unit as several pilots were forced to return early with technical problems, and one was unfortunately killed.

Those who returned early included Sergeant Pilot Arthur Leigh, who got off the ground five minutes late and returned within ten minutes, and Flight Lieutenant Jan Bruinier who was airborne with the rest of the squadron but came back within fifteen minutes. Additionally, Flight Lieutenant Hayter developed oil pressure trouble in the St Omer area and was escorted home by Pilot Officer Lamb and Sergeant Pilot Ingram. It is believed that Eric and Pilot Officer Michael Gardner may also have experienced issues with their aircraft as they returned at 09:10, some 15–25 minutes ahead of the rest of the pilots.

Meanwhile, upon reaching France, the remainder of the wing swept the St Inglevert, St Omer, and Mardyck areas before making its rendezvous with the main formation over Lille. A formation of six Me109Fs was sighted 25,000 feet over St Omer, which No. 54 Squadron endeavoured to attack, without observed result. Formations of four, twelve and fifteen Me109s were also seen in the Lille area. Six of the formation of twelve dived on No. 54 Squadron from 21,000 feet, but caused no damage. The pilots fought back and ultimately claimed one of their attackers destroyed.

No. 603 Squadron turned in behind the formation of fifteen, dived to attack them and claimed one destroyed and one damaged. During these actions, Sergeant Pilot Tabor lost the squadron and was diving to zero feet to head home when he sighted an Me109F with its wheels and flaps down, preparing to land at St Omer-Longuenesse Aerodrome. He swooped on the aircraft and opened fire at just 100 yards range. His target's starboard flap flew off, and then the starboard wing crumpled, detached itself and flew back towards Tabor, just missing him.

The Me109 fell to the ground and was destroyed. On his way out, he also shot up a convoy of lorries travelling towards St Omer, a watch tower in the Fôret de Clairmarais and a ship off Cap Gris Nez.

Wing Commander Stapleton detached himself from the much depleted No. 611 Squadron formation to attack a pair of Me109Fs near Lille. After two brief bursts, one of the Messerschmitts caught fire and spun down, and he claimed it destroyed. Although the remaining pilots of the unit were not involved in any combats, twenty-year-old Sergeant Pilot William Grainger was attacked and shot down.

Underscoring No. 611 Squadron's recent desperate plea for only experienced pilots to alleviate their pilot shortage – which had not been heeded – Grainger had only joined the unit on 17 July and was on his first operational sortie to France. An aircraft, believed to have been his, was seen being attacked south of Lille, after which the pilot baled out. There was, therefore, hope that he had survived and he was only posted as missing. Unfortunately, however, he did not, but what remains unexplained is the fact that he has no known grave.

The wing returned to the coast with the main formation, but concentrated their protection on one bomber in particular, which was lagging behind the others. They crossed out at Gravelines and escorted the straggler as far as Manston.

In the meantime, Bader's Tangmere Wing had also completed its own target support mission, having arrived in France independently via Le Touquet. They saw no sign of the Luftwaffe until shortly before reaching the target, when north of Lille. At that time, a pair of Me109s was seen by No. 145 Squadron, which dived away when the pilots turned to attack them. After orbiting the target area, the wing followed the bombers out, but No. 616 Squadron was chased all the way and repeatedly harassed by numbers of small formations of Me109s. The Luftwaffe failed to inflict any damage on the squadron, but one Messerschmitt was claimed probably destroyed and a second damaged. One of the unit's sections was positioning itself to attack a pair of Me109s, but they were seen, and the enemy aircraft broke to evade them. They were therefore all the more surprised to see one of the pilots bale out of his aircraft; they had not fired a shot!

No. 610 Squadron sighted a formation of four Me109s and commenced an attack, but the aircraft also dived away and evaded. Another pair was subsequently attacked without result, but one pilot took on a further five, which were clearly unaware of his presence, and he claimed two destroyed.

Northolt's Forward Support Wing made landfall between Gravelines and Dunkirk and patrolled ten miles inland. No. 308 Squadron saw a few Me109s and one pilot fired, but no results were observed. On their way back out again, No. 306 Squadron was attacked from above and behind by three Me109s, which broke and dived away without firing as soon as the squadron started to turn towards them. Another twelve Me109s in pairs were seen over Channel, and one pair attacked a pilot of No. 306 Squadron, who successfully evaded.

Finally, North Weald's Rear Support Squadron patrolled the Goodwin Sands to cover the bombers' and escorts' withdrawals. They saw no sign of the Luftwaffe and returned to base, reporting the operation uneventful.

No. 611 Squadron was airborne again with the Hornchurch Wing at 19:35 as escort cover for an abortive operation in which three Stirlings were tasked with attacking Mazingarbe. However, the bombers considered the weather unfavourable and abandoned the operation shortly after leaving the English coast. The bombers and their escorts returned to base and No. 611 was back on the ground by 20:50 hours, ending the day's flying.

Eric was not involved and, in fact, following the morning's operation, he undertook no further operational flying until the afternoon of 27 July. Although there is no evidence, it would be nice to think that he travelled home to Bayston Hill on leave, to celebrate his first wedding anniversary with Peggy.

Over the following six days, the squadron was constantly involved in Circus operations or fighter sweeps. The unit claimed two probably destroyed and one damaged Me109, but Flying Officer James 'Jimmy' Sutton was killed, and two pilots were posted away. This now left the squadron with just thirteen operational pilots. The acute pilot shortage was worse than ever and the arrival of a new pilot on 26 July did nothing to ease the problem: he had only left an OTU just ten days before.

The new NCO pilots spent the morning of 27 July undertaking practice flying, but on account of cloudy and rainy conditions it was not until after lunch that the unit was called upon operationally. Eleven pilots, including Eric, were airborne between 14:25 and 15:55 to patrol Calais at 8,000 feet in cooperation with Kenley's No. 485 Squadron. This was to provide cover for No. 242 Squadron's Hurricanes, which were escorting Motor Torpedo Boats (MTBs) tasked with attacking a Kriegsmarine destroyer and five E-boats off Calais. Neither No. 611 Squadron, providing high cover, nor No. 485 Squadron, providing follow-up cover, saw the Luftwaffe, but No. 242 Squadron, which was flying below cloud, engaged eight Me109Fs that were protecting the vessels. In the series of intensive combats, No. 242 claimed one Me109 destroyed and three probably destroyed, but lost one pilot killed.

This was Eric's first operational sortie in six days, but it was a routine operation and he saw nothing of the fight. Some ten-tenths cloud over the coast rendered visibility impossible and they were unable to assist. However, under the cover of the Luftwaffe's preoccupation with No. 242 Squadron, the MTBs were able to successfully complete their brief and the destroyer 'got a couple of torpedoes in the right place'.[36] No. 611 Squadron returned with nothing to report, and this concluded the day's flying.

Everyone was awoken at 01:30 the following morning when sixty bombers commenced an attack on Greater London, within an area reaching as far west as Reading and as far north as Debden. London itself was not targeted and damage was considered light overall. British heavy- and light-calibre anti-aircraft artillery responded in kind and continued until the last bomber left English soil at approximately 04:15.

Despite a largely sleepless night, it was an early start for the wing in misty conditions just after sunrise. All the pilots gathered at 06:45 to be briefed for an operation, but much to their frustration it was postponed on account of weather conditions. No. 611 Squadron's pilots therefore spent the operational flying day undertaking a convoy patrol and seven Barrow Deep patrols in pairs between 08:30 and 13:35. Eric participated in one of the latter, and was airborne from 10:15 to 11:15, paired up with Sergeant Pilot Richard Turlington. All of the patrols were uneventful.

There was no further operational flying for the rest of the month due to poor weather, providing the squadron with 'a much needed breather',[37] although several hours were spent on practice flying. This allowed five sergeant pilots to be declared fully operational, thereby raising the squadron's total number of operational pilots to eighteen.

It had been a long and intensive month for the unit, and the pilots had logged a massive 857 hours' flying time, of which 625 were operational. Both figures constituted squadron records. However, the month's operations had also exacted its toll, and the unit reported ten casualties – seven killed, two prisoners of war and one man wounded – and they had 'broken more aircraft than ever before'.[38] However, the pilots had also claimed fourteen enemy aircraft destroyed, seven probably destroyed and five damaged.

Three of those destroyed fell to Eric over the course of nineteen operational sorties. This represented a 'strike rate' of roughly one victory for every six sorties. Eric appeared to be back in form; there were no outward signs of nerves or hesitation, as one might expect following a return to operations after a break of over seven months, and he appeared as confident as ever. The wounds he sustained in November 1940 did not seem to be hindering his ability to react to his instincts, to out-fly his quarry, or to fight as he was accustomed. However, was it just a facade?

On 31 July 1941, a photographer arrived at RAF Hornchurch to take a series of now well-known photographs of Eric in the cockpit and on the wing of his Spitfire, holding his dog 'Scruffy' in one. Although the images depict the face of a confident young man, they reflect one that is older than its twenty-two years, and perhaps disclose a hint of weariness. Earlier in the month he had written to his mother saying he had hardly had time to shave, and that,

> About another month of this is about all I can stand, we start at 4.23 in the morning and finish at 11.18 at night so you can see it is pretty tiring. [...] We make on an average three trips a day anything from 60 to 80 miles in [from] the coast, which believe [me] is not all fun.[39]

The enthusiastic young novice of a year before had in fact lost his eagerness to fight; he was now a seasoned veteran with a firm grasp of the job at hand and an understanding of the bigger picture. He was now 'One of the Few', an 'old hand' who had seen more than many other pilots, and who had been knocked down and climbed to his feet again. He had felt the highs of winning a fight and the lows of losing them, and he had lost friends who had not returned.

Decorated by royalty, lauded by the press, respected by superiors and peers alike, idolised by less-experienced pilots who looked up to him for leadership and inspiration, and sought out in the bar, was he perhaps now becoming a man from whom too much was expected – or perhaps too much too soon? Like a sports-man upon whom a nation pins its hopes for gold, did he feel a well-meant pressure to perform and continue pleasing the nation? Was he perhaps pushing himself beyond his limits?

His fellow flight commander, Flight Lieutenant James Hayter, appears to lend credence to this suggestion, stating that it was 'unfortunate at that stage of the war the press were creating aces with all its glamour [and] publicity. I think [Eric] felt he had to better the scores of the likes of Sailor Malan …'.[40]

It did not help that No. 11 Group published monthly lists of the RAF's top pilots. Every man on the list was a double ace as a minimum. The newest list, which included victories up to and including 31 July 1941, showed that Eric had maintained his position of fourth place from the top but was now alone in that position. He had commenced July 1941 with twenty-two victories and had claimed three more with No. 611 Squadron during the month, but No. 11 Group appears to have only credited him with two. Had he been recognised on the list with all three, he would have been equal third with Flying Officer 'Ginger' Lacey.[41]

No.	Name	Sqn	Day	Night	Total
1	Wing Commander Adolph G. Malan, DSO*, DFC*	–	30	2	32
2	Squadron Leader R. Robert Stanford Tuck, DSO, DFC**	257	25	2	27
3	Flying Officer James H. Lacey, DFM*	501	25	–	25
4	Flight Lieutenant Eric S. Lock, DSO, DFC*	611	24	–	24
5	Squadron Leader Michael N. Crossley, DSO, DFC	32	22	–	22
6	Flight Lieutenant Harbourne M. Stephen, DSO, DFC*	130	21	–	21
7	Wing Commander Douglas R.S. Bader, DSO*, DFC*	–	20$\frac{1}{2}$	–	20$\frac{1}{2}$
8	Flight Lieutenant Geoffrey Allard, DFC, DFM* (deceased)	85	19	–	19
8	Squadron Leader Roy G. Dutton, DFC*	19	19	–	19
9	Flight Lieutenant Frank R. Carey, DFC*, DFM	43	18	–	18
9	Pilot Officer Herbert J.L. Hallowes, DFM*	122	17	1	18
10	Flight Lieutenant Alan C. Deere, DFC*	602	17$\frac{1}{2}$	–	17$\frac{1}{2}$
10	Squadron Leader Mark H. Brown, DFC*	1	17$\frac{1}{2}$	–	17$\frac{1}{2}$

Chapter Eight

A Ruddy Awful Waste

August 1941

August 1941 commenced with dull weather and, as a result, there was little activity right across No. 11 Group on 1 August. Rhubarbs (small fighter sweeps at low level in cloudy conditions) were only carried out by Nos 41 and 452 Squadrons with little effect, and Nos 242 and 603 Squadrons were sent out to provide cover for three Blenheims attacking a 6,000-ton tanker off Nieuport, Belgium. Although the strike was successful, two of the Blenheims were shot down by heavy flak, and a Hurricane of No. 242 Squadron was lost in an unfortunate friendly fire incident. No. 611 Squadron spent much of the day on flying practice, intermingled with five uneventful Barrow Deep patrols. NCO pilots carried out almost all the work, but Eric was not involved at all and did not undertake any operational flying all day.

Weather conditions on the second day of the month limited flying to practice sorties until mid-afternoon, when significant weather improvement allowed Nos 41, 54, 71, 111, 306, 485, 609 and 611 Squadrons to undertake independent Rhubarb operations, while No. 609 Squadron also provided withdrawal cover for ten Blenheims following an attack on Cherbourg.

No. 611 Squadron's operational flying today was confined to a window of a little over six hours from around 16:00 hours, and consisted of three Barrow Deep patrols and three Rhubarbs. Although the former sorties were uneventful, the Rhubarbs produced some good results, despite a little flak damage to a number of aircraft. However, for the fifth day in a row, Eric did not participate in operations.

Morning fog cleared around midday on 3 August 1941, and this paved the way for a busy afternoon for No. 11 Group's fighter squadrons. Most were involved in 'fairly intensive'[1] free-ranging Rhubarb operations, while a number of units also undertook convoy patrols, flew sweeps over north-eastern France, or attacked shipping off the French coast. Between them, they claimed a total of six destroyed and one probably destroyed enemy aircraft in the air and one damaged on the ground for no loss, plus an array of ground targets that included small shipping vessels, locomotives, railway facilities, factories and buildings.

Dr Sir Archibald Hector McIndoe CBE MS MSc FRCS FACS (1900-1960). © *Reproduced with the kind permission of East Grinstead Museum.*

Queen Victoria Hospital, East Grinstead, soon after opening in 1936. © *Reproduced with the kind permission of East Grinstead Museum.*

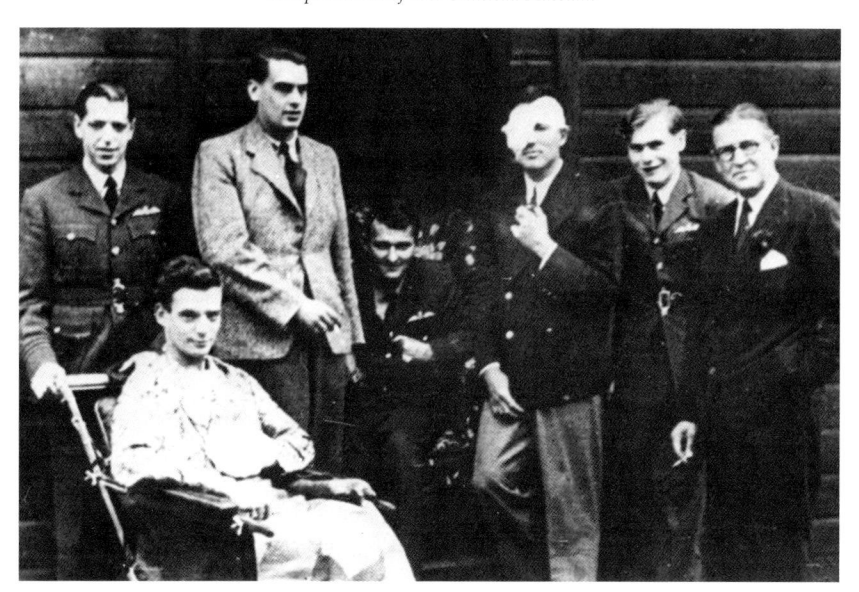

Some of Archie McIndoe's patients at QVH in 1941, including Sqn Ldr Tom Gleave on the far left. McIndoe himself can be seen far right. © *Reproduced with the kind permission of East Grinstead Museum.*

Left: Sgt Plt John McAdam joined 41 Squadron from 6 SFTS with Eric on 18 June 1940. He was shot down and killed off Dover on 20 February 1941. *Source unknown, 41 Squadron Archives collection.*

Below: Eric's Mention in Despatches.
© *Melissa John, via Philip Meyers*

By the KING'S Order the name of
Pilot Officer E S Lock
Royal Air Force Volunteer Reserve
was published in the London Gazette on
17 March 1941
as mentioned in a Despatch for distinguished service.
I am charged to record
His Majesty's high appreciation.

Archibald Sinclair
Secretary of State for Air

Right: The original entry ticket into Eric's investiture at Buckingham Palace on 1 April 1941.
© *Lock and Cornes families.*

1815
Buckingham Palace.
Admit one to witness the Investiture.
1 APR 1941
Lord Chamberlain.

Left: Eric at the investiture for his Distinguished Service Order, Distinguished Flying Cross, and Bar, at Buckingham Palace, 1 April 1941. He is visibly drawn and tired. © *News Syndication; reproduced with their permission.*

A sketch of Eric, perhaps a parting gift, from his time in QVH at East Grinstead. A number of signatures can be recognised including those of Dr Archibald McIndoe and Tom Gleave, and Eric has also signed it. © *Melissa John via Greg Muddell.*

Eric spent a month at Dutton Homestall Convalescent Home, a Red Cross facility two miles from East Grinstead, between late April and late May 1941. © *Knight Frank LLP*

Above: Eric visited the Sentinel Waggon Works in Shrewsbury in June 1941, where he met the staff.
© *Melissa John*

Right: Eric giving a thumbs up for the media to show he was back in the saddle, ca late June 1941.
Crown Copyright expired.

From left to right: Eric, Plt Off Wilfred Duncan-Smith, Fg Off Peter Dexter, and Sgt Plt William Gilmour in an official Air Ministry photograph on 611 Squadron on 7 July 1941. © *Crown copyright expired; Melissa John via Greg Muddell.*

Eric in the cockpit of a 611 Squadron Spitfire Vb, July 1941. *Crown Copyright expired; Melissa John via Greg Muddell*

Capt. Cuthbert Orde's sketch of Eric, which he sat for on 19 July 1941. The image itself is expired Crown Copyright, but this enlargement hangs on the wall of the Eric Lock Bar of Shropshire Aero Club, at the former RAF Sleap, and was photographed there by the author with their kind permission.

Eric with his dog Scruffy in the cockpit of a 611 Squadron Spitfire Vb on 31 July 1941, just four days before he failed to return from operations. *Crown Copyright expired.*

SECRET

PILOTS WITH MORE THAN TWELVE CONFIRMED VICTORIES OBTAINED
WHILE SERVING IN A.D.G.B. (INCLUDING FIGHTER COMMAND, T.A.F.,
B.A.F.F. AND A.A.S.F.) UP TO 29TH FEBRUARY, 1944.

	S C O R E		
	Day	Night	Total
G/Capt. A.G. Malan DSO & Bar, DFC & Bar.	30	2	32
W/Cmdr. B. Finucane DSO, DFC & Bars (Dec'd)	29½	-	29½
W/Cmdr. R.R. Stanford Tuck, DSO, DFC & Bars (PW)	27	2	29
S/Ldr. J.H. Lacey, DFM & Bar	27	-	27
F/Lt. H.S. Lock, DSO., DFC & Bar (Dec'd)	24	-	24
W/Cmdr. J.E. Johnson, D.S.O & Bar DFC & Bar	24	-	24
W/Cmdr. D.R.S. Bader, DSO & Bar, DFC & Bars (PW)	22½	-	22½
W/Cmdr. M.N. Crossley D.S.O.D.F.C.	22	-	22
W/Cmdr. R.F. Boyd, DSO, D.F.C. & Bar	22	-	22
W/Cmdr. D.E. Kingaby, DSO., DFM & Bars	22	-	22
S/Ldr. H.A. Stephen, DSO., DFC & Bars	21	-	21
Fighting French Pilot.	20	1	21
W/Cmdr. A.C. Deere, DSO., DFC & Bar	20¾	-	20¾
G/Capt. J. Rankin, DSO & Bar, DFC & Bar	20	-	20
W/Cmdr. J.R.D. Braham, DSO & Bar, DFC & Bar	1	19	20
W/Cmdr. J. Cunningham, DSO & Bar, DFC & Bar	1	19	20
S/Ldr. D.A.P. McMullen, DFC & Bars	15 7/10	4	19.7/10
F/Lt. G. Allard, D.F.C., DFM & Bar (Dec'd)	19	-	19
S/Ldr. R.G. Dutton, DFC & Bar	19	-	19
F/Lt. K.M. Kuttelwascher, DFC & Bar (Czech)	3	16	19
S/Ldr. H.J.L. Hallowes, DFC., DFM & Bar	18	1	19
S/Ldr. McKellar, DSO., DFC & Bar (Dec'd)	18½	-	18½
W/Cmdr. F.R. Carey, DFC & Bar, DFM	18	-	18
W/Cmdr. M.H. Brown, DFC & Bar (Dec'd)	17½	-	17½
W/Cmdr. C.F. Gray, DSO., DFC & Bars	17½	-	17½
G/Capt. T.F.D. Morgan, DSO., DFC & Bar	11½	6	17½
W/Cmdr. W.D. David, DFC & Bar	17	-	17
Sgt. J. Frantisek (Czech) (Dec'd)	17	-	17
S/Ldr. N. Orton, DFC & Bar (Missing)	17	-	17
W/Cmdr. M.L. Robinson, DSO, D.F.C. (Missing)	17	-	17
W/Cmdr. A.H. Boyd, DSO. DFC & Bars.	15.5/6	1	16.5/6
F/Off. W.L. McKnight, DFC & Bar (Missing)	16½	-	16½
W/Cmdr. W.V. Crawford-Compton DSO, DFC & Bars	16½	-	16½
F/Lt. R.T. Llewellyn, DFM.	16	-	16
S/Ldr. J.G. Sanders, DFC	11	5	16
P/Off. G.L. Nowell, DFM & Bar	16	-	16
W/Cmdr. R.H. Harries, DFC, & Bar.	15¾	-	15¾
S/Ldr. J.W. Villa, DFC & Bar	15¼	-	15¼
S/Ldr. W. Urbanowicz, D.F.C.	15	-	15
S/Ldr. R.F.T. Doe, DFC & Bar.	14½	-	14½
F/Lt. D.A.S. Mackay, DFM & Bar.	14½	-	14½
F/Lt. R.P. Stevens, DSO., DFC & Bar (Dec'd)	-	14½	14½
S/Ldr. J. Ellis, DFC & Bar.	13	1	14
W/Cmdr. J.I. Kilmartin, DFC.	14	-	14
S/Ldr. F.J. Soper DFC. DFM. (Missing presumed killed).	12	2	14
S/Ldr. A. McDowell, DFM & Bar.	13	1	14
W/Cmdr. C.F. Currant, DSO., DFC & Bar	14	-	14
F/Lt. J.A.A. Gibson, D.F.C.	13½	-	13½
S/Ldr. K.W. Truscott, D.F.C.	13½	-	13½
S/Ldr. E.R. Thorne, DFC. D.F.M. & Bar.	12	1	13
G/Capt. G.R. Edge, D.F.C.	13	-	13
G/Capt. J.W. Simpson, D.F.C. & Bar.	11	2	13
W/CMdr. J.A. Kent, D.F.C. & Bar, A.F.C.	13	-	13
S/Ldr. R.F. Hamlyn, A.F.C. D.F.M.	13	-	13
F/Lt. J.C. Dundas, DFC & Bar. (Missing)	13	-	13
S/Ldr. J.C. Freeborn, D.F.C. & Bar.	12½	-	12½
S/Ldr. F.W. Higginson, D.F.C. D.F.M.	12½	-	12½
S/Ldr. T.F. Neil, D.F.C. & Bar.	12½	-	12½
S/Ldr. J. Baldwin, D.S.O.D.F.C. & Bar.	12½	-	12½

Headquarters, No. 11 Group.

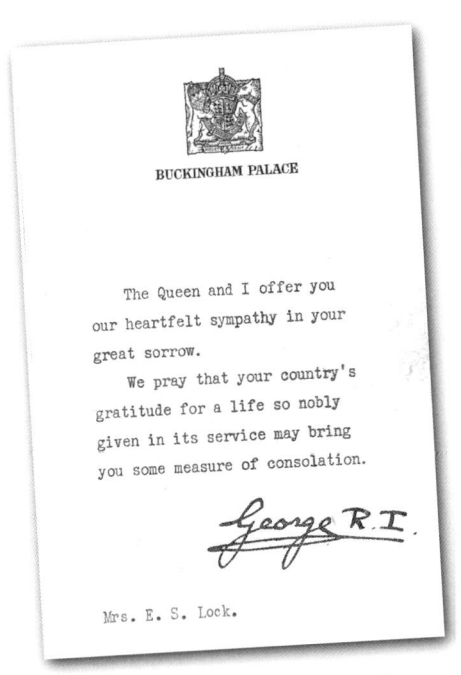

Above left: The condolence letter from Buckingham Palace, which was sent to Peggy Lock in 1942. © *Lock and Cornes families*. **Above right:** The Prestfelde School Roll of Honour, displaying Eric's name. © *Prestfelde School, via Jayne Simmons and Mike Bradbury.*

An enlarged copy of Cuthbert Orde's 1941 sketch of Eric being presented to the Mayor of Shrewsbury, Vic Pierce, by Eric's sisters, ca 1971. © *Unknown via John & Jennifer Milner.*

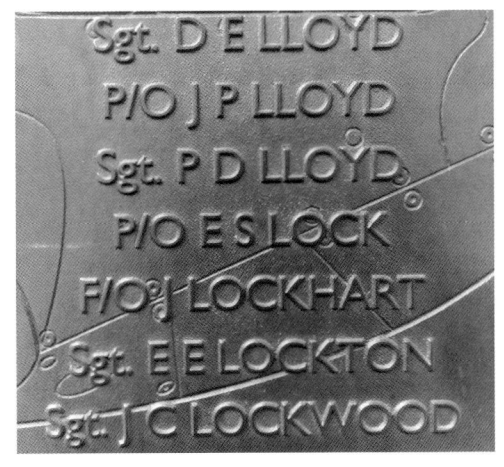

Top left: Eric's name on the Battle of Britain Memorial at Capel-le-Ferne, Kent. © *Andrew Perkins*.
Top right: Eric's name on the Battle of Britain Monument on the Victoria Embankment, London.
© *Paul Abbot*

Above: In 2010, the tailfin of Tornado GR4, ZA600, was painted up as EB-G, representing Eric's Spitfire Ia, N3162, of 5 September 1940. © *UK MOD Crown Copyright (2012)*.
Below: 41 Squadron's Typhoon, ZJ914, replaced Tornado ZA600 as EB-G when ZA600 was scrapped in March 2015. © *Gary Sluffs Johnson*.

The Battle of Britain Memorial Flight (BBMF) also acknowledged Eric when they painted Spitfire IIa, P7350, to represent N3162 in 2011. © *Ady Shaw, Warbirdsphotos*

Right: Eric's Distinguished Service Order.
Below: Eric's Distinguished Flying Cross and Bar. © *Philip Meyers*

The front page of Eric's Combat Report for 5 October 1940. Note that it is dated "5. 9. 40", but the Intelligence Officer has hand-written a note next to it, "? Probably 5.10.40 G. [Gisborough] IO. 41 Sqdn" and someone has also written the number '10' above the date, indicating the month of October. © *41 Squadron Archives*

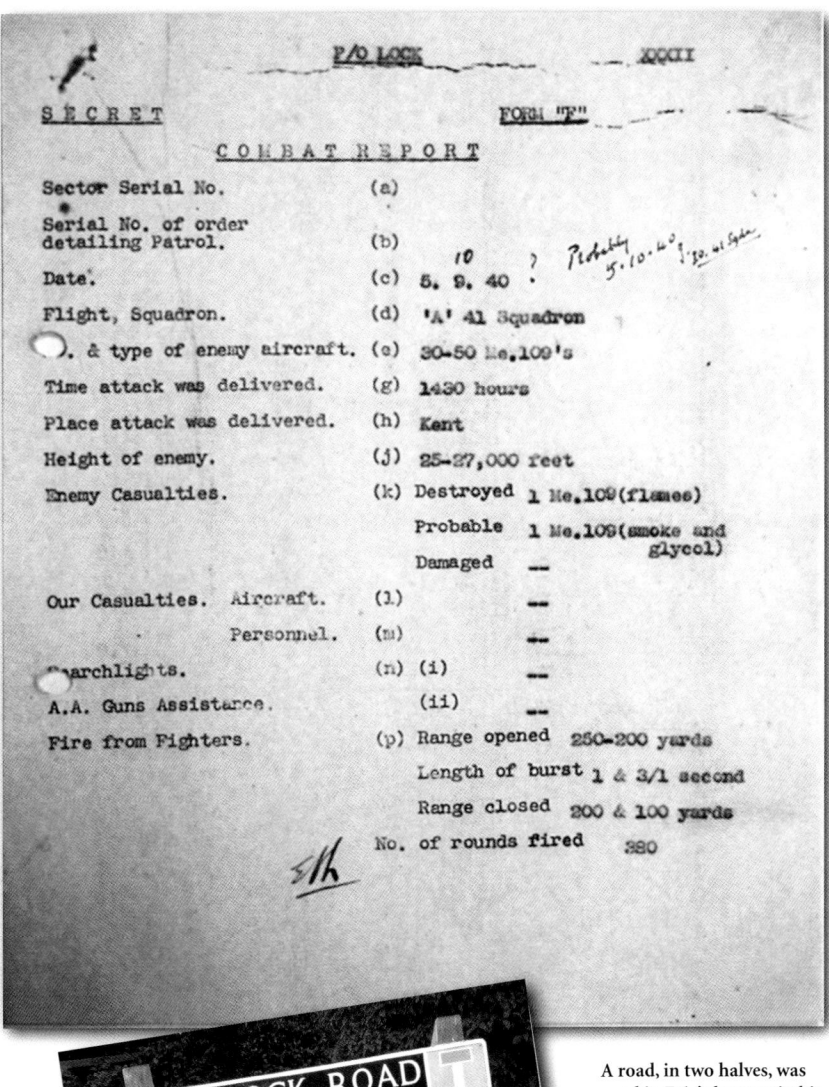

P/O LOCK   XXXII

SECRET   FORM "F"

COMBAT REPORT

Sector Serial No.	(a)	
Serial No. of order detailing Patrol.	(b)	
Date.	(c)	5. 9. 40
Flight, Squadron.	(d)	'A' 41 Squadron
No. & type of enemy aircraft.	(e)	30-50 Me.109's
Time attack was delivered.	(g)	1430 hours
Place attack was delivered.	(h)	Kent
Height of enemy.	(j)	25-27,000 feet
Enemy Casualties.	(k)	Destroyed 1 Me.109(flames)
		Probable 1 Me.109(smoke and glycol)
		Damaged --
Our Casualties. Aircraft.	(l)	--
Personnel.	(m)	--
Searchlights.	(n) (i)	--
A.A. Guns Assistance.	(ii)	--
Fire from Fighters.	(p)	Range opened 250-200 yards
		Length of burst 1 & 3/1 second
		Range closed 200 & 100 yards
		No. of rounds fired 380

A road, in two halves, was named in Eric's honour in his hometown of Bayston Hill in 1966. © *Steve Brew*

A list of Eric's victories on 41 Squadron compiled by the Intelligence Officer, Flt Lt Lord Gisborough, in November 1940. © *41 Squadron Archives*

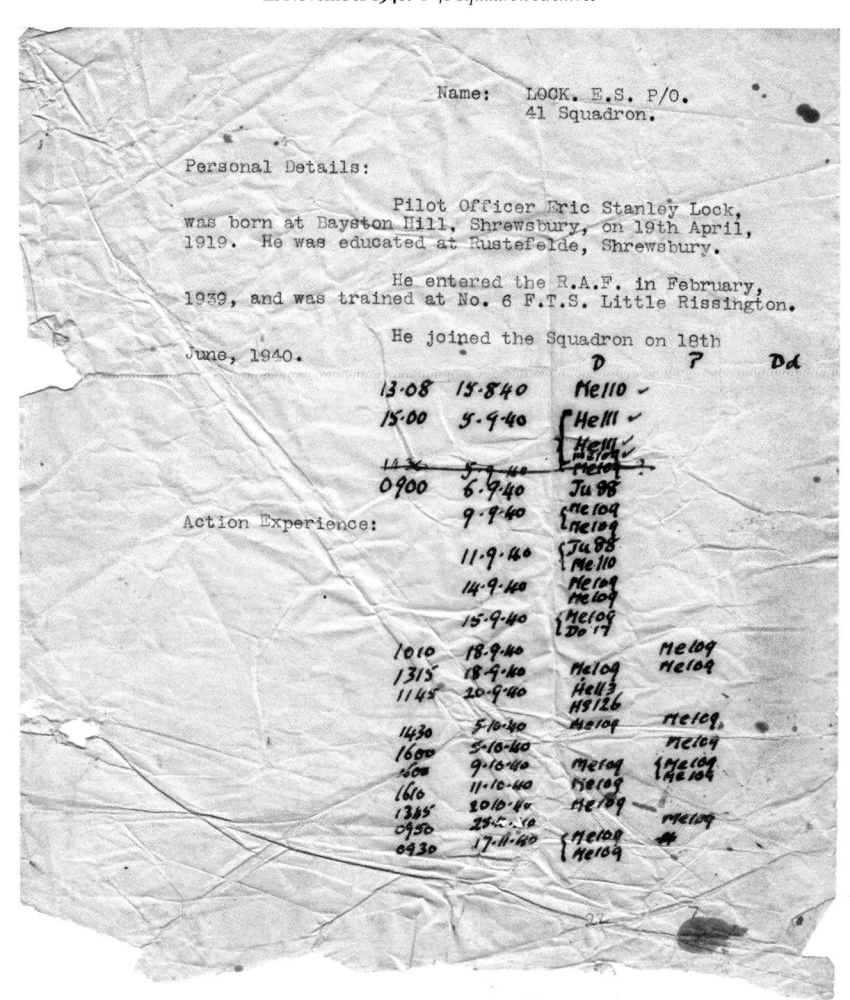

```
Name:   LOCK. E.S. P/O.
        41 Squadron.

Personal Details:
            Pilot Officer Eric Stanley Lock,
was born at Bayston Hill, Shrewsbury, on 19th April,
1919. He was educated at Rustefelde, Shrewsbury.

            He entered the R.A.F. in February,
1939, and was trained at No. 6 F.T.S. Little Rissington.

            He joined the Squadron on 18th
June, 1940.
                              D         P      Dd
            13·08   15·8·40   Me110 ✓
            15·00   5·9·40   {He111 ✓
                             {He111 ✓
                             {Hs126
            14·36   5·9·40   {Me109
            0900    6·9·40    Ju88
                    9·9·40   {Me109
Action Experience:           {Me109
                             {Ju88
                    11·9·40  {Me110
                    14·9·40   Me109
                              Me109
                    15·9·40  {Me109
                             {Do17
            1010    18·9·40                   Me109
            1315    18·9·40   Me109           Me109
            1145    20·9·40   He113
                              Hs126
            1430    5·10·40   Me109           Me109
            1600    5·10·40                   Me109
            ·      9·10·40   {Me109          {Me109
                                             {Me104
            1610    11·10·40  Me109
            1365    20·10·40  Me109  —
            0450    25·10·40
            0430    17·11·40 {Me109
                             {Me109           Me109
```

Flt Lt Eric Lock's Confirmed Victories

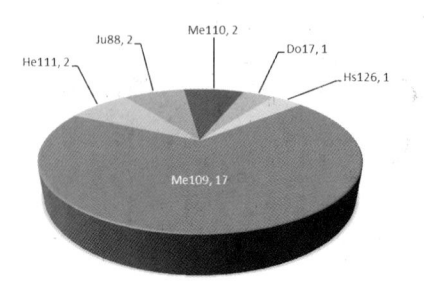

He111, 2; Ju88, 2; Me110, 2; Do17, 1; Hs126, 1; Me109, 17

Left: Charles and Dora Lock with their children Jimmy, Eve, Cissy, Joan and Eric, ca 1926.
© *Lock and Cornes families*

John Meyers & Gwen Beard on their wedding day, Ross-on-Wye, Herefordshire, 14 May 1918.
© *Philip and Richard Meyers*

Peggy and Gwen a few months before their departure for England, 16 March 1925.
© *Philip and Richard Meyers*

Right: Peggy as Miss Shrewsbury with her Uncle Harley & Aunt Elsie Beard, 1937. © *Philip and Richard Meyers*

Below, clockwise: Peggy and Peter with their grandparents, William & Annie Beard, Ross-on-Wye, Herefordshire, ca 1926. The absence of Gwen suggests it was likely taken after her death. © *Philip and Richard Meyers*

Peter and Peggy, Ross-on-Wye, 1933-1934. © *Philip and Richard Meyers*

Peggy, ca 1940. © *Philip and Richard Meyers*

Peggy's brother Peter, ca 1939. © *Philip and Richard Meyers*

Officer Commanding 41 Squadron, Wg Cdr Steve Berry MBE RAF, author Steve Brew, and Mike Bradbury, with a 41 Squadron Typhoon and the Battle of Britain Memorial Flight's Spitfire IIa, P7350, marked up as EB-G to honour Eric Lock, RAF Coningsby, June 2015. © *Stephen Elsworth, BBMF; reproduced with his kind permission*

The Battle of Britain Memorial Flight's Spitfire IIa, P7350, marked up as EB-G to honour Eric Lock.
© *Gary Sluffs Johnson*

A RUDDY AWFUL WASTE   191

No. 611 Squadron's operational flying day commenced early, despite the fog, and included four uneventful Barrow Deep patrols between 05:45 and 08:40 hours. The unit then undertook six Rhubarbs in sections of two, the first of which began just after 09:00. Following lunch, these operations recommenced at 14:30 and continued until just after 16:00. However, 'a serious lack of cloud cover'[2] changed plans and many of the pilots decided to forego the risk and returned early, empty-handed.

Eric was back in the air again after five days off operational flying, and was assigned to one of the afternoon's Rhubarbs. The pilots involved in these operations were as follows:

Rhubarbs, 3 August 1941	Up	Down
Flight Lieutenant James Hayter	09:10	10:10
Sergeant Pilot Arthur Leigh	09:10	10:10
Wing Commander Frederick Stapleton	14:30	15:30
Sergeant Pilot Thomas Ormiston	14:30	15:30
Sergeant Pilot Albert Gray	14:35	15:25
Sergeant Pilot Norman Townsend	14:35	15:25
Flight Lieutenant James Hayter	14:40	15:40
Sergeant Pilot Arthur Leigh	14:40	15:40
Flight Lieutenant Eric Lock	14:45	–
Flight Lieutenant Edmund Cathels (No. 403 Squadron)	14:45	15:45
Pilot Officer Michael Gardner	14:50	16:05
Sergeant Pilot Kenneth Wright	14:50	16:05

Flying Spitfire Vb, W3257, Eric was paired up with No. 403 Squadron's Flight Lieutenant Edmund Cathels in W3242 for a Rhubarb to the Hardelot area. Cathels was undertaking an operational sortie with No. 611 Squadron, possibly with the intention of introducing him to Rhubarb operations in advance of his unit's move to Hornchurch to replace No. 54 Squadron, to enable him better to lead his own pilots on such operations.

They were airborne from Hornchurch at 14:45 hours, and would have reached the French coast approximately twenty minutes later. The lack of cloud cover appears to have curtailed their trip – they were over France for no more than twenty minutes – and were on the way home when Eric spotted a column of German troops and vehicles on a road behind Boulogne-sur-Mer. It is impossible to verify with any real certainty which road this was, but it is possible that it may have been the Route de Saint-Omer, heading north-east from the city, the Route de Desvres, heading east, or the Boulevard de la Laine or Rue Haffreingue, both heading south-east, these being the main roads leading out 'behind' the city, and perhaps the most likely to have been large enough to accommodate a column of troops.

Catching them out in the open, Eric did not want to pass up the opportunity, and decided to strafe them. He advised Cathels, banked, and dived down to deliver his attack, and was last seen 'streaking down a road ... brassing off soldiers on bicycles and whooping over the R/T "Ha-ha, look at the b——s running!"'[3] However, no further communication was received from Eric and he was not seen again.

Flight Lieutenant Cathels arrived back at Hornchurch alone at 15:45 to report the news and the shock sat deep both on the squadron and elsewhere as word spread.[4] Typically candid, No. 611 Squadron's ORB lamented Eric's loss that day, stating that, 'It seems a ruddy awful waste to lose so great a Pilot on so trivial an expedition. It is anticipated that the German Press will make much of LOCK's capture or death.'[5] It was Eric's twentieth operational sortie with the unit, and he constituted No. 11 Group's only casualty that day.

Given the circumstances and his low altitude, it was initially hoped he may have survived the incident and he was only listed as 'missing'. However, left little choice but to get on with the business of war, Flight Lieutenant Richard Barclay, DFC, was posted to No. 611 Squadron that same afternoon to replace Eric as OC A Flight.

Despite hopes for his survival, and yet fears of a field day for the German propaganda machine, nothing was heard in German radio broadcasts. Eric had reassured his mother in one of his last letters home: 'Please don't worry if anything happens to me because nine out of ten times our boys are prisoners of war.'[6] However, nothing was heard at all and, in time, his status was amended from 'missing' to 'missing, presumed killed'. Neither Eric nor his aircraft have been located to this day. In *Spitfire Into Battle* Duncan Smith states:

> At that stage of the war we could ill afford to lose a pilot of 'Locky's' calibre. Experience was becoming a very precious asset and, though losses in combat were inevitable, it seemed senseless to waste valuable experience on 'Rhubarb' operations, which made little difference to the war effort.[7]

Unfortunately, we can only speculate about what may have happened to him. Although the exact circumstances are unknown, the possibility that he was shot down by the Luftwaffe is thought unlikely. It has previously been suggested that Oberleutnant Johann Schmid of JG26 may have been responsible as Eric was No. 11 Group's only fighter loss on 3 August 1941, and Schmid made the Luftwaffe's only claim against an RAF fighter all day – and for a Spitfire no less.

Eric appears to have made his strafing attack around 15:20–15:25 DBST,[8] if one considers a twenty-minute crossing of the Channel to Hornchurch, subtracted from Cathels's arrival there at 15:45. However, Schmid's claim, which was not substantiated and did not identify a location, is recorded to have occurred at 18:32 MET.[9] Considering the fact that Eric was airborne at 14:45, and Schmid's claim was made well over three hours later, Eric's fuel would never have lasted that long. Moreover, it makes no sense for him to have continued flying around alone over occupied territory for any length of time, particularly without any communication or cloud cover.

It is therefore generally assumed that he fell victim to ground fire, probably flak in the Boulogne area, but perhaps even from small-arms fire, such as a rifle or machine gun. This is also the opinion expressed by his fellow No. 611 Squadron pilot, Pilot Officer (later Group Captain) Wilfred Duncan Smith in his autobiography. The damage was also not necessarily visible from the ground, but a 'lucky' shot could have punctured the engine or caused a glycol leak, both resulting in a steady, and possibly rapid, decline in engine performance to the point of seizure. Of course, Eric himself may have also been hit, though not immediately fatally.

This possibility draws a striking resemblance to the deaths of two of the most famous fighter pilots of all time: Captain Manfred von Richthofen ('The Red Baron') and Major Mick Mannock, VC, DSO and two Bars, MC and Bar. While chasing a Canadian pilot at low altitude on 21 April 1918, von Richthofen was engaged by both rifle and machine-gun fire as he passed over the position of an Australian field artillery regiment. He was brought down by a single .303 rifle-calibre round that struck him in the heart; his aircraft was virtually undamaged. Mannock met his end diving low over enemy trenches on 26 July 1918, when he was met by a hail of fire from German infantrymen and his aircraft burst into flames.

Many aircraft are also known to have hit the ground and been buried with their occupants as a result of the speed with which the aircraft impacted with the ground; indeed, such aircraft are still being found today, over seventy years later. However, Eric's low altitude for the strafing attack would have likely precluded such a consequence. Moreover, had his aircraft come down on dry land as a result of the damage it had sustained, it would have been seen and reported. Eric may have been rescued or recovered, but this would have been advised to the British authorities via the usual channels. However, this did not happen.

It is also possible that Eric successfully attacked the column of troops and vehicles and was heading home when hit by coastal flak batteries when crossing out in the Boulogne area. Being a base for German E-boats, the city was well garrisoned. The harbour area was defended by large concrete pill boxes, which housed heavy flak guns, and numerous anti-aircraft batteries also littered the coast, both north and south of the town, armed with light 20mm flak guns and heavy 88mm anti-aircraft artillery.

Considering Eric's proximity to the coast, whether it was small-arms fire or flak that was the culprit, it appears most likely that he and/or his aircraft were hit by ground fire of some type, and he attempted to return across the Channel, but did not make the distance. There is no record of a Mayday being received from him to advise anyone he was in trouble, which may be read as a suggestion that he was wounded or had lost consciousness. However, to remove himself from the area, he would have had to have been in control of his aircraft, at least for some of the time.

Nonetheless, a failure to communicate his predicament does not necessarily imply he was personally incapacitated in any way at all. A commercial pilot consulted on the unexplained loss of another pilot, approximately eight months prior to this event, weighed up the circumstances and concluded: 'I don't think my priority would be to transmit if my aircraft was out of control. No one on the ground can help. One would be very focused on recovering it. We are taught to Aviate, Navigate, Communicate, in that order.'[10]

Eric may also have considered baling out but could not have done so if his altitude was too low to permit him to fully deploy his parachute. He would have therefore sought to gain as much altitude as possible and get himself as close to the English coast as he could. However, the extent of damage sustained by his aircraft may have robbed him of the opportunity. If that were the case, his only option would have been to ditch in the Channel; not a pleasant choice, but perhaps his only one.

There are many examples of similar circumstances to draw upon, one of which is the experience made by Eric's flight commander on No. 41 Squadron, Flight Lieutenant Norman Ryder, in April 1940. Having been hit by return fire from a German bomber at low altitude, he could not climb to a suitable height and was forced to ditch his Spitfire in the North Sea, around fifteen miles off Whitby. He survived the incident and was subsequently able to provide the following chilling account of events:

> I stalled on the water at 65 m.p.h. with a loud crash. [The] aircraft immediately dug its nose in and came to [a] vertical position, tail up, and sank immediately. I think the whole touch down and sinking was simultaneous. My next clear recollection was realising that I was below the surface, and that everything appeared green. I undid my harness and commenced to get clear. The A/C was sinking rapidly and when almost clear my parachute caught under the sliding roof. I then got partly back into the cockpit and out again, and finally

got clear and commenced to swim to the surface. The tail plane passed just in front of my face. Pressure was very great and green light had changed to dull black.[11]

Another example also comes to mind, which relates to the loss of No. 41 Squadron's officer commanding, Squadron Leader 'Elmer' Gaunce, DFC, around fourteen weeks after Eric was lost. Heading into France for an attack on ground targets, his Spitfire was hit by flak, although he was himself unhurt. He advised the other pilots on the operation that he was heading home and they escorted him out.

Despite his intentions, however, the damage sustained by Gaunce's Spitfire was such that, within minutes, he was no longer able to control the aircraft and it rapidly descended to make a heavy and 'very bad landing'[12] in the sea around eight to ten miles off the Cherbourg peninsula. He was not seen to jettison his hood or to evacuate the aircraft, and the weight of the Merlin engine quickly pulled the aircraft under, nose first. As the pilots orbited above him, the tail of his spitfire was visible above the surface for about three seconds, but then disappeared from view as well. Gaunce did not emerge from the water, and in a short time the only trace of his aircraft was a patch of oil on the surface. Was such a frightening scenario the end of Eric, too?

He has no known grave and is therefore formally remembered today on Panel 29 of the Runnymede Memorial, alongside around 20,450 other British and Commonwealth airmen who went missing during the Second World War.

It was a tragic loss of a young man who held so much promise and he would be 'greatly missed'.[13] RAF Hornchurch considered Lock's failure to return 'a severe loss [of a man who] was undoubtedly one of the Sector's star pilots'.[14] One can only imagine that, had he survived, he would have been lauded as one of the greatest British pilots of all time. In fact, as of the end of February 1944, he was still considered the fifth-highest-scoring pilot of Fighter Command – over thirty months after his death.

In his brief war, Eric had seen more fighting and tragedy, felt more fear and pain, and lost more friends than most people do in their entire lifetimes. Such things must scar a man deeply. What stories and anecdotes would his autobiography have therefore included had he survived the war? Where might his career have taken him, and what advice might he have offered to those pilots who followed in his footsteps? What stories might he have told his wide-eyed children, and what memories would he have shared with his colleagues? And who were his mentors, his heroes and his role models? We can but speculate.

All we have of his short life today are a few letters, numerous newspaper reports, and other official documents, which perhaps provide us only a shadow of the man he really was. The Hornchurch ORB gives us a small hint of his character, commenting on 'his cheery, unassuming personality',[15] and Tom Neil recalled him as a 'small, talkative, very bouncy chap [with] a cherubic face'.[16] His fellow flight commander on No. 611 Squadron, Flight Lieutenant James Hayter, was even more candid, referring to him as 'a very likeable cocky little bastard [with] a hell of a reputation as a high scorer'.[17]

Eric left behind a young wife with whom he had recently celebrated his first wedding anniversary. However, the war and Eric's earlier injuries had intervened and prevented any efforts at family planning; sadly, they did not have any children.

When Eric was posted as missing, Peggy is said to have left her parents-in-law's home, where she had been staying while her husband was off fighting, and did not return. At this juncture, she moved back in with her Uncle Harley and Aunt Elsie in Percy Street, Shrewsbury, where she had lived prior to their marriage. Her exact motivation for this move is not known, and may have simply been a feeling of awkwardness – if Eric were not to come home, how long should she stay? – but this was not understood at the time and reportedly caused considerable consternation in the Lock family.

This may have had to do with timing more than anything, as it was not until the summer of 1942, almost eleven months after Eric was posted as missing, that he was formally presumed dead for official purposes. *The Times* advised the public on 3 July 1942 that Eric, who was 'previously reported missing [was] now presumed killed in action',[18] and spoke of 'his magnificent fighting spirit and personal example'.[19] Peggy subsequently received a letter from the King acknowledging Eric's sacrifice, but it was the one letter that no one wished to receive from the palace.

Chapter Nine

Eric's Legacy
The Years Since

Soon after Eric's status was amended from missing to presumed killed, Shrewsbury's iconic department store, R. Maddox & Co. Ltd, released a short biography of Eric titled *The Story of a Brave Shropshire Airman*. The booklet was released with some fanfare at the time and the store set up a large window display, which included photos, Eric's medals and DSO warrant, and a number of his other items, including a portrait of him in oils by an unknown artist.[1] Although rather brief, the booklet was quite up to date at the time, and the lack of any other in-depth work on Eric since then resulted in it being reprinted in 1989 by Nigel Morris in liaison with Eric's sister Joan.

What is curious about the booklet, however, is that it contains an endorsement in the front in Eric's mother Dora's own hand, dated 11 August 1942, which is used as an introduction. Peggy does not appear to have had a hand in the book, which is perhaps reflective of an ongoing rift between her and Eric's family. When Peggy remarried in 1943, any relationship that may have still existed broke irrevocably, and Peggy moved away.

Unfortunately, yet more sadness was to befall the Lock family during the ensuing years. Eric's father Charles died within weeks of the war ending, in September 1945; Eric's older brother 'Jimmy', who had been estranged from the family since at least 1940, died in April 1949 aged just forty-three; and, less than eight months later, Eric's mother Dora also passed away. Charles and Dora were buried in Condover Cemetery, and Eric's name was added to the gravestone. His name was also subsequently included on the Roll of Honour in the Church of England parish Church of Saints Andrew and Mary in Condover, and a brass plaque to his memory also hangs on the north wall.

In 1966, perhaps the greatest memorial to Eric in the Shrewsbury area was erected in Bayston Hill, where he and his family had lived for many years. A new street was created in two separate halves, named Eric Lock Road and Eric Lock Road West. The latter street is also home to the local 1st Bayston Hill Scout Group, which still has an Eric Lock Scout Troop.

In 1969, United Artists released its blockbuster film, *Battle of Britain*, starring Laurence Olivier, Christopher Plummer, Michael Caine, Edward Fox and Susannah York, among others. Queen Elizabeth attended the premiere in London, and regional centres also made events out of their opening nights, attracting local media attention. So, too, in Shrewsbury. The event was held at the French Renaissance-style Granada Cinema on Castle Gates Road, and was attended by the RAF Market Drayton-based AOC 22 (Training) Group, Air Vice-Marshal Eric Plumtree, CB, OBE, DFC, and the mayor of Shrewsbury, Gwendoline Dyas. Also among the invited guests for the gala evening were Eric's three sisters, Eve, Cissy and Joan. A picture of all five appeared in a group photograph in the local press the next day.

Soon afterwards, an enlarged version of the portrait sketched by Cuthbert Orde in July 1941 was framed by Eric's sisters and presented to the new mayor of Shrewsbury, Vic Pierce. It is believed the picture remained with the mayor's office until Shropshire Council moved out of the Guildhall on Dogpole in 2004.[2] It was then offered to the Shropshire Aero Club, based at the Second World War airfield RAF Sleap, near Wem. At the time, the club maintained a lounge on the upper floor of the airfield's control tower, named 'Dave's Loft' after one of the long-term members, Dave Lofts. Eric's portrait was then hung in the lounge, until Eric's younger sister Joan and his nephew Ken visited the club and suggested that the lounge might be renamed in honour of Eric. The club agreed and it was subsequently relaunched as the 'Lock Lounge Café'. Eric's portrait still hangs prominently on the wall, and is accompanied by a number of historical photographs and pieces of memorabilia from the airfield's past.

In more recent times, a memorial bench and plaque to Eric and his parents' memory was unveiled by his sister Joan on The Common at Bayston Hill, which are still there today. It was refurbished in 1990 with the assistance of the Prestfelde School Old Boys Association. A second bench, made of oak and wrought iron, with a further plaque to Eric's memory, was unveiled outside Shrewsbury Castle, at the entrance to Shropshire Regimental Museum, around 1990. In time, the plaque became corroded and the bench weathered and fell into disrepair, but in early 2007 an American citizen, Johnny Wheeler, a long-time member of the Battle of Britain Historical Society, arranged with the curators at the castle museum to refurbish the bench, and Eric's sister Joan agreed to fund a replacement plaque. The local air cadet group, No. 1119 Shrewsbury Squadron ATC, also agreed to provide annual maintenance, and it was still in excellent condition when it was visited in 2015 during the preparation for this book.

In April 2007, Johnny Wheeler also arranged for the Battle of Britain Historical Society to place a plaque dedicated to Eric at his old school, Prestfelde. It includes

ERIC'S LEGACY

two photos, images of a DSO and a DFC, and the citations for Eric's Bar to the DFC and his DSO. Eric's name is also one of thirteen that appears on the school's Roll of Honour, and Prestfelde has a scrapbook dating from the 1940s, which contains a number of clippings about Eric from the local newspapers, dating from the 1930s and 1940s.

There are also a number of more formal memorials to Eric. Aside from the Runnymede Memorial in Surrey, mentioned previously, his name appears formally in at least three other locations.

Fittingly, he is included in the Books of Remembrance in the RAF Church, St Clement Danes, on The Strand in London. Badly damaged by enemy bombing in May 1941, the church was handed over to the Air Council in 1953 and subsequently rebuilt with funds raised through a worldwide RAF appeal. The newly renovated church was re-consecrated in October 1958, 'as a perpetual shrine of remembrance to those killed on active service and those of the Allied Air Forces who gave their lives during the Second World War'.[3] The Books of Remembrance, which include the names of all RAF personnel who have died on active service, were unveiled and dedicated in May 1961.

Eric's name was also included among those on the Battle of Britain Memorial at Capel-le-Ferne, Kent, when it was unveiled by Lady Aitken in July 1999, and on the Battle of Britain Monument on the Victoria Embankment, which was unveiled by Prince Charles and the Duchess of Cornwall in September 2005.

In 2010, as the United Kingdom commemorated the seventieth anniversary of the Battle of Britain, the British Indian Ocean Territory released a series of stamps honouring 'Battle of Britain Aces and Leaders'. The series included portraits of Douglas Bader, Michael Crossley, Bob Doe, 'Ginger' Lacey, Robert Stanford-Tuck, Sir Hugh Dowding and Eric.

That same year, No. 41 Squadron recognised a number of their Second World War pilots by adding 'EB' squadron recognition codes of the era to the tailfins of their entire fleet of Harriers and Tornados. When the Harriers were retired in 2010, the codes were carried over to their new Typhoon fleet and continue to fly today.

One of these aircraft, Tornado ZA600, was painted up to display the code EB-G, representing Eric's Spitfire Ia, N3162, in which he claimed three destroyed enemy aircraft on 5 September 1940 (see Chapter Four). This aircraft became the personal mount of the OC No. 41 Squadron, Wing Commander Rich Davies, and his navigator, Squadron Leader Mark Elsey, and a special commemorative tailfin was displayed on this aircraft for the unit's ninety-fifth anniversary in 2011, which retained the letters EB-G. This aircraft also participated in a flypast over Buckingham Palace for the wedding of Prince William and Catherine Middleton in 2011. The Tornado was scrapped in March 2015 after thirty years' service, but in an effort to continue honouring Eric, it was replaced with Typhoon ZJ914, which was marked up as EB-G on its arrival and was still flying at the time of writing.

In 2011, the Battle of Britain Memorial Flight (BBMF) also recognised No. 41 Squadron's ninety-fifth anniversary by painting up one of their Spitfires, P7350, as EB-G to honour Eric. Being a Battle of Britain veteran itself, it was a fitting salute to the man and his squadron. The Spitfire subsequently participated in many displays and flypasts, including a number over Buckingham Palace. One of the most notable was the mass flight of forty Spitfires and Hurricanes from Goodwood Aerodrome, formerly RAF Westhampnett in the Tangmere Wing, to commemorate the seventy-fifth anniversary of the Battle of Britain in September 2015. The BBMF was still flying this Spitfire with EB-G on its fuselage as this work went to print.

Eric's medals and uniform are on display at Bentley Priory Museum, the headquarters of RAF Fighter Command during the Second World War, but the whereabouts of his flying logbook are unfortunately unknown, and it may have been destroyed.

Alas, this is not a story with a happy ending; it is instead one of pain, sacrifice, heartbreak and death. It is an account of how one family was deeply affected by war, and how one young man paid the ultimate price for his country. Eric belonged to the select club of Churchill's 'Few', but was ranked among an even more exclusive class of men we call aces. What makes his career perhaps even more unique, is that his entire service with the RAFVR extended to a mere thirty months, and his operational flying lasted just under twelve. But if we remove the period Eric was out of action as a result of him being wounded, the achievements of this young man were in fact confined to two brief windows: 9 August–17 November 1940 and 1 July–3 August 1941 – a combined period of just 135 days, or less than twenty weeks of operational flying. Seen as a ratio against his victory claims, this equates to more than one for every week. This is an astounding achievement for any pilot.

Although Eric's final tally was ultimately surpassed by other pilots, this ratio would have decreased by default had he survived. He would have been rested and, in time, promoted and taken off daily operations. However, his sheer number of victories kept him in the top five pilots in Fighter Command until at least early 1944, and he still sits within the top ten of the war. It is for this reason that his name is often mentioned in unison with other great British aces such as 'Johnnie' Johnson, 'Sailor' Malan, 'Paddy' Finucane, 'Ginger' Lacey, Bob Stanford-Tuck, Douglas Bader and Bob Doe.

Yet measuring Eric in this way should not be seen as his ability to kill another man, but rather his prowess in the sky, his flying skills and knowledge of his aircraft, his foresight and calculation, his ability to plan an attack, and his nerve to carry it through. Perhaps luck may have played a role in some way, but his clear thinking is evident in all his operations. Maybe some of his skills were derived from his farm upbringing, where he learned to stalk his target, take his time preparing an attack and then act swiftly and decisively.

All this aside, the fact that Eric died during an operational sortie is perhaps the thing that he should most be remembered for. He was a country boy, a farmer, an average child of the 1920s and 1930s. His family was not poor, but he was also no academic. Had the war not intervened, perhaps his entire life would have been spent on the land. And yet, despite the fact that farming was a reserved occupation, and he could have therefore avoided service altogether, Eric volunteered and chose to serve his country. In this regard, perhaps he was no different to many other young men and women at the time. He recognised there was a job to be done and answered the call to serve, set his family and career aside, and went away to fight for Europe's freedom and to defend Britain's shores. Although just an unassuming farmer's son who did not aspire to greatness, and from whom nothing great was expected, he achieved some spectacular things in his short period of service that few men achieve in their entire lifetimes.

But there was a price to pay. Eric was seriously wounded in November 1940, and if he had not made it back to land on that occasion, he would have likely not survived. That incident left deep physical scars, and anecdotal evidence suggests that it also left psychological scars. Today, we would recognise the symptoms of post-traumatic stress disorder (PTSD), but it did not have a formal name in 1941. It appears that Dr Archibald McIndoe had a grasp of the issue, even if by observation and not by actual medical diagnosis, when he called for a more holistic approach to a man's recuperation than the mere healing of physical wounds alone.

However, in sending Eric to a front-line squadron immediately after his visible wounds appeared healed, the Medical Board at Halton failed to acknowledge any such issue. Although we should not compare his situation with modern medical procedures, with today's awareness of the effects of PTSD, and with our current emphasis on physiotherapy, one cannot but wonder whether a Medical Board in 2015 would have made a different decision about a man in Eric's circumstances. Indeed, while PTSD was not formally recognised in 1941, it does not mean that the psychological effects of Eric's combat and wounding were any different to symptoms we might formally diagnose as PTSD today.

Of course, we could debate at length whether Eric was ready to return to operations and never come to a consensus, but such an exercise would be pointless as it would not change anything. In any case, there is no intention to apportion blame, especially as we cannot know whether it was in fact Eric himself who requested a return to operations; the intent is merely to discuss possibilities in laymen's terms rather than spark unnecessary debate. Ultimately, without access to Eric, to first-hand witnesses, and to medical records – Eric's Service Record is surprisingly scant – we can do nothing but weigh up available evidence, and make assumptions based on the existing data. The simple fact is that there are some things that we will never know.

Even what is available, however, has often been difficult to assess, and research for this work has revealed a multitude of contradictions and inconsistencies between sources. These range from Eric's ancestry, right through his entire life and beyond, and some assertions are absolutely baseless. Most, though, were undoubtedly originally rooted in some long lost fact, but 'Chinese Whispers', superficial research, 'poetic licence', and replicated errors, have rendered some accounts completely useless. Wading through all possible sources to compile as accurate an account of Eric's life as possible has been one of the greatest challenges in compiling this work, and I believe I have been able to set many records straight.

Regardless of these issues, what has stood out throughout my research is that the unassuming youth that joined the RAFVR in early 1939, as one of thousands of other young men, proved he was something special indeed. He foresaw the war and positioned himself for the job he wanted before it started. He fought hard, and anecdotal evidence suggests he played hard. He was a good hunter and a good sportsman. He was an excellent pilot, who was both a team player and able to work competently by himself. He had an analytical mind that was clever at strategising, and could map out his plan of attack before he launched it. He reacted quickly when opportunities presented themselves, or when opponents surprised him. He showed a maturity in his job beyond his years and was respected by superiors and peers alike. When he was knocked down, he got back on to his feet and carried on. He was 'One of the Few', he was decorated, he was popular, and he rose swiftly from anonymity to become a household name both in Shrewsbury and across the country. His name is now known across the world.

But what is it that we really admire in men such as Eric Lock? Their youth and eagerness? Their contribution towards a common goal, and their determination against the odds? Their strong bond with their fellow pilots and their identification with their squadrons? Their bravery, loyalty, honour and altruism in their service to their country? The exhausting job they had and the difficult decisions they faced? Their skill in the cockpit? Their tallies of victories? Their uniform, medals and fame? The ultimate sacrifice that many made? Do we perhaps see elements of ourselves in these men, or characteristics that we aspire to? Is it some of these things or maybe every one of them to some extent?

Perhaps they can all be captured in three basic emotions: sincere awe, deep respect and profound gratitude. They certainly encapsulate my sentiments towards Eric Lock and I hope this has manifested itself throughout this work. Some people are recognised for a life of service, but what makes Eric particularly special is that he earned a country's awe, respect and eternal gratitude in not twenty-two years of his life, not in thirty months of service, not even in twelve months of becoming operational, but in less than twenty weeks.

I hope I have done him justice in this biography by providing previously unknown detail, setting a number of records straight, and attempting to reveal the man behind the legend. His was indeed a short life lived to the fullest and I trust this work helps ensure that he is never forgotten. Wherever he lies, may he rest in peace.

Appendix 1

A Concise Biography

April 1919 – August 1941

- Born Bomere Farm, Bayston Hill, Shrewsbury, Shropshire, 19 April 1919
- Educated Public Elementary School, Bayston Hill, 1924–26
- Educated Clivedon School, Church Stretton, 1926–28
- Educated Shrewsbury Boys High School, Shrewsbury, 1928–29
- Educated Prestfelde School, Shrewsbury, 1929–33
- Employed on family farm, Allfield, and in Bayston Quarry, 1933–39
- Joined RAFVR as AC2 'Airman under Training Pilot' (No. 745051), 17 February 1939
- Promoted to sergeant, 18 February 1939
- 28 E&RFTS (Reid & Sigrist), Meir, 17 February–31 August 1939
- Mobilised, 1 September 1939
- Sent on leave with full pay, 1 September–29 October 1939
- Course 1, No. 4 ITW, Bexhill-on-Sea, 30 October–8 December 1939
- Course 17, No. 6 SFTS, Little Rissington, 9 December 1939–18 June 1940
- Awarded Pilot Badge ('Wings'), March 1940
- Commissioned pilot officer on probation (No. 81642), 18 June 1940
- Posted to No. 41 (F) Squadron, assigned to A Flight, RAF Catterick, 18 June 1940
- First flight in a Spitfire, 21 June 1940
- Married Margaret V. 'Peggy' Meyers, St Julian's Church, Shrewsbury, 27 July 1940
- First operational sortie, 9 August 1940
- WIA (left leg) in Spitfire Ia, N3162, over Thames Estuary, 5 September 1940
- Achieved ace status, 6 September 1940
- Combat damage in Spitfire Ia, R6610, Dungeness–Ramsgate, Kent, 14 September 1940
- Awarded Distinguished Flying Cross, 1 October 1940
- Awarded Bar to Distinguished Flying Cross, 22 October 1940

APPENDIX I – A CONCISE BIOGRAPHY

- Combat damage, force-landed Spitfire IIa, P7314, near Manston, 8 November 1940
- WIA (left arm and both legs) in Spitfire IIa, P7554, twenty miles east of Clacton and crash-landed at Alderton, Suffolk, 17 November 1940
- Admitted to East Suffolk and Ipswich Hospital, Ipswich, 17–23 November 1940
- Admitted to Princess Mary's Hospital, RAF Halton, 24 November–23 December 1940
- Awarded Distinguished Service Order, 17 December 1940
- Admitted to Queen Victoria Hospital, East Grinstead, 23 December 1940–26 April 1941
- Mentioned in Dispatches, 17 March 1941
- Investiture for DSO, DFC and Bar, Buckingham Palace, 1 April 1941
- Admitted to Dutton Homestall Convalescent Home, Ashurst Wood, 26 April–28 May 1941
- Sick leave at home, Shrewsbury, 28 May–25 June 1941
- Confirmed in appointment and promoted to flying officer (WS), 18 June 1941
- Medical evaluation, RAF Halton, 25 June 1941
- Posted to No. 611 (F) Squadron as acting flight lieutenant and OC A Flight, RAF Hornchurch, 27 June 1941
- Became founding member of the Guinea Pig Club in absentia, 20 July 1941
- Failed to return, posted missing, in Spitfire Vb, W3257, in the Boulogne area, 3 August 1941 (Status amended from missing to 'presumed killed', July 1942.)

Appendix II

Victory Claims
June 1940 – August 1941

Exactly how many victories Eric Lock achieved against the Luftwaffe has been the subject of much debate. Various tallies from 1941 to the present differ a great deal, and no two sources appear to agree on the number. Perhaps at times we give such tallies too much weight, but it is a fair question that deserves some clarity.

Perhaps the first issue that requires clarification is that of actual victories versus claims. Although some victories were witnessed and were therefore unequivocal, it is often impossible to say with any certainty how many aircraft a pilot actually destroyed, probably destroyed, or damaged through his own actions. Although there are both proven and suspected cases of over-claiming by pilots, victory claims were generally not made with any ulterior motive, and were reported in the honest belief that a claim was justified. The uncertainty results from numerous factors, not the least of which were the heat of battle, the number of aircraft in the area, claims by other pilots, weather conditions, and evasive tactics by the opponent, to name a few. Combat films were analysed at the time, and it was not uncommon for claims to be upgraded, downgraded, or disallowed altogether. Contemporary research and post-war access to Luftwaffe records has also shed a new light on claims.

In a discussion around such issues many years ago, a respected aviation historian and author once said to me something along the lines of, 'careful historians should only speak in terms of claims', rather than referring to 'actual' victories or making assumptions on specific victories without solid proof. This is a message I took to heart, and it has become a fundamental principle of my writing, both in this work and my earlier histories of No. 41 Squadron.

The simple truth is that contemporary historians and enthusiasts can never really know for certain as we were not there to witness events. Even for those present, certainty is sometimes as limited as it is when police ask multiple witnesses a short time after an incident to describe what happened: often, they have different opinions but are all certain that their version of events is what happened.

APPENDIX II – VICTORY CLAIMS

So, too, of course, in the tempo of battle.

As such, as the title of this appendix suggests, I am discussing claims in this section; that is, those that were actually claimed by Eric, and credits, or what the RAF formally granted him on the basis of his claims. It is therefore a case of 'Eric claimed …', rather than 'Eric shot down …' and, in doing so, this discussion is limited to the facts only, insofar as they can be established today.

To give the reader an idea of the broad range of estimations of Eric's victories, an RAF document dating from July 1941 credits Eric with twenty-two confirmed victories, whereas one for January 1943 states twenty-four; Eric's DSO citation asserts 'at least 22', as do newspaper reports of the award of this decoration; No. 41 Squadron's intelligence officer credited Eric with twenty-two destroyed and seven probably destroyed upon his departure from the unit, but on his arrival on No. 611 Squadron in June 1941 that unit's ORB assigns him twenty-three confirmed victories, to which three more were added the following month. The famous photograph of Eric in his No. 611 Squadron Spitfire in late July 1941 shows him standing alongside a fuselage painted up with twenty-six swastikas, indicating that number of confirmed victories; quoting the American magazine *Life*, the *Daily Express* announced in May 1941 that Eric had 'destroyed 30 Nazi planes' but the text clarifies that the figure comprised twenty-two destroyed and 'at least eight probables'; various websites also record his tally as having been between twenty-one and twenty-six-and-a-half, but all generally appear to place him in the RAF's top-ten scorers.

Investigating some of these figures a little further, there are some initial questions around the number of victories Eric claimed on No. 41 Squadron between August and November 1940 that require some clarification. These are the main issues:

• One source suggests that Eric claimed two victories on 15 August 1940, which is the date upon which he claimed his first victory. A second source states he claimed only one victory, for a Ju88, while a third also states there was one claim, but for an Me110.

   There is no evidence for two victories that day in squadron, station or group records, but confusion around his claims may have stemmed from the fact that no Combat Report for this victory is held in the National Archives' collection (TNA AIR 50/18). However, one has survived in No. 41 Squadron's own archive, which shows that Eric only claimed one victory that day, for an Me110.

• Eric is often credited with claiming five victories in two sorties on 5 September 1940 because two Combat Reports exist for that date, one for three victories and the other two (TNA AIR 50/18, folios 514–515 and 516–517). However, the second pages of each of the Combat Reports, which explain the detail of the actions, differ significantly in context. In the former, Eric is flying as Red 2 at 15:00 hours; in the latter as Yellow 1 at 14:30. However, the squadron was airborne at 09:15, 15:00 and 16:15 on 5 September, and Eric was only airborne once, for the 15:00 operation. There are also other inconsistencies.

Despite initial appearances, it must be concluded that Eric did not make the claims in the latter Combat Report (No. 516–517) on 5 September 1940; they pertain instead to 5 October 1940. The evidence for this lies in the squadron ORB, in Intelligence Reports, and particularly in Eric's original Combat Report in No. 41 Squadron's archives, which includes an annotation by the intelligence officer in red pen after the date 5.9.40: '? Probably 5.10.40 G [Gisborough] IO. 41 Sqdn'. A cross-reference with documentation for 5 October 1940 reveals that Eric made three claims that day: one destroyed Me109 and one probably destroyed Me109 at 14:30, and another probably destroyed Me109 at 16:00. The National Archives has a Combat Report for the latter of these claims (No. 532–533), dated 5 October 1940, but not for the former.

As the circumstances, context and timings of the earlier victories that day fit neatly with Combat Report No. 516–517, it is therefore apparent that this Combat Report is erroneously dated 5 September 1940, and pertains instead to the events of 5 October 1940. Unfortunately, this error has led to the inclusion of two additional victories for Eric on 5 September 1940 (one destroyed and one probably destroyed) in many contemporary works, to which those of 5 October 1940 have also been added on account of evidence in the ORB.

- The two Heinkel 111s claimed destroyed by Eric on 5 September 1940 were possibly shared with other pilots. Contemporary research suggests that one of these aircraft was likely He111, WNr 3338, A1+CR, of 7/KG53, which ditched just off the Nore at 15:30 hours. It is believed the aircraft was initially hit by anti-aircraft fire while bombing an oil storage facility at Thameshaven, and as claims for an He111 were also submitted by No. 17 Squadron's Flying Officer Count Manfred Czernin and No. 73 Squadron's Sergeant Pilot John Brimble, it is possible that this victory was shared with Eric.

  The other aircraft is believed to have been He111, WNr 2632, A1+GR, also of 7/KG53, which went into the sea west of Margate Hook Beacon around 15:30, following the same strike on Thameshaven. It is believed to have also been the same bomber attacked by No. 17 Squadron's Count Manfred Czernin and Sergeant Pilot Clifford Chew, and possibly also by No. 73 Squadron's Squadron Leader Maurice Robinson. Although contemporary analysis likely points to sharing, Eric claimed both destroyed.

APPENDIX II – VICTORY CLAIMS   209

- It has been suggested that Eric shared a destroyed Do17 on 15 September 1940 with Pilot Officer Tom Neil of 249 Squadron. There are several versions of the attack on three Me109s and three Do17s made by the pair, but all differ in some respect. Eric's Combat Report for his victories (TNA AIR 50/18, folios 524–525) suggests that while he and the (then unidentified) Hurricane pilot joined up and attacked the same formation together, they actually claimed one Me109 and one Do17 each.

    It is apparent from Eric's report that he had then already shot down his own Do17 before assisting Tom Neil with the remaining Do17. Although Eric states that they carried out attacks on this aircraft, he clarifies that it was actually 'shot down by [the] Hurricane', which he left to finish off the job and apparently declined a share in the victory. Neither a squadron Intelligence Report for the day, nor a summary of Eric's victories, both held in No. 41 Squadron's archives, make any mention of him sharing any of his victories with Neil.

    Conversely, page one of Tom Neil's Combat Report (TNA AIR 50/96, folios 191–192) states twice that he claimed two Do215s (not Do17s) destroyed but did not claim the Me109s. On the second page, in the detailed report, Neil makes no mention of Eric or the presence of a Spitfire, although someone has written in a different hand at the end of one paragraph 'Shared with EB-E'. However, the front page, summarising Neil's claims for two Dorniers, has not been altered. Eric's claims for this sortie were one destroyed Me109 and one destroyed Do17, and were also not altered to one destroyed Me109 and one destroyed and one shared destroyed Do17s.

- On 7 October 1940, Eric was one of seven pilots who attacked a Do215: 'P/O Lock and P/O Leckie [sic] being last two to attack'.[1] However, only Squadron Leader Don Finlay and Flying Officer John Mackenzie submitted claims for damaging the aircraft, and the last man to fire, Pilot Officer John Lecky, was granted the aircraft destroyed. Eric did not make a claim for damaging the aircraft, even though it is apparent that he damaged it.

The above conclusions are supported by existing Combat Reports and Intelligence Reports, and by a summary of Eric's victories, which was compiled by No. 41 Squadron's intelligence officer upon his departure from No. 41 Squadron. On this basis, his claims on No. 41 Squadron amount to the following: (see next page)

APPENDIX II – VICTORY CLAIMS

Date	Destroyed	Probable	Damaged	Aircraft	Location	Evidence[2]
15.8.1940	1	–	–	Me110	Seaham Harbour	41SA
5.9.1940	2	–	–	He111	Sheppey – Thames Estuary	514 – 515
5.9.1940	1	–	–	Me109E	Sheppey – Thames Estuary	514 – 515
6.9.1940	1	–	–	Ju88	Twenty miles east of Calais	518 – 519
9.9.1940	2	–	–	Me109E	Kent/ Dover	41SA
11.9.1940	1	–	–	Me110	Twenty-five miles south-south-east of Maidstone	520 – 521
11.9.1940	1	–	–	Ju88	Seventeen miles south of Maidstone	520 – 521
14.9.1940	2	–	–	Me109E	Dungeness – Ramsgate	522 – 523
15.9.1940	1	–	–	Me109E	East of London	524 – 525
15.9.1940	1	–	–	Do17	English Channel	524 – 525
18.9.1940	–	1	–	Me109E	Channel off Margate	526 – 527
18.9.1940	1	1	–	Me109E	Gravesend, Kent	528 – 529
20.9.1940	1	–	–	Me109E	Fifteen to twenty miles north-west of Boulogne	530 – 531
20.9.1940	1	–	–	Hs126	Fifteen to twenty miles north-west of Boulogne	530 – 531
5.10.1940	1	1	–	Me109E	West Malling – Ashford	516 – 517 and 41SA
5.10.1940	–	1	–	Me109E	Tonbridge – Maidstone area	532 – 533
9.10.1940	1	–	–	Me109E	Ten miles off Dover	534 and 539
9.10.1940	–	2	–	Me109E	English Channel	534 and 539
11.10.1940	1	–	–	Me109E	Five miles off Dungeness	536 – 537
20.10.1940	1	–	–	Me109E	North of Biggin Hill	538 and 541
25.10.1940	–	1	–	Me109E	South-east of Dover	540[3]
17.11.1940	2	–	–	Me109E	Thames Estuary – Channel	542 – 543 and 535
Unit Total	**22**	**7**	**0**			

APPENDIX II – VICTORY CLAIMS

Twenty-two confirmed victories is also the number quoted in the official citation for his Distinguished Service Order, which was reported many times over in the newspapers at the time. It also tallies with an official RAF list of the top fighter pilots' scores, dating from July 1941.[4]

Another related question that has been posed is: Who was the highest-scoring RAF pilot of the Battle of Britain, as a campaign, isolated from previous and subsequent victories? On the basis of the above list of victories, Eric claimed twenty destroyed and seven probably destroyed enemy aircraft between 10 July and 31 October 1940. It is believed that the top five pilots of the campaign were the following:

Name	Squadron	Nationality	Score
Lock, Eric S.	41	British	20
Lacey, James H.	501	British	18
McKellar, Archibald A.	605	British	17 + 1 shared
Frantisek, Josef	303	Czech	17
Carbury, Brian J.G.	603	New Zealand	15

This data is based on Shores and Williams's in-depth research in *Aces High* (Grub Street, 1994), and the results imply that Eric was possibly not only the highest-scoring British pilot of the Battle of Britain, but also the highest-scoring RAF pilot of the campaign overall. As intimated above, there is always a margin of error, and it is possible that others may debate the numbers or order.

The next issue we face in analysing Eric's victories is the unexplained appearance of an additional victory when he joined No. 611 Squadron in June 1941. Eric claimed no further victories between when he was shot down and wounded on 17 November 1940 and when he joined No. 611 on 27 June 1941. However, on joining his new unit, the ORB recorded, 'POSTING: F/Lt. ERIC STANLEY LOCK, D.S.O., D.F.C. (23 victories) posted to the Squadron from HORNCHURCH as Flight Commander "A" Flight.'[5]

As this is the first time that this figure had been mentioned anywhere up to that date, it is possibly a typographical or transcription error by the person who prepared the No. 611 Squadron ORB that day. However, it is also possible that the error came about as a result of No. 41 Squadron's intelligence officer's record of Eric's victories in his original handwritten list, if it was also sent to No. 611 Squadron. There are several records in No. 41 Squadron's archives of such information being sent to officers commanding or intelligence officers of units to which No. 41 Squadron pilots were subsequently posted. Examples of similar reports are also held that were received from units that posted pilots to No. 41.

One example, dating from January 1941, for a pilot who arrived on No. 41

Squadron from No. 611 Squadron, includes a list of the victories he had had credited to him while on No. 611. Another record, also dating from January 1941, is addressed to the intelligence officer of No. 56 Squadron, and shows a pilot's victory tally on No. 41 Squadron as he was posted to that unit; there are several other examples. Considering this appeared to be common practice at this time, it is quite feasible that a summary of Eric's victories was also sent to No. 611 Squadron on his posting to the unit in June 1941. If so, is it possible that the intelligence officer's handwritten list is a draft of what was sent to the unit?[6] And, considering that one of the victories for 5 September 1940 has been crossed out (effectively a twenty-third victory), did a typed version of this list go to No. 611 Squadron before the error was noted? Could this have been the catalyst for the non-existent twenty-third victory?

There is simply no evidence for a twenty-third confirmed victory while on No. 41 Squadron. Eric's Combat Reports and DSO citation, No. 41 Squadron's Intelligence Reports and ORB, No. 41's intelligence officer's tally, and official RAF tallies, all indicate that Eric had claimed twenty-two victories on No. 41 Squadron. There is no suggestion in any available documentation that there was either an additional victory credited to him, or a probable victory that was raised to destroyed.

It is understood that Eric then added another three victories to his existing claims while on No. 611 Squadron in July 1941, but there is an issue with one of them. The first two victories are not in question; they were reported in the squadron ORB and evidenced by surviving Combat Reports, but a two-fold issue exists with the third, which took place on 14 July 1941.

First and foremost, no Combat Report has survived for the action in which Eric was involved that day, and this robs us of any real opportunity to corroborate any claim. However, what complicates matters further, and unfortunately muddies the waters somewhat, is that the No. 611 Squadron ORB entry that day states that Eric 'had fired at one 109 and saw 3 disintegrate'.[7] On face value, this appears to imply that Eric destroyed three aircraft on the sortie, but no other source or evidence supports this suggestion. There is no subsequent solid or circumstantial evidence that appears to give any credence to the possibility of him simultaneously destroying three aircraft, and contemporary analysts all accept that Eric claimed one Me109F destroyed near Boulogne on this occasion. On this basis, Eric's claims on No. 611 Squadron would amount to the following:

Date	Destroyed	Probable	Damaged	Aircraft	Location	Evidence[8]
6.7.1941	1	–	–	Me109F	North-east of St Omer	197 – 198
8.7.1941	1	–	–	Me109E	St Omer	199 – 200
14.7.1941	1	–	–	Me109F	Near Boulogne	11 Grp ORB
Unit Total	3	0	0			

APPENDIX II – VICTORY CLAIMS

Adding up the scores from No. 41 Squadron between August and November 1940, and from No. 611 Squadron in July 1941, results in a total of twenty-five enemy aircraft claimed destroyed and seven claimed probably destroyed.

All documentary evidence aside, it must also be acknowledged that there is a series of well-known photographs of Eric taken in late July 1941, which show him by the fuselage of a Spitfire, with twenty-six swastikas painted on it: shouldn't this perhaps be taken as 'proof' of his score, despite all other evidence to the contrary?

Do these photographs really prove anything? The point of the photo was not souvenir portraiture for Eric; it was an RAF public relations photograph. It was important for morale and the war effort and, even according to fellow flight commander Flight Lieutenant James Hayter, 'at that stage of the war the press were creating aces with all its glamour [and] publicity'.[9] Accuracy was not the point; inaccuracy was not an issue, and the Ministry of Information was quite an oxymoron, although that is a separate subject in itself.

There is no evidence that Eric ever flew with swastikas on his fuselage and it is perfectly feasible that they were painted on purely for the public relations photo. It is understood that the task of painting them on the fuselage was undertaken by Eric's flight mechanic, LAC Sam Price. His point of reference will possibly have been the squadron ORB, which stated on Eric's arrival that he had twenty-three victories to his credit, and to these were added his three victories during July 1941. Would Eric have physically counted the swastikas immediately before the photo shoot? If he had, and had noticed the number was incorrect, and he asked for it to be corrected, would the photographer have agreed to its removal? Or would he have been more concerned about the time it might take to do so or the possibility that its removal might leave a mark, making it glaringly obvious that it had been removed? And did it really matter anyway? One swastika more wouldn't make a difference to the point of the photograph, and in any case, judging by Eric's rate of successes, he may well have had another victory soon anyway. And the photo would not be publically dated. Eric may have asked for one or all swastikas to be removed afterwards, but there is no evidence either way.

The objective reader might suggest that this is merely clutching at straws, simply making the circumstances suit the argument. Maybe, but the fact still remains that there is simply no proof for a twenty-sixth victory. Although just an assumption, a situation such as that suggested in the last few paragraphs is not outside the realms of possibility. The reality is that there are surviving Combat Reports for claims for only twenty-four destroyed enemy aircraft, and supporting evidence for a twenty-fifth, but there is nothing at all to substantiate a twenty-sixth.

Conversely, if we simply agree that the twenty-six swastikas confirm his true number of victories, the next questions must surely be, 'Which one was the twenty-sixth?', and 'Where is the evidence?' It should also be noted that, ultimately, Fighter Command only credited Eric with twenty-four victories. With that in mind, was there perhaps no victory given on 14 July after all, and it is for this reason that no Combat Report exists for that date?

Approaching this from another angle, no contemporary analysis appears to doubt that Eric claimed three victories on No. 611 Squadron, despite a missing Combat Report for his last victory. Therefore, if Eric should be credited with twenty-six victories by the time he was lost, he must have claimed the first twenty-three on No. 41 Squadron. However, there is no evidence to support this: there are no Combat Reports, Intelligence Reports or ORB entries to corroborate such a claim. There is also no questionable combat that has not been analysed and discounted as a possible additional victory.

On the question of over-claiming, Eric's past behaviour suggests this would be unlikely. On at least two occasions we are aware of, he declined a share in victories: once on 15 September 1940, when he could have justifiably claimed a half share of Pilot Officer Tom Neil's Dornier, and again on 7 October 1940, when he could have submitted some form of claim for another Dornier, which he allowed Pilot Officer John Lecky to finish off and declare destroyed for himself.

The issues discussed above demonstrate a number of plausible possibilities of how a final tally of twenty-six claims and other suggested totals may have been attained, but the evidence does not stack up. The conclusion must therefore be that Eric's total claims were most likely twenty-five destroyed enemy aircraft and seven probably destroyed.

Appendix III

The Lock Family
A Brief Family History

Eric's grandfather, Samuel Lock, moved into the county of Shropshire around 1860, and brought with him the skills of a long line of farmers and animal castrators. The family had spent at least 100 years in rural districts south-east of Worcester and Eric's great-great-great grandparents, William and Ann Lock (née Firkins), had married in the village and civil parish of Croome D'Abitot in Worcestershire's Malvern Hills in February 1758. Between about 1758 and 1770, they brought at least five children into the world: Elizabeth, Mary, Liddy, Samuel and Benjamin. Their youngest boy, Benjamin, born in 1770, would have grown up at a time of some significant moments in history – the American War of Independence in 1776, a new British penal colony established in New South Wales in 1788, and the French Revolution, which commenced in 1789, to name just a few.

In February 1793, France declared war on Great Britain. Within just three years, engagements between the two countries cost Britain some 40,000 lives, many of them in the West Indies. Unfortunately, however, this was barely the beginning, and sporadic but fierce clashes with France and her allies would continue on land and sea for another twenty years.

In March 1797, when Benjamin was twenty-seven, he married Mary Loxley in Cropthorne, a village overlooking the River Avon, approximately twelve miles east of Croome D'Abitot. That year, in a terrifying and unexpected escalation of hostilities, France audaciously sent several armed raiding parties to England and Wales, on one occasion landing troops near Fishguard in Pembrokeshire. That same year the rest of Europe made peace with France, and Britain felt very alone.

Benjamin and Mary produced eight children in a little over ten years. Their first child, Anne, was born seven months after they married, followed by a son, George, who was christened in Cropthorne in March 1799. The family then moved a few miles north-west to Wyre Piddle, presumably following available work, where Luke was christened in July 1800, William in February 1802, Mary in September 1803, Jane in May 1805, Samuel in March 1808, and finally Francis in

September 1809.

The children were born into an era of great historical significance and major events on the world stage. There is little doubt, then, that the Lock family was caught up in the excitement and xenophobia of the 'Rule Britannia' genre, which accompanied a succession of courageous British naval victories in the wake of the French raids.

The first of these was Admiral Jervis's defeat of the Spanish off Cape St Vincent in 1797, when the latter's force outnumbered the British by two to one. This was followed by Admiral Duncan's defeat of the Dutch off Camperdown before the year was out. Horatio Nelson then dealt Napoleon's fleet a crushing blow at Aboukir Bay in 1798, and just three months later, off Donegal, Rear Admiral Warren destroyed or captured seventy per cent of a French squadron sent to land troops in Ireland to aid the revolutionaries there.

There were further clashes in the first years of the new century, but it was Britain's battle against the combined French and Spanish fleets at Trafalgar in October 1805 that was the most spectacular. Within just three hours, Nelson's fleet destroyed twenty-one of the thirty-five vessels amassed against him. The admiral was killed but the country was jubilant – Britannia ruled the waves! It captured the nation's excitement and became legendary in British history.

However, it would take another nine years before Napoleon seemed beaten, when he was forced to abdicate in April 1814. He fled to exile on the island of Elba but, not a year later, he caught Britain off guard when he escaped, returned to France and once again reunited the nation. It was only a matter of months before the emperor once again faced British troops across a battlefield. In a short but bloody campaign at Waterloo in June 1815, Napoleon met his final and decisive defeat at the hands of the Duke of Wellington. With the help of Prussia, the French were crushed and another major victory was written into the annals of British history.

Britain celebrated as her victorious troops came home and the kingdom commenced a lengthy period of relative peace on the international stage. In fact, it would be a full century before Britain's superiority on the seas would again be questioned, but sadly, in the aftermath of Waterloo, the joy was short-lived.

The introduction of new technologies in the form of farming machinery, steam-powered weaving looms and cylinder printing presses, among other recent inventions, had already caused extensive unemployment. The situation was only aggravated after Waterloo when regiments were disbanded and men returned to their villages and towns looking for work. These factors, coupled with low wages and long working hours for those who did have work, only led to further disgruntlement amongst the population. With the economy in recession, the frustration reached boiling point and riots broke out across England and Wales.

APPENDIX III – THE LOCK FAMILY

Set against this background of turmoil and great upheaval at all levels of British society, Benjamin and Mary's oldest son, George, married Maria Waters in St Clement Parish, Worcester, in November 1821. Six months later, their first child, Ann, was born in the village of Pinvin, less than two miles from Wyre Piddle. Following Ann's birth, the little family moved a few miles north-west and settled in White Ladies Aston, where George found work as a castrator.

It was here that another four children were born: Jane in August 1825, Benjamin in September 1827, George Jnr in September 1830 and William in October 1832. The family was on the move again during the mid-1830s, and settled in Kempsey, around four-and-a-half miles south of Worcester, and it was here that another three children were born: James in September 1837, Samuel in March 1840 and finally Maria Jnr in January 1844.

The world was quickly changing around them; education for children was not yet compulsory, but new coal-burning and steam-powered industrial innovations, such as the railways, were just being introduced. By the 1840s, railway tracks, new large roads and canals criss-crossed England and Wales, and rail rapidly overtook horse-drawn vehicles as the main method of transport between major towns and cities. Meanwhile, much of the Continent was in turmoil, and the decade saw populist uprisings sweep many European countries.

Like many other folk at the time, the Lock family was also affected by disease and poverty. George and Maria lost two of their children early, Jane dying before she turned seven, and Maria Jnr as an infant before she was three. Sadly, only two years after Maria Jnr's death in 1847, Maria also died, aged just forty-seven. For a time, George Lock may have juggled young children and household duties with the responsibility of being the main breadwinner: when Maria died, his oldest son was just twenty, and although he was no doubt already pulling his weight with work, the youngest children were still only ten and seven years old.

Around two years later, the 1851 Census provides us with a brief insight into family life. Four of the children were still at home: Ann, aged twenty-eight, Benjamin, a castrator like his father, aged twenty-three, and James and Samuel, both scholars, aged thirteen and eleven, respectively.[1] Being twenty-six, Jane had possibly married by now, and twenty-year-old George and nineteen-year-old William must have been working away from home. However, there were also two visitors in the house: Susan Miles, aged fifty-five, and Susan Collins, possibly her daughter, aged just eleven. In addition, there were also two servants, Mary Andrews, aged sixteen, and Thomas Bills, aged fifty.

Circumstantial evidence suggests that Susan Miles, who is also recorded as Susannah Miles, was probably a widow who was more than just a visitor, and that she and George subsequently married. If gossip had started that there was more to the relationship, they may have had little choice but to marry. However, to what level the relationship really extended is hard to gauge as they were allowed relatively little time together. Sadly, George died approximately three years after the census was taken, in October 1854, aged fifty-five.

We do not know what became of the household after George's death, and can imagine that Susan attempted to hold it together as best she could. We are only able to make assumptions today, but it may be possible that George and Maria's youngest son, Samuel, either did not get on with Susan, or had a falling out with her, as he not only left Kempsey before he was twenty-one, but also the county. The Lock family had not moved from areas just south or south-east of Worcester for almost a century, but by 1861 Samuel had put down roots approximately fifty-six miles[2] away in Condover, Shropshire, a rural district about four miles south-west of Shrewsbury.

Condover had been settled since Anglo-Saxon times and by the 11th century formed a part of both King Edward the Confessor's royal manor and a large royal forest called the Long Forest. It was consequently listed in the Domesday Book in 1086. The modern parish of Condover encompassed the villages of Bayston Hill, Boreton, Chatford, High and Low Condover, Dorrington, Lyth, Ryton, Westley and Wheathall, and was considered of sufficient size to warrant its own station on the Shrewsbury and Hereford railway line. The parish church was the Norman-style church of St Andrew, and the largest building in the parish was Condover Hall, a three-storey Elizabethan-style sandstone residence, which was erected around 1590 and still stands today.

Samuel first appears in documentation as a lodger in Condover in the 1861 Census, in which year the population stood at 1,871 inhabitants. He settled into the area well and, ten years later, was a well-established castrator, aged thirty-one. He had his own home in Ryton Butts, with a housekeeper by the name of Mary Derricutt, aged sixty-one, and a servant, Mary's daughter Elizabeth, who was twenty. In 1872, Samuel married Sarah Steward, who was eleven years his junior, and had been born in Kidderminster, Worcestershire, in 1851. Over the ensuing years, the pair brought six children into the world: Emma Maria in March 1874, Samuel George in October 1875, Henry James in July 1877, Sarah Florence in February 1879, Charles Edward in June 1880 and finally William Steward in September 1883. The 1881 Census shows us that Samuel was thriving, and working as a farmer and castrator at Lower Ryton, and who was employing three labourers on 160 acres of land. The home included five children aged between ten months and seven years, but Sarah had the assistance of two servants, Mary Davies, aged thirteen, and John Morgan, aged twenty-one.

That same year, Sioux Indian Chief, Sitting Bull, surrendered to U.S. troops,

APPENDIX III – THE LOCK FAMILY

ending his infamous stand-off, while in Egypt the following year, British troops occupied Cairo and made the country a British protectorate. In 1883, the world's attention was captured by a series of eruptions of the Dutch East Indies' (Indonesia's) volcanic island, Krakatoa, which culminated in a cataclysmic explosion in August that year, killing at least 36,000 people. The resulting ash cloud caused unusual weather patterns around the globe for several years, and lower than normal temperatures for the following five years. In 1888, Britain's population was horrified by events closer to home, when Jack the Ripper hit the headlines with a series of terrifying murders in London's Whitechapel.

It was also during this decade that compulsory education was introduced in Britain for all children aged between five and thirteen. Aside from its obvious immediate benefits to individuals, it also had the effect of removing child labour from factories and farms, and simultaneously improving the quality of the broader workforce as employees could read, write and comprehend a level of mathematics. It comes as no surprise, then, that in the next snapshot we have of the Lock family, in the 1891 Census, Henry, Sarah, Charles and William are all listed as 'scholars'. Emma and Samuel Jnr, though, aged just seventeen and fifteen respectively, were still at home, but helping on the farm.

Samuel Lock's farm and castration business continued to prosper during these years, and the older children stayed at home working until well into their twenties. Emma married Thomas Cornes, aged twenty-three, in April 1897, but Samuel Jnr learned his father's trade and became a farmer and castrator, too, and Henry turned his hand to butchery. The second youngest, Charles, was employed as a shop assistant by his older sister Emma's husband, Thomas, and by March 1901 only Sarah and William were still without formal employment.

It was also Charles who, despite being the second youngest child of the family, was the second to marry. Living and working in his brother-in-law's home gave him ample opportunity to get to know Thomas's younger sister, Dora, and the couple wed in 1901. Two more of Charles's siblings were also soon married, Sarah to Walter Newnes in 1905, and Samuel Jnr to Edith Furmston in 1907. It was some time, however, before Henry and William finally wed, both ultimately at the age of forty-three, Henry to Annie Goliah in 1920 and William to Elsie Rodenhurst in 1926.

By the 1911 Census, therefore, all but two children had married and moved away, and while Samuel Snr, then seventy-one, was still farming, only Henry, at thirty-three, and William, at twenty-seven, remained working on the property to assist their father. A fourteen-year-old labourer was also employed on the farm, while Sarah, now sixty, received assistance in the home from an eighteen-year-old servant. Samuel died in November 1913, but Sarah survived him by a dozen years, passing away in early 1925, aged seventy-four. These were Eric's grandparents and although he knew his grandmother in his early years, he never met his grandfather.

However, returning briefly to 1901, it is Charles Lock's marriage to Dora Cornes in spring that year that is of most interest to us, as they ultimately became Eric's parents, albeit around eighteen years later. Dora was born in 1879 in Pontesbury, Shropshire, around eight miles south-west of Shrewsbury, the youngest of five children, born to Methodists Peter Cornes (1844–1924) and Rebecca Cornes (née Adams, 1846–1917). Dora's older siblings were Frances Mary (known as Mary), born in 1869, Sarah Ann (known as Ann), born in 1871, Thomas Peter, born in 1874, and Edith Ellen, born in 1877.

As established, Dora's older brother Thomas married Charles's older sister Emma in 1897; Mary also married Edward Banning in late 1895, and Ann wed James Smout that same year. However, while Mary and Edward had a daughter, Frances May, known as Amy, in late 1896, Mary died three years later, possibly in childbirth. This left four-year-old Amy at home with Dora and Edith, and with their parents, Peter and Rebecca, on the 1901 Census, immediately prior to Dora's marriage.

There are, however, a few unusual circumstances surrounding Charles and Dora's nuptials. The main issue is that, although both were resident in the Shrewsbury area, they married some distance away, in the registration district of Fylde, Lancashire. Located between Blackpool and Preston, the area lay approximately 100 miles north of Shrewsbury. It is not clear why they travelled so far to undertake what would normally have been a happy family affair. The trip to Fylde most likely would have been undertaken by horse and cart, at an average speed of a few miles per hour. They could have covered around thirty miles per day, suggesting a travelling time of approximately three to four days in each direction. Perhaps some of the journey could have been done by steam train, but it was nonetheless a significant distance to travel, which raises questions about the acceptance of the marriage within the family.

One might theorise that it may have been that Charles was Anglican and Dora a Methodist, but their older siblings had married without an apparent issue. Or perhaps it was because Dora was a year older than Charles, but this was not likely to be a problem. Unfortunately, there are few facts to clarify circumstances, and we can only make assumptions, based on what little is known. Whatever the reason, the couple subsequently had three children: Evelyn Dora (known as Eve), who was born in January 1904, Herbert Samuel Charles (known as Jimmy), who was born in early 1906, and Sarah Florence (known as Cissy), who was born in June 1907.

There then followed a dozen years with no births. In June 1907, Dora was just twenty-eight, and by the time this period ended, she was only forty. With Charles a year younger than her, they were both in the primes of their lives, and could well

APPENDIX III – THE LOCK FAMILY

have had more children. However, it did not happen and we can only assume that Dora suffered a number of miscarriages. It is also entirely plausible that a child declared on the 1911 Census as having been born alive but since died may have come to the world between Sarah's birth in 1907 and the Census in 1911, but no relevant birth or death records exist. Unfortunately, therefore, this child remains a bit of a mystery. Regardless, by her late thirties, Dora may have considered her child-bearing years were over, and her pregnancy with Eric in late 1918 must have come as quite a surprise.

By the time the Armistice brought an end to the First World War on 11 November 1918, Dora was into her second trimester. Had she lost previous pregnancies, as suspected, she would have taken care every single day and limited her activity on the farm. With Eve now fourteen, Jimmy twelve and Cissy eleven, their parents would have been relying on them to pull their weight with chores during this period. However, the pregnancy continued without concern and, despite odds seemingly stacked against him, Eric was born to the family on Bomere Farm on Easter Saturday, 19 April 1919, after twelve years of trying.

No doubt expected to grow up on the farm and follow in his father's footsteps, as generations of Locks had done before him, this child had different ideas. Little could his parents have dreamed who this new-born would become. He would take the world by storm and rewrite history; he would become a household name, a war hero and a highly decorated ace who would be presented to the King at Buckingham Palace; he would have streets named after him and books written about him; he would have his name engraved in stone and he would earn his country's eternal gratitude.

However, these things would come at a high price. His wife and parents would be visited by the ever-feared delivery boy with his dreaded telegrams; they would see their son battered and broken; they would feel helpless as he suffered in excruciating pain; they would witness his fight for survival; and they would recognise a piece of his character that was gone forever. Then they lost him altogether, shortly after his twenty-second birthday. To make things worse, they had no knowledge of the circumstances – there was no body to bury, no closure and no consolation in their bitter grief. Charles Lock died a broken man only weeks after the Second World War ended, and Dora died just four years later.

The last member of Eric's immediate family, his younger sister Joan, died in July 2009. At the time of this publication there are only a few living male heirs of this line bearing the Lock name – all descendants of Eric's older brother Jimmy. Having married twice, Jimmy's first marriage produced a son, Kenneth, and a daughter, Jennifer, who both lived in Shrewsbury for many years. Another son, Rodney, and a second daughter, Rosemary, were also born during Jimmy's second marriage.

Kenneth had two sons who survive him and live in the London area, while Rodney had two sons, the eldest of whom, Richard, served thirty years in the RAF. Richard has a son named Eric who is studying architecture at Sheffield University, and a second, Anthony, served nine years in the RAF.

Extended members of the family still live in the Shrewsbury area and, although the link to Eric is not always obvious as they have different surnames, they are very much aware of his achievements and his legacy, and they are fiercely and justifiably proud of him. This work could not have been completed without their generous assistance, cooperation and support, and is very much appreciated.

Appendix IV

The Meyers Family

Compiled with the kind assistance of
Simon Davies and Phil Meyers.

Margaret Victoria 'Peggy' Meyers was a descendant of German stock, believed to have been of Jewish origin, whose great grandfather was one Henry Meyers, which was likely an anglicised version of something like Heinrich Meyer or Mayer. He emigrated from Germany to Canada on a route via Switzerland, suggesting the move may have been the result of religious persecution, although this cannot be verified. He ultimately settled in the farming community of Zurich, Ontario, on the eastern shores of Lake Huron, and married Elizabeth Shoemaker (or Schumacher).[1]

A son, Charles Samuel Meyers, was born in the township of Hay, Ontario, on 4 August 1868.[2] On 22 December 1891, aged twenty-three, Charles wed Victoria Sherritt, thereby marrying into an Irish immigrant family from County Leitrim, who were farming in the nearby township of Stanley. It was a large family; Victoria was one of ten girls and one boy, while her father Thomas was one of ten siblings.

Charles and Victoria's first child, Thomas Henry, was born in Blake, Ontario, in late 1892, and there ensued another seven births at roughly two- to three-year intervals: Myrtle Sydella Hay (1894), Mary Jane (1896), John Aaron (1899), Lillian Gertrude (1900), Ada Louise (1902), Eleanor Beryl (1905) and Margaret Irene (1907).

Four years after Margaret's birth, Charles was recorded in the national census as a 44-year-old stonemason residing in Hay. He declared his religion to be Presbyterian and his language German, the latter perhaps a less expected response for someone born and educated in Canada. It is believed that there were three further births to the couple: Alice May Keller, David Campbell and Charles Sherritt. Judging by the previous pattern, we may assume that the latter three births may have occurred around 1909, 1911 and 1913. Charles died in Blake on 26 March 1920.

Charles and Victoria's fourth child and second son, John Aaron Meyers, was born on 29 July 1899. He grew up on the farm and was known as Ernie, or just as 'Ern' by his family. On 13 May 1916, aged only seventeen years and nine months, he enlisted in the 161st Battalion of the Huron Regiment, Canadian Expeditionary Force (CEF), at Hensall, Ontario. The battalion had been on a recruiting drive in the area and many young men eagerly volunteered in the surrounding townships, the pay of $0.75 per day being a clear motivating factor. However, being under age, he required an adult counter-signature on his attestation papers, which he obtained from his aunt Dora Sherritt.

His attestation papers record a young man of a little taller than average height at 5 feet 11½ inches, with a fair complexion, blue eyes and light brown hair. He lists his occupation as a farmer and his religion as Presbyterian. Following a mere five months' training, by which time John had turned eighteen, he was shipped to England aboard the SS *Lapland*, which departed Halifax on 25 October 1916.

Arriving on the Western Front only weeks later, John was deployed on active service during the Battle of Lens, Hill 70, the Third Battle of Ypres and at Passchendaele. During 1917, his battalion was decimated and its survivors, which included John, were posted to other units; the 161st was not re-formed. As a result, John was posted to the 58th Battalion CEF, where he saw out the end of the war.

He was a very good marksman, no doubt partially on account of growing up on a farm, and was consequently employed as a sniper. Occupying strategic vantage points, often in no-man's-land, he also protected working parties that were digging or repairing trenches. His 'conspicuous gallantry' was recognised in particular for his work at Nun's Alley, near Lens, on 30 August 1917, and he was consequently awarded the Military Medal. His citation read:

> He was detailed as a sniper outside the trench, covering the bombing party, and the working company putting in block. He occupied an exposed position for some hours and kept fire concentrated on a low portion of the enemy trench. By his own fire, he accounted for at least six of the enemy.[3]

However, John also suffered from life in the trenches, and is believed to have been exposed to gas. Although no specific incident is recorded, he endured various health and respiratory issues in the years following the war and spent a significant amount of time in hospital.

During leave in England, he was billeted in or near Ross-on-Wye, Herefordshire, where he met Gwyneth Louie Beard. Born in Kington, on the English–Welsh border on 7 March 1898, Gwyneth, who was known as Gwen, was sixteen months older than John. This does not appear to have been a hindrance in the friendship, however, and the young couple fell in love and were married on 14 May 1918.

Following the Armistice, John returned to Canada with his wife and the pair settled in the township of Blake, close to his large family. They did not waste time starting their own family and a daughter, Margaret Victoria, was born in Blake on 6 June 1919. This suggests Gwen was likely pregnant before arriving in Canada.

APPENDIX IV – THE MEYERS FAMILY

The little family subsequently moved to London, Ontario, where John was employed as a police officer with the London City Royal Canadian Mounted Police.

Here in London, a son was born on 23 November 1921, who they named Kenneth William. In time, Margaret became known as 'Peggy' while Kenneth was called 'Peter', a name that he continued to use for the rest of his life. The children were both baptised at St Paul's Church, in Hensall, Ontario, Peggy in January 1920 and Peter in January 1924.

Their mother, Gwen, renewed her passport in March 1922, and it is apparent that a few cracks may have started appearing in the marriage soon after this time, although this is circumstantial. John contracted tuberculosis, which was exacerbated by lung issues resulting from being gassed, and Gwen caught the same illness from John. Fearing a looming death far from home, Gwen left John and returned to her parents in England with her two children in June 1925.

It is apparent that Gwen was still in contact with John up to her departure as a postcard she wrote to her family in England in April 1925 stated that she was visiting him in Victoria Hospital and that he was 'fine', but that he was 'going away too'. The family believes this meant that he was being sent to a sanatorium for convalescence.

Gwen's return to England was clearly some time in the planning. Perhaps it was an amicable split – both John and Gwen fearing pending deaths – but with Gwen acutely feeling the distance from home and family with John in hospital. The large Meyers and Sherritt families around Blake would have welcomed their children, but clearly Gwen would have no part in it and took them with her. It is apparent from family letters that this caused considerable consternation and sadness in the extended family.

By the time Gwen left Canada with Peggy and Peter on 1 June 1925, she was suffering from a cough and reportedly instructed the children not to say anything about it, for fear of not being allowed on, or indeed off, the ship. On their arrival in England, Gwen took Peggy and Peter to the home of her parents, William and Annie Beard, in Ross-on-Wye. Perhaps the trip was originally only intended as a brief visit, but before the year was out, Gwen succumbed to her tuberculosis and died. However, instead of being returned to their father in Canada at this time, Peggy and Peter were taken in by Gwen's parents.

Ten years later, when Peggy was sixteen and Peter was not quite fourteen, their lives changed yet again, when they were rocked by two further deaths in the family. Their grandmother Annie died in spring 1935 aged sixty-three, and their father, although some distance away in Canada, died of his tuberculosis in London, Ontario, on 8 August 1935, aged just thirty-six. As a result, Peggy and Peter were split up and found homes with separate relatives.

Peggy was sent to live with Gwen's brother and sister-in-law, Harley and Elsie Beard in a two-up, two-down railway house near the shunting yards at 59 Percy Street, Shrewsbury, but Peter stayed in Ross-on-Wye, moving in with Gwen's younger sister Katherine ('Kay') and Newton Winder. As Harley and Elsie had their own children, Peggy was in good company with younger cousins, and completed her education in Shrewsbury's Lancasterian School, behind the town's prison in Beacall's Lane.

Peggy was a tall girl, who was considered both clever and beautiful. When she was eighteen, she entered the Miss Shrewsbury competition, which was a regional heat of the national Miss England contest. She won the regional competition in 1937 and was crowned Miss Shrewsbury, but was not placed in the ensuing Miss England heats. This did, however, earn her a little local celebrity status. It was also this year that she is understood to have met Eric Lock at a dance. Little is known today about their romance, but they were married in St Julian's Church in Shrewsbury on 27 July 1940, by which time the war was under way, and Eric was a general duties officer pilot in the RAF. Peggy's brother Peter was the best man, and Eric's younger sister Joan was Peggy's bridesmaid. Peter joined the Royal Navy only two days later.

When Eric was posted as missing in August 1941, Peggy is said to have left her parents-in-law's home, where she had been staying while her husband was off fighting, and did not return. She moved back in with her Uncle Harley and Aunt Elsie in Percy Street, Shrewsbury, and it is believed to have been here in July 1942 that she received news that Eric was now presumed dead for official purposes. Peggy took yet another knock, similar to those that had filled her life before: once again, a piece of her life was taken from her. Reacting in the only way she knew, with the resilience and tough skin she had built up since she was small, she pulled herself up off the ground and got on with life.

In July 1943, she married Flight Lieutenant Robert Lloyd Rees Davies, a tall and slim man who was known as Lloyd. Commissioned in the RAFVR from LAC on 8 April 1941, he was promoted to flying officer six months later, and to flight lieutenant in April 1943. On 15 August 1944, he was awarded the Distinguished Flying Cross for his service with No. 25 Squadron, in which he was lauded as 'a highly skilled and courageous pilot whose example has been inspiring'.[4] Then based at Coltishall, he had been credited with successfully attacking a large number of enemy airfields and railway lines, and with destroying three enemy aircraft.

Following the war, Lloyd and Peggy moved to Rayleigh Road, Stoke Bishop, near Bristol, with their first child, Simon, who had been born in 1944. During this time, Lloyd was a pilot for BOAC and the family lived in a house near the Clifton Suspension Bridge. A second son, Nigel, was born here in 1948. However, despite flying around the Middle East in this role, and even meeting the Shah of Iran on one occasion, Lloyd did not find the job fulfilling and subsequently left BOAC.

In September 1949, he and Peggy moved to Chardstock, on the eastern fringe of Devon's Blackdown Hills, where they bought a house named 'The Court' for £6,250. The land was formerly a part of the Chardstock Manor estate and included outbuildings, a garden and an orchard. However, within a year, Lloyd applied for re-admission to the Royal Air Force. He was offered a short service commission as a flight lieutenant in the RAF in November 1950, which required him to relinquish his commission as a flight lieutenant in the RAFVR. The appointment, which allotted him a seniority in his rank of 30 October 1948, comprised eight years on the Active List and four years in the Reserve.

The RAF posted him to RAF Biggin Hill as its chief flying instructor, and Peggy and the two boys moved with him. It was in Bromley, Kent, therefore, that a third son, Jonathan, was born in June 1951. Four months later, Lloyd's short service commission was amended to a permanent commission. It was not until December 1951, however, that Lloyd and Peggy were able to sell their previous house in Chardstock, but they were able to do so for a small profit.

On 23 March 1953, Lloyd was promoted to squadron leader and posted to command No. 603 (City of Edinburgh) Squadron (RAuxAF), then based at RAF Turnhouse, near Edinburgh, Scotland. The family moved with him and took up residence in the officers' mess on the station. At this time, the unit was flying Vampire FB.3s and FB.5s, but also used Meteor T7s for training. The squadron was sent to RAF Sylt in Germany with their aircraft for their two-week annual summer camp and air firing practice that July. However, while driving an RAF Land Rover on 10 July, Lloyd was involved in a collision with a Volkswagen near the US Army's Flint Kaserne in Bad Tölz, and was killed, barely five months into his tenure. It is believed that the other driver, a German officer, was intoxicated.

Not surprisingly, Peggy took the loss very hard. One year later, having been widowed twice by the age of thirty-four, she returned to Canada to raise her three boys. Seeing little prospect for the children in the United Kingdom, she felt her boys might do better in her country of birth. In any case, the English pound sterling was worth much more in Canada, at around two dollars and seventy cents to the pound in July 1954, which meant her RAF pension would stretch that little bit further. It was a courageous decision.

Peggy and the boys arrived in Canada on 23 July 1954, but the hard times did not end there. The boys' boarding school tuition at Upper Canada College in Toronto was paid for by the RAF Benevolent Fund, but Peggy was required to fund their uniforms and activities, while maintaining a home in London, Ontario, on precious little income.

She found work difficult to come by and although she was an accomplished seamstress and knitter, she could not earn enough from these skills to support the family. However, like all the hardships and knocks she had taken until now, she faced these new challenges with resolve and determination. She sold land and clothing to make ends meet, and managed to raise her three boys into men that their father, and no doubt Eric Lock, would have been proud of.

Peggy was an intelligent, artistic, charming and beautiful woman, an insatiable reader with an impeccable taste in clothing and furniture, who always maintained her high standards. However, she was convinced she must be a jinx on her partners, and never remarried. Moving often, constantly seeking a discouragingly elusive sense of security, she suffered from depression in her forties and fifties. She felt she had little in common with her Canadian relatives and never grew roots in any community. As her boys grew up and left home, she found herself quite isolated, and her health began to fail. She died of liver disease in London, Ontario, in the spring of 1978, aged just fifty-eight.

Although, on face value, Peggy's personal life story may not seem a happy one, as the author of this work and, in one sense, an objective story teller, I have discovered a real admiration for her. If ever there was a person who epitomises resilience, it is Peggy, and indeed her brother Peter, who was of the same ilk. Knocked down multiple times, they got back on their feet and carried on. Taken from their childhood home and their father, then losing their mother, father and grandmother within a few years of each other, they were then split up and lived some distance apart.

As if that was not enough, only a few years later, when Peggy thought life was improving and the scars were healing, her husband was severely wounded in the war. Having nursed him back to health over several months, he was killed only weeks after returning to operations. Once again, Peggy picked herself up and subsequently remarried. As time passed and she had children, life settled down and at last took on an air of normality. However, twelve years after losing her first husband, her second was also killed on active service. How many tragedies can one person take in their brief life?

She was a tough and indomitable woman; one to be admired. Every time she was knocked down, she got up again. It was hard, and it had a major effect on her personally, but she rolled with the punches, pulled up her sleeves, and just kept on keeping on. She is an exceptional example to us all, and her legacy lives on in her sons, and no doubt in their own families.

I hope that, through these pages, this gutsy woman will be remembered for the sacrifices she made and the price she paid, giving every piece of herself for her children. I also hope her grandchildren, great grandchildren, and subsequent generations will find her life and values an inspiration for their own.

Notes to Text

Chapter One – Growing Up in Shrewsbury

1. There remains no explanation why Charles Lock and Dora Cornes travelled 107 miles north to the Fylde Registration District (roughly between Blackpool and Preston) to get married. Was it a forbidden marriage between an Anglican and a Methodist? Dora's brother had married one of Charles's sisters four years before this, so that was unlikely to be the reason. Perhaps Dora was pregnant, but no child survived, so maybe she had lost it? This theory is supported by evidence provided in the 1911 Census, which suggests that one child of the marriage had died. Despite searches, however, no relevant birth can be located.
2. It has been suggested that Eric climbed the Long Mynd to watch the gliders of the Midland Gliding Club and on one occasion met aviation pioneer Amy Johnson, who was the first woman to fly solo from London to Australia. However, this cannot be substantiated. What can be established is that the club did not commence flying from the Long Mynd until summer 1934, around six years after Eric left Clivedon School, when he was fifteen. Further, while Amy Johnson did in fact visit the club, this occurred in 1938, when Eric was nineteen. Drawing these facts together, it is quite possible that the anecdote is true, but it would have occurred some years after Eric attended Clivedon School.
3. The facts surrounding this family story have proven difficult to corroborate. While anecdotes suggest that the flight was made from Prees Heath, around twenty-three miles north of Bayston Hill, it has been established that Sir Alan Cobham's Flying Circus never operated from this location. In fact, the closest Cobham came to Prees was Whitchurch, which he visited on 9 September 1933, some six months after Eric's birthday. The Flying Circus made another visit to Whitchurch on 6 July 1934, which is a closer date to his birthday, but a year after it is purported to have taken place. Moreover, some accounts suggest that Eric's flight was undertaken in de Havilland DH61 Giant Moth G-AAEV, but it is unclear how such a precise aircraft identification has come about, as that particular aircraft was only used by the Flying Circus until the end of the 1929 season, approximately four years before Eric is supposed to have flown in it. In fact, the aircraft was sold to Imperial Airways in late 1929 and crashed in Rhodesia in January 1930, so cannot have taken part in the air shows in 1933 or 1934. The only other circumstantially fitting possibility is that Cobham's rival company, the 'British Hospitals Air Pageant', visited Shrewsbury on 4 May 1933, less than a month after Eric's fourteenth birthday. Supporting this possibility, in an interview to a newspaper in late 1940 after Eric was awarded the DSO, his mother Dora told the reporter that he had taken his first 'flip' in an air show at Shrewsbury.

Chapter Two – Flying Training

1. Extract from prime minister Neville Chamberlain's speech at No. 10 Downing Street on 30 September 1938, upon his return from meeting the German chancellor, Adolf Hitler. This information is licensed under the terms of the Open Government Licence (http://www.nationalarchives.gov.uk/doc/open-government-licence).
2. *Flight* magazine, 14 July 1938, Flight Global, Quadrant House, The Quadrant, Sutton, SM2 5AS, UK.
3. Meir is today a suburb of Stoke-on-Trent.
4. Extract from the radio address by prime minister Neville Chamberlain from the Cabinet Office of No. 10 Downing Street, 3 September 1939. This information is licensed under the terms of the Open Government Licence (http://www.nationalarchives.gov.uk/doc/open-government-licence).
5. *Flight* magazine, 23 November 1939, Flight Global, Quadrant House, The Quadrant, Sutton, SM2 5AS, UK.

6. This changed after the Dunkirk evacuation in May/June 1940, and the children were relocated to safer areas of England.
7. The minimum hours were increased even further in practice, to over 200 hours by late 1941. Nonetheless, King's Regulations (KR 811) still stated until at least late 1944 that eighty hours were the minimum.
8. Extract from prime minister Winston Churchill's speech, '*War Situation*', to the House of Commons, 18 June 1940, House of Commons Hansard, Parliamentary Archives, HC Deb, 18 June 1940, vol. 362 cc 51–61. This information is licensed under the terms of the Open Parliament Licence.

Chapter Three – Posted to Operations
1. *Flying Made My Arms Ache*; Squadron Leader R.W. 'Wally' Wallens, DFC, retd, 1990, Self Publishing Association Ltd.
2. Excerpt from a letter from Group Captain Norman Ryder, CBE, DFC, to Andy Long, dated 15 June 1992; reproduced with Andy's kind permission.
3. *One of 'The Few': The Memoirs of Wing Commander Ted 'Shippy' Shipman AFC*, John Shipman, 2008, Pen & Sword.

Chapter Four – Battle of Britain Ace
1. Source: *German Air Forces Available for Attack on England and to Aid in Invasion*, Appendix B to No. 11 Group Operation Instruction No. 14, dated 18 September 1940, TNA AIR 25/198.
2. Intelligence Report, Reconstruction of Enemy Raid – 15.8.40., No. 41 Squadron archives.
3. Ibid.
4. Ibid.
5. Ibid.
6. Ibid.
7. Combat Report for Flight Lieutenant Norman Ryder, No. 580, 15 August 1940, TNA AIR 50/18.
8. Combat Report for Pilot Officer Eric Lock, 15 August 1940, No. 41 Squadron archives.
9. *One of 'The Few': The Memoirs of Wing Commander Ted 'Shippy' Shipman AFC*, John Shipman, 2008, Pen & Sword.
10. This aircraft was Me110D, WNr 3155, M8+CH, of 1/ZG76, whose crew were Oberleutnant Hans Ulrich Kettling (pilot) and Obergefreiter Friedrich Volk (wireless operator). Both men were captured and spent the rest of the war as POWs in Wales and Canada. Kettling later attested to having been subjected to two separate strikes, one disabling his starboard engine, and the other disabling his port engine, destroying his windscreen and wounding Volk. This appears to fit neatly with Shipman's and Bennions's attacks.
11. *Luftwaffe Over the North*, Bill Norman, 1997, Pen & Sword, ISBN 0850525292, and reproduced with Bill's kind permission.
12. Extract from prime minister Winston Churchill's speech, 'War Situation', to the House of Commons, 20 August 1940, House of Commons Hansard, Parliamentary Archives, HC Deb, 20 August 1940, vol. 364 cc 1165–1167. This information is licensed under the terms of the Open Parliament Licence.
13. This information has been extracted from a distribution list attached to an Intelligence Report for 21 August 1940 in No. 41 Squadron's archives. The list only contains ranks and surnames; forenames and initials have been added, and corrections made, by the author.
14. Entry in propaganda minister Dr Josef Goebbels's diary on 27 August 1940, as quoted in *Der Jahrhundertkrieg*, Guido Knopp, Econ, 2001, ISBN 9783430155168.
15. *Flying Made My Arms Ache*; Squadron Leader R.W. 'Wally' Wallens, DFC, retd, 1990, Self Publishing Association Ltd.
16. Both Flying Officer Wallens and Pilot Officer Cory are listed on the No. 41 Squadron ORB's F541 as having flown Spitfire I, X4021, on the 15:00 hours patrol on 5 September 1940. As X4021 is understood to have been the aircraft seriously damaged when Wallens force-landed, it is unclear which aircraft was being flown by Cory.
17. Both Flight Lieutenant Webster and Flying Officer Morrogh-Ryan are listed on the No. 41 Squadron ORB's F541 as having flown Spitfire Ia, R6635, on the 15:00 hours patrol on 5 September 1940. However, as parts of Webster's aircraft were located after this attack marked 'R6635', it is apparent that it was Webster who was flying this aircraft. It is unclear, therefore, which aircraft was being flown by Morrogh-Ryan.
18. The two Heinkel 111s claimed by Eric that day were possibly shared with other pilots. Contemporary evidence suggests that one of these aircraft was likely He111H-3, WNr 3338, A1+CR, of 7/KG53,

NOTES TO THE TEXT   231

which ditched just off The Nore at 15:30 hours. It is believed the plane was initially hit by anti-aircraft fire while bombing an oil storage facility at Thameshaven, and subsequently attacked by fighters, thereunder Eric, No. 17 Squadron's Flying Officer Count Manfred Czernin, and possibly also No. 73 Squadron's Sergeant Pilot John Brimble. Two of the crew, Feldwebel A. Maier and Unteroffizier H. Lenger were rescued by Royal Navy patrol boats, but the remaining three, Feldwebel Erwin Agner, Unteroffizier Rudolf Armbruster and Gefreiter Alexius Nowotny remain missing, presumed dead. The other aircraft is believed to have been He111H-2, WNr 2632, A1+GR, also of 7/KG53, which went into the sea west of Margate Hook Beacon around 15:30, following the same raid on the oil storage facility at Thameshaven. It is believed to have been attacked by Eric, No. 17 Squadron's Count Manfred Czernin and Sergeant Pilot Clifford Chew, and possibly also No. 73 Squadron's Squadron Leader Maurice Robinson. The entire crew was lost: Feldwebel Hermann Bohn, Unteroffiziers Karl Bickl, Fritz Bolz and F. Rosenberger and Gefreiter K. Haak.

19. There are two Combat Reports for Eric for 5 September 1940 in National Archives file AIR 50/18 (Combat Reports, No. 41 Squadron), numbered 514–515 and 516–517, which suggest he claimed four destroyed and one probably destroyed enemy aircraft on this date. However, the second pages of each of the Combat Reports, which explain the detail of the actions, differ significantly in context. In the former, Eric is flying as Red 2; in the latter as Yellow 1. The time of attack also differs, the former taking place at 15:00 hours and the latter at 14:30. There are also other inconsistencies. It is now clear that, despite appearances, Eric did not make the claims in the latter Combat Report (No. 516–517) on 5 September 1940; they pertain instead to 5 October 1940. The evidence for this lies in documents in No. 41 Squadron's archives, particularly the original typed and signed Combat Report, which also includes an annotation by the intelligence officer, Flight Lieutenant Lord Gisborough, stating in red pen after the date 5.9.40, '? Probably 5.10.40 G [Gisborough] IO. 41 Sqdn'. A cross reference with Intelligence Reports for 5 October 1940, also in No. 41 Squadron's archives, reveal that Eric made three claims that day, one destroyed and one probable Me109s on a patrol between 13:32 and 14:54 hours, and another probable Me109 on a patrol from 15:36 to 16:42. The National Archives has a Combat Report for the latter of these patrols (No. 532–533), but not the former. As the circumstances, context and timings of the earlier victories that day fit neatly with Combat Report No. 516–517, it is therefore apparent that Combat Report 516–517 is erroneously dated 5 September 1940 and pertains instead to events of 5 October 1940. As such, only the victories contained in Combat Reports 514–515 are included in the text for 5 September 1940.
20. As a whole on 5 September 1940, No. 11 Group had sustained losses of eight pilots killed in action, seven wounded and two injured, but also claimed sixty-four victories against the Luftwaffe during the day's two raids: twenty-eight destroyed, twenty-two probably destroyed and fourteen damaged.
21. Combat Report for Pilot Officer Eric Lock, No. 518, 6 September 1940, TNA AIR 50/18.
22. This aircraft is believed to have been Ju88A-1, F1+DP, of I./KG76, which crashed at Evere, Belgium.
23. Excerpt from a letter to Andy Long from Flight Lieutenant Roy Ford, dated 6 March 1993; reproduced with Andy's kind permission.
24. Combat Report for Pilot Officer Eric Lock, 9 September 1940, No. 41 Squadron archives.
25. Ibid.
26. Ibid.
27. No. 11 Group ORB Appendix, 11 September 1940, TNA AIR 25/197.
28. *Composite Combat Report, 41 Squadron, 1810–1900 hours, 14.9.40*, No. 41 Squadron archives.
29. Combat Report for Pilot Officer Eric Lock, No. 522, 14 September 1940, TNA AIR 50/18.
30. Ibid.
31. Ibid.
32. This was possibly Unteroffizier Valentin Blazejewski in Me109E-7, WNr 2014, of 6/LG2, who was captured unhurt. This aircraft may also have been attacked by Pilot Officer John Lloyd and Sergeant Pilot William Rolls of No. 72 Squadron.
33. No. 11 Group ORB, 15 September 1940, TNA AIR 25/193.
34. Post-war research places the total number of aircraft destroyed on 15 September 1940 closer to thirty-four bombers and twenty-six fighters destroyed, and twenty bombers seriously damaged.
35. Pilot Officer Tom Neil became the officer commanding No. 41 Squadron in September 1942 and held the post for approximately ten months.
36. Combat Report for Pilot Officer Eric S. Lock, No. 524, 15 September 1940, TNA AIR 50/18.
37. Ibid.
38. There are at least four conflicting accounts of these actions provided by the two men involved. These date from the same day, late October 1940, and 2007.

- Eric's Combat Report for his victories (TNA AIR 50/18, folios 524–525) suggest that while he and the (then unidentified) Hurricane pilot joined up and attacked the same formation of Me109s and Do17s in unison, they actually claimed one Me109 and one Do17 each. It is apparent from his report that Eric had already shot down his own Do17 before assisting Pilot Officer Tom Neil with the remaining Do17. Although Eric states 'we carried out ½ and beam attack[s]' on the remaining aircraft, he clarifies that it was actually 'shot down by [the] Hurricane', apparently declining a share in the victory over the third Dornier. Neither a squadron Intelligence Report for the day, nor a summary of Eric's victories, both held in No. 41 Squadron's archives, make any mention of him sharing any of his victories with Neil;
- Page one of Tom Neil's Combat Report states twice that he claimed two Do215 (not Do17s) destroyed but did not declare the Me109s. On the second page, in the detail of the report, Neil makes no mention of Eric or the presence of a Spitfire, and although someone has written in a different hand at the end of one paragraph 'Shared with EB-E', the front page has not been altered. It is unclear when this comment was added;
- In a radio broadcast of an interview with Eric and Tom Neil on 22 October 1940, it was suggested that Neil shot down two Me109s and Eric one, after which Neil shot down a Do17 by himself. The second Dornier is hardly mentioned, but the third was attacked by both men, and finished off by Eric as Neil's ammunition ran out;
- In a 2007 letter (Neil to Wheeler, 30 May 2007), Neil states that Eric had observed him shooting down two Me109s, and that they had then shared the destruction of a Do17. Having circled the wreck in the sea, they then flew back to the coast together, which conflicts with Eric's Combat Report that he 'left the other DO 17 being chased by the Hurricane', but was joined by the Hurricane again over the coast.

It is not possible to verify today what in fact occurred with any real certainty, but as this work is based on 'claims', and Eric claimed one Do17 and one Me109 destroyed in his Combat Report, and Tom Neil claimed two Dorniers in his, and clarified in subsequent accounts that the two Me109s were also shot down by him, this is the version used in this account.

39. *London Gazette*, issue 34958, 1 October 1940. This information is licensed under the terms of the Open Government Licence (http://www.nationalarchives.gov.uk/doc/open-government-licence).
40. Ibid.
41. *Intelligence Patrol Report, 41 Squadron 0907-1033 hours, 18.9.40*, No. 41 Squadron archives.
42. Combat Report for Pilot Officer Eric Lock, No. 528, 18 September 1940, TNA AIR 50/18.
43. Combat Report for Pilot Officer Eric Lock, 20 September 1940, No. 41 Squadron archives.
44. The Heinkel He113 was a fictional Luftwaffe fighter used as a propaganda and disinformation strategy by Germany. Actually a He100D, only twenty-two were built as prototypes and production aircraft, as they were not accepted for operational use by the Luftwaffe. However, Germany's propaganda minister, Joseph Goebbels, used the opportunity to announce that a new fighter had entered service and photographed the aircraft at several German airfields in varying paint schemes and fabricated unit designations. Claims were also made that the aircraft had proven itself in combat in Denmark and Norway. British Intelligence took the misinformation seriously, and it was some time before the falsehood was recognised. By that time, however, RAF pilots had claimed many victories over the type. The aircraft they had taken credit for were in fact Me109Es, which was the only single-seat fighter in full operational use by the Luftwaffe during the Battle of Britain.
45. Combat Report for Pilot Officer Eric Lock, 20 September 1940, No. 41 Squadron archives.
46. Ibid.
47. Ibid.

Chapter Five – Great Courage

1. Combat Report for Pilot Officer Eric Lock, No. 516, 5 October 1940 (erroneously dated 5 September 1940), TNA AIR 50/18.
2. Ibid.
3. *Intelligence Patrol Report, 41 Squadron – 1332-1454 hours 5.10.40*, No. 41 Squadron archives.
4. Combat Report for Pilot Officer Eric Lock, No. 532, 5 October 1940, TNA AIR 50/18.
5. Entry for 7 October 1940 in the logbook of John Mackenzie, RNZAF, AFMNZ.
6. Pilot Officer Edward Wells's attack is based on a statement by Flying Officer John Mackenzie in his logbook on 7 October 1940. However, the squadron F541 that day does not show him flying on this patrol. This is possibly an erroneous substitute for Pilot Officer Robert Boret, who is listed on the F541 and is also mentioned by Mackenzie on his Pilot Service Record.
7. Pilot Service Record for Flying Officer John Mackenzie, No. 41 Squadron archives.

NOTES TO THE TEXT 233

8. Combat Report for Pilot Officer Eric Lock, No. 534, 9 October 1940, TNA AIR 50/18.
9. The aircraft destroyed by Eric is believed to have been Me109E-4, WNr 1573, of 9/JG54, which was flown by 26-year-old Leutnant Josef Eberle. His body was washed ashore near Harwich on 26 October 1940, and he is buried today in the German Military Cemetery at Cannock Chase.
10. No. 11 Group ORB Appendix, 11 October 1940, TNA AIR 25/198.
11. Combat Report for Pilot Officer Eric Lock, No. 536, 11 October 1940, TNA AIR 50/18.
12. Ibid.
13. RAF Hornchurch ORB, 11 October 1940, TNA AIR 28/384.
14. *London Gazette*, issue 34976, 22 October 1940. This information is licensed under the terms of the Open Government Licence (http://www.nationalarchives.gov.uk/doc/open-government-licence).
15. Combat Report for Pilot Officer Frederick Aldridge, No. 19, 17 October 1940, TNA AIR 50/18.
16. *Fighter Command Combat Report, Intelligence Patrol Report – 41 Squadron – 20.10.40*, folio 508, TNA AIR 50/18.
17. Ibid.
18. Combat Report for Pilot Officer Eric Lock, 25 October 1940, No. 540, TNA AIR 50/18, and No. 203, TNA AIR 27/428.

Chapter Six – Shot Down and Wounded
1. This information has been extracted from a distribution list attached to an Intelligence Report for 4 November 1940, held in No. 41 Squadron's archives. The list only contains ranks and surnames; forenames and initials have been added by the author.
2. The No. 41 Squadron ORB states on 9 November 1940 that Eric was forced to land at Manston 'owing to his aircraft being damaged by enemy action'; however, this is believed to be an erroneous entry that should have appeared in the ORB on 8 November, instead. No. 41 Squadron did not see any action at all on 9 November and several records, including the RAF Hornchurch ORB, refer to his action as having occurred on 8 November.
3. These numbers are taken from an Intelligence Report for the operation held in No. 41 Squadron's archives. However, there appears to be a little disagreement about the numbers as the RAF Hornchurch ORB states there were 'about 40 Me.109s and He113s', while the No. 11 Group ORB Appendix states the formation consisted of '60 He113s and Me109s'. (Note, though, that the He113 did not exist; it was only a fabrication of German propaganda.) In his Combat Report, Flight Lieutenant Tony Lovell estimated that the formation consisted of approximately thirty Me109s, while Pilot Officer Frederick Aldridge put the number closer to seventy aircraft, noting in his Combat Report that there was one formation of twenty aircraft followed by a second of fifty.
4. *Intelligence Patrol Report, 41 Squadron (0800–0938 hours)*, 17.11.40, No. 41 Squadron archives.
5. RAF Hornchurch ORB, 17 November 1940, TNA AIR 28/394.
6. Entries on these pilots' Combat Reports on 17 November 1940 suggest that this was the order in which victories were achieved. It should, however, be noted that Flight Lieutenant Lovell stated his combat took place at 08:50 hours, which is slightly earlier than the commencement time for the battle stated in the No. 11 Group ORB Appendix. Alternatively, Eric's Combat Report declares his combats took place at 09:30, but this is the time the squadron is recorded in the ORB as having landed back at Hornchurch. However, he did not write his own Combat Report as he was wounded in the engagement. A report written by him (CR 535, TNA AIR 50/18), at a much later date, outlines his combats but does not give a time. Based on previous performance, though, it is highly unlikely that his combats and victories took place this long into a battle that commenced at 09:00. It is most probable that all the combats happened within a five- to ten-minute timeframe between 09:00 and 09:10 hours.
7. Combat Report for Pilot Officer Frederick Aldridge, No. 26, 17 November 1940, TNA AIR 50/18.
8. No. 41 Squadron ORB, 17 November 1940, TNA AIR 27/424.
9. Combat Report for Flying Officer John Mackenzie, No. 563, 17 November 1940, TNA AIR 50/18.
10. Combat Report for Pilot Officer Eric Lock, No. 543, 17 November 1940, TNA AIR 50/18.
11. Undated subsequent Combat Report for Pilot Officer Eric Lock, No. 535, for 17 November 1940, TNA AIR 50/18.
12. RAF Hornchurch ORB, 17 November 1940, TNA AIR 28/394.
13. It is not possible to match Nos 41 and 603 Squadrons' claims on 17 November 1940 with available Luftwaffe records. JG54 reported the loss of only two pilots, and a third who force-landed at Ostend, Belgium, having run out of fuel. The two pilots who failed to return were Oberleutnant Roloff von Aspern, Staffelkapitän of 5/JG54, and Oberfeldwebel Wilhelm Donninger of the same Staffel; the pilot who force-landed was from 2/JG54. However, it is known that several Me109s from

14. JG54 returned with combat damage. Additionally, JG26 reported the loss of their Staffelkapitän, Oberleutnant Eberhard Henrici, who also went into the sea.
14. Spitfire IIa, P7544, was salvaged and sent to Westland Aircraft Ltd in Yeovil, Somerset, for repairs on 30 November 1940. The aircraft was rebuilt and returned to service with No. 266 Squadron on 31 March 1941.
15. Some accounts suggest that Eric climbed out of his cockpit and doused flames on his aircraft before help arrived. This can be discounted as most unlikely for several reasons. First of all, Eric states he was unable to open his hood. Had he been able to do so, he would have done this in the air and possibly parachuted to safety rather than risk his life in a virtually uncontrolled forced landing. Further, it is suggested that despite having his arm broken in two places, machine gun and/or cannon wounds to his left leg and right knee, and suffering from the effects of significant blood loss and shock, he still managed to climb out of the cockpit unaided. Thirdly, once out of his cockpit and safe, he would have had little incentive or reason to extinguish a fire, let alone have had the strength to do so. He is unlikely to have been able to stand and his wounds would have been his paramount concern – certainly greater than the fact his aircraft may have been on fire.
16. Sulfa powder, or sulphanilamide, which was marketed in the United Kingdom as M&B 693, was an antibacterial drug used widely from 1938. It was the first and only antibiotic available before penicillin. Sprinkled on to open wounds before bandaging as an immediate treatment, it was credited with saving thousands of lives during the Second World War. Sulfa powder was ultimately issued to every American soldier as a part of his personal first-aid pouch.
17. Service record of Flight Lieutenant Eric S. Lock, RAF Disclosures, Trenchard Hall, RAF Cranwell, Sleaford NG34 8HG.
18. There have been suggestions that Eric also sustained burns, but this is incorrect and is more likely an assumption based upon the fact that he was subsequently admitted to the Queen Victoria Hospital in East Grinstead for skin grafting, or stories that he put flames out on his aircraft, or both. As most patients at QVH were given skin grafts for burns, the assumption is understandable, but is nonetheless incorrect.
19. RAF Hornchurch ORB, 28 November 1940, TNA AIR 28/394. There is an anomaly in the entry in the RAF Hornchurch ORB, which states that Eric's total number of enemy aircraft destroyed to that point in time was twenty-one, whereas all other records give the total as twenty-two. The citation for Eric's Distinguished Service Order in the London Gazette even goes so far as to say that the total was 'at least twenty-two'.
20. *Daily Mail*, 10 December 1940.
21. Citation for the award of the Distinguished Service Order to Pilot Officer Eric Lock, 17 December 1940, *London Gazette*, issue 35015. This information is licensed under the terms of the Open Government Licence (http://www.nationalarchives.gov.uk/doc/open-government-licence/).
22. *Daily Mail*, 10 December 1940.
23. The mayor's son, Flying Officer Harry M. Steward, was killed in action on 16 July 1944.
24. *Shrewsbury Chronicle*, 13 December 1940.
25. Ibid.
26. As recounted by Joan Stather to John Wheeler via Hamish Evans, 2006.
27. Macmillan and Co. Ltd, London, 1942, but reprinted numerous times since.
28. Flying Officer Richard Hillary in *The Last Enemy*, Macmillan and Co. Ltd, London, 1942, p. 194.
29. Ibid., p. 176 and pp. 177–78.
30. Ibid., pp. 190–91.
31. Ibid., p. 191.
32. Ibid.
33. Flight Lieutenant Richard Hillary was ultimately released from QVH and returned to flying but was killed in a flying accident during a night-time training flight in a Blenheim of No. 54 OTU on 8 January 1943. Flying Officer Tony Tollmache also returned to service but was killed in a motor vehicle accident in Paris in 1977.
34. No. 41 Squadron ORB, 20 February 1941, TNA AIR 27/425.
35. Letter from Sir Walter Monkton, KCVO, KC, MC, director-general of the Ministry of Information, London, addressed to Eric, dated 11 March 1941. © Melissa John.
36. As recounted by Joan Stather to John Wheeler via Hamish Evans, 2006.
37. Ibid.

Chapter Seven – Back to Work
1. No. 611 Squadron ORB, 27 June 1941, TNA AIR 27/2110.

NOTES TO THE TEXT   235

2. The number of victories quoted here cannot be substantiated with solid evidence. Combat Reports, newspaper reports, the citation for his DSO, and other documentation from Eric's time on No. 41 Squadron all point to twenty-two enemy aircraft destroyed and seven probably destroyed.
3. Extracted from *Appendix to Part II of 11 Group Intelligence Bulletin No. 215, Fighter Command Pilots with more than Twelve Confirmed Victories. (Up to 30th June, 1941)*, 30 July 1941, TNA AIR 25/200, with forenames added and some corrections made by the author.
4. No. 611 Squadron ORB, 29 June 1941, TNA AIR 27/2110.
5. Barrow Deep is one of three main shipping channels in the North Sea, leading into the Thames Estuary to the Port of London. It is located approximately ten miles off the Essex coast. The other two main shipping routes are Black Deep Channel and Princes Channel. In essence, a 'Barrow Deep' patrol implied that the squadron was maintaining routine patrols along a section of one of the main British shipping routes off the Essex coast.
6. RAF Hornchurch ORB, 1 July 1941, TNA AIR 28/384.
7. Ibid.
8. No. 611 Squadron ORB, 2 July 1941, TNA AIR 27/2110.
9. Contemporary evidence suggests Broadhurst was attacked by Hauptmann Josef Priller of JG26.
10. RAF Hornchurch ORB, 4 July 1941, TNA AIR 28/384.
11. No. 11 Group ORB Appendix, Circus 32, 4 July 1941, TNA AIR 25/200.
12. Combat Report for Flight Lieutenant Eric S. Lock, No. 197, 6 July 1941, TNA AIR 50/173.
13. Ibid.
14. RAF Hornchurch ORB, 6 July 1941, TNA AIR 28/384.
15. Combat Report for Sergeant Pilot William Gilmour, No. 115, 6 July 1941, TNA AIR 50/173.
16. Ibid.
17. Ibid.
18. No. 611 Squadron ORB, 6 July 1941, TNA AIR 27/2110.
19. RAF Hornchurch ORB, 7 July 1941, TNA AIR 28/384.
20. No. 611 Squadron ORB, 7 July 1941, TNA AIR 27/2110.
21. RAF Hornchurch ORB, 8 July 1941, TNA AIR 28/384.
22. Ibid.
23. No. 11 Group ORB Appendix, Circus 39, 8 July 1941, TNA AIR 25/200.
24. Ibid.
25. Combat Report for Flight Lieutenant Eric S. Lock, No. 199, 8 July 1941, TNA AIR 50/173.
26. Ibid.
27. Combat Report for Sergeant Pilot Norman Townsend, No. 303, 8 July 1941, TNA AIR 50/173.
28. Combat Report for Flying Officer Peter Dexter, No. 86, 8 July 1941, TNA AIR 50/173.
29. Ibid.
30. RAF Hornchurch ORB, 8 July 1941, TNA AIR 28/384.
31. No. 611 Squadron ORB, 12 July 1941, TNA AIR 27/2110.
32. Ibid., 14 July 1941.
33. Ibid., 14 July 1941.
34. Ibid., 16 July 1941.
35. Ibid., 17 July 1941.
36. No. 611 Squadron ORB, 27 July 1941, TNA AIR 27/2110.
37. Ibid., 29 July 1941.
38. Ibid., 31 July 1941.
39. Undated letter from Eric to his mother. As the text of the letter refers to him achieving his first victory on No. 611 Squadron the day before, this suggests it was written on 7 July 1941. © Melissa John.
40. Letter from James C.F. Hayter to Christopher John, dated 16 July 1994. © Melissa John.
41. Extracted from *Pilots with more than Twelve Confirmed Victories (Up to 31st July, 1941)*, No. 11 Group ORB Appendix, August 1941, TNA AIR 25/200, with forenames added and some corrections made by the author.

Chapter Eight – Ruddy Awful Waste

1. No. 11 Group ORB, 3 August 1941, TNA AIR 25/200.
2. RAF Hornchurch ORB, 3 August 1941, TNA AIR 28/384.
3. No. 611 Squadron ORB, 3 August 1941, TNA AIR 27/2110.
4. Flight Lieutenant Edmund Cathels was shot down and captured approximately three weeks later, on 27 August 1941 – the same day as the author's great uncle, who was on No. 41 Squadron – and they

are believed to have been transported to Dulag Luft in the same train together.
5. No. 611 Squadron ORB, 3 August 1941, TNA AIR 27/2110.
6. Undated letter from Eric to his mother. As the text of the letter refers to him achieving his first victory since returning to operations the day before, this suggests it was written on 7 July 1941. © Melissa John.
7. Duncan Smith, Group Captain W.G.G., DSO, DFC, *Spitfire into Battle*, Arrow Books, 1981.
8. DBST = Double British Summertime. This was the time in the United Kingdom from 4 May to 10 August 1941, and equated to both GMT+2 and Middle European Time (MET). This implies that it was the same time in the United Kingdom as it was in France on 3 August 1941.
9. Fighter claims, *Oberkommando der Luftwaffe, Chef für Ausz. und Dizsiplin, Luftwaffen-Personalamt* [Head of Training and Discipline, Luftwaffe Personnel Department] L.P.(A.)V. *Filme, Bundesarchiv-Militärarchiv*, Freiburg, Germany, Film C. 2036/II Nr. 69278/42.
10. Correspondence with R. Vince Hogg, June 2010.
11. Combat Report for Flight Lieutenant Norman Ryder, No. 566, for 3 April 1940, dated 5 April 1940, TNA AIR 50/18.
12. Intelligence Report, *Rhubarb Operations Target 212-213-214 (Distilleries), 41 Squadron, 1445–1550*, 19 November 1941, No. 41 Squadron archives.
13. RAF Hornchurch ORB, 3 August 1941, TNA AIR 28/384.
14. Ibid.
15. Ibid.
16. Letter from Thomas F. Neil to Johnny Wheeler, dated 30 May 2007; reproduced with Johnny's permission.
17. Letter from James C.F. Hayter to Christopher John, dated 16 July 1994, and reproduced with Melissa John's permission.
18. *The Times*, p. 7, issue 49278; column D, 3 July 1942.
19. Ibid.

Chapter Nine – Eric's Legacy
1. In 2007, the oil painting of Eric was hanging in the office of the officer commanding, No. 1119 (Shrewsbury) Squadron ATC, at Copthorne Barracks, although he had no idea how it came to be there. At the time of writing, however, this rather unique piece of history was no longer in the squadron's possession, and its location was once again unknown.
2. 'Dogpole' is the name of a street in Shrewsbury.
3. http://www.raf.mod.uk/stclementdanes/history/since1958.cfm, rtrvd Sep 2015

Appendix II – Victory Claims
1. Entry for 7 October 1940 in the logbook of John Mackenzie, RNZAF, AFMNZ.
2. Entries in this column refer to the folio numbers in the National Archives file TNA AIR 50/18 (Combat Reports, No. 41 Squadron), or to the No. 41 Squadron archive ('41SA'). Combat Reports in No. 41 Squadron's archive are kept in chronological order but do not have reference numbers.
3. There is only a front (summary) page for Eric's Combat Report of 25 October 1940 in TNA AIR 50/18. However, a copy can be found in TNA AIR 27/428 (No. 41 Squadron ORB Appendices, May–December 1940) in folios 202–203.
4. *Appendix to Part II of 11 Group Intelligence Bulletin No. 215, Fighter Command Pilots with more than Twelve Confirmed Victories. (Up to 30th June, 1941)*, 30 July 1941, TNA AIR 25/200.
5. No. 611 Squadron ORB, 27 June 1941, TNA AIR 27/2110.
6. No. 41 Squadron's archive contains a large number of original, handwritten draft documents, such as Combat Reports, that were subsequently typed up, signed and formally submitted.
7. No. 611 Squadron ORB, 14 July 1941, TNA AIR 27/2110.
8. Entries in this column refer to the folio numbers in the National Archives file TNA AIR 50/173 (Combat Reports, No. 611 Squadron), or to No. 611 Squadron's Operations Record Book (ORB).
9. Letter from James C.F. Hayter to Christopher John, dated 16 July 1994. © Melissa John.

Appendix III – The Lock Family
1. These are the ages listed in the 1851 Census (TNA HO107/2042) but it is acknowledged that they differ slightly from the ages generated by the birth and christening dates in the parish records, which are mentioned earlier in the text. The intention of this paragraph is to illustrate what the census document records on the Lock household.
2. This distance is measured on a modern route via Worcester, Kidderminster and Bridgnorth.

Appendix IV – The Meyers Family

1. Elizabeth is recorded in the 1901 Census in Toronto as a widow who was born in Germany on 9 July 1845 and emigrated to Canada in 1852. She died in Toronto on 3 June 1914, aged sixty-nine.
2. Another record states that Charles was born on 16 August 1867. His siblings appear to be Christopher, born 1870, and Otto Frederick, born 7 January 1880.
3. Service record for 654827 Lance Corporal John Aaron Meyers, Library and Archives Canada.
4. Citation for the award to 63457 Flight Lieutenant R. Lloyd R. Davies of the DFC, 15 August 1944, *London Gazette*, issue 36656. This information is licensed under the terms of the Open Government Licence (http://www.nationalarchives.gov.uk/doc/open-government-licence).

Index

A

Abbeville Marshalling Yards,	156
Abyssinia,	11, 32
Acklington,	32, 46
Adams, Dennis,	93, 99–100, 120
Aden Protectorate,	30, 32
Adlertag [Eagle Day],	45
Air Council,	199
Air Defence Great Britain (ADGB),	12
Air Fighting Zone,	10
Air Force Cross (AFC),	32, 150
Air Ministry,	9, 10–11, 14–16, 20, 24, 29, 164
Air Service Training,	17
Air-Sea Rescue (ASR),	141–142, 146
Aircraft Storage Unit,	24
Airspeed Oxford,	24–25
Aitken, Lady,	199
Alderton,	127–129, 205
Aldridge, Frederick,	110, 116, 122, 125–126
Allard, Geoffrey,	189
Allfield Farm,	7, 21, 204
Allison, Jack,	35, 54, 56
American Indians,	142, 218
American War of Independence,	233
Amputation,	130
Angus, Robert,	122, 141, 142
Anson, Avro,	24, 25
Antibiotics,	130–131, 135
ap Ellis, Augustine,	24, 26
Armée de l'Air,	10–11
Armistice,	9, 30, 221, 224
Armstrong Whitworth Aviation,	17
Arques,	174
Ashford,	62–63, 78, 81, 97, 103, 115, 210
Ashurst Wood,	143, 205
Ateliers d'Hellemes Accumulator Factory,	183
Audax, Hawker,	24, 25
Australia,	137, 182, 193
Austria,	13
Austro-Hungarian Empire,	13
Auxiliary Air Force,	12–13, 20
Auxiliary Territorial Service (ATS),	36
A. V. Roe (Avro),	17

B

Bader, Douglas R. S.,	155, 166, 185, 189, 199–200
Bad Tölz,	227
Baker, Aubrey,	113, 122
Baker, Henry (Harry),	81, 85
Balloon barrage,	91, 98, 101
Bamberger, Cyril (Bam),	96
Banning, Edward,	220
Banning, Frances Mary, *see Cornes, Frances Mary*	
Banning, Frances May (Amy),	220
Barclay, Richard,	192
Barnard Castle,	48, 50, 52
Barrow Deep Channel,	180
Barrow Deep patrols,	151, 179, 187, 190–191
Battersea,	115
Battle of,	
Amiens,	29
Arras,	29
Britain (campaign),	27–28, 35, 37, 39, 43, 45, 53–55, 63, 77, 83, 107, 117, 121–122, 137, 140, 144, 147–150, 160, 180, 182, 199–200, 211
Britain (film),	198
Britain Historical Society (BOBHS),	198
Britain Memorial,	199
Britain Memorial Flight (BBMF),	200
Britain Monument,	199
Cambrai,	29
France,	28
Lens,	224
Messines,	29
the Somme,	29
Ypres,	224
Bayston Hill,	
Common,	198
Eric Lock Road,	197
Lyth Hill Road,	2, 6–7, 145
Public Elementary School,	2, 204
Scout Group,	197
(Village of),	1–2, 6, 15, 21, 24, 131, 145, 186, 197, 204, 218
Women's Institute,	145
Bayston Quarries,	3, 7–8, 21, 204
Beachy Head,	39, 65, 119, 124
Beamish, Victor,	86

INDEX

Beard,
  Elsie, 226
  Gwyneth Louie (Gwen), *see Meyers, Gwyneth Louie (Gwen)*
  Harley, 36, 226
  William, 225
  Annie M., 225
Beardsley, Robert (Bob), 90, 119, 122
Belgium, 3, 11, 22, 29, 31, 33, 43–44, 147, 190
Bennions, George (Ben), 35, 37–38, 40–41, 47–52, 54–55, 57–58, 61–62, 65, 67–69, 73, 78, 81, 84–88, 90, 94, 121, 146, 182
Bentley Priory Museum, 200
Berck-sur-Mer, 155, 173, 181
Bergues, 155
Berlin, 20, 54
Bett, Patrick J., 22
Bexhill-on-Sea, 21–23, 101, 204
Biggin Hill, 44, 56–57, 86, 90, 95, 102, 105, 106, 108–113, 115, 119–120, 123–124, 128, 153–156, 159, 165–167, 170, 173, 176–177, 183–184, 210, 227
Birch, Percy Y., 17
Blackpool, 220
Blake (Ontario), 223–225
Blenheim, Bristol, 32, 151, 153–156, 158, 176, 180, 190
Blitz, The, 43, 54, 94
Blitzkrieg, 33
BOAC, 226–227
Bomber Command, 12, 25, 54, 182
Bomere Farm, 1, 3–7, 144, 204, 221
Bomere Pool, 4
Bomere Wood, 4
Books of Remembrance, 199
Boret, Robert, 49, 54, 96, 103
Boreton, 218
Bouchier, Cecil, 55
Boulogne, 91, 124, 165, 167, 177–178, 191, 193, 205, 210, 212
Boyd, Robert F., 150
Boyle, John, 35, 41, 54, 56–58, 62, 68–69, 80, 84
Briggs, Michael, 122
Brimble, John, 208
British Cabinet, 9–11
British Government, 10, 11, 13, 18–19
British Indian Ocean Territory, 199
Brittan, James R., 17
Broadhurst, Harry, 150, 154, 156, 163, 164
Bromley, 71, 227
Brown, Mark H., 189
Brown, Peter, 112–113, 116, 118, 122, 141–142
Bruinier, Jan, 160, 163, 169, 174, 184
Buckingham Palace, 75, 143, 199–200, 205, 221
Bulldog, Bristol, 30
Burne, Thomas, 133
Burway, 5

C

Calais, 64, 105, 123, 152, 175, 178, 186, 210
Canada, 8, 35, 57, 65, 67, 71, 76, 78–79, 84, 182, 193, 223–225, 227–228
Canadian Expeditionary Force (CEF), 223
Canterbury, 62, 78, 91, 141, 152
Capel-le-Ferne, 199
Cap Gris Nez, 84, 124, 178, 185
Carey, Frank R., 189
Carr-Lewty, Robert, 35, 40, 54, 55, 57, 62
Carter Guy, 32, 55
Carter Leslie, 103, 107, 123, 160
Cassel, 154–155
Cathels, Edmund, 191–193
Catterick, 27, 30, 32, 33–35, 39–41, 45, 48–51, 54–56, 146, 182, 204
Census, 217–218, 220–221, 223
Chain Home Radar, 44
Chalder, Harry, 85
Chamberlain, Neville, 13, 18, 19
Chardstock, 227
Charles, Edward F. J. (Jack), 181
Chatford, 218
Chatham, 64, 84, 85, 95–96, 101, 110, 118, 126
Cherbourg, 190, 195
Cheshire, 1, 7–8, 144
Chew, Clifford, 208
Chief Whirling Thunder, 142
Chocques, 151–152, 155, 158, 164, 165
Chocques Power Station, 151, 155, 156, 163–165, 170
Christmas, 6, 24, 136
Church Fenton, 32
Church Stretton, 5, 204
Churchill, Winston, 28, 33, 53, 200
Circus operations,
  No. 28, 151
  No. 31, 153
  No. 32, 156
  No. 35, 159
  No. 36, 162
  No. 38, 164–165
  No. 39, 167
  No. 40, 170
  No. 46, 174
  No. 48, 176
  No. 52, 180
  No. 54, 183
Clacton, 82, 123, 125–126, 128–129, 152, 183, 205
Clivedon School, 5, 204
Coastal Command, 12
Collins, Susan, 217
Coltishall, 153, 162, 173–174, 226
Committee of Imperial Defence, 10
Communist Party, 11
Condover, 1, 218
Condover Church of St Andrew & Mary, 197
Condover Cemetery, 197
Condover Hall,
Cornes,
  Dora Evelyn, *see Lock, Dora Evelyn*
  Edith Ellen, 220
  Frances Mary (Mary), 220
  Peter, 220

Rebecca (née Adams), 220
Sarah Ann (Ann), 220
Thomas, 219
Thomas Peter, 220
Cory, Guy, 35, 40, 54–55, 58, 61–62, 69, 71, 109–110, 119, 122
Council for the Protection of Rural England, 24
Cranwell, 31, 63, 150
Croome D'Abitot, 215
Cropthorne, 215
Crossley, Michael N., 150, 189, 199
Croydon, 16, 56, 120, 123
Cunliffe-Owen Aircraft Factory, 71
Czechoslovakia, 13, 18, 139, 182, 211
Czernin, Manfred, 208

D

Daily Mail, 134
Daladier, Édouard, 13
Darling, Edward, 35, 39, 41, 54, 56, 65, 69, 78–80, 88, 89
Davies,
 Jonathan, 226
 Nigel, 226
 Rich, 199
 Robert Lloyd Rees (Lloyd), 226–227
 Simon, 223, 226
 Thomas, 7
Deal, 68, 71–72, 76, 101, 105, 109–110, 121, 152
Debden, 44, 55, 124, 176, 178, 187
Declaration of War, 19, 22, 30, 135
Deere, Alan C., 189
De La Warr Pavilion, 22, 23
Demon, Hawker, 30
Desvres, 165, 191
Detling, 57, 173
Dewar family, 144
Dexter, Peter, 164, 172–173, 177, 178
Digby, 149, 153, 162
Dig for Victory campaign, 21
Dishforth, 45
Distinguished Flying Cross (DFC), 17, 21, 29, 31–32, 40, 44, 55, 63, 85, 107, 134, 143, 150, 181, 189, 192, 195, 198–199, 204, 205, 226
Distinguished Flying Medal (DFM), 150, 161, 189
Distinguished Service Order (DSO), 17, 29, 132–133, 143, 150, 156, 189, 193, 197, 199, 205, 207, 211–212
Doe, Bob, 199–200
Domesday Book, 2, 36, 218
Do17, Dornier, 56–58, 62–64, 79–83, 115, 209–210
Do215, Dornier, 57, 78–79, 83, 99, 119, 209
Dorrington, 218
Dover, 37–39, 43, 56, 58, 63 68, 70, 71, 72, 76, 78–79, 84–85, 87–89, 91, 95–96, 98–99, 101–102, 104–107, 110–111, 118, 121, 141–142, 162, 210
Dovey, Rev. Kendal, 6
Dovey, Edith, 6
Dowding, Sir Hugh, 52, 92, 199
Duncan Smith, Wilfred, 164, 168, 193

Dungeness, 56, 65–67, 71–72, 76–77, 81, 83, 87, 90, 95–102, 104–109, 111, 115, 118–120, 123–124, 162, 173, 175–176, 178, 204, 210
Dunkirk, 27, 30–31, 43, 63, 139, 149, 152, 155–156, 161, 170, 172, 175, 178, 180, 183, 185
Durham, 51–52
Duchess of Cornwall, 199
Dutton, Roy G., 189
Dutton Homestall Convalescent Home, 143–145, 205
Duxford, 149, 156, 159, 170, 174
Dyas, Gwendoline, 198
Dyce, 32, 46
Dymchurch, 100, 106

E

East Grinstead, 94, 134–136, 143, 181–183, 205
Eastington, 6, 7, 145
East Suffolk & Ipswich Hospital, 127, 129, 131, 136, 205
Edinburgh, Duke of, 183
Edmonds, Godfrey, 139
Egerton Park Pavilion, 22
Egypt, 9, 219
Elementary and Reserve Flying Training School (E&RFTS), 12, 15, 16, 17, 20, 204
Elsey, Mark, 199
England, 22, 24, 27, 30, 43–45, 53, 54, 67, 83–84, 105, 119, 122, 124, 134, 145, 147, 166, 197, 215–217, 224–226
English Channel, 3, 21, 27, 33, 37–38, 43–45, 62–64, 66, 71, 84, 88–91, 97–104, 110–111, 114, 119, 123, 126, 128, 141, 147, 152, 155–158, 160, 162–165, 166, 168, 170, 172–176, 178, 186, 193–194, 210
Essex, 35, 53, 58–60, 78, 87, 120–121

F

Fair, Donald, 173
FE8, Royal Aircraft Factory, 29
Feeley, Brian, 171–172
Felixstowe, 124, 126, 128
Fighter Command, 12, 44, 144, 150, 195, 200, 214
Finlay, Donald, 76, 93, 95–96, 99, 100, 102–103, 109, 111–112, 199, 122–124, 132, 180, 209
Finucane, Paddy, 200
First World War, 3, 8, 9, 17, 21, 24, 26, 29, 32, 35, 135, 142, 180, 221
Fives-Lille Engineering Works, 158–159
Fleet Air Arm, 43
Flint Kaserne, 227
Flying Training School, 16, 21, 24
Folkestone, 37, 72, 99, 110, 115, 119, 120
Ford, Roy, 49, 54–55, 58, 61–62, 67, 122
Flying Circus, Sir Alan Cobham's, 6, 7, 16
Fractures, 130, 138
France, 3, 10, 11, 13, 18, 19, 28–29, 31, 33, 37, 39, 43–45, 61, 64, 66, 81, 84, 89, 99, 101, 103–104, 141, 147, 155, 157–158, 165, 173, 178–180, 182, 184–185, 190–191, 195, 215
Franco-Prussian War, 130
French Revolution, 215

INDEX

Fury, Hawker, 24, 25, 30, 114
Fylde, 1, 220

G

Gamblen, Douglas, 35, 38
Gardner, Michael, 179, 180, 184, 191
Gaunce, Lionel (Elmer), 195
Gauntlet, Gloster, 16
German Air Fleets, 44–45, 52, 53
Germany, 9, 11, 13, 17–20, 23, 28–29, 31, 33–34, 43–44, 55, 223, 227
Gillies, Harold, 134–135
Gillingham, 27, 87
Gilmour, William, 157–158, 161, 164, 172, 179
Gisborough, Lord, 40, 208
Gleave, Tom, 139, 140, 182
Gloster Aircraft Company, 17
Goebbels, Josef, 54
Goliath, Annie, 219
Goodwin Sands, 173, 186
Goodwood Aerodrome, 200
Grainger, William, 185
Gravelines, 152, 154–156, 158–159, 162–164, 166–168, 170, 171, 173–177, 179, 184–185
Gravesend, 38, 62–63, 76, 78, 88, 98, 102, 210
Gray, Albert, 191
Great Britain, 3, 9, 10, 11, 13, 19, 21, 27–29, 33, 44, 52, 83, 215
Greenwich, 71, 112
Group,
  2 (Bomber), 151, 153, 156, 176
  3 (Bomber), 159, 162, 165, 167, 170, 174, 183
  9 (Fighter), 145
  10 (Fighter), 44, 120
  11 (Fighter), 39, 41, 44, 57, 65, 71, 74, 77–79, 83–85, 89–90, 94–98, 100–102, 105–106, 108–113, 115, 118–121, 146, 150, 155, 162, 177, 188, 190, 192
  12 (Fighter), 44, 120, 145, 153, 155, 156, 158–159, 162–164, 170, 173–175
  13 (Fighter), 32, 41, 44, 52–53, 145
  16 (Bomber), 156
  22 (Training), 198
  26 (Training), 14, 16
  50 (Training), 16
Guinea Pig Club, 181–182, 205
Gyll-Murray, John E. C. G. F., 17

H

Hainault Farm, 55
Hall, William D., 17
Hallowes, Herbert J. L., 189
Halton, 131–132, 134, 136, 144–145, 201, 205
Hardelot, 154, 164, 166–167, 170, 173–178, 191
Harrier, Hawker Siddeley, 199
Harrow, Handley Page, 24
Hart, Hawker, 17–18, 24, 25, 149
Hartlepool, 32, 34
Harvard, North American Aviation, 24–27, 30, 33
Harwich, 87, 128
Hastings, 79, 97, 101, 105, 115, 118
Hawker Aircraft Company, 17, 67
Hayter, James, 151, 153, 156, 160, 163, 166, 168, 174, 184, 188, 191, 196, 213
Hazebrouck, 154–155, 163, 177, 180
Hazebrouck Marshalling Yards, 153, 162–163, 176
Healy, Terence, 117, 122–123
Heelas, Eric T., 17
He111, Heinkel, 31, 39, 45–46, 51–54, 57, 59–62, 67–70, 72–74, 79–83, 89–90, 119, 208, 210
He113, Heinkel, 56, 91, 107
Hendon, 14, 146, 149
Hensall (Ontario), 223, 225
Herne Bay, 109, 125–126, 128
Hillary, Richard, 137–140, 143
Hind, Hawker, 17, 25, 149
Hitler, Adolf, 9, 11, 13–14, 18–19, 27–28, 33, 54, 83, 147
Hogg, Ralph, 122
Hood, H. R. L. (Robin), 31, 33, 35, 37–38, 40, 54, 56–59, 62–63, 67
Hornchurch, 30, 35, 38–40, 44, 54–57, 59–64, 67, 69–70, 72–73, 75–78, 80–95, 97–98, 100–106, 108, 111–112, 114–116, 118, 121, 123–125, 128, 132, 137, 142, 146, 149–160, 162–171, 173–177, 180–184, 186–187, 191–193, 195–196, 205, 211
Horsham Cottage Hospital, 94
Hounds, South Shropshire, 7
House of Commons, 19, 27, 53
Howitt, Ted, 35, 54, 55, 57, 60–61, 70–72, 76, 122
Hs126, Henschel, 91, 107, 210
Hugo, Petrus, 133
Hurricane, Hawker, 25, 38, 44, 59, 62, 66, 71, 81–82, 89, 94, 98, 151, 153, 156, 159, 162, 165, 167, 170, 174, 176, 179, 183, 186, 190, 200, 209

I

Infection, 130, 131, 132, 135, 139, 140, 143
Ingram, Sgt Plt, 184
Initial Training Wing (ITW), 20–23, 27, 204
Inner Artillery Zone (IAZ), 10, 76, 98, 109, 120
Ipswich, 124, 129, 131, 205
Ipswich Hospital, *see East Suffolk & Ipswich Hospital*
Isle of Grain, 80
Isle of Man, 7, 145
Isle of Sheppey, 60, 62–63, 90, 96, 102, 105, 109, 110, 118
Isle of Wight, 39, 43
Italy, 11, 19, 21–22, 121

J

Johnson, Johnnie, 200
Ju87 (Stuka), Junkers, 38, 123
Ju88, Junkers, 35, 41, 45–46, 48, 49, 52, 57, 59, 61–62, 64, 67, 69, 70, 72–74, 79, 84, 89, 91, 101, 120, 207, 210

K

Kayll, Joseph R., 150

Kempsey, 217, 218
Kenley, 38, 44, 56, 90, 95, 97, 101–102, 105, 106, 109, 115, 119, 123–124, 151–153, 156, 158–159, 162, 165, 167, 170, 173–174, 176, 178, 183, 186
Kent, 53, 56, 60, 62–64, 66, 72, 75–76, 83, 87, 90, 93–94, 96–97, 101, 104–106, 109–110, 112, 119–120, 122, 124, 199, 204, 210, 227
Kenton Bar, 32
Kidderminster, 218
Kilner, Tommy, 134–135
King Edward the Confessor, 2, 218
King George VI, 8, 14, 132, 143, 196, 221
King's Regulations, 26
Kirton-in-Lindsey, 156, 159, 170
Koukal, Josef, 139
Kriegsmarine (German Navy), 186
Kuhlmann Chemical Factory, 151, 155, 156, 163–165, 170

L

Lacey, James H. (Ginger), 150, 188–189, 199–200, 211
Lamb, Plt Off, 184
Lancasterian School, 226
Langley, Gerald, 27–28, 30–35, 39, 46, 53, 54, 55, 73, 78–79, 83, 92, 140
Last Enemy, The, 137
Lecky, John, 96, 99–100, 106–107, 209, 214
Leeming, 34–35
Leigh, Arthur, 156–157, 184, 191
Lens, 162, 167–168, 170, 224
Lens Power Station, 151, 166, 167
Le Touquet, 152, 153, 158, 162, 175, 177–181, 185
Lille, 158–159, 162, 170–173, 183–185
Lille Power Station, 159, 170
Link Trainer, 17–18
Linton-on-Ouse, 45
Lipton, Celia, 136
Lister, Robert, 67, 71, 75
Little Rissington, 24, 204
Lloyd, Philip, 109
Lloyd George, David, 9–10
Lock,
  Ann, 217
  Anne, 215
  Ann (née Firkins), 215
  Anthony, 222
  Benjamin, 215, 217
  Charles Edward, 1–4, 6–8, 21, 131, 143, 145, 197, 218–221
  Dora Evelyn (née Cornes), 1–4, 6, 21, 131, 143, 197, 219–221
  Edith (née Furmston), 219
  Elizabeth, 215
  Emma Maria, 218–220
  Eric (great nephew), 222
  Ethel Mary Joan (Joan), 4, 6, 21, 36, 131, 136, 139, 143, 197–198, 221, 226
  Evelyn Dora (Evie), 1–2, 6, 200
  Francis, 216
  George, 215, 217–218
  Henry James, 218–219
  Herbert Samuel Charles (Jimmy), 1–3, 6, 197, 220, 221
  James, 217
  Jane, 215, 217
  Jennifer, 221
  Kenneth, 221–222
  Liddy, 215
  Lounge Café, 198
  Luke, 215
  Maria (née Waters), 217–218
  Mary, 215
  Mary (née Loxley), 215, 217
  Richard, 222
  Rodney, 221–222
  Rosemary, 221
  Samuel, 1, 217–218
  Samuel George, 218–219
  Sarah (née Steward), 218–219
  Sarah Florence, 218–219
  Sarah Florence (Cissy), 1, 2, 6, 198, 220–221
  Susan/Susannah (née Miles), 217–218
  William, 215, 217
  William Steward, 218–219
London, 10–11, 14, 16, 19, 44, 54, 56, 64, 67, 71–72, 75, 77–79, 81, 83–85, 87, 90, 94, 95, 96, 98, 100–102, 105–106, 108–112, 115, 118–121, 136, 142, 143, 187, 198–199, 210, 219, 222
London Gazette, 142, 145
London (Ontario), 225, 227–228
Long Forest, 2, 218
Long Mynd, 5
Lovell, Tony, 35, 37, 40, 48, 50, 52, 54–55, 57, 60, 63–65, 78, 82–83, 94, 96, 105, 111–112, 120–122, 125, 128, 180
Lovett, Reginald, 59
Luftwaffe, 19, 28, 30, 31, 33–35, 37–42, 44–49, 51–54, 56–58, 60, 64–67, 71, 74–78, 83, 85–86, 89–91, 93–98, 100–102, 105–109, 111–115, 118–120, 122–124, 126, 140, 141, 146–147, 152, 154, 158, 160, 164, 166–168, 172, 174, 176–177, 178, 181, 183, 185–186, 192, 206
Lympne, 91, 93
Lysander, Westland, 142

M

MacCarthy, Dr J. Aidan, 22
Mackenzie, John, 35, 38, 41, 49, 52, 54–55, 64–65, 67, 68, 73–74, 81, 85, 89–90, 97, 99–100, 116–119, 121–122, 125–126, 128, 209
Maddox, R. & Co Ltd, 197
Magister, Miles, 17
Maidstone, 56, 62, 64–65, 67, 71, 74, 76, 84, 86–87, 91, 95–99, 101–102, 106, 108–111, 115–117, 119, 123–124, 210
Maintenance Unit, 24
Malan, Adolph G. (Sailor), 150, 188–189, 200
Mannock, Mick, 193
Manston, 37, 39, 56, 84, 89–90, 102, 111, 123, 125, 159, 160–161, 170–171, 174, 185, 205
Mardyck, 161, 184
Margate, 61–62, 88, 106, 210

INDEX

Margate Hook Beacon, 208
Market Drayton, 198
Martlesham Heath, 120, 127–128
Masonic Lodge, 145
Master, Miles, 25, 33
Matlaske, 126, 156, 159, 170
Mazingarbe Power Station, 167, 186
McAdam, John, 27–28, 30–35, 40, 54, 56, 79, 92, 103, 108, 118, 122, 140–142
McHugh, Martin, 153
McIndoe, Dr Archibald, 94, 134–139, 143–144, 146, 181–182, 201
Me109, Messerschmitt, 37–40, 56–63, 65–72, 74, 76–91, 93–113, 115–120, 123, 125–128, 130–132, 141, 152–173, 175–179, 181, 183–184–186, 208–210, 212
Me110, Messerschmitt, 45–52, 72–74, 79, 81, 103, 128, 207, 210
Meares, Stanley, 151
Medical Board, 201
Megarry, Herbert, 27
Meir Aerodrome (RAF Meir), 14–16, 18–20, 24, 204
Memorial bench, 198
Mention in Dispatches, 22, 29, 142, 205
Meole Brace, 2
Mesopotamia, 9
Meteor, Gloster, 227
Metropole Hotel, 22
Meyers,
  Ada Louise, 223
  Alice May Keller, 223
  Charles Samuel, 223
  Charles Sherritt, 223
  David Campbell, 223
  Eleanor Beryl, 223
  Elizabeth (née Schumacher/Shoemaker), 223
  Gwyneth (Gwen) Louie (née Beard), 224, 225
  Henry (Heinrich), 223
  John Aaron (Ernie), 223–225
  Kenneth William (Peter), 36, 225–226, 228
  Lillian Gertrude, 223
  Margaret Irene, 223
  Margaret Victoria (Peggy), 8, 21, 35–36, 131, 143, 145–147, 186, 196–197, 204, 223–228
  Mary Jane, 223
  Myrtle Sydella Hay, 223
  Phil, 223
  Thomas Henry, 223
  Victoria (née Sherritt), 223
Midland Aircraft Repairs, 16
Mileham, Denys, 96, 122, 125, 128
Military Cross (MC), 17, 29, 44, 134, 142, 150, 193
Military Medal (MM), 29, 224
Ministry of Defence, 22
Ministry of Information, 142, 213
Mitchell, Alfred, 3
Mölders, Werner, 140
Monkton, Sir Walter, 142
Morehen, Joseph, 27
Morphine, 129, 131–132
Morris, Brenus, 184

Morris, Nigel, 197
Morrison, John S. F., 21, 22
Morrogh-Ryan, Oliver, 35, 40, 48, 52, 54–55, 58, 61, 62,
Mounsdon, Mark, 139
Mowlem, Rainsford, 134
Munich Agreement, 13, 18

N

National Archives, 100, 207, 208
National Aviation Day, 6, 16
National Farmers' Union, 145
National Flying Services, 16
Neil, Tom, 82, 196, 209, 214
Netherlands, 33, 44, 147, 216, 219
Nevendon, 58–59
Newby, Rev. Leonard, 36
Newcastle, 32, 47
Newhaven, 119, 124
Newnes, Walter, 219
Northolt, 29, 44, 79, 111, 123, 151–153, 155–156, 158–159, 162–163, 165, 167, 170–171, 174–176, 183, 185
North Foreland, 65, 67, 77, 83, 96, 121, 152, 154, 157, 160, 163–164, 166, 174, 184
North Sea, 3, 30, 34, 41, 45, 194
North Weald, 38, 44, 82, 121, 125, 155–156, 159, 162, 170, 174, 176, 183–186
Norwell, John (Jock), 85, 89
Nun's Alley, 224

O

Officer of the Most Excellent Order of the British Empire (OBE), 55, 134, 198
Old Porch House, 5
O'Neill, Desmond, 107
Operation *Adlerangriff* [Eagle Attack], 45
Operation *Seelöwe* [Sea Lion], 43, 83
Operational Training Unit (OTU), 179, 186
Operations Record Book (ORB), 85, 95, 100, 132, 150, 177, 192, 196, 207, 208, 211–214
Orde, Cuthbert, 180, 198
Ormiston, Thomas, 191

P

Panter, John, 177
Parish, Clare, 18,
Park, Keith, 44, 74
Pas-de-Calais, 151, 153, 156, 159, 162, 165, 167, 170, 174, 176, 183
Peake, Harald, 180
Pearson, Edith & Evelyn, 5
Penicillin, 131–132, 135
Physiotherapy, 144, 146, 201
Pierce, Vic, 198
Pilot Badge (Wings), 25–26, 36, 204
Plastic surgery, *see skin grafting*
Plumtree, Eric, 198
Poland, 18–20, 45, 182

INDEX

Pony Club, 7
Pontesbury, 220
Poole, 95, 97
Portsmouth, 43, 71, 77, 95
Post-Traumatic Stress Disorder (PTSD), 201
Precious Bane, 4
Prestfelde School, 5–7, 134, 198–199, 204
Price, Sam, 213
Prince Charles, 199
Prince William, 199
Princess Mary's Hospital (Halton), 131–132, 134, 136, 144–145, 205
Prisoners of War, 29, 41, 45, 81, 117, 147, 150, 154–156, 158, 160, 162, 173, 175, 177, 187, 192
Pritchard, Thomas, 36
Prussia, 18, 216

Q

Queen Elizabeth II, 198
Queen Victoria Hospital (QVH), 94, 134, 136, 137, 140, 143–144, 146, 181, 205

R

Radar, 34, 38, 44
Railway Air Services, 16
Ramsgate, 43, 76, 77, 102, 105–106, 108, 112, 204, 210
Rearguard, 48, 65, 68, 69, 70, 86, 98, 104, 106, 113, 115, 123, 141, 171
Red Cross, 143–144
Reeves, John, 152
Reid & Sigrist Ltd, 17, 204
Reid, George H., 17
Reserve Command, 16
Reserved occupation, 3, 21, 201
Restemeyer, Werner, 47
Rhubarb operations, 190–192
Richardson, Alfred C., 17
Richthofen, Manfred von, 193
Roadstead operations, 180
Roberts' Marine Mansions, 22
Robinson, Maurice, 208
Rochester, 102, 110
Rochford, 44, 57, 72, 93, 98–99, 102–103, 111, 114–115, 119, 125, 128, 149
Rodenhurst, Elsie, 219
Roll of Honour, 197, 199
Romford, 101, 108
Ross-on-Wye, 224–226
Rotary Club, 145
Royal Air Force (RAF), 9–14, 16–17, 21–22, 24–25, 27, 29–31, 33–34, 36, 38, 42–47, 52–55, 63, 65–66, 70–71, 76–77, 82–83, 86–87, 90, 94–95, 98, 101, 107, 120, 133–136, 142, 144, 147, 149, 161, 181–188, 192, 199, 207, 211–213, 222, 226–227
Royal Air Force Benevolent Fund, 227
Royal Air Force Volunteer Reserve (RAFVR), 8–9, 12–16, 20, 22, 24–25, 36, 63, 200, 202, 204, 226, 227
Royal Albert Hall, 136
Royal Canadian Mounted Police, 225
Royal Navy, 43, 226
Royal Naval Air Service, 17, 21
Runnymede Memorial, 195, 199
Ryder, Norman, 31, 35, 40, 46, 48, 52, 54–58, 60–68, 71–73, 75–76, 78–79, 80, 83, 90–91, 99, 100, 108, 115–116, 119–120, 122, 180, 194,
Rye, 101, 115–116, 164–165, 167
Ryton, 218

S

Sackville Garage, 22
Sackville Hotel, 22
St Alban's Preparatory School, *see Prestfelde School*
St Clement Parish, 217
St Clement Danes (RAF Church), 199
St Omer, 123, 153–155, 157–158, 160, 162, 164–165, 168, 173–175, 178–179, 184–185, 212
St Omer Longuenesse Aerodrome, 184
St Omer Ship Lift, 174
Salop Licenced Victuallers' Association, 145
Saul, Richard, 32
Sayers, James, 54
Schmid, Johann, 192, 193
Scotland, 32, 139, 145, 227
Scott, William, 35, 38, 40, 54–55, 65, 66, 69
Seaham Harbour, 46–49, 52, 210
Searl, Francis H. L., 22,
Second World War, 29, 65, 133, 142, 195, 198–199, 200, 221
Secretary of State for Air, 19, 142
Sentinel factory, 145
Service Flying Training School (SFTS), 20, 23–28, 140, 146, 204
Sevenoaks, 73, 98, 110, 115, 117
Sherritt, Dora, 224
Shipman, Edward (Ted), 34–35, 47, 50–54
Shoeburyness, 105, 154
Shomere Pool, 4
Sholto Douglas, William, 150
Shoreham, 69, 120
Shrewsbury,
  ATC, 1119 Squadron, 198
  Beacall's Lane, 226
  Castle, 198
  Castle Gates (road), 198
  Dogpole (road), 198
  Eric Lock Road, 197
  Granada Cinema, 198
  Guildhall, 198
  High School for Boys, 5, 204
  London Road, 5
  Mayor, 134, 198
  Miss (competition), 8, 226
  Music Hall, 8
  Percy Street, 196, 226
  St Julian's Church, 35–36, 204, 226
  Swan Hill, 5
  (Town of), 1–2, 4, 5, 8, 35–36, 133–134, 137, 145,

INDEX 245

196–198, 202, 204–205, 218, 220–222, 226
Town Council, 134
Shropshire, 1, 4, 7, 133–134, 139, 197, 204
Shropshire Aero Club, 198
Shropshire Journal, 145
Shropshire Regimental Museum, 198
Sigrist, Frederick, 17,
Sinclair, Archibald, 142
Singer Le Mans, 7–8
Siskin, Armstrong Whitworth, 30
Skin grafting, 134–140, 143–144, 146, 181
Sleap, 198
Smith, Forgrave M., 150
Smith, Norman J., 162
Smout, James, 220
Snipe, Sopwith, 29
Sopwith Aircraft Company, 17
Southampton, 71, 93, 108, 120–121
South Foreland, 100–101, 110
Southend, 59, 71–72, 81, 105, 154–156, 176–177
Spitfire, Supermarine, 25, 30, 32–34, 38, 44, 48, 50–51, 54, 59–60, 62, 66, 69, 71–75, 85, 87–89, 102, 106, 107, 110, 112, 114, 117–118, 122, 123, 125, 128, 130, 141, 149, 150–151, 153–154, 156–157, 159, 161–162, 164–167, 170, 172, 174, 176, 178–179, 183, 187, 191–192, 194–195, 199–200, 204–205, 207, 209, 213
Spotter, 71, 76, 84, 90
Squadrons,
 1 (RAF), 64–65, 151, 189
 1 (Canadian), 57, 65, 67, 71, 76, 78–79, 84
 3, 183
 17, 57, 65, 71, 76, 79, 83–84, 114, 124, 128, 208
 19, 57, 150, 162, 174, 189
 24, 146
 25, 226
 32, 38, 150, 189
 41, 27–32, 35–42, 44–47, 51–57, 62–67, 71–72, 75–79, 82–87, 89–90, 92–105, 106, 108–115, 118–125, 128, 132–133, 137, 140–141, 146, 149–151, 160, 180, 182, 189–190, 194–195, 199, 200, 204, 206–214
 43, 57, 64, 189
 46, 57, 65–67, 71, 76, 78–79, 83–84, 87, 125
 54, 38, 40, 55–56, 150, 151, 153–154, 156, 159–160, 162–163, 165, 167, 170, 172, 174–177, 180–181, 183–184, 190–191
 56, 38, 156, 159, 170, 173–174, 212
 64, 38
 65, 156, 159, 170, 173
 66, 57, 64–65, 67, 71, 76, 78–79, 83–84, 89, 106, 124, 128, 180
 71, 156, 159, 162, 170–171, 176, 183, 190
 72, 46, 47, 52, 57, 65–67, 71, 76, 78–79, 83–84, 86, 90, 105, 176–177, 183,
 73, 57, 59, 64–65, 71, 75–76, 78–79, 84, 208
 74, 37, 96, 124, 151, 153–154, 156, 159, 160, 165–166
 79, 47, 52, 56, 57, 64
 85, 189
 92, 67, 71, 76, 78–79, 83–84, 86, 89–90, 106, 114–115, 151, 153–154, 156, 159–160, 165, 166–167, 170, 176, 183,
 111, 56, 57, 64–65, 190
 112, 189
 123, 180
 124, 179–180
 130, 150, 189
 145, 151–154, 156, 158–159, 162, 165, 167, 170, 173–174, 176, 178, 183, 185
 213, 67, 71, 76, 79, 84, 89
 215, 24
 219, 32, 40, 46, 47, 52
 222, 56–57, 65, 67, 71, 75–76, 78–79, 83–84, 87, 90, 94, 99, 101–105, 113, 115, 123, 150, 159, 162, 167, 170–171, 176, 180
 229, 67, 71, 76, 78–79, 84, 114
 242, 156, 159, 162, 170–171, 174, 176, 180–181, 186, 190,
 249, 57, 64–65, 67, 71, 76, 78–79, 82–84, 87, 120, 125
 253, 46, 57, 66–67, 71, 75–76, 78–79, 84, 90, 124, 128
 256, 153
 257, 65–66, 71, 76, 78–79, 83–84, 124, 128, 150, 155, 162,174, 189,
 258, 151, 153–154, 156, 159, 165, 167, 170, 174, 176
 266, 92, 150, 153, 155
 302, 123
 303, 57, 64, 66–67, 71, 76, 78–79, 84, 87, 95, 151–153, 155, 159, 162, 165, 170–171, 174–175, 183, 211
 306, 151–152, 159, 167, 170, 174, 176, 185–186, 190
 308, 151–153, 156, 159, 162–163, 165, 170–171, 174–175, 183, 185
 312, 151, 153–154, 156, 159, 165, 167, 170, 174, 176
 401, 153, 155, 162
 403, 184, 191
 452, 190
 485, 153–154, 156, 159, 165, 167, 170, 173–174, 176, 178, 183, 186, 190
 501, 38, 56–57, 64–67, 71, 75–76, 78–79, 83–84, 86–87, 123–124 128, 150, 189, 211
 504, 66–67, 71, 76, 78–79, 83–84
 600, 137
 601, 57, 64, 156, 159, 170
 602, 67, 71, 79, 84, 176, 178, 183–184, 189
 603, 46, 56–57, 65–67, 71–72, 75–76, 78–79, 83–84, 86–87, 90, 99, 101–102, 105, 111–113, 115, 118–119, 124–125, 137, 150–154, 156, 158–159, 160, 162, 164–165, 167, 170–172, 174–177, 183–184, 190, 211, 227
 605, 46, 52, 66–67, 71, 78–79, 83–84, 101, 123, 211
 607, 46, 52, 67, 71, 76, 79, 84
 609, 153–154, 156, 159, 165, 167, 170, 176–177, 183–184, 190
 610, 92, 151–154, 156, 158–159, 165, 167, 170, 173–174, 176, 178, 183, 185
 611, 92, 114, 123, 146, 148–156, 158–160, 162–168, 170–172, 174–181, 183–188, 190–193, 196, 205, 207, 211–212
 615, 123
 616, 151–154, 156, 158–159, 162, 165, 167, 170, 173–176, 178, 183, 185
Staffordshire Sentinel, 15
Stalin, Josef, 11,
Stanford Tuck, R. Robert, 150, 189–200
Stapleton, Frederick S., 150, 152–153, 156–157, 160, 163,

166, 168, 170–171, 174–175, 177, 181, 184–185, 191
Stephen, Harbourne M., 150, 189
Steward, Harry, 134
Stirling, Short, 158–160, 162–167, 170–171, 174, 183, 186
Stoke-on-Trent, 14–17
Stoke-on-Trent Aerodrome, *see Meir Aerodrome*
Stoke-on-Trent Council, 15–16, 19
Story of a Brave Shropshire Airman, The, 197
Sulfa powder, 129–130, 135, 140
Summers, Sgt Plt, 172
Surrey, 53, 97, 112, 199
Surrey Docks, 71
Sussex, 21, 53, 87, 90, 94, 97, 100, 122, 134
Sutton Harness, 33
Sutton, James (Jimmy), 186
Sylt, 227

T

Tabor, Sgt Plt, 184
Tangmere, 44, 69, 83, 146, 151–156, 158–159, 162, 165–167, 170, 173–176, 178, 183, 185, 200
Tankerville Villa, 2–3, 6,
Ternhill, 16, 149
Thames / Thames Estuary, 57, 60–62, 64–66, 72, 75, 90, 101–102, 104–105, 108, 115, 118–120, 122–128, 204, 210
Thomas, Eric H., 150–151, 153, 160, 163, 168, 174, 177
Tiger Moth, de Havilland, 17
Times, The, 10, 85, 196
Tindall, Lewis S., 17
Tollemache, Tony, 137, 138
Tonbridge, 74, 78, 98, 106, 115, 117, 210
Tornado, Panavia, 199
Towers-Perkins, Bill, 182
Townsend, Norman, 169, 172, 191
Training Command, 12, 16
Treaty of Versailles, 9, 18
Trenchard, Sir Hugh, 9
Trentham Institute, 17
Tuberculosis, 225
Tunbridge Wells, 72, 97, 106
Turlington, Richard, 187
Turnhouse, 32, 46, 227

U

United Kingdom, 29, 135, 199, 227
United States, 28–29, 182
Upper Canada College, 227
Usmar, Frank, 27–28, 30–35, 39, 46, 51–55, 79, 87, 92, 140, 146
Uxbridge, 9, 44

V

Vampire, de Havilland, 227
Vickers Armstrong, 17, 25, 114
Victoria Cross (VC), 133, 193
Victoria Embankment, 199

Walker, James, 100, 103, 104
Wallens, Ronald (Wally), 35, 39–41, 51–52, 54–59, 63, 146
Webb, Mary, 4
Webster, Terry, 31, 35, 37–40, 54–57, 59, 60, 63, 74
Weeks, Peter, 182
Wellington, Vickers, 24,
Wells, Edward (Hawkeye), 99–100, 110–111, 117–119, 122
West Malling, 27, 74, 90, 97, 101, 113, 173, 210
Western Front, 29, 32, 136, 224
Westhampnett, 200
Westmoreland, Joshua J., 22
Wheeler, Johnny, 198
Whitby, 31, 40, 45, 53, 194
Whitechapel, 36, 219
White Ladies Aston, 217
Williams, Tom, 157–158
Winchelsea, 100, 119
Winder, Katherine (Kay), 226
Winder, Newton, 226
Women's Auxiliary Air Force (WAAF), 21
Wood, Sir Kingsley, 19
Woolwich, 71, 101, 123
Worcester, 215, 217, 218
Worcestershire, 1, 215, 218
Worthing, 87
Wright, Kenneth, 191
Wyre Piddle, 215, 217

Y

Yorkshire, 27, 32, 35, 41, 146
Ypres, 160, 224

Bibliography and Sources

41 Squadron Archives, RAF Coningsby: *Analysis by Types of Enemy Aircraft Shot Down by Squadrons Under the Control of Hornchurch (3.9.39 – 3.11.40)*, original typed, undated document, ca Nov 40; Combat Reports for ES Lock, original documents, unnumbered & un-indexed, for 15 Aug 40, 9 Sep 40, & 5 Oct 40; *Pilot Service Record*, unreferenced & un-indexed, for ES Lock; Intelligence Reports, original documents, unnumbered & un-indexed, for 27-29 Jul 40; 15 Aug 40; 5-9,14-15,17-18,23-24,27-30 Sep 40; 5,7,9,11,17,20,25&30 Oct 40; 11,17&27 Nov 40.

RAF Disclosures, Trenchard Hall, RAF Cranwell: Service Record for 81642 Eric Stanley Lock.

The National Archives, Kew: *Aerodromes*: Stoke on Trent, Meir, Staffordshire, Stoke on Trent Corporation, TNA AVIA 2/779; *Aerodromes:* Licences: Stoke-on-Trent (Meir) Aerodrome Licence, TNA AVIA 2/1197; *Air Ministry and Ministry of Defence: Operations Record Books, Groups*, 11 Group RAF, TNA AIR 25/193 (May 26-Dec 41), 197 (Appendix Sep 39-Sep 40), 198 (Appendix Oct-Dec 40), & 200 (App May-Aug 41); *Air Ministry and Ministry of Defence: Operations Record Books, Groups*, 13 Group RAF, TNA AIR 25/232 (Jul 39-Dec 40); *Air Ministry and Ministry of Defence: Operations Record Books, Miscellaneous Units*, 6 SFTS, TNA AIR 29/558; *Air Ministry and Ministry of Defence: Operations Record Books, Miscellaneous Unit*s, 4 ITW, TNA AIR 29/632; *Air Ministry and Ministry of Defence: Operations Record Books, Royal Air Force Stations*, RAF Catterick, TNA AIR 28/141; *Air Ministry and Ministry of Defence: Operations Record Books, Royal Air Force Stations*, RAF Hornchurch, TNA AIR 28/384; *Air Ministry and successors: Operations Record Books, Squadrons*, No. 41 Sqn, TNA AIR 27/424 (1 Apr 23-31 Dec 40) & 428 (Appendix May-Dec 40); *Air Ministry and successors: Operations Record Books, Squadrons*, No. 611 Sqn, TNA AIR 27/2110; *Air Ministry: Combat Reports, Second World War, Fighter Command*, No. 41 Sqn, Oct 39-May 45, TNA AIR 50/18; *Air Ministry: Combat Reports, Second World War, Fighter Command*, No. 249 Sqn, Jul 40-Dec 43, TNA AIR 50/96; *Air Ministry: Combat Reports, Second World War, Fighter Command*, No. 611 Sqn, Sep 39-Apr 45, TNA AIR 50/173.

Private Collections, Personal Accounts and Unpublished Records: Bradbury, Mike, *Flight Lieutenant Eric Stanley Lock DSO, DFC & Bar, 1919-1941*; Sales Prospectus for the Auction of Bomere Farm by E. R. Brisbourne Esq, dated 10 Apr 56; via Tim & Sarah Adkins.

Periodicals: *The Times*, Times Newspapers Ltd, London, editions of 3 Apr 41 & 3 Jul 42 (obit); *The Daily Mail*, Associated Newspapers Ltd, edition of 10 Dec 40; *The Daily Sketch*, now defunct (1909-1971), edition of 29 Mar 41; *The Daily Telegraph*, Telegraph Media Group Ltd, edition of 3 Apr 41; *Flight magazine* (Flightglobal Archive), various editions of 1920-1940; Shrewsbury Chronicle, editions of 17 Jul 31, 14 Jul 33, 19 Oct 40, & 13 Dec 40; *Wellington Journal & Shrewsbury News*, now defunct (1874-1965), editions of 15 Jul 33 & 7 Dec 40.

Published Works: Brew, Steve, *Blood, Sweat and Courage, 41 Squadron RAF 1939-1942*, Fonthill Media, 2014; Cooke, William, *Wings over Meir; The Story of the Potteries Aerodrome*, Amberley Publishing, 2010; Duncan Smith, Gp Capt, W. G. G., DSO DFC, *Spitfire into Battle*, Arrow Books, 1981; Foreman, John, *Battle of Britain: The Forgotten Months, November and December 1940*, Air Research Publications, 1988; Foreman, John, *RAF Fighter Command Victory Claims of World War Two, Part Two, 1 January 1941-30 June 1943*, Red Kite, 2005; Franks, Norman L. R., *Royal Air Force Fighter Command Losses of the Second World War, Vol. 1, 1939-1941*, Midland Publishing, 1997; Guy, John, *30s & 40s Britain* (Snapping Turtle Guides), Ticktock Entertainment Ltd UK, 2003; Her Majesty's Stationery Office, London, *The Air Force List*, Crown copyright, editions of 1938-1960; Her Majesty's Stationery Office, London, *The Royal Air Force Retired List 1973*, Crown copyright, 1973; Hillary Richard, *The Last Enemy*, Macmillan and Co. Ltd, London, 1942; Jefford, C. G., *Observers and Navigators: And Other Non-pilot Aircrew in the RFC, RNAS and RAF*, The Crowood Press Ltd, 2001; Maddox R., and Co Ltd, *The Story of a Brave Shropshire Airman*, 1942, printed by Wildings; re-printed ca 1989 (Nigel Morris); Morgan, Eric B., & Shacklady, Edward, *Spitfire; The History*, Key Books, 1987-2000; Overy, Richard, *The Battle of Britain: Myth and Reality*, Penguin Books, 2010; Ramsey, Winston G. (editor), *The Battle of Britain Then and Now*, Battle of Britain International Ltd, 1989; Ramsey, Winston G. (editor), *The Blitz Then and Now, Vol 1* (3 Sep 39-6 Sep 40), Battle of Britain Prints International Ltd, 1987, and Vol 2 (7 Sep 40-16 May 41), 1988; Rawlings, John, *Fighter Squadrons of the RAF and their Aircraft*, Crecy Publishing, 1993 (revised edition); Shores, Christopher, & Williams, Clive, *Aces High, A Tribute to the Most Notable Fighter Pilots of the British and Commonwealth Forces in WWII*, Grub Street, 1994; Smith, Richard C., *Hornchurch Eagles, The Life Stories of Eight of the Airfield's Distinguished WWII Fighter Pilots*, Grub Street, 2002; Williams, Peter, & Harrison, Ted, *McIndoe's Army, The injured airmen who faced the world*, Pelham Books Ltd, 1979.

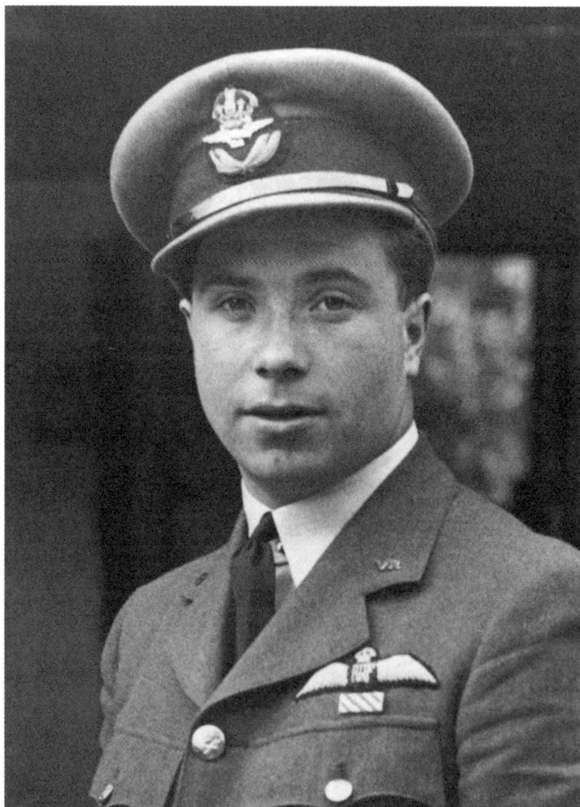